THE ACHIEVEMENT MOTIVE

by

DAVID C. McCLELLAND
JOHN W. ATKINSON
RUSSELL A. CLARK
EDGAR L. LOWELL

With a New Preface with Hindsight
by JOHN W. ATKINSON

IRVINGTON PUBLISHERS, Inc., New York

HALSTED PRESS Division
JOHN WILEY & SONS
NEW YORK   LONDON   SYDNEY   TORONTO

Distributed by HALSTED PRESS
A division of JOHN WILEY & SONS, New York

Library of Congress cataloging in publication information:

McClelland, David Clarence.
    The achievement motive.

    Bibliography: p.
    Includes index.
    1. Achievement motivation. I. Title.
BF683.M2   1975   153.8   75-37826
ISBN 0-470-01390-7

Printed in The United States of America

A New Preface with Hindsight
by John W. Atkinson

There is a photograph of a young David McClelland sitting on a grassy knoll at Yelping Hill in West Cornwall, Connecticut in the summer of 1950. He is surrounded by three somewhat younger men in shorts and shirtsleeves, looking and feeling as old, wise, and cocksure as their early Wesleyan mentor. One of the three already had a hurried Ph.D. from Michigan behind him. The other two were well on their way to ones at Yale and at Harvard. They had been away from the academic scene for a war and had returned mature beyond their years and as full of steam (if not of wisdom) as the long, lean fellow in the middle they knew, with affection, as "Dreamy Dave." The acorn they planted together at Yelping Hill that summer has become an oak. (The near-sighted still consider it an overgrown weed!)

A reader who stumbles upon this reissued edition, a quarter of a century later, may be helped by a sketchy outline of the shape of things that developed as viewed by one of those "present at the creation."

Even as the repeatedly redrafted manuscript went to press, including as much as we could of what had happened between 1947 and 1953, the need for affiliation (Shipley & Veroff, 1952) and sexual motivation (Clark, 1952) had joined hunger and achievement motivation in the list of motivational states shown to have a demonstrable effect on the content of imaginative thought, and there were already 22 names including 7 doctoral dissertations included in the list of *n* Achievement titles (p. 377).

A

By 1958, similar results in studies of need for power (Veroff, 1957), fear (Walker, Atkinson, Veroff, Birney, Dember, and Moulton, 1958), and aggression (Feshbach, 1955) justified our calling attention in the follow-up book, *Motives in Fantasy, Action, and Society* (Atkinson (ed.), 1958), to the fact that we had now as comprehensive a list of kinds of motivation *studied by the same method* as one could find anywhere in the psychological literature. In this second progress report, the first rapid growth of the main stem from the seed seemed impressively healthy. Old investigators and new branched out along the lines of the three-pronged argument for the validity of fantasy measures presented in this initial volume. I refer to the sensitivity of thematic apperception or fantasy to experimental arousal of motivation; to its ability to assess relatively stable and general individual differences in the strength of motives as expressed behaviorally in a variety of ways; and to its ability to reflect individual differences in the antecedent formative life histories of individuals.

McClelland and co-workers at Wesleyan and later Harvard had begun to concentrate on the social origins and consequences of achievement motivation, a topic he had treated particularly well in an earlier text (McClelland, 1951, pp. 346–352; 445–458). Later he presented in *The Achieving Society* (1961) his theses concerning the role of achievement motivation in the calculated risk-taking of entrepreneurial activity, in the historical rise and decline of societies as shown by motivational analysis of samples of popular literature in relation to indices of economic development, and in religious and family influences affecting the development of nations. Here he used the new method of measuring achievement motivation explained in this book the same way the radiocarbon method derived from contemporary physics is being used to date events of the distant past. That branch of activity has extended to an interest in changing motivation, dealt with by McClelland and David Winter in *Motivating Economic Achievement* (1969), by deCharms in *Enhancing Motivation:*

Change in the Classroom (1976), by McClelland and Steele (1972) and in related work by Litwin and Stringer (1968). These and other books I mention are sources of numerous citations for the ever growing number of problems in sociology, economics, political science, education, and business administration (for example, Rosen, Crockett, and Nunn, 1969) to which the ideas first presented here have made a contribution.

In addition to *The Achieving Society* (1961), the branch of research emphasizing development of achievement motivation includes Veroff (1965), Heinz Heckhausen's timely review of a growing international literature in *The Anatomy of Achievement Motivation*—to say nothing of his many important theoretical and empirical contributions to the study of motivation before and since—and a collection of important contributions from varying research approaches co-authored and edited by Charles P. Smith in *Achievement-related Motives in Children* (1969).

Another strand from the early work focused on power motivation. For this motive, as originally studied by Joseph Veroff, was represented, along with the needs for achievement and for affiliation in the scoring manuals, self-training coding materials and substantive studies of the 1958 collection, edited by Atkinson. More recently David Winter has developed and expanded on work by Veroff (see also Veroff and Veroff, 1972) and by Uleman (1972) to produce a more complete scoring definition for *n* Power which he has used with great success in exploring aspects of power behavior in *The Power Motive* (1973). The distribution and effects of *n* Power had been examined along with others in a study of national characteristics by Veroff, Atkinson, Feld, and Gurin (1960), based on thematic apperceptive measurement of motivation in a national sample survey. The intensive analysis of issues relating to personality and role arising in that work is presented in *Marriage and Work in America* (1970). Then it turned out that *n* Power was heavily involved as a cause and consequence of alcohol consumption as shown in an extensive study of cultural and individual drinking patterns by McClelland, Davis, Kalin, and Wanner (1972). Finally McClelland has carried out an analysis of the role of power motivation in society, analogous to what he did in *The Achieving Society*, in his latest book, *Power: The Inner Experience* (1975).

Still others have worked on the need for affiliation as reported by R. Boyatzis in the McClelland and Steele volume (1973), but our knowledge of this motive remains still relatively undeveloped.

In retrospect, our theoretical chapter (Chapter 2), written back in the early fifties, is stronger as criticism of the then dominant drive-reduction theory of reinforcement than as construction of an alternative relevant to our own empirical work on motivation. Nevertheless it is still part of the literature on the nature of pleasure and pain as reviewed, for example, by Walker and others in *Pleasure, Reward and Preference*, edited by Berlyne and Madsen (1973). A Michigan branch of the tree has focused persistently on the theoretical *problem of motivation*, defined programmatically by Kurt Lewin as $B = f(P, E)$, as distinct from the *problem of development*, $P = f(H, E_f)$. In the former, individual differences in personality (motive) are independent variables interacting with the immediate social environment as antecedents of contemporaneous behavior. In the latter, personality (motive) is a dependent variable, the product of heredity and formative social environment. The distinction is emphasized in *An Introduction to Motivation* (Atkinson, 1964), a text that puts the work in historical context and which helped to breathe new life into the cognitive theories of motivation proposed earlier by Tolman and Lewin that had been formalized as decision theory (see also Vroom, 1964; Lawler, 1973). Continual systematic study of the effects of individual differences in *n* Achievement yielded A *Theory of Achievement Motivation* (1966) edited by Atkinson and Norman T. Feather which made contact with McClelland's emphasis of risk-taking in entrepreneurship and included the landmark study of persistence by Feather (1962). It focused attention on the problem of change from one activity to another (Atkinson & Cartwright, 1964). A decade-long cenceptual analysis of this fundamental problem produced a reconstruction of the theory of motivation by Atkinson and David Birch in *The Dynamics of Action* (1970). Now, finally, we have a general theory of an *active* individual rather than the merely *reactive* individual of traditional conceptions worked out within the old S–O–R paradigm. The person whose behavioral life is now characterized as a continual stream of activity, involving change from one to another, and continuity in motivation contingent upon continual interaction of personality (motive) and environment (incentive), is active in two senses: (a) always already doing something when the scientific observer first takes notice; and (b) already actively motivated to engage in any number of alternative activities before the *stimulus situation* of interest to the observer (the starter's gun of traditional theories) even occurs. The most recent compilation along this branch is *Motivation and Achievement*, edited by Atkinson and Joel O. Raynor (1974). It has emphasized the identification of the various components of motivation (most recently the fear of success, Horner, 1968), and the details of the latter's influence on action. In it, Raynor emphasizes the more distant future expected consequences of a present activity and, in so doing, formulates a more general theory of achievement motivation which recovers the 1957–1966 version as the simplest case. In addition, the theory and evidence on achievement motivation catches up with the Yerkes-Dodson Law and agrees with the proposal of many others that the relationship of strength of motivation to efficiency of performance is curvilinear. And all of the previous empirical work and theory is recovered within the new conceptual framework, the dynamics of action, with all the deductive power attributable to David Birch's mathematical elaborations. *Motivation and Achievement* (1974) identifies the dual role of motivation on action: a curvilinear effect on efficiency of performance and a positive monotonic (approximately linear) effect on persistence or time spent in an activity. So it can distinguish achievement in the short run (intellective performance on a given occasion) and in the long run (overall academic performance, productivity in a career, and soon). Computer programs in the appendix of that book for the dynamics of action, and for dealing with the interdependence of motivation and ability on cumulative achievement, bring the work well into the orbit of educational testing, contemporary discussion of the meaning of I.Q., and test theory more generally. The contact with McClelland's emphasis of achievement in society is more obvious.

We can report, as this new edition goes to press, that computer simulation of the operant imaginative behavior emitted on the occasion of being confronted with a series of pictures, based on the programs written and refined by Robert Seltzer, James Sawusch, and Kenneth Bongort (since 1971) demonstrates that *construct validity does not require internal consistency reliability in thematic apperception* (Atkinson & Bongort, 1975). In other words, the theory of motivation evolved over twenty five years using the TAT method to diagnose individual differences in *n* Achievement, presented in this volume, initially, is now being turned around to explain the properties of the measuring instrument itself as the theory of heat explains the behavior of mercury in a thermometer. The implications of this, simply put, are: (a) that content analysis of the stream of operant imaginative thought (thematic apperception) has a more solid theoretical foundation than ever before and must, I believe, be considered the most promising and virtually untapped resource for future study of personality and in social psychology more generally; and (b) having developed a *psycho* logic to substitute for the *statistical* logic of the normal curve of distribution heralds a new era for diagnostic test theory and assessment of personality. We are quite obviously moving from an era dominated by the statistical logic of the normal curve of distribution (because there was nothing else), which encouraged a cautious and *defensive* strategy among psychologists concerning the complexities of their subject, into the era of computer simulation of behavioral processes, which encourages an *offensive* strategy, the attempt to conceptualize those processes. The new genie spells out, with most enviable precision, the implications of the simplest principles (for example, the principle of a change in activity) applied to very complex antecedent conditions (that is, a five story TAT taken by 30 Ss who differ in strength of achievement motive). It can and does show in its printouts and graphs that the strength of a person's inclination to achieve, *though based on a constant motive*, when tracked continuously from one moment to the next, does not dart about a *true score*, first way up, then the next moment a little down, then up again, as one expects by chance to produce a distribution of variations that are independent in direction and amount and conveniently describable as normally distributed error variance (with all that implies). General application of this logic was the crutch that psychology needed to move at all early in this century. Now it is archaic. All the elaborate deductive elaborations of a simple set of *a priori* assumptions introduced and elaborated by men of genius gave us test theory and factor analysis. Among those who accept it all as infallible doctrine, it has produced the psychometric suspicions that have annoyed us like mosquitoes for a quarter of a century. It is now clear that the psychology of the future belongs to the psychologists and not to the statisticians. But the statisticians better know how to think mathematically and converse with the computer.

The front edge of the basic science of motivation, as I see it, is the task of integrating something like the dynamics of action and the more highly articulated cognitive conceptions being developed by Heinz Heckhausen (1973) and Bernard Weiner (1974). The approaches are complementary, and their point of union is discussed by Birch, *et al.* (1974).

How can this introductory bridge between the past and

A Truncated Guide for Readers

Atkinson, J.W. (Ed.). *Motives in Fantasy, Action and Society.* Princeton: Van Nostrand, 1958.

Atkinson, J.W. *An Introduction to Motivation.* Princeton: Van Nostrand, 1964.

Atkinson, J.W., & Birch, D. *The Dynamics of Action.* New York: Wiley, 1970.

Atkinson, J.W., & Bongort, K. Explorations using computer simulation to comprehend TAT measurement of motivation. Paper presented August 30, 1975 at 83rd *Annual Convention of American Psychological Association* in Chicago.

Atkinson, J.W., & Cartwright, D. Some neglected variables in contemporary conceptions of decision and performance. *Psychological Reports,* 1964, *14*, 575–590.

Atkinson, J.W., & Feather, N.T. (Eds.). *A Theory of Achievement Motivation.* New York: Wiley, 1966.

Atkinson, J.W., & Raynor, J.O. (Eds.). *Motivation and Achievement.* Washington, D.C.: V.H. Winston (Distributed by Halsted Press of John Wiley & Co.), 1974.

Berlyne, D.E. and Madsen, K.B. *Pleasure, Reward, Preference.* New York: (Academic Press, 1973).

Birch, D. Measuring the stream of activity. *Michigan Mathematical Psychology Publication.* MMPP 72-2, Michigan Mathematical Psychology Program. Ann Arbor: University of Michigan, 1972.

Birch, D., Atkinson, J.W., & Bongort, K. Cognitive control of action. In B. Weiner (Ed.), *Cognitive Views of Human Motivation.* New York: Academic Press, 1974, pp. 71–84; 91–98.

Birney, R.C., Burdick, H., & Teevan, R.C. *Fear of Failure.* New York: Van Nostrand-Reinhold, 1969.

deCharms, R. *Enhancing Motivation: Change in the Classroom.* New York: Irvington, 1976.

Feather, N.T. The study of persistence. *Psychological Bulletin,* 1962, *59*, 94–115. Also in J.W. Atkinson and N.T. Feather (Eds.), *A Theory of Achievement Motivation.* New York: Wiley, 1966.

Feshbach, S. The drive reducing function of fantasy behavior. *Journal of Abnormal and Social Psychology,* 1955, *50*, 3–11.

Heckhausen, H. *Hoffnung und Furcht in der Leistungsmotivation.* Verlag Anton Hain: Meisenheim am Glan, 1963.

Heckhausen, H. *The Anatomy of Achievement Motivation.* New York: Academic Press, 1967.

I

Heckhausen, H. Intervening cognitions in motivation. Ch. 9 in *Pleasure, Reward, Preference*. New York and London: Academic Press, 1973, pp. 217–242.

Horner, Matina S. *Sex differences in achievement motivation and performance in competitive and noncompetitive situations*. Unpublished doctoral dissertation, University of Michigan, 1968. Included in J.W. Atkinson and J.O. Raynor (Eds.), *Motivation and Achievement* (1974) above.

Lawler III, E.E. *Motivation in Work Organizations*. Monterey: Brooks/Cole, 1973.

Maehr, M.L. *Socio Cultural Origins of Achievement*. Monterey: Brooks/Cole, 1974.

McClelland, D.C. *Personality*. New York: Wm. Sloane, 1951.

McClelland, D.C. *Power: The Inner Experience*. New York: Irvington Publishers, 1975.

McClelland, D.C. *The Achieving Society*. Irvington.

McClelland, D.C. *Assessing Human Motivation*. New York: General Learning Press, 1971, 20 pp. (a)

McClelland, D.C. *Motivational Trends in Society*. New York: General Learning Press, 1971, 23 pp. (b)

McClelland, D.C., Davis, W.N., Kalin, R., & Wanner, E. *The Drinking Man: Alcohol and Human Motivation*. New York: Free Press, 1972.

McClelland, D.C., & Steele, R.S. *Motivation Workshops: A Student Workbook for Experiential Learning in Human Motivation*. New York/Morristown, N.J.: General Learning Press, 1972.

McClelland, D.C., & Steele, R.S. *Human Motivation: A Book of Readings*. Morristown, N.J.: General Learning Press, 1973.

McClelland, D.C., & Winter, D.G. *Motivating Economic Achievement*. New York: Free Press, 1969.

Rosen, B.C., Crockett, H.J., Jr., & Nunn, C.Z. *Achievement in American Society*. Cambridge, Mass.: Schenkman Publ. Co., 1969.

Smith, C.P. (Ed.). *Achievement-related Motives in Children*. New York: Russell Sage Foundation, 1969.

Uleman J.S. The need for influence: development and validation of a measure, and comparison with the need for power. *Genetic Psychology Monographs*, 1972, *85*, 157–214.

Veroff, J. Development and validation of a projective measure of power motivation. *Journal of Abnormal and Social Psychology*, 1957, *54*, 1–8.

Veroff, J. A scoring manual for the power motive. In J.W. Atkinson (Ed.), *Motives in Fantasy, Action, and Society*. Princeton: Van Nostrand, 1958.

Veroff, J. Theoretical background for studying the origins of human motivational dispositions. *Merill-Palmer Quarterly*, 1965, *11*, 3–18.

Veroff, J., Atkinson, J.W., Feld, S., & Gurin, G. The use of thematic apperception to assess motivation in a nationwide interview study. *Psychological Monographs*, 1960, *74* (12 Whole No. 499).

Veroff, J., & Feld, S. *Marriage and Work in America*. New York: Van Nostrand-Reinhold, 1970.

Veroff, J., & Veroff, J.B. Reconsideration of a measure of power motivation. *Psychological Bulletin*, 1972, 78, 279–291.

Vroom, V.H. *Work and Motivation*. New York, Wiley, 1964.

Walker, E.L., Atkinson, J.W., with Veroff, J., Birney, R., Dember, W., & Moulton, R. The expression of fear-related motivation in thematic apperception as a function of proximity to an atomic explosion. In J.W. Atkinson (Ed.), *Motives in Fantasy, Action, and Society*. Princeton: Van Nostrand, 1958, pp. 143–159.

Weiner, B. (Ed.). *Achievement Motivation and Attribution Theory*. Morristown, N.J.: General Learning Press, 1974.

Winter, D. *The Power Motive*. New York: Free Press, 1973.

Zander, A. *Motives and Goals in Groups*. New York: Academic Press, 1970.

Preface

THIS BOOK contains a summary of research on the achievement motive conducted mainly at Wesleyan University during the period January 1, 1947, to January 1, 1952, under the continuous moral and financial support of the Office of Naval Research. We initially planned to publish our findings in a series of short articles (cf. McClelland, Clark, Roby, and Atkinson, 1949), but as time went along it became clear that our accumulated research data had begun to form an over-all picture of achievement motivation which could best be brought to focus in the form of a book. Such a book, we believe, will be of general interest for several reasons.

First, it provides a practicable method of measuring one of the most important human motives, a method, moreover, which in all probability can be applied to other motives with equal success. Those who are especially interested in this side of our work will want to concentrate on Chapter IV which provides a detailed discussion of the scoring method and on Appendix I which contains a set of stories which can be scored by the researcher and then compared with our scoring of these stories which is reported in Appendix II.

Secondly, the book contains what we believe to be an important contribution to psychological theory—at least to the theory of motivation. Those who are concerned mainly with this aspect of our work will find the core of our ideas in Chapter II.

Finally, the book contains a great deal of information about the achievement motive and related variables, and we feel that most readers, being interested in the total problem, will want to read the whole book. For only if they do, will they discover what we have discovered—that concentration on a limited research problem is not necessarily narrowing; it may lead ultimately into the whole of psychology. In personality theory there is inevitably a certain impatience—a desire to solve every problem at once so as to get the "whole" personality in focus. We have proceeded the other way. By concentrating on one problem, on *one motive,* we have found in the course of our study that we have learned not only a lot about the achievement motive but other areas of personality as well. So we feel that this book can be used as one basis for evaluating the degree to which a "piecemeal" approach to personality is profitable, an approach which proceeds to build up the total picture out of many small experiments by a slow process of going from fact to hypothesis and back to fact again. At the moment it may seem like a poor alternative to immediate, over-all assessment methods, but it is our present feeling that in the long run it will be at least as profitable.

This is a report of research in progress. It was first written in the summer of 1950, and it has been rewritten by one or another of us several times since then. One of the difficulties has been that after something has been written up, new data often appear which cast a somewhat different light on the picture. The present report is no exception. In desperation we finally decided to "freeze" our knowledge and report our findings as of a certain date. The result is that as this goes to press, we know that certain findings or interpretations have been superseded by newer ones. The reader should keep this in mind: we do not regard anything in this report as final. It is truly a report of research in progress, a report which we hope will be of some assistance to others in their work and perhaps serve to stimulate them to check and extend our findings.

This book is the result of a co-operative enterprise. The problem of organization of co-operative research is important and complicated. It may be useful to record at this point who did the research, how our program operated, and what we consider to be some of its advantages and disadvantages. Surprisingly enough, most of the data reported here were collected by college seniors working on Honor's theses or by first-year graduate students. Looking back, we are inclined to draw two tentative conclusions from this fact. First, these students were able to complete fairly significant research projects considerably before the Ph.D. thesis which usually has been regarded as the stage at which significant research begins. There were several reasons for this, some peculiar to this period in history and some not. Most of the students were much older than usual because of the war. If this is a factor, it suggests that maturity has more to do with research capacity than years of previous training in psychology. Another possible explanation may be that practically all the students, even the seniors, had had experience with at least one prior research project for which they had assumed primary responsibility. At Wesleyan it has always been the practice to teach psychology by involving students as soon as possible in the research process. Thus, after a semester of guided experience with laboratory experiments, all majors spend the second semester in following up a research problem of their own, usually in co-operation with one or two other students. When the best of these students become seniors, they undertake a year-long research problem and write a thesis in connection with this work. By their first graduate year the students who follow this course have accumulated experience with two independent research projects and are, therefore, as prepared as many Ph.D. candidates to conduct a significant piece of research on their own. They have one further advantage over the Ph.D. candidate in that they do not yet feel the pressure to be completely original, to break entirely new ground, to invent a new approach to a research problem.

A second generalization which this research enterprise suggests is that in the long run considerable autonomy in research pays very high dividends. The men who conducted the research reported here were seldom, if ever, simply given a research problem because it fitted somewhere into a co-ordinated research program, being conducted by the senior author. In fact many of them as assistants expected that they would be given a number of routine tasks to perform in order to get their pay. Instead, because of the generous policy of the Office of Naval Research in making these grants for exploratory research, it was possible to permit each of these men to work out some problem that *he* thought was significant. The only restrictions placed on his efforts were that his research had to have something to do with achievement motivation and that it had to make use of the general method of measuring motivation which had been adopted. This last restriction may seem a little rigid, but it seemed preferable to the alternative of obtaining results which might be due either to differences in the method of measurement *or* the particular variables investigated.

With the stimulation of being able to work on their own research problem within these broad limits, most of the students were able to carry out a project in which they became ego-involved (or should we say achievement-oriented?). As a result, many became in every sense of the word full partners in the total enterprise. This method of procedure may result in less efficient research progress (although we are not even convinced of this in the long run) than assigning someone a specific task in a planned program, but it certainly should help to produce better psychologists—psychologists who can think for themselves and carry out their own research projects.

As the result of the type of co-operative enterprise we have been describing, this book has been contributed to by many more people than the four whose names appear on it. We four are simply representatives of a much larger group—representatives who sat down one summer and tried to report the various research projects in some kind of co-ordinated fashion. In making our many acknowledgments we would like to single out in particular Joseph Veroff, who was closely associated with the research for three years. Also deserving particular thanks for important contributions are Benjamin Simon, M.D. and Jules Holzberg, Ph.D., both at one time with the Connecticut State Hospital at Middletown, who were anchor men in the clinical study of thirty undergraduates which we made in order to explore the role of achievement motivation in the total organization of personality. Others who have made important contributions to this book and whose assistance is gratefully acknowledged are: Richard Alpert, David Angell, Robert C. Birney, Roger Brown, Esther (Laden) Cava, Gerald A. Friedman, William Lee, Alvin M. Liberman, John Martire, Robert Moulton, John Perkins, Thornton B. Roby, Alvin Rosenstein, Thomas Shipley, Nicholas Verven, Bernice Weinberger, Sue Wilcox, Marian Winterbottom, and Josef Zatzkis. In addition to these specific individuals, both students and faculty in seminars at the University of Michigan, Harvard University, and Wesleyan University have given us much valuable criticism and advice. A special word of thanks is due Irene Parmelee and Elspeth Cowie, who have struggled with the manuscript in its final form.

The assistance of the Office of Naval Research also deserves particular acknowledgment. From the very beginning—from the initial encouragement of Captain C. W. Schilling on through the constant support and help of Dr. J. W. Macmillan and Dr. H. E. Page—the ONR's attitude has been everything that could be desired from a fund-granting institution. It has proceeded on the philosophy that the research worker is the best judge of what he ought to be doing, and it has never attempted to short-circuit long-run theoretical development in favor of immediate practical advantage to the Navy. In fact, it has never even suggested to us what our research objectives should be. More than this, its staff has helped us when we

Table of Contents

CHAPTER VI. GENERAL APPLICABILITY OF THE N ACHIEVEMENT SCORING SYSTEM

CHAPTER VII. THE MEASURING INSTRUMENT . 185

List of Figures

xvii

List of Tables

xix

THE
ACHIEVEMENT MOTIVE

❧CHAPTER I❧

Introduction

THIS REPORT represents an attempt to summarize the results of five years of intensive research into the nature of achievement motivation. Our purpose in writing it has been twofold. On the one hand, we have felt the need to bring together the many diverse findings accumulated over this period in an attempt to develop some kind of a theory that would at least begin to put them in order. On the other hand, the measure of achievement motivation that we have developed has seemed promising as a research tool, and we are eager to have others use it and extend this general approach to the study of other motives. The problems uncovered in the course of this research have been so numerous and complex that we feel their solution will require the co-operative effort of many scientists.

The idea which initially gave impetus to the research was the commonplace one that motivation theory, especially with respect to human motivation, is greatly in need of development. In some areas psychologists have made relatively good progress in recent years. For example, in the study of "learning" the journals are filled with research contributions and with the kind of controversy that indicates a fairly advanced stage of theoretical development. The same can be said of the study of perception to a lesser, but ever increasing, extent. The work of Bruner (1951), Postman (1951), and their associates has reopened old theoretical questions and stimulated new interest in this traditional area of psychological knowledge. But the study of motivation lags behind.

To be sure, the concept of motivation occupies a prominent

1

position in the theoretical systems of many learning theorists. However, these men have been primarily concerned with explaining learning, not motivation, which they have tended to treat in a rather narrow fashion, basing their conception largely on the manipulation of a limited range of "noxious" or deficit stimuli (produced by electric shock or by food and water deprivation). There is a definite lack of experimental work involving humans and "secondary" drives. It has been only recently that the "secondary" or "acquired" drives have been subjected to close scrutiny in their own right. Even in this recent work the tendency has been to employ animal subjects, with an emphasis on fear acquired as a result of electric shock. Of course psychoanalytically-oriented psychologists have written extensively about human motivation but with, as yet, little emphasis on experimentation.

In such a state of affairs, the greatest need appeared to be the discovery of some standard method of measuring human motivation. Theoretical advances in any field seem to wait upon the development of methods of measurement. Motivation has no long-established methods of measurement such as "trials to reach a criterion," "errors," and so on, which are employed in learning, or the psychophysical methods employed in perception. Psychologists have been able to find a stopgap solution to this problem in the field of animal motivation, chiefly for the hunger drive, by controlling strength of motivation in terms of hours of deprivation. Such a method of control or measurement, however, is of little value in the study of human motivation and is not even exactly applicable to many biological drives. Our purpose, then, has been to develop a method of measuring human motives and to use the method in collecting data which would contribute to a theory of motivation.

In approaching the problem we were guided by two ideas —one based on psychoanalytic thinking about motivation, another based on experimental investigations of animal motivation. From the former we accepted the hypothesis, which appears to be amply supported by Freud's original work on dreams, by years of psychoanalytic experience, and by the clinical success of Murray's Thematic Apperception Test, that an excellent place to look for and measure the effects of motivation is in fantasy. Unlike many previous workers with the dynamic content of fantasy, we felt that it was unjustifiable to attempt to draw sound inferences about the strength of motivation on the basis of the fantasy material alone. It was here that we accepted the notion from experimental studies of animals that motives could be experimentally aroused and their intensity controlled by manipulating arousal conditions. Our problem, then, boiled down to the attempt to arouse and control the intensity of a human motive and to measure its effect on imagination or fantasy. By using standard experimental design, we could hope to establish which characteristics of fantasy could be attributed solely to the introduced variable, namely, the aroused motivational state. In this way we would not be forced to make any a priori assumptions as to what characteristics of fantasy indicate the presence and intensity of a certain motive. Instead, we would discover the diagnostic characteristics by our empirical, experimental procedure.

To avoid starting with two unknowns at once, we decided to test first the hypothesis that fantasy will readily reflect the effects of a condition like hunger which is generally accepted as a motive. This procedure also had the advantage of helping us standardize an instrument for sampling imaginative behavior. The initial experiment in this series by Atkinson and McClelland (1948) demonstrated that subjects deprived of food for one, four, and sixteen hours will write brief imaginative stories that are increasingly concerned with food deprivation, food-getting activities, hunger, and the like. It was assumed that an approximate measure of the intensity of the hunger motivation of a particular individual would be an algebraic sum of those characteristics in his stories which had been shown to increase or decrease significantly in frequency with increasing hours of food deprivation. A rough n Food (need for food) index thus derived predicted fairly well how long the person had been without food. Although the index was only approximate, partly because n Food is clearly not just a simple function of hours of food deprivation and partly because we did not refine it further, we felt that it had demonstrated that fantasy could reflect the presence and intensity of motivation sensitively.

From that point on, we devoted our attention to the achievement motive, primarily because there seemed to be a set of operations which had been frequently used in the laboratory for arousing it. These centered around procedures for producing ego-involvement and experimentally-induced experiences of success and failure (cf. Alper, 1946; Nowlis, 1941; Rosenzweig, 1943; and Sears, 1942). The chief purposes of our report here are to show in detail the effects of various arousal conditions of this sort on imaginative behavior, to demonstrate how we derive a measure of achievement motivation from these effects—a measure which will often be referred to as n Achievement after Murray (1938)—and to show the relation of n Achievement to various other types of behavior. Although our initial approach to this problem was purely empirical, and although most of the data to be reported were collected with an empirical, exploratory frame of reference, we have always been guided by some more or less implicit theoretical assumptions that we have become more and more motivated to make explicit as we have reviewed our work. That is, the findings to be reported here stand on their own feet as empirical data about human motivation collected in a relatively new way, but they will achieve wider significance only as they can be related to a general theory of motivation and behavior. Consequently, we have attempted to state as explicitly as possible what some of our theoretical assumptions were to begin with or are now since we have reviewed our findings. It might be more impressive to "predict" some of our findings on the basis of our theory now that we have developed it, but this would not represent accurately the actual process of induction and deduction that has led to the theoretical formulation. Nevertheless, in whatever way we arrived at some of our proposals for a theory, we are for the time being stuck with them and want to state them in such a way that they will account for some of our present findings, make predictions for future experiments, and perhaps suggest experiments which will test their validity as compared with alternative theories of motivation.

Therefore, our report includes a theory of motivation which, if we had had it when we started, would have led to the design of "cleaner" experiments and which should lead to better experiments in the future. The reader may be impressed at certain points by the lack of congruence between our theory and the way we collected our data. If so, we can only protest that the data came first and the theory second, and that in the future we should do better. We regard what is reported here only as an interim report—a report of work in progress. If our ideas change as often and as radically in the next five years as they have in the last five, much in this report will be outmoded very soon. To repeat, our reason for writing it has been to clarify our own thinking and to make available to other investigators an instrument for measuring human motivation which we have found promising.

CHAPTER II

Toward a Theory of Motivation

2.1 Introduction. In our struggles with empirical studies of motivation in the last four or five years, we could scarcely have avoided formulating some general ideas, however vague, about a theory of motivation. The very process of trying to discover conditions for experimentally arousing a motive has forced us to consider just what a motive is, and the study of its many effects on imagination and behavior has continuously raised for us certain theoretical problems which demand solution. Probably the most insistent challenge to our theoretical imagination has come from trying to understand the manner in which a motive is acquired. It is this question as much as any other which forced us to reopen apparently settled issues, just as it did for Mowrer (cf. 1950).

What follows then is an attempt at a theory of motivation. It has not been forced upon us by our data in any specific sense. That is, we believe that our data stand on their own feet and should be taken account of by any theory of motivation that may ultimately be proposed. The data have *suggested* a particular set of theoretical proposals, but they do not *demand* the proposals in any rigorous fashion. It would be fairer to say that the theory has grown out of the continuous study of motivational problems that we have had to make in order to collect our data and interpret them. In this connection it is worth noting that our theory has developed from an empirical study of motivation rather than learning, and thus differs in its origin from most other theories of motivation which have developed primarily, though not exclusively, from an empirical study of *learning* phenomena.

One word of caution is in order before we begin our survey of the present status of motivation theory. In what follows we have restricted ourselves to rather large generalizations, both because of limitations of space and because our purpose at this stage is only to rough out our own proposals for a new theory and our objections to other theories. In many cases we have mentioned data which we feel represent the *main trend* of research, although we know that, in many instances, the problem is not yet completely solved, and that what seem like theoretical difficulties to us have been adjusted in one fashion or another by the theorists involved. We have not felt that we could or should go into a detailed discussion of these "adjustments," some of which become exceedingly involved and technical, nor have we felt capable at this stage of stating the kind of precise, functional relationships that Brown and Farber (1951) insist constitute a "real" theory. Instead we would argue for the importance of an intermediate, somewhat flexible stage in theory development when hypotheses are stated which can be empirically tested and gradually refined in the course of testing until precise functional relationships can be stated. It is for this reason we have labeled the chapter "Toward a Theory of Motivation." We are chiefly interested not in rigorously disproving present motivational theories but in illustrating what seem to us to be some of their difficulties, so that we can lead more easily into an exposition of our alternative tentative hypotheses in which we assume the reader will be mainly interested.

2.2 **Difficulties with current motivational theorizing.** Psychologists have reached a rather unusual degree of agreement with respect to the general nature of motives. The common assumption running through most contemporary theories is that motives are "deficit" tensional states which energize organisms until relief is obtained or "equilibrium" restored. Broadly conceived, this "tensional" theory of motivation has received support from such widely different sources as Freud (part of the time), Hull (1943), Miller and Dollard (1941), Murray (cf. Kluckhohn and Murray, 1948), and Mowrer (1950).

Yet to us this basic conception has not appeared entirely adequate. There have always been those who have objected to it like Young (1949), Hebb (1949), Maslow (1953), or Allport (1937), but their objections have carried more weight with us than with many others who have continued to write elementary textbooks, at least, as if motivation is primarily a matter of energy released by an upset equilibrium. The idea that motives are essentially "tensional" in nature and energize organisms certainly has its difficulties which vary somewhat according to the way in which the tension is conceived. Hebb (1949) has objected vigorously and effectively to the notion of a motive as an *energizer*—as a concept which is needed in order to explain the activity of the organism. He argues that the organism is already active and that the motive concept is needed to explain the *directedness* of activities rather than their over-all intensity level. For him, variations in the amount of overt activity are not necessarily a function of the intensity level of some "central tensional state," but are more probably a function of variation in the *patterning* of neural activity.

A behavioral excitation, an increase in some bodily activity, is not necessarily a sign of increased neural activity either in the brain as a whole or in some part of it. The point is well illustrated by the process of getting drunk. A small amount of alcohol may be an excitant—socially, and in its immediate net effect on behavior—but this, of course, does not prove that alcohol is a neural excitant. . . . The behavior of the drunk may be produced because alcohol, depressing *all* neural cells, depresses some more rapidly than others and so changes the pattern of firing throughout the cerebrum (Hebb, 1949, pp. 209, 210).

In short, he is arguing that a connection between behavioral "tension" or activity and neural "tension" is by no means necessary or as obvious as it might appear to be. The same point has been made by Brown and Jacobs (1949), who state that one should abandon "the rather limited assumption that drives, when functioning as energizers, always lead to more vigorous overt or random action" (pp. 752–753). These authors recognize the difficulty with the usual common-sense conception of drives as energizers of activity, but hope to retain the energizing concept by restricting its meaning to activation of a habit.

Other difficulties with the tension notion arise when it is conceived essentially as a negative affective state derived primarily from painful experiences. Thus, Mowrer (1950) has conceived of secondary motivation primarily as anxiety over the possibility of painful sensations arising from the failure to satisfy primary biological needs.

All the basic needs are types of discomfort and are in the broad sense "painful" . . . Human beings are capable of being motivated, not only by organic needs (discomforts) that are immediately present and felt, but also by the mere anticipation of such needs (1950, p. 29).

In discussing, for example, how a trainer may come to have positive reward value for a bird who is being taught to talk, Mowrer states,

The bird (baby) discovers that when it is alone it may get hungry, thirsty, cold, hurt. On the other hand, when the trainer is present, these discomforts vanish. Therefore, the presence of the trainer is an important stimulus element in the total situation, serving to convert it from situation-in-which-I-may-be-uncomfortable (helpless) to situation-in-which-everything-will-be-allright (1950, p. 726).

In short, being alone is a cue which evokes anxiety or fear of discomfort for the bird. The trainer has symbolic reward value because he has been associated with reduction in anxiety. In this way, anxiety for Mowrer comes to be the key to all motives. "At the level of ego psychology, there may be said to be only one master motive: anxiety" (Mowrer, 1952, p. 423).

There are several objections to the "discomfort" or "anxiety" explanation of tension as a motivational state. In the first place, McMurray (1950) has reported the case of a girl who apparently has never felt pain or shown any of the usual physiological reactions to pain.

> After a day on the beach she had to inspect her feet carefully for cuts. She claimed on many occasions to have received deep cuts from shells which she had not noted until this inspection. At no time had she ever reported any form of ache or pain, such as headache, earache, toothache, stomachache or menstrual pain. The whole of her ordinary activities of living from birth had repeated, again and again, the same theme of tissue damage that had gone unnoticed or been looked on indifferently. Frostbites in winter were frequent. Burns from hot objects and from overlong exposure to the sun had also been numerous (1950, p. 5).

When she was subjected in the laboratory to ordinary tests of pain threshold, she gave no objective reports of feeling pain nor did she show any of the disturbances in blood pressure, heart rate, and the like which normally accompany pain. In short, she appeared to be as free of sensory discomforts as any person could be, and yet so far as could be judged, she seemed to be a normal, highly intelligent girl whose personality did not show any marked defect. But if motives are built essentially on discomforts of one sort or another, how could she fail to show some gross apparent defect in development?

Mowrer (1950, p. 725) himself suggests that the discomfort notion may be inadequate in his discussion of "the precise nature of the gratification which a dog derives from close association with a human master." This appears as a special problem to him because he recognizes that the attachment of dog to master may occur without the master

ever having served as a means of removing the dog's discomforts (by feeding him, etc.). One of Mowrer's corre-
spondents suggests that stroking the dog as a source of special
pleasure may be the explanation. Mowrer confirms the fact
that "it is well known among the keepers of parrots and
parakeets that they love nothing better than to have their
'necks scratched'" (1950, p. 725), but then he does not go
on to consider the logical possibility that certain types of
sensory stimulation are innately pleasurable just as certain
other types are innately painful. Psychologists have had difficulty in considering this possibility seriously. That is, we
have been very willing to assume that certain kinds of stimulation give rise innately to pain and discomfort and act as motives but unwilling to assume that other kinds of stimulation
give rise innately to pleasure. Recently several experiments
have confirmed the type of observation reported by Mowrer
about parrots under more controlled conditions. Thus Sheffield and Roby (1950) have confirmed earlier results of Young
(1949), which may be interpreted as showing that saccharine
has certain innate reward values for producing learning that
cannot readily be explained in terms of its association with
need reduction. Similarly Sheffield, Wulff, and Backer (1951)
have reported that male rats will learn to run to copulate with
a receptive female even though prevented from reaching orgasm (tension-reduction); and Weiner and Stellar (1951)
have demonstrated that rats show a preference for salty water
which "does not depend on experience" and which "does not
depend crucially upon any physiological effect of salt being absorbed in the gut, for it shows up too soon after drinking begins." "Harlow *et al.* give convincing evidence that
monkeys manipulate the manipulatable without any need-
reduction or reinforcement in the usual sense of these terms"
(Nissen and Semmes, 1952). In short, the evidence for certain innate "gratifications" has seemed to us very convincing
on a priori, phenomenological, and experimental grounds,

and we have felt in consequence that any theory of motivation should take account of the active comforts and pleasures of life as well as the discomforts, tensions, and their relief.

2.3 **Review of various motivational models.** Having considered what we feel is a general shortcoming of motivational theorizing, let us specifically examine some of the current theoretical systems. Table 2.1 has been constructed to show the various sources and behavioral consequences of motivation as conceived by different theorists. Although it is true that not all theorists have thought of the motive construct in exactly this way, it has proved possible in nearly every instance to fit their ideas into this type of theoretical framework. The reason this has been possible is that all theorists. agree that there are certain special types of conditions which give rise to motives, and nearly all theorists agree that motivated behavior is in some way distinguishable from unmotivated behavior. Brown and Farber (1951) constitute a partial exception to the general rule as far as the response side of the equation is concerned. That is, while they argue that all intervening variables like emotion or motivation must be defined in terms of "antecedent conditions, concomitant states, *and* responses" (1951, p. 470), they themselves find that attempts to achieve classificatory groupings of emotions on the response side have been "notoriously futile." "The procedure of categorizing certain responses as emotional and others as nonemotional becomes unnecessary and undesirable. . . . At any given instant, the topography of a given bit of behavior may reflect the action of numerous hypothetical determinants: habits, motivations, inhibitions, response-produced stimulations, perceptions, and (perhaps) emotions" (1951, p. 470). For them, all of these variables are preferably defined in terms of special sets of antecedent conditions rather than in terms of unique response patterns, since the latter are always jointly determined by all the other intervening variables in the hypothetical system. With this exception, however, which is a practical rather than a theoretical matter, most theorists have felt that the presence of motivation can be detected from some characteristic way in which it influences behavior.

Table 2.1 has been further arranged in order to show which types of behavioral effects are usually (but not always) associated by a theorist with which particular types of antecedent conditions. Thus, for example, those theorists who have thought of a motive as being aroused through an increase in stimulus intensity have also usually thought of the motive as showing itself through an increase in response vigor or output. The parallelism, however, is not exact, and there is no logical necessity for correlating any particular response definition of a motive with any particular stimulus definition of a motive. There certainly are theorists whose theoretical positions cut diagonally across the table, and there are others who adopt a pluralistic position, like Melton who argues (1941) that motives energize, direct, and select behavior. Nevertheless, the arrangement has seemed useful particularly in isolating at least four major types of theoretical models that have been constructed for motivation, including our own.

2.4 **The survival model.** One of the earliest and certainly one of the most influential ways of thinking about motivation was to start with the notion of survival of the species or of an individual member of the species. This idea, which was central to the doctrine of evolution, has had an extremely powerful influence on psychologists as widely different in other respects as Freud and Hull. Psychoanalysis and behavior theory could unite in the belief that life is a struggle for survival and that Mother Nature or Divine Providence must have provided organisms with some innate signals which would warn of approaching threats to survival (cf. Hull, 1943,

TABLE 2.1. Motive as a hypothetical construct conceived as based on various kinds of antecedent conditions and as being reflected in various types of behavior

Possible *sources* of	MOTIVES	as reflected in *types of behavior*
1. Biologically defined survival needs— food deprivation, etc. (Hull)	"Survival model"	1. Adaptive responses which permit or promote survival (need reduction)
2. Stimulus intensity (Miller and Dollard)	"Stimulus intensity model"	2. (*a*) Increased response output (*b*) Improvement in performance (learning)
3. Stimulus patterns of particular sorts	"Stimulus pattern model"	3. Response patterns
(*a*) Stimulus situations which evoke varying degrees of correspondence between expectancy and perception (Hebb)		(*a*) Organized direction of behavior, the relatedness of a series of acts
(*b*) Stimulus situations which evoke incompatible response tendencies producing frustration (Brown and Farber)		
		(*c*) Distinctive response patterns measured in the brain, through autonomic effects, or in overt behavior
4. Cues paired with adaptation level discrepancies innately producing affect (McClelland, *et al.*)	"Affective arousal model"	4. Goal-oriented "free" choice with habit and situational factors minimized, known, or randomized
		(*a*) Approach-avoidance under the above conditions
		(*b*) Frequency with which classes of goal-oriented thoughts (*R*'s) are chosen for inclusion in fantasy

p. 17). These signals are tripped off by certain biological needs, such as the need for food or water, and serve to make the organism active until it finds some way of putting an end to the need. Therefore motives can be aroused by creating biological needs and their presence can be inferred, at least to some extent, by the adaptive or need-reducing nature of behavior. To be sure, this has always created some difficulties as far as maladaptive responses or habits are concerned (see Maier's study of frustration-produced "behavior without a goal" [1949]); but on the whole, the idea behind this theoretical model is beautiful in its simplicity and it can probably be found in every elementary psychology textbook today. Certain difficulties with this model may be summarized briefly. In the first place, some survival needs produce a motive and some do not. For example, it is now known that vitamin B_{12} is necessary for the production of erythrocytes, and without B_{12} the organism will suffer from pernicious anemia and die. Yet a person suffering from anemia or B_{12} deficiency behaves in no way like a motivated person, at least as determined by any of the usual measures of motivation. Another example would be the breathing of carbon monoxide which leads to sudden death and certainly to a tissue need, but which apparently produces no activity or behavior suggestive of a state of motivation. If anyone feels that these are merely isolated exceptions to the biological-need theory of motivation, a very brief perusal of medical literature should convince him of the great number of pathological organic conditions that by definition constitute tissue needs, but which do not give rise to any kind of "driving" stimulus or motive. Granted this fact, it follows that the presence of a biological need is not a reliable index of the existence of a motive.

In the second place, it is often hard to determine just what the organism's survival needs are, since there are so many possible ones and it often depends on what point of view you take whether you decide a particular one exists or not. Take the invasion of the body by foreign protein, for example. From one point of view you might argue that the biological need is to fight this invasion. So the body in its "wisdom" mobilizes antibodies. But the antibodies may produce anaphylactic shock and in extreme cases death. So it turns out that the biological "need" for antibodies produced death. In the same way, satisfying even a dependable need like the need for food may have side effects that ultimately produce death. Thus the connection between so many often contradictory bodily "needs" and motives is in practice very difficult to work out in precise terms.

A third difficulty with the assumption that all motives are ultimately derived from or dependent on primary biological needs is that biological needs provide only a very partial basis for explaining how behavior is guided and controlled, particularly in lower animals. Thus Kohn (1951) has demonstrated that milk introduced into a rat's mouth or into its stomach will produce a change in its behavior long before the milk could be absorbed in the gut so as to produce a change in biological need. Similarly, the experiments cited above by Sheffield and Roby (1950) and by Sheffield, Wulff, and Backer (1951), with respect to the effects of saccharine and sexual stimulation on learning, argue for a more direct control of behavior through afferent stimulation rather than through slower-acting changes in biological need states. The evidence for such afferent control of behavior in lower animals is overwhelming, as Hebb and others have pointed out. For example, in discussing how spiders spin a highly specific kind of web or birds build a nest of a particular design, Hebb (1949, p. 167) says,

All this means that the behavior, though it cannot be called reflex, is still continually under sensory influence, more or less direct. At each stage in the construction the muscular activity varies with circumstance and is such as to produce a certain perceptual effect. This indirect sensory control is demonstrated whenever accident destroys part of the structure. The muscular activity then does not continue in a predetermined sequence, but reverts to an earlier stage, in such a way as to restore the missing parts. Since the behavior is continually responsive to such events, it must be under afferent influence throughout.

He further points out that as you go up the phylogenetic scale, the amount of sensory control decreases, but this seems no reason to assume a sharp discontinuity between lower animals and man as to the importance of sensory influences in guiding behavior. (See also Tinbergen, 1951.) The paradox can be put very simply this way: In lower animals, biological needs like hunger, thirst, and pain do not provide a very complete means of describing how behavior is directed and controlled. In fact, animals often do things under afferent influences which are clearly the opposite of any conceivable "biological need" as normally defined, such as when a moth flies into a flame. Yet with human beings we commonly discard the notion of afferent control and think of motivation almost wholly in terms of needs which must be satisfied if the organism is to survive. As we shall show in a moment, we have returned somewhat to this notion of afferent control in our proposals for a theory of motivation.

A fourth difficulty with the biological need theory of motivation has been discussed at length in another connection by McClelland (1951), who points out that the extraordinary persistence and strength characteristic of learned human motives argues against their continued dependence on biological needs. In other words, despite all the arguments about continued partial reinforcement, it remains difficult (though not impossible) to conceive of a social motive like the achievement drive as continuing to be influential in a man's life because it brings him food, shelter, and relief from tissue needs. A related difficulty arises from trying to figure out how a motive can be *acquired* when the primary drives are weak and non-persistent, as they normally would be in adulthood. One not very satisfying way out of this difficulty is, of course, to assume that motives cannot be learned in later life but can be formed only in infancy when the primary drives are relatively important. Such a state of affairs is possible, but it does not seem probable. In view of the known flexibility of the human learning mechanism, why should it not be possible to form new motives at any time in life? Finally, at the simple empirical level we have found no evidence in our data to indicate that the achievement motive is perceived as instrumental to or associated with the satisfaction of primary biological needs. That is, by the experimental manipulation of achievement-related arousal conditions we were able to get increases in achievement imagery (Chap. V), but a count of achievement-associated imagery leading to food-getting, pain-reduction, survival, and so on has revealed no accompanying increase in the achievement-oriented, as contrasted with the relaxed, condition. It may appear simple-minded of us to expect such a connection in imagination, but *why not,* if the achievement motive is thought to be associated with satisfying these biological needs even in adulthood?

We should not conclude from this that biological needs have no connection with motivation. They probably do, through the capacity of many of them to produce affective arousal or cues that will be regularly associated with affective change, as we shall see later on (Section 2.14). They must have some connection with the mechanisms that control and direct behavior or the species would not have survived. But the connection is not close enough to work well theoretically. Our over-all conclusion is that to approach motivation through trying to identify tissue needs is inaccurate and unnecessarily restrictive. Motivation theory built on such a base does have a simplicity that is very attractive, but it may have been obtained at too great a cost (cf. Hebb, 1949, p. 179).

2.5 **The stimulus intensity model.** Implicit in Hull's system is another idea about motivation which has been developed most fully by Miller and Dollard (1941). This idea, which is also extremely attractive in its great simplicity, is that "a drive is a strong stimulus which impels action. Any stimulus can become a drive if it is made strong enough. The stronger the stimulus, the more drive function it possesses" (Miller and Dollard, 1941, p. 18). Again, however, the simplicity is a little deceptive. At first glance it would appear that any strong stimulus, such as a loud noise, a hunger pang, or an electric shock, will produce a motive whereas conversely a decrease in stimulation such as a reduction in noise level, or in electric shock, would be rewarding. Yet, such a notion raises some obvious objections. Often decreases in stimulation appear to cause an increase in motivation (e.g., a dark night), whereas an increase in stimulation may cause a decrease in motivation (e.g., a light on a dark night). Miller and Dollard recognize this possibility—in fact the "dark night" example is their own (1941, p. 65)—but they argue that one must take into account the organism's past learning and the *total* amount of stimulation. Presumably the person who is alone on a dark night has a more active brain because of anxiety based on past negative experiences with absence of visual stimulation in the dark. "The light may produce a moderate increase in the amount of stimulation reaching him through the eyes, but a marked decrease in the amount of stimulation from anxiety responses" (Miller and Dollard, 1941, p. 65). But this explanation only adds to our difficulties. For the theory has now lost some of its simplicity and becomes exceedingly hard to test crucially if we must always take into account past experience and total stimulation every time we try to decide whether a strong stimulus will be a drive or a reward. That is, the advantage of this type of theoretical model arises partly from the fact that one can presumably arouse a motive by increasing a particular peripheral stimulus intensity. But a good deal of the advantage is lost if we must take these other factors into account.

Furthermore, there is other evidence which seems to cast doubt upon the adequacy of the stimulus intensity model. As Hebb points out (1949, p. 185), decreases in total afferent activity, as in the regeneration of cutaneous nerves, are often accompanied by marked hyperalgesia. Cattell and Hoagland (Morgan, 1943, p. 266) in an investigation, the intent of which was to determine if there was such a thing as a "pure" pressure receptor, stimulated the skin of a frog with an interrupted air jet. They showed that the nerve fibres activated by this stimulation responded at their maximum rate (300 per second) but the frog showed no activity that would indicate the presence of a motive to avoid this stimulation which, in terms of intensity (frequency of firing), was as strong a stimulation (for the number of fibres involved) as the frog was capable of experiencing. Finally, pain seems to be a very effective source of avoidance motivation, yet according to present evidence it is probably the *slow firing C* fibres which are singularly effective in mediating pain.

What this evidence seems to add up to is that although strong stimulation often does give rise to pain or negative affect and thus provides a source of motivation, it does not always produce negative affect. And when it does not, it appears not to be a source of motivation. Therefore, negative affect would seem to be the causative motivational factor and not strong stimulation per se. The connection between stimulus intensity and strong central motive states is so imperfect and complex that at best stimulus intensity can be considered only one of the antecedent conditions for arousing a motive, and we must search further for other antecedent conditions.

On the response side, the model has also been criticized. For one thing, it is by no means necessary that increases and decreases in response output result from changes in the *in-*

tensity of neural activity. "A decrease of bodily activity does not always mean a decrease of neural activity; sleep may consist only of a change of the combinations in which cortical cells fire—i.e., may essentially be hypersynchrony, with no decrease of total activity" (Hebb, 1949, p. 211). Thus the idea behind the stimulus intensity model, that strong afferent stimulation leads to strong central neural activity which leads to strong response activity, appears to be much too simple. It is more probable that changes in patterns rather than in intensity levels of central neural activity are involved. Even if one sticks to the intensity idea, there are difficulties with it. Sometimes apparent increases in central neural activity lead to decreases (instead of increases) in overt responsiveness, as in the "freezing" behavior that Brown and Jacobs (1949) observed in anxious rats. Furthermore, apparent decreases in central neural activity, such as may result from alcohol in the blood, may lead not to decreases in overt behavior but to hyperactivity. And so forth. In short, it is by no means so obvious as it might appear that "the various needs evoke actions which increase in intensity and variety as the need becomes more acute" (Hull, 1943, p. 65). Again we are not arguing that there is *no* connection between amount of activity and motive level (see Table 2.2, Sections 8.1 and 8.2) but only that the relationship is complex and that therefore some other measure of motive strength may be preferable. It is perhaps because of such considerations that Miller, as well as Brown and Jacobs (1949), argues for learning, rather than increased activity, as the chief criterion for inferring the existence of a drive. He states that "the ultimate test of drive and reward is their ability to produce the learning and performance of new responses" (in Stevens, 1951, p. 436). This version of the "stimulus intensity" hypothesis should really be rephrased to read, "a drive is a strong stimulus whose existence can be inferred from learning." Such a statement follows by definition from Miller's (and also Hull's) system, since drive reduction is *essential* for learning according to the system (cf. Dollard and Miller, 1950, p. 26). Therefore all learning indicates that a drive has been present. One difficulty with this idea is that it leaves contiguity-learning theorists out on a limb with no way of telling whether motivation is present. That is, for them learning can occur without motivation as in the latent learning experiments. Therefore, if latent learning can be accepted as a fact, learning is not a sure sign that motivation has been present. In any case, learning per se is not of much use in telling us what *kind* of motive has been operating, which limits the usefulness of this measure for many purposes.

2.6 The stimulus pattern model. Of those theorists who hold a position somewhat similar to ours, Hebb has been probably the most persistent critic of the motivation models so far discussed. What does he have to offer in their place? In its most general form, his model replaces the notion of stimulus intensity with the notion of variations in neural patterning. He begins by defining motivation as a hypothetical construct with certain *neural* attributes. "The term motivation then refers (1) to the existence of an organized phase sequence, (2) to its direction or content, and (3) to its persistence in a given direction, or stability of content" (1949, p. 181). The crucial factor here is whatever serves to *limit* "the variety of conceptual activity" so as to cause it to persist in a given direction. Whatever succeeds in this respect may be called a motive. But what are the factors which succeed in this way? Can any generalizations be made as to what antecedent conditions may be considered motivating because they serve to limit conceptual processes? Hebb considers how such specific states as pain and hunger may serve as motives, but the nearest he comes to a general statement seems to involve the size of the discrepancy between expectation and perception. In a general way he states, "what I

postulate is that, up to a certain point, lack of correspond-
ence between expectancy and perception may simply have
a stimulating or 'pleasurable' effect . . . ; beyond this point,
a disrupting (or unpleasant) effect" (Hebb, 1949, p. 149).
More specifically, the size of the discrepancy can be discussed in four stages. In the first stage, when the discrepancy
is largest, the organism may feel pain which is "a disruptive
somesthetic event." It may serve to control learning (and
hence be classified as a motive) "by disrupting one phase sequence, leaving another unmolested" (p. 182). In the second stage, when the discrepancy is a little less, the pain
stimulus may get organized into a phase sequence and help
it to persist. Then "we must regard the stimulus as essentially motivating: just as a blow of a whip may be motivating
and energizing to a race horse who appears already to be
exerting himself to the utmost" (1949, p. 190). In the third
stage, there is still some discrepancy between expectation and
perception but it is now relatively small and the organism
may feel pleasure. Hebb's favorite example here is the pleasure which derives from reading a detective story in which
the elements are somewhat familiar but the outcome unfamiliar. The last stage is when no discrepancy exists at all
between expectation and perception, in which case the phase
sequence tends to run off with great speed or be short-cir-
cuited. In this situation the person is bored, as in reading
the same detective story for a second time, and may ultimately fall asleep. According to this view, the second and
third stages of moderate discrepancy between expectation
and perception are most apt to be motivating in that they
foster the continued development and persistence of a phase
sequence in a given direction. The first stage may be motivating indirectly by knocking out a competing phase sequence; and the last is the very opposite of motivation, since
the short-circuiting of the phase sequence leads to its disap-
pearance rather than persistence, a notion which can be in-

voked to account for satiation or cessation of motivated behavior. In short, for Hebb's theory one must know the relationship between past learning and present perception in order to set up a motive.

So much for the antecedent conditions which give rise to motivation, at least in so far as they can be ascertained without reading into Hebb's treatment more than he intended. What about a motive's effect on behavior? As the definition quoted above suggests, the characteristic of behavior which marks it as motivated is its "persistence in a given direction," at least if we assume that the persistence in a given direction of a phase sequence results in the same effect on overt behavior. Again for him it is the *organization* of behavior rather than its intensity which requires the motive concept. A live organism is an active organism and no strong stimuli are needed to get it moving. What is needed is some kind of a concept which will account for the interrelatedness of a series of acts or the persistence of a sequence of acts. Oddly enough, it was a somewhat similar observation which led Freud to emphasize the importance of motivation. That is, he found it necessary to employ the motive concept in his clinical practice to explain the connectedness of queer, apparently unconnected symptomatic acts.

It seems to us that the chief difficulty with Hebb's system is just the opposite of that which creates problems for the two previously discussed models. They are perhaps too simple to account for all the facts. His is so general that the experimentalist trying to work with such a model is hard put to know when he is working with a motive or how to measure its effects. For how can we know whether a phase sequence is organized or not? What are the criteria an experimentalist can use for distinguishing an organized direction of behavior from a disorganized direction of behavior? Or, on the other side of the picture, how can we measure the discrepancy between expectation and perception? Such discrepancies would have to be determined rather precisely if we were going to predict ahead of time whether or not they would lead to pleasure or pain. Otherwise one might naively argue that barely failing to get admitted to college, for example, ought to be pleasurable. Since we are talking about hypothetical phase sequences, why is it not fair to assume that the phase sequence resulting from the hope of getting into college is modified only slightly when the director of admissions says that the candidate was good enough in *almost* every respect? It may be retorted that the difference between getting into college and not getting constitutes a major shift in phase sequence, but the point is that the neurological model in itself is not much help in establishing the antecedent conditions for determining the size of such discrepancies. These still have to be defined in some kind of measurable terms. The model would appear to be better for *post hoc* explanations as to why pleasure or pain arose than for predicting ahead of time what effect a particular set of antecedent conditions is going to have. Still, Hebb's ideas have proved immensely stimulating to us, and our own theory in many respects picks up where he leaves off.

Hebb's model is only one among several which could be classified under this heading. Brown and Farber (1951), for example, have worked out a kind of miniature system for one motive, which demonstrates how frustration may arise and serve as a motive, in a way which classifies their approach as an example of the stimulus pattern view of motivation. In a fashion very similar to Whiting's (1950), they argue that frustration is produced by the conflict of two incompatible response tendencies. Thus, any antecedent condition which is capable through learning of arousing incompatible response tendencies has the power to evoke the frustration motive. Here the necessary antecedent condition for a motive is the attaching of incompatible response tendencies to the same situation. As we have seen, Brown and Farber do not feel that frustration as a motive can be easily identified via the complex topography of behavior, so that one would have to classify their approach as a kind of "truncated" stimulus pattern model with no special criteria on the response side (see Table 2.1).

On the other hand, there are those theorists who think of motivation primarily in response terms and argue that certain distinctive response patterns would reveal best the fact that an emotion or perhaps a motive is aroused. These distinctive response patterns may be located in the central nervous system, as in Hebb's discrepant phase sequences, or in autonomic responses, or in overt behavior. One could argue, for example, that certain autonomically-controlled visceral responses are the best measure of the presence of a motive like fear. Such a theory would detect the fear motive not from any increase in response output, or from its ability to produce learning, or a directed sequence of behavior, but from a peculiar or unique patterning of physiological responses, caused perhaps by the discharge of adrenalin or adrenal corticoids into the bloodstream. Finally, Morgan and Stellar (1950) have pointed out how certain overt behavior patterns may also be used to infer the presence of motives or emotions. A cat is a good example because it has very distinctive response patterns for fear (spitting, arched back, stiff legs), for rage (leaping, scratching), and for pleasure (purring, relaxation). It is this type of criterion for the presence of a motive rather than the one given elsewhere in his book which Hebb is using when he states that "Hunger is defined here as the tendency to eat" (1949, p. 190). Such an attempt to find characteristic response patterns produced by motives may have its value in dealing with certain limited types of motives, particularly in lower animals when the problem is more one of identifying instinctive response patterns. But with higher animals the capacity for learning is so great that it would be surprising to discover any very specific fixed pattern of response tendencies associated with any particular motive. It was just this line of reasoning, together with a lot of empirical evidence, that discouraged experimentalists from attempting to distinguish emotions from one another on the basis of their motor or physiological effects (cf. Landis, 1924). Still, as will be pointed out, our theory of motivation relies on certain characteristic patterns of verbal behavior for distinguishing one motive from another, and perhaps ultimately for distinguishing the approach and avoidance aspects of a given motive. The difference seems to be that the common element in verbal response patterns and in approach-avoidance behavior is of a much higher order of abstraction than the common element in the bodily response patterns under discussion above. Our method of classification works better perhaps because it allows a greater flexibility in variation of the response elements in a given pattern, since the pattern is defined in terms of some higher order meaning of the response elements (e.g., in the case of the achievement motive, in terms of words which signify "affect in connection with evaluated performance").

2.7 **The affective arousal model.** Our reservations with respect to contemporary motivation theory have led us to attempt to rough out proposals for an alternative theory which may now or ultimately meet some of these objections and handle the data at least as well as the other models discussed. We are well aware of the incompleteness, as of this writing, of our theoretical thinking, but we will attempt to state our views as precisely and forcefully as we can in the hope that we can stimulate more serious discussion and experimental testing of motivational theory. At several points we will be obliged to present alternative hypotheses, since we do not as yet have the data to decide between them. But we agree with Hull and others that the only way to make progress in a field is "to stick one's neck out" and to state implicit theoretical assumptions as explicitly as possible.

Our definition of a motive is this: *A motive is the redintegration by a cue of a change in an affective situation.* The word *redintegration* in this definition is meant to imply previous learning. In our system, all motives are learned. The basic idea is simply this: Certain stimuli or situations involving discrepancies between expectation (adaptation level) and perception are sources of primary, unlearned affect, either positive or negative in nature. Cues which are paired with these affective states, changes in these affective states, and the conditions producing them become capable of redintegrating a state (A') derived from the original affective situation (A), but not identical with it. To give a simple example, this means that if a buzzer is associated with eating saccharine the buzzer will in time attain the power to evoke a motive or redintegrate a state involving positive affective change. Likewise, the buzzer if associated with shock will achieve the power to redintegrate a negative affective state. These redintegrated states, which might be called respectively *appetite* and *anxiety,* are based on the primary affective situation but are not identical with it.

The term *change in affect* is used in two separate senses. It refers on the one hand to the fact that *at the time of arousal* of a motive, the affective state which is redintegrated must be different from the one already experienced by the organism, and on the other hand to the *possibility* that *at the time of acquisition* of a motive, the affective state with which the cue gets associated must be undergoing a change. We are agreed that a "change in affect" at the time of arousal in the first sense must occur, but we see two possibilities on the acquisition side of the picture—one, that the association is with a *static* affective state; the other, that it is with a *changing* affective state. To elaborate this point further, the first

alternative states simply that any cue associated with a situation producing affect will acquire the power to evoke a
"model" of that situation (A') which will serve as a motive.
The second alternative requires that the cue be associated
with a *changing* state—of going from "shock" to "no shock"
or from neutrality to pleasure, and so forth. The difference
between the two possibilities is illustrated in the following
diagram:

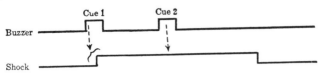

According to the first hypothesis, both cue 1 and cue 2 should
be capable of evoking an avoidance motive, since they have
both been paired with the affective state arising from shock.
According to the second, alternative hypothesis, cue 2 should
have weak or nonexistent motivating power since it has not
been associated with a *change* in affect. It should be possible
to determine which of these alternatives is correct by experimentation along these lines. Finally, it should be repeated
that both hypotheses assume that the redintegrated affect *at
the time of arousal* must represent a change over the present
affective state of the organism.

   In the discussion so far there has been some ambiguity as
to just what is redintegrated—the affective state or change,
the conditions which produced it, or both. Actually, the ambiguity reflects some uncertainty as to which alternative is
correct and also some difficulty in expressing simply exactly
what happens. By far the most likely possibility is that both
the situation *and* the affect it produces are redintegrated. Thus
the redintegrated "situation" defines the goal in the usual
sense (e.g., sugar in the mouth), and the redintegrated "affect" (e.g., reaction to the sugar in the mouth) determines
whether the goal is motivating or not. For the sake of sim-

plicity, phrases like redintegrated "affective state" or "affective change" are used throughout this chapter to refer both to the affective reaction itself and the situation which produced it.

Two main questions connected with the concept of redintegrated affective state still remain to be answered. Why, first of all, should we have decided to base motives on affect? Secondly, how are we to determine the existence of affective arousal? It will be difficult to do complete justice to these questions, but a word on each may help indicate the progress of our thinking.

2.8 **Why affect as a basis for motives?** We have decided to base motives on affective arousal, following Young's lead (1949) for several reasons. In the first place, it seems apparent that the motive concept will be useful only if it has some kind of a limited base. That is, if all associations are motivating, then there seems no particular reason to introduce the concept of motivation to apply to a particular subclass of association. Thus the associations involved in forming motives must be in some way different from other types of associations. And we have chosen affective states as the basis for motives rather than biological needs or strong stimuli because of the limitations of those concepts already discussed. A more positive reason for choosing affective states as primary is that they are "obviously" important in controlling behavior, at least at the common-sense level. The hedonic or pleasure-pain view of motivation is certainly one of the oldest in psychological thinking and can be traced at least to Plato's *Protagoras*. Furthermore, in order to get motives in the laboratory we commonly pair cues with affective states resulting from shock, saccharine in the mouth, food deprivation, and the like. Operationally we manipulate states which we know subjectively will produce pleasure and pain when we work with motives.

Another reason for choosing affect as the basis for motives rather than tissue needs, etc., is the overwhelming evidence for the importance of selective sensitivity in guiding and directing behavior in lower animals. Tinbergen (1951) has collected dozens of cases which illustrate how special stimuli are required to release a particular "consummatory" response particularly in submammalian species. Young (1949) has repeatedly called attention to the different palatability of various foods for the white rat. Weiner and Stellar (1951) have demonstrated unlearned salt preferences in the rat. And so forth. The list could easily be extended. The usual reaction by theorists to these facts is to assume that they are not characteristic of the human animal, which is obviously much more dependent on learning than on innate reactions to particular "releasing" stimuli. The difference is nicely highlighted by Ford and Beach (1951), who show how human sexual behavior is much less dependent than the behavior of lower animals on particular external signs and internal hormonal conditions.

But all of this seems no reason to assume a sharp discontinuity between man and other animals with respect to the factors controlling behavior. Rather we have been struck by the possibility that man's behavior may also be guided by selective sensitivity to particular kinds of situations. The difference may be one of degree rather than kind. With man the "releasing" situations may be much less specific than the dot on a gull's beak which releases pecking behavior of a gull chick, but they may exist just the same (Section 2.10). And the consummatory reactions elicited by such situations may also be much less specific and rigid than the pecking, fighting, courting responses shown in lower animals; in fact, the interesting possibility pursued here is that in man these specific overt reactions to "releasing" stimuli are attenuated and occur instead as diffuse reactions of the autonomic nervous system signifying what we usually call "affect." Thus our motivational system for man has been constructed to parallel the analysis of instinctive behavior in lower animals made by Tinbergen (1951) and others. Certain types of situations (Section 2.10) innately release reactions which are diffuse and covert in man rather than specific and overt, but which are consummatory in the same sense in that they ultimately exhaust themselves. These diffuse reactions are what we mean by affect, and they can be observed either through verbal reports and autonomic reactions, or inferred from approach and avoidance behavior, as we shall see in the next section. Man's advantage over lower animals lies precisely in the wider range of situations which will produce affect and in the lack of overt specificity of the affective reaction. Thus he can build a wide variety of motives on a much broader base, but to our mind it is essentially the same base as that which is responsible for guiding and directing the behavior of lower animals.

2.9 **Behavioral effects of affective arousal.** But how do we propose to define pleasure and pain or affective arousal? We certainly do not intend to fall into the trap of arguing that pleasurable sensations are those that lead to survival, and painful ones those that ultimately lead to maladaptation and death. This answer lands us back in the same difficulties that face the biological need theory of motivation. Let us first attempt to define affect by anchoring it on the behavioral side. It might seem more logical to consider first the antecedent conditions of affect (see Section 2.10) rather than its behavioral consequences, but the behavioral approach is more familiar because it is the one that has been customarily employed in attempts to measure affect or pleasure and pain (cf. Lindsley in Stevens, 1951). Thus, at a certain gross level, one can distinguish affective states from other states by the effects of autonomic activity—changes in respiration rate, in electrical skin resistance, in blood pressure, and the like. Thus one might initially state as a generalization that an affective state is present whenever the *PGR* shows a significant deflection, and that anyone who wants to establish a motive can simply pair cues with such deflections or the conditions which produced them. Autonomic accompaniments of emotions may not be perfect indexes of their presence, but they are sufficiently good to provide a very practical basis for deciding in a large number of cases that affective arousal has occurred.

Since autonomic measures apparently cannot be used at the present time to distinguish sensitively between positive and negative affective states, we will need to attack this problem in some other way. There are several possibilities. Among humans, expressive movements can readily be interpreted as indicating pleasant or unpleasant feeling states, particularly facial expressions (Schlosberg, 1952). Impromptu vocalizing seems also to be a good indicator of mood. Probably the most sensitive and frequently used index to hedonic tone is verbal behavior. If the person says "I dislike it," "I'm unhappy," or "it hurts," we take it as a sign of negative affect. If he says "I feel good," or "I like it," we take it as a sign of positive affect. One difficulty with these expressive signs is that they are not infallible. They can all be "faked," or changed by learning.

And what about animals? They can't talk, it would be difficult to try to interpret the facial expression of a rat or an elephant, and no one has made a careful study of animal vocalization patterns in response to pleasure and pain. In the case of some animals, certain innate response patterns are readily interpreted as signifying positive or negative affect —e.g., purring or spitting in the cat; licking, tail-wagging, or growling in the dog, and so on. More attention should be given to the study of the expressive signs of affect, but until it is, we must be satisfied with stopgap measures. Probably the most useful of these with adult animals is simple preference or approach behavior in contrast to avoidance behavior.

Sometimes there are reflex responses that are clearly approach or avoidance in nature—e.g., sucking, grasping, swallowing, spitting, vomiting, blinking—and in some instances they may provide direct evidence of positive or negative affective arousal. That is, eye-blinking in response to a puff of air, if accompanied by an autonomic response, would give evidence that affect was present and that this affect was negative in nature. Cues paired with the air puff would in time come to elicit an avoidance motive (as indicated by the presence of an avoidance *response*—the conditional or anticipatory eye-blink). But since reflexes are few in number and sometimes hard to classify as approach or avoidance (e.g., the knee jerk), better evidence for the existence of affective arousal is to be found in *learned* approach and avoidance behavior (locomotor, manual, verbal). There is an apparent circularity here, because what we are saying is that we can tell whether affective arousal occurred only after the organism has learned an approach or avoidance response in the service of a motive. Are we not first making a motive dependent on affective arousal and then saying we can find out whether affective arousal occurred if a motive has been formed which leads to approach or avoidance behavior? The answer is "Yes, we are," but the argument is not completely circular (cf. Meehl, 1950). Thus in one experiment we can determine that salty water leads to learned approach or preference behavior in the rat and we can then *infer* from this that it produces positive affective arousal. This inference (that salty water "tastes good" to the rat) can then be used as the basis for new learning experiments, theorizing, and so on. In this way we can gradually build up classes of objects, situations, response categories, or sensations which must produce affective arousal and then try to generalize as to what they have in common, as we have later on in this chapter (Section 2.10). In brief, the notion here is to use autonomic responses to indicate the presence of affect and approach and avoidance (either learned or reflex) to distinguish positive from negative affect.

There is one misconception which may arise in connection with this definition that it is well to anticipate, however. The terms *approach* and *avoidance* must not be understood simply as "going towards" or "away from" a stimulus in a spatial sense. Thus "rage," when it goes over into attack, is an "avoidance" response, even though it involves "going towards" something. *Avoidance* must be defined in terms of its objective—to discontinue, remove, or escape from a certain type of stimulation and not in terms of its overt characteristics. Attack has, as its objective, removal of the source of stimulation in the same sense that withdrawal does. *Approach* must also be defined functionally—i.e., it is any activity, the objective of which is to continue, maintain, or pursue a certain kind of stimulation. Because of the ambiguity involved in using these terms, it might be better to substitute others like *stimulus enhancement* or *stimulus reduction,* but approach and avoidance have the advantage of common usage and if it is understood that they are used in a functional sense, difficulties should not arise in using them as the primary means of defining positive and negative affect on the response side. It is perhaps worth noting that Dearborn (1899) and Corwin (1921) came to the same decision long ago after recording involuntary "pursuit" (extension) and "withdrawal" (flexion) movements to pleasant and unpleasant stimuli, respectively.

2.9.1 *Distinguishing the effects of affect and motive.* Analytically speaking, there are three events involved in the development of a motive, any of which may have observable and distinguishable behavioral effects. In order of occurrence, they are:

A. The situation producing affect

B. Redintegration of (A)

C. Response learned to (B)

We have discussed the problem of measuring the behavioral

effects of A in the previous section. How can the effects of A and B be distinguished, if at all? The simplest assumption would seem to be the one that Hull made years ago (1931), to the effect that a cue paired with a goal response will evoke a fractional anticipatory portion of it. The notion behind this is that the redintegrated response is like the original but fractional in nature, that is, consisting of a portion of the total goal response which is perhaps less in intensity or duration. The difficulty with this idea has been discussed at some length by Mowrer (1950). In general, the objection is similar to the one made against the substitution hypothesis in conditioning experiments. That is, formerly it was commonly assumed that in conditioning the conditioned stimulus simply substituted for the unconditioned stimulus in evoking the unconditioned response. But, as Hilgard and Marquis (1940) point out, the conditioned response is in fact often quite different from the unconditioned response. It is not necessarily a miniature replica or fractional portion of the original unconditioned response. For example, there is evidence that the normal response in rats to the primary affective state produced by shock is squealing, defecating, and intense variable behavior, whereas the normal response to anticipation of shock (e.g., to fear) is different, probably crouching (Arnold, 1945). The evidence that crouching is the normal response to fear is not conclusive, as Brown and Jacobs (1949) point out, because it can be eliminated by certain experimental procedures; but the probability is still fairly great that the response to fear differs in important ways from the response to shock. Therefore it would seem unwise at this state of our knowledge to assume that the fear response is just a partial copy of the shock response. At the phenomenological level, it seems that shock produces two distinguishable response elements—pain, which is the immediate reaction to shock, and fear, which is the anticipatory redintegration of the pain response. These two responses are clearly different. That is, if one's teeth are hurt by drilling in the dentist's chair, the sight of the chair may evoke a subjective feeling we label fear, but it does not evoke a "fractional" pain in the teeth.

When we consider the third event in the sequence of motive formation—namely, the responses learned to the redintegrated affect—the picture becomes even more complex. Our position is that the genotypic responses to redintegrated positive or negative affect are "functional" approach or avoidance. Thus from avoidance we can infer that negative affect has occurred if we lack a direct independent response definition of negative affect. But at the phenotypical level, the responses learned to redintegrated negative or positive affect may be very varied. A rat can be trained to run at as well as away from a shock (Gwinn, 1949). Rage and fear are genotypically avoidance responses, but phenotypically the former involves approach and the latter withdrawal. Similarly, love and contempt or scorn are genotypically similar in that they both involve attempts to maintain a source of stimulation, but phenotypically love involves "going towards" an object and scorn involves "keeping your distance" from the scorned object. A classification of emotions on a pleasant-unpleasant dimension and on an attentive-rejective one succeeds in ordering satisfactorily nearly all the facial expressions of emotion, according to Schlosberg (1952), a fact which tends to confirm our position that one must distinguish basically between positive and negative affect on the one hand and learned reactions to it, however classified, on the other. If the learned reactions are classified as to whether they phenotypically involve "going towards" or "away from" something, as they were approximately on Schlosberg's attentive-rejective dimension, then one gets a fourfold table in which Love, Contempt, Rage, and Fear represent the four major types of emotional reactions.

But obviously such classifications of phenotypic reactions can vary tremendously. The important points to keep in mind theoretically are (1) that they are surface modes of reaction with two basic objectives—to approach or maintain pleasure and to avoid or reduce pain, and (2) that they are acquired and hence take time to develop and show characteristic individual differences.

2.9.2 *Measuring motives through their effects.* The fact that the learned reactions to motives may vary so much suggests that it may be difficult to identify motives through their effects. The first problem is to decide at what point the stream of behavior indicates the presence of a motive. It may be helpful to begin the analysis with a simple case in which the behavior produced by affect can be distinguished from that which reflects the subsequent redintegration of affect. Consider the startle reaction (Landis and Hunt, 1939). A pistol shot produces varied autonomic and reflex effects which are signs of affective arousal. The fact that this arousal is negative can be inferred after the longer latency "voluntary" avoidance responses appear which are signs of an avoidance motive cued off by the shot or its "startle" effects because of the former association of such cues with negative affect. A necessary inference from this is that the first time startle is elicited (as perhaps in the Moro reflex in infants), it should not produce the longer latency co-ordinated avoidance behavior which Landis and Hunt observed in adults.

This suggests that one of the important ways in which motivated behavior may be identified is in terms of the *co-ordination* of responses or in terms of some kind of a response *sequence,* which terminates when the organism arrives somewhere with respect to a source of affect. The terms *approach* and *avoidance* imply a sequence of responses which has a *goal*—e.g., arriving at or away from a situation producing affect. Perhaps the point can be clarified by referring to our response definitions of a motive in Table 2.1. The general definition is "goal-oriented free choice with habit and situational factors controlled." Under this we have placed approach and avoidance behavior, the only criterion one can use with animals, and the choice of certain "classes of goal-oriented thoughts" for inclusion in fantasy, the criterion we have used in measuring achievement motivation. These criteria are similar in implying choice responses with respect to a goal. We mean by the term *goal* here the same thing we meant earlier when we were distinguishing between genotypic and phenotypic approach and avoidance, between the functional significance of an act (e.g., avoiding a stimulus) and the modality of the act itself (which may involve attacking the stimulus). The goal is the functional significance of the act. Let us be more specific. Any response an animal makes involves choice in a sense. Any succession of responses also involves co-ordination in the sense of alternation of effector pathways, and so on. But only when the succession becomes a sequence which results in approach to or avoidance of a situation can we argue that there is evidence for the existence of a motive.

In dealing with verbal responses in a story the problem is simpler. Many thoughts (e.g., "the boy is happy") indicate the presence of affect, but only those thoughts chosen for inclusion which imply affect in connection with a particular situation are evidence for the existence of a motive (e.g., "the boy wants to do a good job"). In this example, "wanting to do a good job" defines an end situation which would produce positive affect (see Section 2.13), and the fact that the subject chooses to include such a statement is taken as evidence that he is motivated for achievement. That is, he has made a "goal-oriented" choice by making a statement about an achievement situation ("good job") which would inferentially produce positive affect (the boy "wants" it). Thus with such a measure of motivation we do not need the evidence of a co-ordinated though perhaps variable sequence of responses with a certain end, since the end ("good job") is directly stated, and it is this end state, with its accompanying affect rather than mere co-ordination, which seems to be the necessary criterion for deciding that behavior is showing evidence of the existence of motivation.

In short, in verbal behavior the "redintegrated affective situation" may be reflected directly and need not be inferred from a sequence of responses signifying approach and avoidance.

But why in the definition do we insist on "free" choice with certain factors controlled? The argument runs like this. Since general locomotor approach and avoidance are learned so early and so well in the life history of the organism, they can be utilized in normal animals to test the strength of a motivational association, provided the testing situation is a "free" one—provided the rats' "habits" are normal and provided the situation is a normal one for the rat. That is, it would be fair to test for the existence and strength of a rat's hunger motive by measuring the number of times he runs toward food as compared with other objects when placed on an open table top, provided his past experience has been "normal." But obviously if his past experience has not been normal—if he has lived in a vertical cage with no chance to walk in a horizontal dimension, if he has never had the opportunity to connect the sight of food with certain affective states (taste, reduction in hunger pangs), if he has been taught to run only when mildly hungry and to sit when very hungry—then the situation will not give a "fair" measure of his hunger motive. The number of times he ends up in the vicinity of the food could still be recorded in such cases, but it might be a measure of things other than hunger. It would measure hunger according to our argument if, and only if, it made use of a highly overlearned response (i.e., a "normal" habit) in a situation which did not clearly evoke incompatible responses (i.e., a "normal" situation).

In a sense, this is fairly similar to the state of affairs when a human being is telling a story in response to a picture. That is, for most subjects putting thoughts into words or verbalizing is a highly overlearned response. Furthermore, in the fantasy situation no particular set of responses is supposed to be perceived as especially appropriate. Fantasy is a "free" response situation, provided the picture is not too structured. It might not be for a certain class of persons, for professional writers, for example, because they may have learned a particular set of responses to use in such a situation, just as the rats who have been trained to sit still when hungry have learned a particular set of responses which prevent us from measuring their motivation in the usual way. But except for professional authors, individuals should have no particular set of verbal response tendencies which seem appropriate because of past experience with such situations. In contrast, if we ask a subject if he would like to get a good grade in a course, the fact that he answers "yes" is of no particular significance for diagnosing his achievement motivation, because we can assume that he will have learned that this is an appropriate response to such a question. Here the social reality or the modal cultural pattern determines his response. It is just for this reason that we prefer pictures which are not so structured as to elicit one particular response by common social agreement. We want the restraints on the free choice of responses by the subject reduced to a certain necessary minimum.

Furthermore, the fantasy situation is "free" because the testing conditions do not place any external constraints on the responses which are possible. Thus the subject can write about anything—about killing someone, committing suicide, touring the South Seas on a pogo stick, having an illegitimate child, and so forth. Anything is symbolically possible. Thus the choice of response patterns is not limited by what can be done under the conditions in which the motive strength is to be tested. Here our measure of human motivation has a great advantage over measures of animal motivation, but in both cases the problem is the same: to minimize or know the situational and habit determinants of behavior. This position fits into the general theoretical framework described elsewhere by McClelland (1951) in which he argues that behavior is determined by situational (perceptual) factors, by habit (memory) factors, and by motivational factors. It follows that if one wants a particular response to reflect motivation primarily, the strength of the other two determinants must either be known, minimized, or randomized. In the elementary state of our present knowledge, the best procedure would appear to be to use highly overlearned responses in "free" situations. There is, therefore, some theoretical justification for our empirical finding that motives can be measured effectively in imagination.

2.10 Antecedent conditions for affective arousal. Let us now focus our attention on the all-important problem of identifying the antecedent conditions which produce affective arousal. For if we know them, we are in a position, according to the theory, of knowing how to create a motive by pairing cues with those conditions, according to the principles discussed in the next main section on *the acquisition of motives* (2.11). Considering the antecedent conditions for affective arousal inevitably gets us into some ancient controversies over what causes pleasure and pain (McDougall, 1927; Beebe-Center, 1932; Dallenbach, 1939; Hebb, 1949). There is not the space here to review these controversies or to attempt to resolve them. Instead, we can only indicate what appears to us to be a promising approach to a general theory. This approach can only be outlined roughly here in the form of a series of propositions which seem promising to us but which will require experimentation and more detailed exposition in further publications.[*]

[*] D.C.McC. and R.A.C. are largely responsible for Section 2.10, which was written after the main body of the text had been completed.

2.10.1 *Affective arousal is the innate consequence of certain sensory or perceptual events.* It is probable (though not necessary) that the basic mechanism (see proposition 2) which gives rise to *sensory* pleasantness (e.g., sweetness) and unpleasantness (e.g., bitterness) is similar to that which gives rise to pleasantness-unpleasantness at a more complex perceptual level (pleasant music vs. dissonant music). In this connection we use the term *sensory* to refer roughly to simple variations in stimulus dimensions (e.g., stimulus intensity), whereas *perceptual* refers primarily to more complex variations in stimulus events.

2.10.2 *Positive affect is the result of smaller discrepancies of a sensory or perceptual event from the adaptation level of the organism; negative affect is the result of larger discrepancies.* The salt curve in Figure 2.1 illustrates this postulated

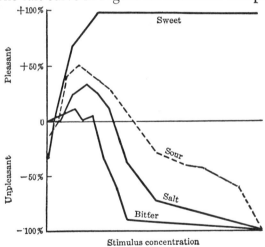

FIG. 2.1. Preponderance of "pleasant" or "unpleasant" judgments in relation to the concentration of a sapid solution. The ordinate gives per cent "pleasant" minus per cent "unpleasant." The abscissa is proportional to the concentration, the full length of the baseline standing for 40 per cent cane sugar, for 10 per cent salt, and for .004 per cent quinine sulphate (all by weight). Data of R. Engel, after Woodworth, 1938.

relationship from the hedonic reactions to increasing salt concentrations in the mouth. Fifty years ago it was a commonplace assumption that increasing sensory intensity in *any* modality produced a pleasantness-unpleasantness curve like this (Beebe-Center, 1932, p. 166). The new feature of such a curve for us is that, like Hebb, we would plot it not against increasing intensity as such but against size of discrepancy between the stimulus (perception) and the adaptation level of the organism (expectation). Such a modification has several advantages which we will enumerate, but among them is the fact that it brings the "discrepancy hypothesis" as to the source of affect within the realm of quantitative testing according to Helson's formulae (1948) for determining adaptation level and discrepancies from it. In the discussion which follows we have obviously leaned heavily on Helson's formulation of the concept of adaptation level.

2.10.3 *Natural adaptation levels for various sensory receptors differ.* Such a hypothesis is apparently essential to a discrepancy hypothesis because of the known fact that some receptors give rise most readily or "naturally" to pleasantness and others to unpleasantness. In Figure 2.1 the two curves for sweet and bitter sensations illustrate this point. Thus sugar appears to give rise to pleasurable sensations across the entire range of stimulus intensity. In terms of the discrepancy hypothesis, this suggests that a discrepancy from the natural adaptation level (*AL*) large enough to produce unpleasantness is not possible. The bitter curve, on the other hand, is quite different: here nearly all intensities of stimulus concentration tested give rise to negative affect. The fact that the absolute threshold for sugar is considerably above what it is for bitter (Pfaffman in Stevens, 1951) suggests the following interpretation. The threshold for sweet is relatively high and the range of stimulation to which it is sensitive sufficiently narrow so that large discrepancies from *AL* which probably lies near the threshold are impossible. With bitter the threshold is so low that small fractions of the maximum concentration used in Figure 2.1 still represent fairly large discrepancies from an *AL* near the threshold. At this stage of our knowledge easy generalizations must be avoided, but it seems obvious even now that ultimately the natural *AL* for a receptor will turn out to be somewhere near its threshold (modified perhaps by the normal stimulation impinging on it) and that the size of the discrepancies which will yield positive and negative affect will be a joint rational function of the three constants in receptor functioning—the lower threshold, the upper threshold, and the Weber fraction.

What is clearly needed is a survey of all sensory qualities in terms of the discrepancy hypothesis as to what produces positive and negative affect. Such a survey cannot be attempted here both because of space limitations and because of the obvious complexity of some of the problems to be solved. Take pitch, for example. At first glance, it would look as if a few moments at the piano would easily disprove the discrepancy hypothesis. If two notes of small discrepancy in pitch, such as C and C-sharp, are played together in the middle pitch range, the effect is normally unpleasant; whereas if two notes farther apart in pitch, such as C and E, are played together, the effect is pleasant. Isn't this just the reverse of what our hypothesis would predict? It is, unless one considers the fact that two notes fairly close together produce a larger number of audible beats per second than two notes farther apart. It has long been recognized (Woodworth, 1938, p. 515) that unpleasantness is a function of these beats which represent discrepancies from an evenly pitched sound. Thus if size of discrepancy is measured in terms of "frequency of beats," it appears that the two tones close together are *more discrepant* than those farther apart and should therefore be more unpleasant. But this is only the beginning of what could be a thorough exploration of the esthetics of music according to this principle. Variables which appear to influence the pleasantness of combinations of tones, for example, include the absolute pitch of the two tones, the pattern of overtones, simultaneity vs. succession in sounding the two tones, and the like.

Or to take one more example—that of color. If our *AL* theory is correct, one would have to predict that dark-skinned peoples of the world would have different color *AL*'s from looking at each other than would light-skinned people. Consequently, the discrepancy in wavelength terms from the *AL*'s which should yield maximum pleasure in countries like India and the United States ought to be different. In these terms one might explain the fact that in India red is the most preferred color and white is the color of mourning, whereas in the United States blue-green is most preferred and black is the color of mourning (Garth, *et al.*, 1938). It is at least suggestive that nearly complementary skin color bases should produce complementary pleasant and unpleasant colors, but the most important point to note here is that our theory would argue for a *natural* basis for color preferences based on dominant or recurrent experiences rather than for a purely accidental basis subsequently reinforced by culture, as current thinking would appear to emphasize. Obviously such natural preferences can be changed by the culture or by the individual through particular experiences (e.g., there are plenty of American children who prefer red), but the point is that U.S. and Indian populations as groups should show different color preferences according to the principle that moderate discrepancy from different skin color *AL* bases will yield pleasure in colors of different wavelength composition.

These two examples should be sufficient to illustrate the deductive fertility of the discrepancy hypothesis and also the need for the kind of careful analysis of different sensory qualities which is beyond the scope of this introductory treatment.

2.10.4 *A discrepancy between adaptation level and a sensation or event must persist for a finite length of time before it gives rise to an hedonic response.* There are several reasons for making this assumption. In the first place, Beebe-Center and others have noted that certain types of sensations—e.g., taste, smell, pain—give rise to affective responses more readily than others—e.g., sight, hearing. A possible explanation for this fact would be "receptor lag" or "AL lag." That is, for the first group of sensations AL may change rather slowly, so that the discrepancy caused by a new stimulus will last long enough to give an hedonic report. In taste and smell, for instance, there appear to be purely "mechanical" reasons for the relative slowness with which previous concentrations of stimulator substances are changed by new substances. Thus a change might occur at one point in the receptor surface while the rest of the surface was still responding to earlier chemicals. In vision and hearing, on the other hand, the AL appears to respond rapidly to new sensations so that only major shifts in intensity will cause a discrepancy from AL to persist long enough to give rise to an hedonic response.

A second reason for the discrepancy-persistence hypothesis is that the hedonic j.n.d. seems to be larger than the sensory j.n.d. That is, in all modalities the discrepancies required to produce a just noticeable difference in hedonic tone seem to be larger than those required to produce a report of a difference in sensation. Unfortunately, adequate data on this point are apparently not available at present, although the problem is one that may be attacked easily experimentally. What is needed is a repetition of some of the standard psychophysics experiments in which hedonic judgments are called for under exactly the same conditions as judgments of *heavier, brighter, longer*, and so on. Usually these two types of judgments have been made separately. It would not be surprising if the hedonic j.n.d. turned out to be some function of the Weber fraction for each modality. The meaning of all this in terms of the present hypothesis is simply that a larger than just noticeable sensory difference is required to maintain a discrepancy over AL long enough to give rise to a just noticeable hedonic effect.

A third reason for the discrepancy-persistence hypothesis is simply to avoid making the whole of behavior affectively toned. After all, every sensory event might be considered, at least in some marginal sense, a discrepancy from some "expectation" and should therefore lead to some kind of affective arousal, were it not for some principle requiring a minimum degree of stability in the expectation or *AL* so that a discrepancy from it *could* persist. In short, the simple occurrence of an event is not sufficient to set up an *AL* such that any further modified occurrence of that same event will produce a discrepancy sufficient to cause affect. Rather the *AL* must be built up to a certain minimum level of stability through successive experiences, as in memory or psychophysical experiments, before discrepancies from it will produce affect. A case in point is provided by Hebb's young chimpanzee which did not fear a detached chimpanzee head until it had formed through experience a stable expectation of what a chimpanzee should look like (Hebb, 1949).

2.10.5 *Discrepancies from adaptation level will give rise to a positive-negative affect function in either direction along a continuum.* In many instances, events can differ from expectation only uni-directionally. Thus after the shape of the human figure has been learned, discrepancies can occur only in the direction of being less like the expected shape. But with many dimensions, particularly intensity, discrepancies are bi-directional and may have somewhat different affective consequences depending on their direction. For example, does a decrease of so many j.n.d.'s from an *AL* have the same hedonic tone as an increase of the same number of j.n.d.'s?

The simplest assumption is that the hedonic effect is the same regardless of the direction of the discrepancy. But the evidence for the assumption is not very convincing. It consists for the most part of some early experiments in esthetics such as the one summarized in Figure 2.2. Angier (1903) simply asked his subjects to divide a 160 mm line unequally at the most pleasing place on either side of the midpoint. The results in Figure 2.2 were obtained by averaging the frequencies of choices per 5 mm unit between 5–25 mm, 25–45 mm, 45–65 mm, 65–75 mm discrepancies, and plotting them with the

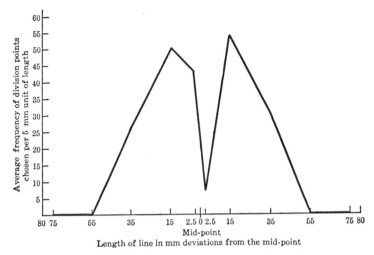

FIG. 2.2. Unequal division points of a straight line chosen as most pleasing. From Angier, 1903.

actual frequencies for the 5 mm discrepancies on each side of the midpoint. Since Angier did not permit his subjects to choose the midpoint and since he forced them to make half of their judgments on either side of the midpoint, the data do not really test our hypothesis crucially. He should rather have let a large number of subjects choose any division points at all along the line. Still, Angier's introspective data from his subjects led him to conclude that "most of the subjects, however, found a *slight* remove from the center disagreeable" (1903, p. 550). Furthermore it is clear that his subjects did not like to divide the line near its extremities on either side. In short, there is evidence for the typical hedonic curve for discrepancies *in both directions* from the center which must be assumed to represent some kind of an *AL* based on symmetry, balance, and so forth. A similar bimodal preference curve for rectangles of different width-length ratios is reported by Thorndike (see Woodworth, 1938, p. 386), if the exactly balanced ratio of .50 is taken as the *AL*.

When an attempt is made to discover the same principle in the operation of sensory modalities, however, the situation becomes complex. Consider Alpert's data in Figure 2.3 as an example. The lower curve, which again is the typical hedonic function for discrepancies from *AL*, was obtained in the following way. Subjects inserted one eye in a translucent "Ganzfeld" about the size of an egg cup. Around the outside of the cup, red lights were placed so as to produce inside it a diffuse red light covering the entire visual field and presumably stimulating largely only one set of receptors—the cones. In the center of the cup a small spot subtending about 18 degrees of visual arc was distinguishable from the rest of the field by a hazy dark line, produced by the fact that the spot was separately illuminated from behind. First the subject adjusted the illumination of the reddish spot until it matched the reddish "Ganzfeld" in all respects as closely as possible. Then the experimenter set a Variac which also controlled lamp voltage for the spot in such a way that if he switched off the "constant" lamp just adjusted by the subject and switched on the "variable" lamp for about two seconds, the subject got a glimpse of the spot as more or less intense than the surrounding "Ganzfeld." The subject made a judgment of pleasantness-unpleasantness on a scale of $+3$ to -3 *after* the "variable" lamp had been switched off and the "constant" lamp back on. Each subject made four judgments at each of the lamp voltage settings shown on the abscissa of Figure 2.3. The "spots" of different intensity were presented in random order four separate times. The procedure was duplicated for different illuminations of the "Ganzfeld" (i.e., for different adaptation levels). There were 10 subjects and the two curves in Figure

2.3 represent the average judgments of all of them under two adaptation level settings—one in which the "Ganzfeld" illumination was low (< .5 foot candles) and the other in which it was high (about 3 foot candles according to G.E. photom-

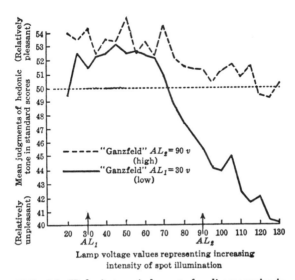

FIG. 2.3. Hedonic tone judgments for discrepancies in spot illumination above and below low (AL₁) and high (AL₂) "Ganzfeld" illuminations. Red light, 10 subjects making 4 judgments at each lamp voltage value. Data from Alpert, 1953.

eter). Each subject's judgments under all conditions were converted to a common scale of standard scores with a mean of 50 and an SD of 10. Thus the fact that the dotted line in Figure 2.3 is above 50 throughout most of its course means that most of the subjects' judgments in this condition were above their individual hedonic means *for the whole series of judgments* (including a series with a moderate AL not reproduced here).

Three conclusions can be drawn from Figure 2.3: (1) When the AL is low, and the receptors are close to the "resting" state, increases in stimulation produce first positive affect and then negative affect as postulated in Section 2.10.2. See solid line in Figure 2.3. (2) When the *AL* is high, well above the resting state, all increases in stimulation tend to produce negative affect and all decreases tend to produce positive affect. See dotted line in Figure 2.3. (3) There is no marked evidence in these curves either (*a*) for large decreases in stimulation leading to negative affect or (*b*) for stimulation around the *AL* producing a neutral hedonic response. Neither (*a*) nor (*b*) should be considered as conclusive negative evidence, however. With respect to (*a*), common experience suggests that eating ice cream after drinking coffee is more painful than under normal conditions. On the surface, it would appear that this is because the low temperature of the ice cream represents a much larger discrepancy downwards from the heightened *AL* of the mouth or teeth produced by drinking coffee. But the problem is complicated by the fact that the heat and cold receptors may be different and related in an unknown way. That is, ice cream may not be a decrease in stimulation for warm receptors but an *increase* in stimulation for cold receptors. The virtue of using red illumination in the present experiment is that it presumably limits the effects of stimulation largely to one set of receptors—the cones. In short, the question of whether decreases in stimulation ever produce negative affect and of whether the hedonic curve is therefore alike on both sides of *AL* must be left open at the present time.

With respect to (*b*) there is a slight (though probably insignificant) dip in the lower hedonic curve for values of the spot which are close to those of the "Ganzfeld" *AL*. It can be argued that the reason the dip is not more striking is that at least two other *AL*'s are operating in this situation. The first is the natural or physiological *AL* of the receptor which here and in other similar figures seems to lie somewhere around the threshold of the receptor. The illumination of the "Ganzfeld" was apparently close enough to this value for the lower curve in Figure 2.3 not to produce a major modification in its shape. The second AL is that produced by the *series* of spot stimuli of varying intensity. This can be calculated by Helson's formula (1947) to be equivalent to a lamp voltage value of around 63 volts, which is considerably *above* the "Ganzfeld" AL value and which may interact with it in some way to obscure further the dip in hedonic tone for values approximating AL. Generally speaking, the principle appears to hold for the lower curve if the AL is taken to be the physiological AL, and for the upper curve if the AL is taken to be the "Ganzfeld" value. Although both of these assumptions seem reasonable, once again the question must be considered open as to whether values approximating the AL always tend to take on a neutral hedonic tone, at least until we have more accurate ways of figuring out how AL's are shifted by exposure to various experiences.

2.10.6 *Increases and decreases in stimulus intensity can be related to motivation only if adaptation level and learning are taken into account.* Our view of motivation differs from Miller and Dollard's (1941) in two important ways. First, the effect of changes in stimulus intensity must always be referred to AL, and second, such changes produce affect immediately and motives only through learning. More specifically, an increase in stimulus intensity (a "drive" for Miller and Dollard) provides the basis for a motive only if it represents a large enough discrepancy from AL to produce positive or negative affect. It elicits a motive only if it or the situation producing it has been associated with such affect in the past. A decrease in stimulus intensity (a "reward" for Miller and Dollard) either provides the basis for an approach motive if it produces positive affect or removes the cues which have been redintegrating negative affect and thus eliminates an avoidance motive. Thus "drive" and "reward" in Miller and Dollard's sense are seen to be special cases of a more general theory.

Let us leave aside for the moment the question of whether motives or drives are always learned and look more closely at the question of the relation of stimulus intensity to AL. For us, it is not intensity per se which is important but discrepancy from AL. It follows that many strong stimuli will be unpleasant, but not all. It depends on over-all AL. Thus if a person is in dim illumination (bottom curve in Figure 2.3), a light with a lamp voltage value of 90 will produce marked negative affect; but if the illumination is already that bright, the same light will produce a rather indifferent response (upper curve in Figure 2.3). It is for this reason apparently that biting one's lips or otherwise hurting one's self helps relieve pain.

2.10.7 *Changes in adaptation level, with attendant hedonic changes, may be produced by somatic conditions.* This is an obvious point and a few illustrations will serve to demonstrate its importance. The somatic conditions may be either chemical (hormonal) or neurological in nature. Pfaffman and Bare (1950) have demonstrated that the preferences for lower salt concentrations shown by adrenalectomized rats cannot be explained by a lowering of the *sensory* threshold of the nerves responding to salt. An explanation in our terms would simply be that the central AL has been lowered by chemical changes in the bloodstream so that lower salt concentrations on the tongue will produce a pleasurable discrepancy from it. That is, Pfaffman and Bare found that the lower concentrations had always produced action potentials in the gustatory nerve, although they did not produce preference behavior in the normal rat. The reason for this in our terms is that they were sufficiently near the normal AL not to evoke preference behavior. Figure 2.4, which is plotted from Harriman's data (1952), shows in detail what happens to salt preferences in adrenalectomized rats when salt has been removed from their diet. The solid curve shows the amount of salty water of different concentrations consumed by normal rats on a normal diet (including about 1 per cent salt) when they could choose between it and distilled water. The dotted curve shows the same results for the adrenalectomized animals on a salt-free diet.

The solid curve shows substantially the same relationship

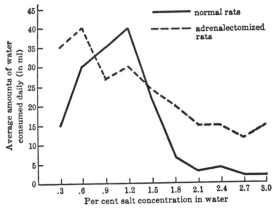

FIG. 2.4. Data plotted from Harriman (1952) showing average amounts of salty water of different concentrations consumed by normal (solid line) and adrenalectomized rats (dotted line) on a salt-free diet.

obtained for humans as presented in Figure 2.1 and it can be explained by the same assumptions—namely, that the AL for salt is somewhere below .3 per cent salt but above the absolute threshold for discrimination of salty from non-salty water which is at least as low as .01 per cent concentration of salt (Pfaffman and Bare, 1950). The AL empirically is that concentration which a rat will not consistently approach or avoid as compared with distilled water. The dotted curve suggests that for the operated animals the AL has now moved to lower concentrations, so that a .3 per cent solution represents a "pleasurable" discrepancy whereas before it was relatively "neutral." The fact that formerly preferred concentrations (.9 per cent and 1.2 per cent) are now *less* preferred also supports the idea that the AL has been lowered, since these now represent larger (and therefore less pleasant) discrepancies from it. But how about the tail end of the dotted curve? Should not the adrenalectomized animals find the high salt concentrations even less pleasant than the normals, if their AL has been lowered? According to the discrepancy hypothesis they should, but these data are not conclusive evidence that they do not. That is, the operated animals may find the strong concentrations even more unpleasant than the normals do, but drink more of them in short "swallows" because the "aftertaste" remains pleasant longer. In other words, if the salt solutions dissipate according to a negative decay function, there may be an appreciable time period after exposure to a strong concentration when the stimulus is pleasant, if the AL is low as in operated animals. Thus the operated animals may drink for the pleasant after-taste of strong concentrations; the normal animals may not because the dissipating solution reaches the higher AL sooner. At least the possibility is worth exploring.

In this fashion, changes in positive and negative affect resulting from the same stimulation on different occasions can be accounted for by chemical effects on AL. Such a hypothesis should be especially valuable in accounting for changes in the pleasurableness of sexual sensations accompanying certain hormonal cycles in lower animals (cf. Ford and Beach, 1951). Similarly Head's observations on the effects of thalamic lesions show that neurological damage can affect AL. Take this case, for example: "In one case a tube containing water at 38° C applied to the normal palm was said to be warm, but the patient cried out with pleasure when it was placed on the affected hand. His face broke into smiles and he said, 'Oh! that's exquisite,' or 'That's real pleasant'" (quoted in Beebe-Center, 1932, p. 391). Or another: "When a pin was lightly dragged from right to left across the face or trunk of one of the patients suffering from a lesion affecting the left side, she exhibited intense discomfort as soon as it had passed the middle line. Not only did she call out that it hurt more, but her face became contorted with pain. Yet careful examination with algesimeters showed that on the affected side her sensitivity to such stimulation was, if anything, slightly lowered" (Beebe-Center, 1932, p. 390). It is difficult to think about such findings in any other terms but some neurological effects on a central AL such that identical stimulations would produce different effects.

An interesting consequence of this proposition is that it suggests a reason why the sources of positive and negative affect may be different for different physiques. Thus if the AL for kinaesthetic sensations from large well-developed muscles is higher, it would be easy to understand why more activity would be required to get pleasurable discrepancies from the AL than for a weaker physique with lower kinaesthetic AL. In fact, one should argue that the amount of activity which produces pleasure for the mesomorphic physique (and consequently approach motives) might well produce too large a discrepancy, negative affect, and avoidance motives for the ectomorph. It might not be too far-fetched to attempt to account for the dominant sources of pleasure in each of Sheldon's somatotypes (1940) in terms of different AL's set up in different sensory modalities by different types of physiques. The argument would run something like this: The endomorph appears to get most of his pleasure from his gut because the AL for gut sensations is relatively high for such physiques and it takes gut sensations of greater intensity (or variety) to produce the discrepancies necessary for pleasure; the mesomorph appears to get most of his pleasure from his muscles because the AL for kinaesthetic sensations is relatively high and more variations in kinaesthetic sensations are required to give pleasure; the ectomorph appears to get more of his pleasure from minimal sensory stimulation because the AL for skin sensations is so low that moderate deviations from it give pleasure, and so forth. Such hypotheses are obviously incomplete and highly tentative, but they can certainly be tested experimentally and made more precise by isolating such physique types and determining their hedonic thresholds for various sensory qualities.

Finally, this proposition provides a basis for explaining Freud's libidinal development hypothesis, which has proven so fruitful clinically but so difficult to understand in terms of traditional "objective" theories of motivation. The explanation runs briefly as follows: "Erogenous zones" are skin areas where AL's are so low that relatively light tactual stimulation gives rise to sufficient discrepancies from AL to yield pleasure. If Freud is correct, it should be possible to demonstrate objectively that a constant tactual stimulus will give rise to pleasure responses in infants more readily in certain areas than in others. For the mouth, this seems well established, if the sucking response is taken as indicative of pleasure (i.e., because it is an approach response). For the anal and genital regions the facts are less well established. Freud's second hypothesis is that the erogenous sensitivity of these regions shifts as the child matures. In our terms, this simply means that changes in somatic conditions, produced here by maturation, modify AL's so that, as in the case of Head's patient, the same stimulus has a different hedonic effect. For example, the innate AL to mouth stimulation may increase with age so that touching the lips in the same way no longer yields pleasure and, at the same time, the anal region may become especially sensitive to tactual stimulation, and so on. The rise and fall in sensitivity of these various skin areas can certainly be measured behaviorally and understood in terms of physiologically produced changes in AL.

2.10.8 *Changes in adaptation level, with attendant hedonic changes, may be produced by experience.* This proposition opens up a whole new area that needs careful experimental exploration. We know some things but not nearly enough about how this happens. Thus Helson (1948) has demonstrated how an anchor or a series of stimuli can modify an *AL* in various modalities. His formulae even make assumptions as to the relative weights of background and figural stimulations in determining an *AL* produced by a series of stimuli. Furthermore, we know that hedonic judgments show the same type of central tendency, contrast, and assimilation effects that led Helson to formulate his notion of *AL* (Beebe-Center, 1932). This is as it should be, because as *AL*'s shift in the "physical dimensions of consciousness" there should be corresponding shifts in hedonic reactions if they are a function of the size of discrepancies between new stimuli and the sensory *AL*. But the most clear-cut evidence we know of which demonstrates that the hedonic curve is shifted as a function of shifts in sensory *AL* is that which has already been presented in Figure 2.3 and discussed in Section 2.10.5. (See also Beebe-Center, 1932, p. 238.)

In the absence of more such data at a more complex level, we must work with qualitative observations to some extent. Take Hebb's treatment of the "fear of the strange" as a point of departure. "About the age of four months the chimpanzee reared in the nursery, with daily care from three or four persons only and seeing few others, begins to show an emotional disturbance at the approach of a stranger (Hebb and Riesen, 1943). The disturbance increases in degree in the following months. . . . Chimpanzees reared in darkness, and brought into the light at an age when the response (to a strange face) would be at its strongest, show not the slightest disturbance at the sight of either friend or stranger. *But* some time later, after a certain amount of visual learning has gone on, the disturbance begins to appear exactly as in other animals" (Hebb, 1949, pp. 244–45). He also reports that "a model of a human or chimpanzee head detached from the body" produces marked affective arousal in half-grown or adult chimpanzees but not in younger chimpanzees. From all this he concludes that "the emotional disturbance is neither learned nor innate:

a certain learning must have preceded, but given that learning the disturbance is complete on the first appearance of certain stimulus combinations" (Hebb, 1949, p. 245). This is the crux of the matter as far as our theory of the conditions necessary for affective arousal (either positive or negative) is concerned. An *AL* must be built up in certain areas of experience (though it appears to be innately given for sense modalities) and then increasing discrepancies from that *AL* give rise first to positive and then to negative affect, as in Figure 2.1. *The AL may be acquired, the affective reactions to discrepancies from it are not;* they appear maximally the first time the discrepancy occurs and with less intensity thereafter because the new experience automatically interacts with the *AL*, changes it, and thereby reduces the discrepancy. Hence there is ultimate boredom or adaptation to pain or pleasure (satiation) as we shall see in a moment.

2.10.9 *Events can differ from expectations on a variety of dimensions.* The example we have chosen from Hebb to illustrate the preceding point is important because, unlike the sensory *AL*'s which we have been discussing, it deals with changes in *patterns* of stimulation rather than with changes in *intensity* levels. Thus we have to expand the *AL* concept to include expectations about shapes (e.g., faces) or any other events that the organism has had occasion through past experience to build up expectations about. This expansion, while absolutely necessary for a complete theory, raises certain practical problems in defining the size of a discrepancy between expectation and perception—a variable which we must be able to determine quite precisely if we are going to be able to predict whether a given discrepancy will give rise to positive or negative affect.

Basically, the problem is one of isolating dimensions along which two events can differ and then attempting to define degrees of difference objectively. Thus the events can differ in intensity, extensity, clarity, quality, certainty, and so on, and traditional psychophysics gives us plenty of cues as to how degrees of difference along these dimensions can be determined. So far we have talked largely about intensity differences, but differences in quality (or similarity) can be treated the same way. Thus one would predict on the basis of the discrepancy hypothesis that an artificial language consisting of highly probable syllabic combinations would be more amusing than one consisting of highly improbable syllabic combinations, or that nonsense syllables that sounded like English (NOQ) would be more amusing than ones that didn't (VOQ). And so forth. The research along these lines that needs to be done appears almost limitless.

Most events, of course, can differ from expectation in a variety of ways. Suppose a rat runs down an alley, turns left, proceeds three or four steps further, finds and eats a food pellet of a certain size and consistency. If this series of events occurs with sufficient frequency, we argue that the rat has built up a chain of associations of high probability or certain "expectations" as to what will happen. But these expectations, redintegrated partially when the rat is placed in the maze, may fail to be exactly confirmed in a variety of ways. An obstacle may delay him so that it takes him longer to get to the food. We may substitute mash for a food pellet, or a large pellet for a small one. He may eat the food where it is or pick it up and carry it somewhere else to eat it. And so forth. According to the discrepancy hypothesis, certain predictions about this process can be made. So long as the animal is uncertain in his expectations (i.e., is still learning the habit), there will be a tendency to limit the variability of responses so as to increase the probability of expectations until events represent only moderate and hence pleasurable deviations from them. But once the habit is overlearned the animal will tend to introduce variations once more—now to *increase* uncertainty to a "pleasurable" level. In short, exactly confirming certain expectations produces boredom and a tendency to discontinue the act unless enough minor variations are permitted to produce positive affect. The evidence for this hypothesis from animal learning is considerable. Thus the tendency toward variability in routine behavior has been found by many learning psychologists and is perhaps best illustrated by Heathers' (1940) report that rats alternate the paths they choose to get food when either is equally good. They are apparently operating according to the same general principle when they prefer a path to food with a barrier in it to an unobstructed path to food (Festinger, 1943), or prefer seeds which are difficult to crack open to seeds which are not so difficult (Yoshioka, 1930). Other similar examples of "inefficient" preferences have been collected by Maltzman (1952). In these and other such cases, the rat may prefer what looks like an inefficient response because it involves minor variations from expectation along such dimensions as time delay, spatial location, size of expected object, nature of expected object, and so forth—variations which according to the discrepancy hypothesis should yield pleasure. Research on this problem has to be done with care because as soon as the modification is major (for example, when the time delay becomes too long), then, of course, negative affect results and the preference of the animal is reversed. To complicate the matter even more, one should know how certain, or overlearned, the expectations are before predicting the effects of variations from them. If the expectations are of low probability, then confirmation should produce negative affect as in "fear of the strange." If they are of moderate probability, precise confirmation should produce pleasure (as in reading a detective story or playing solitaire). If the expectations are of high probability, then precise confirmation produces boredom or indifference (as in reading over again the detective story one has just finished, to use Hebb's example). The hedonic effects of the interaction of degrees of certainty of an expectation on the one hand, and degrees of deviation of an event from that expectation on the other, have yet to be worked out experimentally, but there is no reason why they could not be, using either animal or human subjects.

2.10.10 *Frustration is a source of negative affect.* A special note is in order as to where the notion of frustration or conflict as a drive (Whiting, 1950; Brown and Farber, 1951) fits into this scheme. Frustration in their terms results essentially from competition of response tendencies in such a way that F (frustration) is increased by reducing the difference in strength between the two opposed tendencies and also by increasing the absolute strength of both of them. Such statements are completely in line with our assumptions, with some exceptions to be noted in a minute. That is, we too would argue that the more nearly equal in strength two response tendencies are, the more they would give rise to negative affect (F); because such competition means that if either response is made, the expectation based on the other is not confirmed; or that if neither is made, both are unconfirmed. Similarly, the effects of nonconfirmation should be greater, the greater the strength of the response tendency. There are two differences between our scheme and theirs, however: (1) We would argue that when the size of the discrepancy between the stronger and weaker response tendencies is large, there should be a stage when the competition of the weaker response tendency should give rise not to frustration but to pleasure, if the stronger tendency is confirmed. This would require a modification in their formula for computing F such that for a certain range of discrepancies between the two tendencies it would yield negative F values (signifying pleasure). (2) They treat F as if it were a drive, whereas in our terms F in itself is simply negative affect and does not become a motive until anticipations of it or by it are elicited.

2.10.11. *The achievement motive develops out of growing expectations.* So far our scheme has been stated in fairly abstract form. A concrete example involving the development of the achievement motive may help explain its application in practice. Suppose a child is given a new toy car for Christmas to play with. Initially, unless he has had other toy cars, his expectations (or AL's) as to what it will do are nonexistent, and he can derive little or no positive or negative affect from manipulating it until such expectations are developed. Gradually, if he plays with it (as he will be encouraged to by his parents in our culture), he will develop certain expectations of varying probabilities which will be confirmed or not confirmed. Unless the nonconfirmations are too many (which may happen if the toy is too complex), he should be able to build up reasonably certain expectations as to what it will do *and confirm them.* In short, he gets pleasure from playing with the car. But what happens then? Why doesn't he continue playing with it the rest of his life? The fact is, of course, that his expectations become certainties, confirmation becomes 100 per cent, and we say that he loses interest or gets bored with the car; he should get bored or satiated, according to the theory, since the discrepancies from certainty are no longer sufficient to yield pleasure. However, pleasure can be reintroduced into the situation, as any parent knows, by buying a somewhat more complex car, by making the old car do somewhat different things, or perhaps by letting the old car alone for six months until the expectations about it have changed (e.g., decreased in probability). So, if a child is to continue to get pleasure from achievement situations like manipulating toy cars, he must continually work with more and more complex objects or situations permitting mastery, since, if he works long enough at any particular level of mastery, his expectations and their confirmation will become certain and he will get bored. The situation is analogous to the experiments by Washburn, Child, and Abel (cf. Beebe-Center, 1932, p. 238) which show that pleasure decreases on successive repetitions of simple popular music, whereas it increases on successive repetitions of severely classical music.

In the first instance, expectations or AL's are readily formed and confirmed to the point of boredom, whereas they take much longer to form with classical music—so long in fact that some people never expose themselves to such music often enough to get pleasure from having them confirmed. Thus pleasure from anything—be it mastery, music, or modern art —depends on a moderate degree of novelty, which has to become ever greater as expectations catch up with it. But note that there are limits on this developmental process: not every child will develop a very high level achievement motive or esthetic appreciation motive. In the first place, there are limits placed by native intelligence: the possibilities of a toy car or a comic book may never be exhausted as far as a moron is concerned because they never become certain enough for him to be bored over trying them out. Thus one would expect some kind of a correlation between the mastery level involved in n Achievement for a given person and his intelligence.

In the second place, there are limits placed on the development of n Achievement by the negative affect which results from too large discrepancies between expectations and events. Thus Johnny may develop expectations as to what a model airplane or a solved arithmetic problem looks like, but he may be unable to confirm these expectations at all, or only very partially. The result is negative affect, and cues associated with these activities may be expected to evoke avoidance motives. To develop an achievement approach motive, parents or circumstances must contrive to provide opportunities for mastery which, because they are just beyond the child's present knowledge, will provide continuing pleasure. If the opportunities are too limited, boredom should result and the child should develop no interest in achievement (and have a low n Achievement score when he grows up). If the opportunities are well beyond his capacities, negative affect should result, and he may develop an avoidance motive as far as achievement is concerned. Since a fairly narrow range of circumstances will conspire to yield a high achievement approach motive, it would not be surprising to discover that individuals or groups of individuals in different cultures differ widely in the amount of achievement motivation they develop.

2.10.12 *In human adults adaptation levels are numerous and complex so that a single event may have several hedonic consequences.* Take flunking out of school, for example. One might argue that if the student half expected it, he should feel pleasure since his expectation is confirmed. Although it is true that he may get some fleeting satisfaction from having predicted correctly, this is more than outweighed by the nonconfirmation of other expectations built up over his whole life history such as doing a good job, being a professional man, etc. So far we have been dealing largely with low level expectations and *AL's* taken one at a time for the sake of simplicity, but obviously in real life situations, after the person has matured, the calculus of pleasure and pain becomes exceedingly complex. Consider, for example, the traditional argument used against hedonic theories of motivation to the effect that adults at any rate frequently do things, out of a sense of duty or what not, which are distinctly unpleasant. What about the martyr, for example? Can he be seeking pleasure or avoiding pain? The answer is "yes," in the larger sense in which positive and negative affect are defined here. If a man builds up a conception of the Universe—an expectation of the way in which moral or spiritual laws govern it and his place in it—which is sufficiently firm and well defined, it may well be that the anticipated nonconfirmation of such an expectation through transgression of those laws would produce sufficient negative affect so that a man would choose the lesser negative affect of burning at the stake. One of the virtues of our view of motivation is precisely that it permits the development of new, high level motives as experience changes the person's expectations or adaptation levels. Whereas the rat or the child may be primarily governed by variations from sensory or simple perceptual expectations, the adult will be ruled by discrepancies in higher level cognitive structures (beliefs) which may lead to action in direct opposition to simple sensory pleasures and pains.

2.11 **The acquisition of motives.** Now that we have considered the possible antecedent conditions for affective arousal, what about the parallel problem of the antecedent conditions for motive formation? By our definition of a motive, the solution to this problem is straightforward. A motive is formed by pairing cues with affective arousal or with the conditions, just discussed, that produce affective arousal. These cues may be unconnected with affective arousal or they may be response-produced cues resulting from affective arousal. That is, the following sequence of events may occur:

Large discrepancy⟶Negative⟶Autonomic⟶Distinctive- - ⟶Avoidance
　　from AL　　　　affect　　response　　　cues　　　motive

The first three links in this chain are unlearned (as indicated by solid arrows), but the last link is a learned association (as indicated by a broken arrow) based on previous pairings of such autonomic cues with negative affect. Thus the cues for setting off a motivational association may lie in the behavioral effects of the affect itself. Take Hebb's half-grown chimpanzees, for example. The sight of a detached plaster head produces negative affect that leads to diffuse autonomic responses which have been associated with negative affect in the past and which consequently evoke fear (the redintegrated portion of negative affect). Fear in turn elicits co-ordinated avoidance responses which continue until the situation which touched off the sequence changes—e.g., until the head is out of sight, or if that is impossible, until the animal "adapts" to it.

But the main point is that affect is the innate result of certain discrepancies between expectations and perceptions. A motive is the learned result of pairing cues with affect or the conditions which produce affect.

2.11.1 *The acquisition of motives of different strength.* Since motives are learned, the conditions for their acquisition that we must consider are largely those which are traditionally called the "laws of learning." That is, the strength of a motivational association should be a function of the same factors, such as contiguity, which have been assumed to govern the strength of any association. But what exactly is meant by the term *strength of a motive?* At least three meanings can be distinguished. Strength may refer to the likelihood or *probability* that a motive will be aroused by a particular cue; it may refer to the *intensity* of the motive once aroused; or it may refer to the pervasiveness or *extensity* of the motive, by which is meant the variety of circumstances under which it will appear. Table 2.2 has been prepared to summarize very briefly the different variables which we believe will influence these three aspects of motive strength and also the response variables by which these aspects of motive strength may be most conveniently measured. As in Table 2.1 the sequence across the table from antecedent variable to hypothetical construct to response variable is not exact or exclusive. Thus "rate of affective change" almost certainly influences motive intensity as well as motive dependability.

Most of the variables in the table are fairly self-explanatory and are drawn with one or two exceptions from prevailing theories of the factors which influence learning. Probably the simplest way to explain how they are all supposed to operate is to choose an hypothetical example which will illustrate each of them in turn. Let us take a frog as our experimental animal and place him in a water-filled container which is equipped with a platform onto which he can jump if he wants to. Let us further suppose that pouring hot water on a frog will evoke a negative affective change. Leaving aside for a moment the

TABLE 2.2 Motive strength as a hypothetical construct conceived as varying in three dimensions, each of which is determined primarily by certain
antecedent variables and measured primarily by certain response variables

Antecedent variables influencing	Dimensions of MOTIVE STRENGTH	as reflected in the most relevant response variables
1. Frequency of association of cue with affective change 2. Contiguity between cue and affective change 3. Rate of affective change	Motive Dependability	Probability that a choice response will occur per unit time
4. Amplitude of affective change	Motive Intensity	Intensity of the choice response (Response ampli-tude, number of R's per unit time, latency or speed of R)
5. Variety of cues connected with affective change	Motive Extensity	Variety of cues eliciting R or resistance of choice re-sponse to extinction

problem of how the frog acquired the instrumental response
necessary for avoidance, we can further assume that the goal-
oriented choice response we will be interested in observing
here is whether or not he jumps out of the water onto the platform. As a conditioned stimulus we may use anything to which
he is sensitive, say a light touch on the head. Now we begin
the conditioning procedure and pair the touch on the head
with a "shot" of hot water. The first two antecedent variables
in the table then are the familiar conditioning variables, which
state simply that the more frequently the cue (touch) is
paired with the affective change (produced by hot water)
and the more contiguous the association, the greater the probability that the motive will be aroused, as can be demonstrated by the greater frequency of the avoidance response of

jumping onto the platform for a given number of taps on the head. The third variable, *rate of affective change*, is, on the other hand, a relatively unfamiliar one, although it has been used by Gwinn (1949) to explain certain effects of punishment in rats. What it states is that if the temperature in the water is changed slowly so that the affective change is spread out over time, it will produce a less dependable affective association. Or to turn this statement around, the more rapid the affective change, the more effective it is in producing a motivational association. There is little evidence that we know of which supports the importance of this variable directly, although it has seemed to us to follow logically from some of our other assumptions. That is, a slow change in water temperature would presumably raise the adaptation level so that the temperature increase from beginning to end would provide less discrepancy from *AL* at any given moment, and hence less negative affect, than would the same increase over a shorter period of time. By this interpretation, rate of change reduces to a special case of amplitude of the affective change, the next variable to be considered. That is, the more rapid the change, the greater the affect; and the greater the affect, the stronger the motive. Rate of change may also exert an influence indirectly through its effect on contiguity. Often the initial change in affect (as produced by an increase in temperature) provides cues that get associated by contiguity with further changes in affect (discomfort from the heat), but if the connection has been noncontiguous, as in slow changes in temperature, it will provide a more imperfect means of eliciting anticipatory negative affect.

The *amplitude of affective change* in our frog experiment could be controlled not only by rate of change but more simply by varying the temperature of the hot water. The assumption is that up to a certain point the hotter the water, the more vigorous would be the response to the conditioned stimulus (touch). The vigor of the response could be measured by the number of responses made per unit time (if he were blocked from escaping), by the latency of the avoidance response, by its speed, or by the strength of pull against a thread attached to some kind of recording instrument.

Our fifth variable, the variety of cues connected with affective change, also represents something of a new emphasis. The reason for its inclusion becomes quite apparent in the light of some recent studies by V. F. Sheffield (1949) and by McClelland and McGown (1953). These authors were interested in explaining why it was that extinction takes longer after partial reinforcement during learning. Both researches come to the conclusion that the reason for the delay in extinction is that some of the cues present during extinction were also present during acquisition in the partially reinforced group, namely, those cues resulting from non-reinforcement. This can be interpreted further as follows. It means in effect that the greater the similarity between the cues in the extinction and the acquisition conditions, the longer the extinction will take because the animal will find it harder to distinguish between extinction and acquisition conditions. In the ordinary learning experiment, where the animal has received 100 per cent reinforcement or reward, he is commonly extinguished under conditions of zero reinforcement. This constitutes such a major change in stimulating conditions that he can discriminate the difference without too much difficulty and learn that a different response is appropriate under such markedly changed conditions. But the perceptual difference between 50 per cent reinforcement in learning and zero reinforcement in extinction is not so large, and the animal should therefore take longer to make the discrimination and learn not to respond in extinction. To generalize this example a little, we can state that *the greater the variety of cues to which a response is attached, the harder it will be to extinguish it completely,* because the more difficult it will be to reinstate all the original cues and extinguish the response to them. Therefore, the more varied or irregular the conditions of acquisition, the more generalized the association will be and the harder it will be to extinguish it by any specific non-reinforcement. In our hypothetical frog experiment there are a number of ways in which the cue conditions during acquisition could be varied. We could use different conditioned stimuli (light and sound as well as touch); we could *vary* the time between the conditioned stimulus and unconditioned stimulus (hot water); we could sometimes fail to introduce the hot water after the conditioned stimulus (partial reinforcement), and so on. A rough measure of the generalized nature or extensity of the affective association is *the number of trials* it takes the animal to give up making the avoidance response completely when any particular conditioned stimulus is presented repeatedly without the unconditioned stimulus. That is, the more general the association, the harder it should be for the animal to discriminate the new situation (extinction) from the old (acquisition). So he should take more trials to extinguish. In passing it should be noted that, since "trials to extinction" measures primarily, though not exclusively, the *extensity* aspect of motive strength, it may not give exactly the same results as measures of other aspects of motive strength, such as strength of pull, latency, speed, and so forth.

Another, perhaps more direct, test of extensity of an association would be to explore the limits of the generalization gradients from some particular conditioned stimulus. Thus, one could certainly predict that the generalization gradients would be much wider for animals trained under a variety of conditions than those trained very regularly with a particular stimulus of a particular intensity, and so on.

These three aspects of motive strength are of great importance at the human level. We expect to find with further research that there are some subjects whose achievement motive is aroused by a great variety of cues. Other subjects may have achievement motives which are aroused only by very specific situations (e.g., playing cards, winning at football, making feminine conquests). People will also vary in the intensity as well as the extensity of their motives. Some will have an intense desire to succeed at cards, others only a mild desire in this area but an intense desire to get good grades in a course. It should be possible to plot for each individual a graph which would show the intensity of his achievement motive or achievement *interest*, in each of several different areas. Our present measure of *n* Achievement represents a kind of averaging out of these two variables so as to obtain one index for each person. Motive dependability is in a sense the primary aspect of strength, since a motive must be first aroused before its intensity and extensity can be measured. The best measure here seems to be the regularity with which a given cue, if repeated over and over again, will give rise to the achievement motive. Thus we might find some subjects who wanted to win at cards all the time; others only part of the time and some not at all. On the face of it, there seems no reason to assume that this variable is perfectly correlated with intensity. It is at least logically possible that a subject who is only occasionally aroused might, if aroused, show a very strong achievement motive. Conversely, a person who is always aroused by a particular situation might be aroused at a relatively low level of intensity. It is in these terms that some of the picture differences discussed in Chapter VII can best be explained. To sum up, we expect to be able to measure independently at the human level the three aspects of motive strength theoretically distinguished here—e.g., dependability, intensity, and extensity. Motives also differ in kind as well as in strength, of course (see Sections 2.12, 2.13), so that the complete description of a motive will have four dimensions—quality (goal or scoring definition), extensity, intensity, and dependability.

2.12 **Types of affective change and types of motives.** As previously indicated, it is possible to distinguish two aspects of motives based on whether the choice response made involves approach or avoidance. These two types of behavior seem sufficiently different to warrant speaking of two different aspects of motivation. For one thing, Miller (1944), Clark (1952), and others have commonly assumed that approach and avoidance gradients differ markedly in slope. For another, we have found fairly convincing evidence in our own data for two aspects of the achievement motive, one of which seems characterized by defensiveness and a fear of failure, the other by increased instrumental striving and hope of success. Finally, if we consider the way in which motives are supposed to be learned, some should be acquired under circumstances in which pleasure results from successful achievement, whereas others should be acquired under circumstances in which negative affect results from failure.

In addition to these two basic aspects of motivation, there is at least the logical possibility of two other types which would result from other kinds of affective change. Thus the two types we have already mentioned might be thought of as resulting primarily from first, an increase in pleasure (an approach motive) and, second, from an increase in pain (an avoidance motive). But, at least theoretically, cues may also be associated with a decrease in pain or with a decrease in pleasure. One would expect the former to lead to approach behavior and the latter to avoidance behavior of a sort. At the present writing, however, there is very little evidence for the existence of either of these aspects of motivation, despite the current popularity of the notion that stimulus reduction is particularly important in motivation theory. Thus in a preliminary experiment Lee (1951) has shown that a cue paired with *onset* of shock will lead to intense avoidance behavior when presented in a new situation, whereas a cue associated with *offset* of shock will not lead to approach behavior, as it should, but to a somewhat less intense avoidance behavior. It may be that reduction in shock gains its apparent "rewarding" effect because it removes cues arousing an avoidance motive and not because it is in itself a positive goal. In common-sense language, a rat may learn to run off a charged grid not because the "safety box" attracts him (approach motive) but because the grid cues off an avoidance or fear motive which is no longer cued off in the safety box so that he stops running when he gets there. On the whole, however, further exploration of motives based on *decreases* in affective states is definitely called for.

2.13 **Definition of a particular motive.** Considering the problem of types of motives leads into the question of defining particular motives. How do we conclude a human being or a species of animal has a particular motive? How many motives are there? How do we know there is such a thing as an "Achievement" motive? And exactly how do we distinguish the Achievement motive from the Affiliation motive or the Food motive? Suppose we begin by referring back to our earlier description of a motive. "A motive is the learned result of pairing cues with affect or the conditions which produced affect." We might attempt first to distinguish one motive from another in terms of the type of cues which give rise to the affect. That is, the sight of food could give rise to the Hunger motive, the sight of mother to the Affiliation motive, the sight of school books to the Achievement motive. Although there is some basis for distinguishing motives in this way, it soon becomes apparent on further analysis that such an approach is not precise enough. The sight of mother, for instance, may arouse all three motives: the need for Food, the need for Achievement, or the need for Affiliation. And anyway why shouldn't we then speak of the need-for-mother motive?

What about the type of affect? Can we classify motives on this basis? Obviously not, since we have distinguished in general only between "positive" and "negative" affective changes which must be common to all types of motives from hunger to achievement. In terms of the definition, then, this leaves as the only remaining possibility distinguishing motives in terms of the "conditions which give rise to affect." But what exactly is meant by the word *conditions* here? To specify what it means should provide us with a basis for classifying motives. One thing it could refer to is the type of *response* necessary to produce affect. Thus we might identify hunger in terms of the "eating" response, the Affiliation motive in terms of making contact with others, the Achievement motive in terms of the "working" response, and so on. Such an approach has an appealing simplicity, but it is insufficient for at least two reasons. In the first place, dynamic psychologists have argued very convincingly that the very essence of motivation is its capacity to elicit *alternative* behavioral manifestations. As Frenkel-Brunswik puts it, "Overt behavior and the underlying motivational tendencies may vary independently in a statistical sense. . . . It is well known that exaggerated friendliness may serve, or even be the direct result of, strong destructive tendencies" (1942, p. 127). In the second place, such a way of defining motives does not fit in with our earlier discussion of the conditions which produce affect.

If we refer back to that discussion, it immediately becomes obvious that the conditions for affective arousal involve not actions so much as *expectations* * (or adaptation levels) and *the results of action* in terms of how far they confirm expectations. So to be consistent, motives should be distinguishable primarily in terms of the *types of expectations* involved, and secondarily in terms of the types of action, in so far as they exist, which confirm those expectations in varying de-

* Since expectations are in turn lawfully based on repeated exposure to certain stimuli or situations, we are not avoiding here the definitional problem simply by naming a process within the organism (cf. Table 2.1 and Section 2.10).

grees and thus yield positive or negative affect. For instance, in a general way we might speak of a "Gregariousness" motive which should involve expectations about the presence of other people similar to ones seen previously and the confirmation of those expectations based on appropriate types of action—e.g., associating with people. Such a motive should develop out of the perceptual expectations the infant develops about his mother and other people (see the earlier discussion of Hebb's "fear of the strange") and it should therefore be relatively universal, occurring in all seeing babies (and in a different form in non-seeing ones), and probably also in animals (cf. Scott, 1945, on gregariousness in sheep).

It is meaningful then to speak of motives "common to all men" (and animals) to the extent that conditions can be identified which will give rise regularly to affective change either through biological or cultural arrangements. Let us take hunger first as a biological example and then consider the Achievement motive as a cultural one.

The need for food is in our terms a compound motive because it is based on two types of affective change; one the innate pleasure from sucking and tasting, and the other based on the reduction in internal stimulation arising from food deprivation. The first is sometimes called appetite, the second hunger. Hull, et al. (1951) have demonstrated on a dog with an esophageal fistula that either food in the mouth alone or food in the stomach alone is reinforcing (will cause the dog to learn), thus supporting the view that the food motive has two components, although they take the view that the pleasure in eating is learned, not innate as we are assuming here (cf. also Kohn, 1951). We define the motive in terms of the adaptation levels in the mouth and in the stomach which can ordinarily be changed only by the consequences of certain acts—chewing and swallowing food. Incidentally, conditions can occur which will produce one or the other of these affective changes *alone*, but cues associated with such conditions are not ordinarily conceived of as arousing the hunger motive. Thus saccharine will produce positive affective change in the mouth and a desire for saccharine may develop despite its non-nutritive character, yet such a desire is not ordinarily conceived by itself as defining the presence of the hunger motive. This serves to underline the fact that the food motive may become very complex, since different eating habits may develop different adaptation levels which in turn may make previously disliked tastes pleasurable (e.g., beer or oysters). The one apparently unchanging aspect of the motive is the negative affective state produced internally by metabolism which always serves as a motive because it has *always* been paired with further negative and positive affective changes (from going without or obtaining food).

Now what about achievement? What adaptation levels or expectations distinguish this motive from others? Clearly the expectations are built out of universal experiences with problem-solving—with learning to walk, talk, hunt or read, write, sew, perform chores, and so forth. The expectations also involve standards of excellence with respect to such tasks. The tasks can be done quickly and efficiently or clumsily and slowly. They can also be done better or faster than someone else. Some of the pleasure that develops out of mastering tasks is undoubtedly intrinsic. That is, the child develops gradually certain expectations about what self-locomotion or a toy car will do for him and gets pleasure from confirming these expectations as long as they remain somewhat uncertain. So everyone has the rudiments of an achievement motive. But stronger achievement motives probably require for most (though not necessarily all) children some structuring of performance standards, some *demands* by the parents and the surrounding culture. The child must begin to *perceive performance in terms of standards of excellence* so that discrepancies of various sorts from this perceptual frame of reference (AL) can produce positive or negative affect. The surest sign of such a frame of reference is *evaluation* of a performance in one of our TAT stories—e.g., "the boy has done a *good* job."

Such a frame of reference is absolutely essential, but by itself it is not a motive any more than the adaptation level to sweet in the mouth is a motive. Both are simply standards which make the production of affect possible. Just as certain types of substances in the mouth produce discrepancies from taste AL's which are pleasurable, certain types of performance produce positive, negative, or no affective changes in terms of previously established perceptual standards of performance. What then becomes crucial in scoring stories for achievement motivation is detecting *affect in connection with evaluation*. A boy may have an achievement frame of reference, perhaps because of stress on achievement by his parents. He may write often of "successful businessmen," of contests for prizes, and so on, but unless there is some sign of affect over performance we cannot be sure that he is *personally involved*, that he sees his own performance in terms of these standards, that the affective result which defines a motive theoretically is really present. Thus we look in the stories for some sign of involvement such as directly stated affect ("He is *unhappy* because he flunked the exam") or desire ("He *wants* to become a successful businessman"). (See Chap. IV.) Thus our scoring definition for n Achievement is ultimately consistent with our theoretical conception of what constitutes a motive.

This definition of the Achievement motive in terms of *affect in connection with evaluated performance* leaves considerable room for variation as to the type of performance which may be involved, just as it should according to Frenkel-Brunswik's argument about the alternative manifestations of a motive. Thus a Navaho may want to be a good sheepherder (cf.

Chap. VI), an American boy a good businessman. Young males in our culture usually evaluate work or career performance so that references to leadership potential and intelligence increase their n Achievement scores (Chap. VI). But young American females may not respond to standards evaluating the same type of performance (Chap. VI). Instead, their standards of excellence apparently are more concerned with behavior connected with social acceptability. Thus Field found (1951) that social rejection of women raised their n Achievement scores and Frenkel-Brunswik reports (1942, p. 186) that for girls "attractive appearance" correlated highly with rated n Achievement. Whether the performance be grooming, playing football, landing a job, or herding sheep, it can give evidence of an achievement motive if there is affect or involvement connected with evaluation of it (doing it well, and so on). It should not be assumed, of course, that the presence of these signs means the person has actually done well at the task in question. There is no *necessary* connection between high achievement motivation and more efficient performance. The standards in terms of which a person evaluates his performance may be quite low objectively or the affect over performance could be predominantly negative because of repeated failures. In either case, a poor performer could show evidence of high achievement motivation. Still, this should be the exception rather than the rule, since an achievement approach motive at least requires performance that must be fairly close to expectations to yield pleasure; and as performance does approximate expectations, the expectations must increase if it is to continue to yield pleasure. Therefore there should be a significantly positive but moderate correlation between n Achievement and the actual efficiency of performance of various sorts (see Chap. VIII).

The number of motives possible then is determined by the number of expectations which psychologists can find which occur fairly universally and which frequently result in affective changes through confirmation or nonconfirmation. We will make no attempt to enumerate such common motives here, but it seems to us that with these two limiting criteria it should be possible to come out with not too long a list of motives common to all men. To mention just one further example to illustrate the general applicability of the criteria, it is equally obvious that all human individuals everywhere associate with other human individuals, and these associations develop expectations which are intrinsically and extrinsically loaded with affective changes. Thus the two major criteria are present for assuming that an Affiliation motive will develop in all men to a greater or lesser degree. Furthermore, we have done enough experimental work (cf. Shipley and Veroff, 1952) to show that an Affiliation motive can be aroused and measured according to the same technique used here for measuring the Achievement motive.

2.14 **Biological needs and motivation.** In an earlier section (2.4) where we discussed the inadequacies of the survival model of motivation, we tried to avoid the premature conclusion that there is no connection between tissue needs and motivation. There undoubtedly is such a connection through the capacity of many biological needs to produce affective arousal. The species which have survived are probably those for which there is a fairly pronounced correlation between tissue needs and affective states.

Now according to our theory, how could we explain the fact that the longer an animal is deprived of food the more motivated he appears to become? Since most psychologists have been accustomed to thinking of biological need states as the primary sources of motivation, this is a very important question for us to discuss. In the first place, it is clear that in terms of our theory food deprivation does not produce a motive the first time it occurs. The lack of food in a baby rat or a baby human being will doubtless result in diffuse bodily changes of various sorts, but these do not constitute a motive until they are paired with a subsequent change in affect. More specifically, if the organism is to survive, the cues subsequent to food deprivation must always be associated with eating, and eating results in two types of affective change—pleasurable taste sensations, and relief from internal visceral tensions. Thus internal (or external) cues resulting from food deprivation are associated very early and very regularly in all individuals with positive affective change, and thus they become capable of arousing the hunger *motive* with great dependability. But this still does not explain why the motive gets stronger as food deprivation is increased from 10 hours to 24 or 36 hours. Several explanations for this are logically possible. For example, it could be argued that longer deprivation gives rise to distinctive cues which have been paired with greater subsequent changes in affect. Food tastes better after longer deprivation, and so on. As we have just pointed out, we consider amount of affective change one of the principles governing the strength of a motive. Another possible explanation is somewhat simpler than this. It is based on the assumption that as food deprivation increases, the cues to which it gives rise become more insistent (occur with greater frequency, and the like) and thus elicit with greater regularity the hunger motive. With lesser degrees of motivation, the hunger motive may be cued off occasionally but will yield its place from time to time to other associations. As the deprivation increases, the hunger association is cued off more and more regularly until it dominates the associative processes of the organism.

Such a way of thinking about the hunger motive throws light on several phenomena which have puzzled those who think of food deprivation itself as producing the hunger motive. It is one good explanation for the need to habituate animals in learning experiments, for example. According to this view, one of the consequences of habituation is to associate external cues (being picked up by the experimenter) with the affective changes resulting from eating, so that in time *the experimenter will become a dependable means of arousing the hunger motive.* The value of pre-feeding the animal can be explained in a similar manner. It has been found that if a hungry or thirsty rat is given a nibble of food or a few cc. of water before he starts working on an experimental day, he performs better and appears more motivated (Maltzman, 1952). This has seemed somewhat paradoxical to those who think of eating or drinking as producing a reduction in need or motivation. But in our view a bite to eat should also produce cues which arouse a motive based on past association of such cues with the pleasures of eating. In short, pre-feeding produces additional cues for arousing the food motive complex which in turn serves to make the animal perform slightly better.

What this adds up to is that we have redefined the whole problem of so-called primary and secondary drives. That is, from our point of view *all drives (motives) are learned.* Affective arousal, on which motives are based, is essentially primary (unlearned), although the adaptation levels which govern it can obviously be changed by experience. So the traditional distinction between *primary* (biological need) motives and *secondary* (learned or social) motives has disappeared. Instead, we may speak of primary affect and secondary motives if we like. Or we may even speak of primary and secondary motives, if it is understood that both involve learned associations but that the cues involved in the former are primarily biological rather than primarily social in nature. For example, after the food motive is learned, the cues which set it off occur as a result of body metabolism with great certainty and regularity; and in this sense they might be called primary cues as opposed to cues which occur less regularly as a result of social interaction and the like. But even this distinction seems somewhat confusing to us, since some social cues are also quite inescapable (e.g., those arising from the interaction of mother and child). And furthermore some biological cues (e.g., those resulting from certain autonomic responses) give rise to motives (fear) which are not ordinarily conceived of as "primary." In our opinion, it really seems somewhat preferable to discard the distinction between primary and secondary motives altogether.

2.15 **Rewards and motives.** What does a reward do to an affective association as we have defined it? How is it that rewards seem to put an end to motives? We must begin by distinguishing sharply between what has commonly been called primary reward and secondary reward. For us these are quite different phenomena, although, as their similar names suggest, they have commonly been assumed to be alike. In fact, a secondary reward has often been spoken of as a substitute for the primary reward and as getting its secondary reinforcing power from association with the primary reward. There seems to be a fundamental paradox in this assumption, however, for the simple reason that whereas a primary reward (e.g., food) is assumed to tend to put an end to motivated behavior (by reducing the need or drive), a secondary reward (e.g., a click associated with food) is thought of as maintaining the motivated behavior (e.g., bar-pressing). The paradox has been neatly exposed by Simon, Wickens, Brown, and Pennock (1951), who demonstrated that a secondary "reward" has no capacity to reduce the strength of the thirst drive. The paradox results, we believe, from a fundamental misconception of the nature of the secondary "reward."

But let us consider first the nature of a primary reward. In most general terms, the "rewarding state of affairs" appears to be correlated with the actual occurrence of the change in affect which is anticipated or redintegrated. Such an event— the occurrence of an affective state—often gradually disrupts the motive. Eating slows hunger; orgasm, the sexual drive;

success, the achievement motive. But why? In simplest terms, the answer is that the occurrence of the affective state (1) changes the hedonic adaptation level of the organism, and (2) removes cues that have been associated with affective changes. Take eating as an example. Suppose looking at one's watch, coupled with certain internal sensations, arouses the food motive which leads to going home for lunch. Eating lunch disrupts the food motive partly because the external and internal sensations which contribute to arousing the motive have been directly removed by eating and partly because pleasure from eating interferes directly with appetite (anticipation of pleasure from eating). Eating itself stops in time either because it is no longer pleasurable (through changes in taste adaptation levels) or because satiation cues begin to appear which redintegrate negative affect through past experience with overeating. The person ordinarily will not eat again until the taste and stomach adaptation levels have drifted back to the point where either a positive or negative affective change can again be redintegrated and hunger or external cues are again present to redintegrate such a change.

One virtue of this scheme is that it appears to handle a difficulty that Miller and Dollard (1941), Allport (1937), Hebb (1949), and others have repeatedly found with the notion of reward. In a nutshell, the problem seems to be this: What makes an organism stop doing something pleasurable? As Miller and Dollard put it (1941, p. 66): "If some stimuli are inherently pleasant and rewarding, however, it is difficult to see why responses producing these stimuli should ever stop short of extreme fatigue or other shifts introducing unpleasant stimulation." Allport's repeated objection to the law of effect has been that it ought to lead people to repeat monotonously things they have done with reward before, such as taking the same courses or reading the same novel over and over again. Our notion of what produces pleasure takes care of this objection. As we have shown, pleasure is dependent on adaptation level or expectation which can be changed in a number of ways, not the least of which is the occurrence of the pleasant event itself. Thus a person will not continue eating sugar indefinitely because of marked changes in adaptation level (cf. Woodworth, 1938), nor will he continue to play with the same toy forever for the same reason (see Section 2.10.11).

But what about the occurrence of negative affect? Does it disrupt a motive in the same way that positive affect does? Usually not. It probably would change the hedonic level in time so that the size of the increases in pain which can be redintegrated are reduced, if the pain were produced by a steady state type of stimulus, but this is usually not the case. There are two other important differences between positive and negative affect. In the first place, adaptation levels would have to be shifted farther than for positive affect to get rid of all negative affect, since by definition negative affect is dependent on larger discrepancies from adaptation level. And there may very well be limits on how far adaptation level can shift. In the second place, the cues which elicit negative affective changes are like the ones produced by the negative affect itself. Thus if a person is afraid of being hurt and is hurt, the pain may simply provide further cues for eliciting the fear motive. This is not necessarily true, of course: a spanking may disrupt a fear motive just because it has been associated with the end of negative affect. But the point is that the reverse is much more commonly true. Negative affect more often contains cues which redintegrate further increases in pain. The situation with positive affect is different. Positive affect is more often redintegrated by cues (from deprivation, and so forth) which are actually *removed* rather than reintroduced by its occurrence.

Now what about the phenomenon which has been referred to as "secondary reward"? From our point of view, a poker chip or a click which has been repeatedly associated with food is simply another cue which gets the capacity to evoke an anticipated change in affect. Each is a means of arousing a motive and should in no sense be thought of as a substitute for the primary affective or reward state itself, as the term *secondary reward* suggests. In experiments by Wolfe (1936) and Cowles (1937) chimpanzees showed approach behavior toward food tokens because those tokens were now capable of redintegrating a positive affective change on account of their past association with eating. In an exactly similar manner the animals should have shown approach behavior toward the experimenter, the vending machine, or other objects or cues consistently associated with the affective changes resulting from eating. That is, the tokens have no special "substitute reward value" which is different from that which the vending machine, for example, has. The animal should "like" (e.g., approach) both of them because of their past association with positive affective changes. In this case *extinction* can be seen as a process in which a cue or a response-produced cue (e.g., bar-pressing) gradually loses its motive-arousing capacity through its repeated association with new consequences (lack of pleasure from eating, frustration, fatigue, and so on). This argument is in essential agreement with Liberman's view (1944) of the extinction process as a competition between two associations or response tendencies. (Compare also Mowrer's [1950] and Hull's [1943] views of extinction as involving work, which, in our terms, may result in negative affect.)

2.16 **Emotions and motives.** It may appear a little cavalier to have blithely assumed up to this point that motives are based on affect when the whole weight of psychological tradition supports the opposite view—namely, that affect is the by-product or accompaniment of motives. McDougall is particularly eloquent on this point (1927) and of course the whole psychoanalytic tradition starts with the assumption of the libido, an innate urge which produces pleasure if gratified and displeasure if frustrated. In fact, such a view is so widely held and so obviously "sensible" that some explanation of how our theorizing accounts for it is definitely called for.

The best approach seems to be to try and explain in our terms the observations which have led to the view that striving is primary, affect secondary. First, frustration of motives leads to anger, fear, and similar types of negative affect. Is this not evidence that the motive comes first? Let us be more specific. Johnny wants an ice cream cone. The cue of the ice cream wagon redintegrates anticipation of pleasure from eating one. But he can't find a dime and nobody will give him one. Result: negative affect. Why? First, we should make it clear that the positive "taste" affect on which the motive (wanting the ice cream cone) is based is different from the negative affect which results from not getting it. Second, the negative affect is the result of the nonconfirmation of the expectation of getting and eating an ice cream cone. Furthermore, one could safely predict that the amount of negative affect from nonconfirmation will be a direct function of the perceived probability of getting the ice cream (estimated from the frequency with which he has gotten it in the past) and of the size of the positive affective change redintegrated (how much he "likes" ice cream). In both cases, as certainty increases and as amount of pleasure anticipated grows greater, nonconfirmation produces a larger discrepancy from expectation and negative affect is necessarily larger.

A second observation suggesting that affect is secondary is that food doesn't taste good unless one is hungry. Drinking water may be unpleasant if one is not thirsty, and so on. Doesn't this suggest that positive and negative affect from particular stimulation is dependent on the state of various drives? Superficially it does, but again in our terms it is clear that the reason the food or water is no longer pleasant is that AL's have been shifted by previous stimulation or internal bodily conditions. This part of the argument can simply be rephrased to state that affect is dependent on the relation of stimulation to AL.

A third observation is that intense motives produce affect which may interfere with or facilitate performance, and so on. Thus a person who wants intensely to succeed on an exam may get so anxious and upset, so disturbed by negative affect, that he cannot proceed. Again is this not evidence that affect comes from motivation, rather than the reverse? Here our explanation must recall the fact that a motive involves in part the redintegration of an affective state or change. Fear or anxiety is in a sense the "redintegratable" portion of pain or negative affect. Obviously, if the original affect on which it is based is intense, the redintegrated affect may also be intense and may grow more so if frustration occurs, according to the mechanism described above. Thus the redintegrated affect may be strong enough to interfere with performance. An interesting idea suggested by this analysis is that various named emotions may refer either to redintegrated affect—e.g., fear, anxiety, lust, appetite, and so forth—or to affect itself—e.g., grief, disgust, laughter, and so on.

Actually none of these observations can argue conclusively that motives cannot result from affect anyway. Because affect *results* from motives in various ways, this is no reason to assume that it cannot therefore be the *cause* of motives. So all we have attempted to do is show how and why according to our theory affect apparently accompanies motives in the ways described.

2.17 **Learning and motivation.** Although we have tried to restrict ourselves to hypotheses about the nature of motivation, we have been forced inevitably to consider how learning (acquisition of responses) fits into the picture. Even now we are incapable of making any kind of complete analysis of learning theory in the light of our assumptions about motivation, but we do feel an obligation to make some highly tentative suggestions as to how the two kinds of theorizing may ultimately be fitted together. One thing is clear: in our discussion of how cues get to be associated with changes in affect we have said nothing specifically about the need for reinforcement in the Hullian sense. On the surface, at least, our approach would seem to imply a contiguity theory for learning several types of associations—$S \rightarrow S$, $S \rightarrow R$, $S \rightarrow$ affective change, and so forth. Granted for the moment that this is so, how then do we explain the obvious fact that motives facilitate learning or at least performance? How do we account for what McGeoch (1942) calls the "empirical" law of effect? The usual assumptions have been that motives make the organism active, that in the course of this activity a response will occur which will be followed by need reduction, and that somehow or other this need reduction or reward will "reinforce" or "forge" a connection between the situation and the response which results in need reduction. The mysterious part of this process has been the third step ever since Thorndike first formulated the law of effect. How is it that this after-effect produces a connection between the two events which preceded it?

Our conception of motivation adds nothing in particular to the understanding of the first two steps in this process. Motivation does seem to activate particular response hierarchies in the organism, even though this does not always result in increased overt activity. Some of the responses in the hierarchy are followed more promptly by "positive" affective change (increase in pleasure, decrease in pain). But why do such responses appear more and more readily the more closely they have been associated with the final affective change? We believe that an important clue to the understanding of how these "affective effects" control and direct behavior is to be found in the study of instinctive behavior in animals. During the early days of behaviorism, it was common to think of an instinct as unfolding in the form of a rigid, non-varying series of response elements. Now the conception is quite different. Now we tend to think of response elements which vary considerably *so long as their sensory or perceptual effect is the same* or relatively constant. Consider a moth flying toward a light, a fish maintaining pressure on his head receptors as he swims against the current, a fly maintaining his equilibrium as he speeds through the air, a male moth fluttering several miles in pursuit of a supersonic noise given off by the female moth, or a male dog pursuing the scent given off by a female dog in heat. In all of these instances, response patterns may vary over an extremely wide range, but they are always controlled and directed by their sensory effect.

A simple and economical description of what happens in instances like this would run somewhat as follows. Take a male dog who has just had a whiff of the scent of a female in heat. Let us suppose further that this scent is innately pleasurable for him, which means that he will make instrumental approach responses which maximize this effect, if such responses are available to him from previous learning (cf. Beach and Gilmore, 1949). Now our problem is to discover just how he learns to make appropriate approach responses to this particular sensory "delight." Let us assume that the scent arouses him and causes a lot of variable behavior. In the course of this, he may turn his head in the wrong direction, but this decreases the pleasant effect. Now he turns in another direction which may increase the effect. Gradually or quickly he learns to make those compensating responses which will keep the sensory effect maximal. The process seems to be quite analogous to the "governor" or servo-mechanisms described by Wiener (1950).

Now let us try to apply this analysis to the functioning of motives in human beings. As we have pointed out earlier, it is doubtful if human beings are controlled as directly by afferent stimulation as are lower animals, but the mechanism of control may be similar. The only difference is that now behavior is controlled not so much by afferent stimulation but by anticipation of affective change, i.e., instead of sensory stimulation being innately pleasurable, the cue has been associated with pleasurable affective changes. We will need to assume further that the motive or the anticipation of affective change is in itself somewhat pleasurable or painful, just as the affective state is on which it is based. This is not such a gratuitous assumption in the light of our earlier analysis of what causes positive and negative affect. That is, by definition the redintegrated positive or negative affect constitutes a discrepancy from the present hedonic state of the organism. Such a discrepancy should be pleasant or unpleasant, depending on how large it is. Furthermore, the longer it persists, the more likely its affective character is to change because of shifts in adaptation level. Thus dreaming about a positive affective change (a trip to Florida in winter) should initially be pleasurable, but if unaccompanied by instrumental activity, it should gradually lose its pleasurable quality through the mechanism for producing boredom by confirmation of certainties as described above. If it were not for the boredom mechanism, the pleasurable character of anticipated affective changes might actually interfere with the acquisition of responses necessary to bring the change (goal) about.

If the anticipated change is pleasurable in itself, then we can argue that the animal will learn to perform those acts which cue off the affective change state most dependably. Consider a rat running toward food. The last response he makes just before eating produces stimulation which is most strongly associated with affective change, both because of its nearness to the change in time and because of the relatively greater frequency with which it is associated with the change as compared with response-produced cues farther from the goal. Instrumental approach responses are those which cue off more and more dependably the anticipated increase in positive affect. Instrumental avoidance responses are those which remove the cues with increasing dependability which redintegrate negative affect. To repeat: the only additional assumption that we must make is that these redintegrated states are in themselves pleasurable and painful. They therefore have the capacity to guide and direct behavior just as afferent stimuli innately do for lower animals.

The important thing to note about this sketch of instrumental learning is that we have described somewhat more fully how the after-effects of behavior control the sequence of associations leading to the behavior. To review the argument once more:

Suppose we make the simple assumption that motivation is not necessary to produce an association (e.g., that associations are produced by contiguity or some other such principle). Then the problem is to explain why motivation often facilitates problem-solving or instrumental learning. This we have done by stating (1) that the organism seeks to maximize pleasure and minimize pain, (2) that responses which cue off anticipated pleasure will be made preferentially, (3) that in a problem-solving situation some responses will tend to be more closely associated with pleasure, and (4) that these responses will tend to be repeated since they cue off anticipated pleasure more dependably. A somewhat oversimplified picture of the sequence of events is given below. Suppose an animal is allowed to explore a simple T maze of the sort illustrated. He is always put in at X, which we will label Sx for stimulus conditions at X, and he may turn left (R_l) or

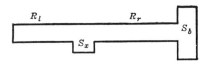

right (R_r) in which case he arrives at an end box (S_b). The contiguous sequences of events that occur on repeated exploratory trials are listed on the left. On the right are listed their associational counterparts as shown by broken arrows and (′) signs:

$$S_x \longrightarrow R_l \qquad\qquad S_x \dashrightarrow R_l'$$

$$S_x \longrightarrow R_r \qquad\qquad S_x \dashrightarrow R_r'$$

$$R_r \longrightarrow S_b \qquad\qquad R_r \dashrightarrow S_b'$$

$$\qquad\qquad\qquad\qquad S_x \dashrightarrow R_r' \dashrightarrow S_b'$$

The column on the right indicates associations that occur symbolically. That is, R_l' is not actually turning left as in the left-hand column; it is the redintegrated portion of R_l (or CNS counterpart of R_l). R_l' may lead to R_l, but whether it does or not depends on the strength of this as compared to other associations or whether R_l' cues off an affective change. Now suppose we introduce an affective change (A) by giving the animal a little something to eat in the box ($A+$) so that a new association is formed.

$$S_b \longrightarrow A+ \qquad\qquad S_b \dashrightarrow A'+$$

Now if we place the animal back at X, the following competing associations occur:

The argument runs that the anticipation of affective change ($A'+$) somehow *weights* or gives precedence to the bottom associative chain, so that it tends to continue and grow stronger until it erupts into action. Whether the animal will immediately run to the food in this situation is, of course, a function of a number of variables, such as the strength of the various associative connections, the similarity between S_b and S_b', the absence of non-instrumental, short-circuiting associations such as $S_x \dashrightarrow S_b' \dashrightarrow A'+$ and the like.

One advantage of this way of conceiving the effects of motivation on learning is that it provides a kind of solution to the problem of whether there are two types of learning—one based on contiguity and the other on reinforcement. According to this view, learning results from contiguity but it is especially influenced by the presence of a motivational association based on the past contiguity of cues and affective states. A motivational association thus becomes one very important way of producing positive transfer and takes its place with other associations (based on similarity, and so forth) that also produce transfer. Mowrer's position that there are two types of learning is similar though not identical with ours. Thus he argues (1950) that the contiguity principle operates for events mediated by the autonomic nervous system and the reinforcement principle for events mediated by the central nervous system. We too feel that associations involving the two nervous systems are different but not in the same way. Both are formed by contiguity, but those which involve the autonomic system are motivational associations and as such markedly influence (facilitate or disrupt) other associative chains.

Once more let it be emphasized that it would be presumptuous to argue that this is anywhere near a complete picture of the learning process. It is intended only to give a clearer picture of how we believe the redintegration of an affective change may control associational processes. Thus, rats stop going up blind alleys because these responses cue off the pleasure from eating less dependably than correct responses. They press a bar so long as this response evokes or redintegrates the affective change (pleasure from eating) previously associated with bar-pressing. Redintegration of negative affective change may disrupt an associational sequence, but this may help an animal solve a problem only slightly if there are a large number of alternative approaches to it. Perhaps the chief merit of our scheme is that it attempts to go beyond or behind the idea that reward somehow "forges" a connection between an S and an R. At least our intention has been to

CHAPTER III

Arousing the Achievement Motive and Obtaining Imaginative Stories

MANY PROCEDURES were employed in the present research to manipulate the intensity of achievement motivation in groups of subjects. These procedures involved attempts to control the degree to which achievement motivation was aroused by manipulating the cues in achievement-related instructions, the cues in achievement-related tasks, and the experiences of success and/or failure in these achievement-related tasks. The different arousal conditions were devised by various combinations of these three factors.

There were six experimental conditions. They will be referred to as Relaxed, Neutral, Achievement-oriented, Success, Failure, and Success-Failure. Male college subjects were used throughout. Each of the different experimental procedures preceded the measure of motivation used, e.g., a group Thematic Apperception Test (TAT). Because of the familiarity of the term TAT, it will be used often in this text as a shorthand way of referring to our method of sampling fantasy. However, there are certain differences between our method and Murray's classical use of the TAT (1938): (1) We often employ pictures different from those employed by Murray and his followers. (2) We use a group testing procedure in which the pictures are projected on a screen, and the subjects write their own stories with an imposed time limit. (3) Our scoring system, although borrowing somewhat from Murray's need-type of analysis, is quite different. The procedure for the administration of the TAT was standard throughout and can be summarized briefly as follows:

3.1 **Collecting stories.** Four 8½ x 14 inch sheets of paper clipped together were handed to each subject. On each sheet four sets of questions were printed. The sets of questions were spaced on the sheet so that one quarter of the page was allowed for writing about each of them. The four questions, adapted from Murray (1938), were intended to insure complete coverage of a plot. They were:
1. What is happening? Who are the persons?
2. What has led up to this situation? That is, what has happened in the past?
3. What is being thought? What is wanted? By whom?
4. What will happen? What will be done?

The experimenter read the following instructions:

This is a test of your creative imagination. A number of pictures will be projected on the screen before you. You will have twenty seconds to look at the picture and then about four minutes to make up a story about it. Notice that there is one page for each picture. The same four questions are asked. They will guide your thinking and enable you to cover all the elements of a plot in the time allotted. Plan to spend about a minute on each question. I will keep time and tell you when it is about time to go on to the next question for each story. You will have a little time to finish your story before the next picture is shown.

Obviously there are no right or wrong answers, so you may feel free to make up any kind of a story about the pictures that you choose. Try to make them vivid and dramatic, for this is a test of *creative* imagination. Do not merely describe the picture you see. Tell a story about it. Work as fast as you can in order to finish in time. Make them interesting. Are there any questions? If you need more space for any question, use the reverse side.

The room was then darkened for 20 seconds while the first picture was projected on a screen before the subjects. After 20 seconds the picture was turned off, the lights were turned on, and the subjects began writing. The experimenter kept time, and after a minute had been allowed for each question, would say, "All right, it is about time to go on to the next question." When the subjects had been writing for 30 seconds on the last question, the experimenter would say, "Try to finish up in 30 seconds." At the end of the final minute he would begin to prepare for the next picture, allowing no more than 15 seconds more than the required time for finishing the stories. The lights would be dimmed and the next picture projected on the screen for 20 seconds, and so on without interruption until all four stories had been written. The four pictures used in these particular six experiments will be designated *B, H, A*, and *G* (in order of presentation). The first two of these are reproduced in Figure 3.1. The second two were from the Murray TAT series (TAT 7BM, "father-son" picture; and TAT 8BM, "boy and operation scene" picture). A complete description of all the pictures used in the course of our research appears in Appendix III. This standard procedure for obtaining stories was imbedded in a variety of contexts or atmospheres described below.

3.2 **Arousing the achievement motive in various experimental conditions.** The basic assumption underlying our attempts to produce changes in the content of imaginative stories was that the achievement motive could be manipulated experimentally in much the same way as the hunger motive normally is in the animal laboratory. The analogy with hunger proved misleading, as will soon be apparent, since it led us to expect that the degree of arousal would be a direct function of *deprivation* (e.g., failure) and an inverse function of *satiation* (e.g., success). Thus the particular choice of the six arousal conditions to be described was dictated in part by a mistaken notion of the nature of the achievement motive. That is, in the beginning our focus of attention was on manipulation of success and failure with the expectation that a "Success" group would show the lowest n Achievement, a "Neutral" group a moderate amount, and a "Failure" group the highest amount. Later it became apparent that the motive had to be aroused by instructional cues and the like before its course could be affected by success and failure, so that our attention shifted to methods of arousal and away from what happened to the motive after it was aroused. Thus the first three experimental conditions—Relaxed, Neutral, and Achievement-oriented—represent roughly three degrees on an n Achievement arousal continuum, whereas the second three conditions —Success, Failure, Success-Failure—represent three possible outcomes for aroused motives, outcomes which may also affect the degree of arousal but do not in themselves produce it.

3.2.1 *Relaxed condition.* The experimenter was introduced to a group of college subjects as a graduate student. He made every effort to give the subjects the impression that there was really very little importance attached to a series of paper and pencil tasks that they were to perform. The tasks were presented as tests in the developmental stage that had been devised recently and were now being used to collect data to shed some light on their value. Subjects were not asked to sign their names. The experimenter attempted to create the impression that he was really not taking the situation very seriously but was just trying out some new ideas. He joked a little, showed no signs of ego-involvement himself in the situation, and so on. He was probably aided in all this by the fact that it was a beautiful summer day.

The paper and pencil tests used were a four-minute anagrams task, a three-minute scrambled-words task, a different four-minute scrambled words task, and four motor-perseveration tests in each of which the subject had to write something as often as possible in the normal manner for one minute and then backwards or in some unusual manner for another minute. The tests were chosen in part as a basis for a factor analytic study by Clark (1948) and are described in detail by him.

FIG. 3.1.A. Picture B, which was used in the standard series for eliciting stories to be scored for n Achievement.

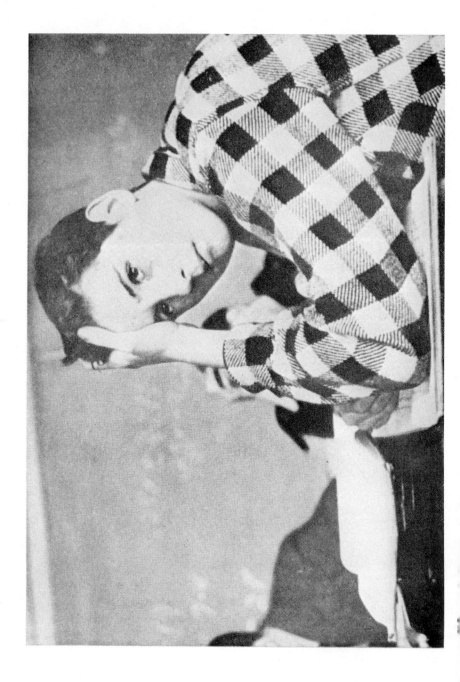

In this research, the chief function of the various paper and pencil tests was to provide a possible avenue for the presentation of achievement cues and a means of producing experiences of success and failure.

For the Relaxed condition every effort was made to minimize the achievement-related cues in the instructions, and there probably was no experience of success or failure, since subjects had no way of knowing how well they did on the tasks or any basis for expecting to know how well they should do. It should be pointed out, however, that the tasks themselves and the classroom situation probably did provide some minimal achievement cues. Following this 20-minute period of performing paper and pencil tasks under very relaxed conditions, another experimenter appeared to administer the group TAT with the standard procedure previously described. The tests were administered to a large summer session class at a large university which included both men and women, but only the men's records were used.

3.2.2 *Neutral condition.* The word *neutral* is used to describe the condition in which the imaginative measure of achievement motivation was presented without any extensive attempts to manipulate the motivation of the subjects. In the Relaxed condition real efforts were made to de-emphasize the importance of the situation to the subjects. In other conditions to follow, an effort was made to increase the intensity of motivation. The purpose of procedures preceding the measure of motivation in the Neutral condition was neither to depress nor to increase the level of motivation but rather to keep it "normal," so as to obtain a measure of the motivation subjects brought with them to the situation. In other words, our intention here was to measure the motivation level elicited by the cues of everyday school life. Thus, the experimenter did not joke or display the offhand manner shown in the Relaxed condition. Instead, he was introduced as a graduate student who was making a psychological investigation for his Master's thesis. He explained to the class that he wanted to establish some norms for his tests and that their serious cooperation was necessary if the results were to be meaningful. The subjects were told that they would be asked to take some tests, but they were not told what psychological capacities the tests would measure. After this attempt to gain the cooperation of the students, the group TAT was administered as usual.

After the group TAT, subjects were given specific instructions for a twelve-minute anagrams task (see Clark, 1948). In this one condition the actual performance of the task followed the administration of the TAT. This was done to avoid any slight possibility of contaminating the TAT with subjective feelings of success and failure which might result from the task performance and also to collect data on the relationship between imaginative n Achievement and subsequent performance (see Chap. VIII). The subjects in this experiment were all male undergraduates in a large elementary psychology class of about 160 students.

3.2.3 *Achievement-oriented condition.* In the Relaxed and Neutral conditions there was no intentional introduction of achievement cues other than those involved either in the tasks themselves or the classroom situation. The Achievement-oriented condition (referred to as Ego-involved by McClelland *et al.*, 1949) is the first in which the experimenter made a deliberate attempt to bring in additional achievement-related cues. After being introduced as Mr. X from W—— University who was conducting a serious psychological investigation, he made the following introductory remarks from memory:

The tests which you are going to take indicate, in general, a person's level of intelligence. They were taken from a group of tests which were used to select Washington administrators and officer candidates for the OSS during the past war. Thus, in addition to general intelligence, they bring out an individual's capacity to organize material, his ability to evaluate situations quickly and accurately—in short, these tests demonstrate whether or not a person is suited to be a leader. The present research is being conducted under the auspices of the Office of Naval Research to determine just which individuals possess the leadership qualifications shown by superior performance on these tests.

Subjects were then given a 12-minute anagrams test, instructions for which were the same as that for the Neutral condition (see Clark, 1948). This test was followed as usual by the group TAT. To make certain that a high level of motivation would be maintained, the experimenter preceded the standard instructions for the TAT by saying: "This test involves, among other things, creative intelligence. Listen carefully so you can do your best." A second experimenter then came forward and administered the TAT according to the standard procedure.

It is worth noting here that achievement-involving the TAT directly, like this, may sometimes frighten impressionable subjects into incoherence in their stories (cf. Chap. VII). In general, our method has been to arouse achievement motivation *before* the TAT is administered and to note its after-effects on imaginative stories which are written following relatively neutral instructions given by a different experimenter. The reason for using a new experimenter is to suggest a break between the achievement-oriented instructions and the TAT itself, so that subjects in writing their stories will not be too inhibited by fears that they are not appearing "intelligent." Achievement-involving the TAT directly, as in the case of the group reported here, did not cause any apparent inhibition in the story writing, but a similar procedure once used with a group of timid freshmen produced a startling "freezing" of the imaginative stories. The individuals in this latter group qualified their stories to such an extreme extent that it was impossible to score them. The problems raised in this connection will be dealt with more fully later.

Essentially, the Achievement-oriented condition was one in which additional achievement cues in the form of special instructions were introduced to heighten the motivation of subjects but without any subsequent induction of feelings of success or failure. The subjects in this condition were men (mostly ex-GI's) attending psychology classes at a large university.

3.2.4 *Success condition.* In the Success, Failure, and Success-Failure conditions, achievement-related instructions were introduced to heighten the motivation of subjects as in the Achievement-oriented condition. In addition to this, attempts were made to induce feelings of success and/or failure. The same paper and pencil tests that were used in the Relaxed condition were presented as highly achievement-related, and in the Success condition the subjects were led to believe that their performance on them was very good by means of the following procedure.

The experimenter was introduced as a person who would administer some tests. Subjects were given a pamphlet containing the tests already described for the Relaxed condition. The first test (anagrams) was preceded only by instructions on how to perform it. (This was done because a separate purpose required comparable situations with respect to this particular test for the Success, Failure and Success-Failure groups.) Upon finishing this task, the subjects were requested to count up the number of words they had completed and record it on a score sheet provided for that purpose. Following this, they filled out a questionnaire calling for name, high school and college attended with estimated class standing in each, IQ (if known), and an estimate of their general intelligence (above average, average, or below average). The purpose of these items was to heighten the achievement motivation of subjects by making it known that the scores on these tests would be associated with one's name and a number of other achievement-related facts.

Looking at his watch, the experimenter said that perhaps he would have sufficient time to tell the subjects about the nature of these tests. He then proceeded in a serious and impressive manner with an explanation of the tests:

The tests which you are taking directly indicate a person's general level of intelligence. These tests have been taken from a group of tests which were used to select people of high administrative capacity for positions in Washington during the past war. Thus, in addition to general intelligence, they bring out an individual's capacity to organize material, his ability to evaluate crucial situations quickly and accurately—in short, these tests demonstrate whether or not a person is suited to be a leader.

The present research is being conducted for the Navy to determine which educational institutions turn out the highest percentage of students with the administrative qualifications shown by superior scores on these tests. For example, it has been found that W—— University excels in this respect. You are being allowed to calculate your own scores so that you may determine how well you do in comparison with W—— students.

The experimenter then quoted norms which were low enough to permit the majority of the subjects to surpass the W—— students with respect to the anagrams test. W—— was used as a frame of reference partly because the experimenters were known to have come from there, and partly because the subjects employed were from nearby colleges and would normally feel a certain desire to surpass W—— students. At the completion of all the tests, subjects computed and added their scores for each test, and low norms were again quoted for the entire battery of tests so that most of the subjects would succeed. Then another experimenter administered the group TAT in the usual fashion. The subjects in this experiment were obtained from psychology classes at a large university which contained both men and women, although only the men's records were used.

3.2.5 *Failure condition.* The procedure for the Failure condition was identical with that of the Success condition with one exception. The norms quoted for both the initial test and the battery as a whole were so high that the majority of the group fell below them and presumably experienced feelings of failure. The subjects were undergraduates in all male psychology classes at a liberal arts college.

3.2.6 *Success-failure condition.* This condition differed from the Success and Failure conditions only with respect to the norms quoted after the initial test and at the end of the battery. The norms cited for the first test were low, as in the Success condition, so that the majority of subjects succeeded. However, the norms quoted for the whole battery were those of the Failure condition, i.e., very high, so that the majority of subjects failed on the greater part of the test after having been led to expect success. The subject population was the same as for the Achievement-oriented condition—e.g., male students (mostly ex-GI's) at a large university.

The effect on imaginative stories of these various experimental conditions, which presumably define different intensities of n Achievement, will be discussed in Chapter V. But first, attention must be directed to the imaginative stories obtained and the kind of analysis made of them.

to arouse different intensities of achievement motivation immediately prior to the administration of the measure. The purposes of the present chapter are: (1) to make clear the theoretical position implicit in the kind of content analysis that has been made of thematic stories in both the hunger and achievement studies, and (2) to describe in detail the various achievement-related categories which are scored in obtaining the n Achievement score from imaginative stories.

4.1 Relation of scoring categories to the adjustive behavioral sequence. Our classification of many of the aspects of the behavior and experiences of characters in imaginative stories reveals an implicit acceptance of the kind of descriptive categories elaborated by many different psychological theorists in conceptualizing adjustive overt behavior. Thus, we perceive the behavioral sequence originating when an individual experiences a state of need or a motive (N). (The symbols in parentheses are used throughout to denote the various scoring categories.) He may also be anticipating successful attainment of his goal ($Ga+$) or anticipating frustration and failure ($Ga-$). He may engage in activity instrumental (I) to the attainment of his goal which may lead to the attainment of the goal ($I+$) or not ($I-$). Sometimes his goal-directed activity will be blocked. The obstacle or block (B) to his progress may be located in the world at large (Bw) or it may be some personal deficiency in himself (Bp). He may experience strong positive and negative affective states while engaged in solving his problem, i.e., in attempting to gratify his motive. He is likely to experience a state of positive affect ($G+$) in goal attainment, or a state of negative affect ($G-$) when his goal-directed activity is thwarted or he fails. Often someone will help or sympathize with him—[nurturant press (Nup)]—aiding him in his goal-directed behavior. This, in brief, is our analysis of the behavioral sequence. It is presented schematically in Figure 4.1. Note that the five states an individual may experience (Need, Positive or Negative Anticipatory Goal States, Positive or Negative Affective States) are located within the person in this diagram. Instrumental Activity is denoted by the arrows suggestive of trials and errors in the problem-solving attempt. A Block (which also may be located within the person) is denoted as a barrier that must be overcome if the goal is to be attained. The symbol for Nurturant Press is another person with an arrow in the

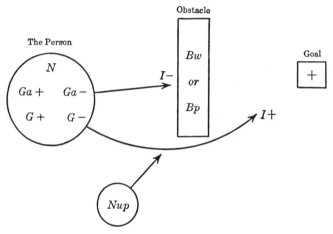

FIG. 4.1. Position of the scoring categories in the adjustive behavioral sequence.

direction of the goal indicating aid of some sort. And finally, the goal is indicated by a plus sign. The goal defines whether or not the various anticipations, affective states, instrumental acts, and so forth of the person are achievement-related or are related to some other motive. Presumably these categories may be used to describe the behavioral sequence no matter what the goal of the individual. For this reason, major attention must be directed to the definition of what constitutes an achievement goal.

4.2 **Procedure in scoring a story.** The remainder of this chapter will be devoted to careful definitions, with examples, of all our scoring categories, beginning with the most important definition of all—the definition of what constitutes achievement imagery. The categories are arranged in the approximate order in which scoring decisions are made as one reads through a story. Each story is scored separately and a given category can be scored only once per story.

The process of describing a category obviously takes much longer than using it once it is understood. So the complexity and detail of the next pages should not be taken as evidence that the scoring system is intrinsically complex, hard to learn, and tedious to apply. On the contrary, it can be learned with reasonable scoring reliability (over .90) in a week's time, and once learned can be applied to a single story in about the length of time it takes to read the story. Around a minute per story is not exceptionally fast scoring. The scoring criteria have to be spelled out in detail here for two reasons: (1) because the scoring involves simple *classifications of response elements* by objective criteria rather than the more complex *judgments* often involved in scoring TAT's clinically; and (2) because there are many arbitrary decisions that have to be made in any system of content analysis to handle the response elements which refuse to fit readily in any category. Thus, in nine cases out of ten, scoring is a very simple matter, but the scoring definitions must be spelled out in sufficient detail to handle the one case in ten which causes trouble.

4.3 **Definition of Achievement Imagery (*AI*).** The scorer must first decide whether or not the story contains any reference to an achievement goal which would justify his scoring the sub-categories (Need, Instrumental Activity, and so on) as achievement-related. By achievement goal is meant *success in competition with some standard of excellence*. That is, the goal of some individual in the story is to be successful in terms of competition with some standard of excellence. The individual may fail to achieve this goal, but the concern over competition with a standard of excellence still enables one to identify the goal sought as an achievement goal. This, then, is our generic definition of n Achievement. In the definitions of criteria for scoring Achievement Imagery that follow, it will become apparent that we include certain types of imagery in which there is no explicit statement in the story concerning competition with a standard of excellence. For these particular criteria it is our feeling that the evidence is sufficient for a fairly safe *inference* that competition with a standard of excellence is implicitly involved.

Competition with a standard of excellence is perhaps most clear when one of the characters is engaged in competitive activity (other than pure aggression) where winning or doing as well or better than someone else is the primary concern. Often, however, competition with a standard of excellence is evident in the concern of one of the characters with how well a particular task is being done, regardless of how well someone else is doing. Any use of adjectives of degree (good, better, best) will qualify so long as they evaluate the excellence of performance. Stories are scored for Achievement Imagery *only* when one of the criteria listed below is met. Although competition with a standard of excellence is implicit in all three criteria, as pointed out above, the phrase is used to denote the first criterion in which concern over how well the activity is being done is most explicit.

4.3.1 *Competition with a standard of excellence. a.* One of the characters in the story is engaged in some competitive activity (other than pure cases of aggression) where winning or doing as well as or better than others is *actually stated* as the primary concern. Wanting to win an essay contest, or an apprentice wanting to show the master that he, too, can fix the machine, are typical examples.

b. If one of the characters in the story is engaged in some competitive activity (other than pure cases of aggression), but the desire to win or do as well as or better than others is *not explicitly* stated, then (1) affective concern over goal attainment, and (2) certain types of Instrumental Activity are considered as indicating that the desire to compete successfully with a standard of excellence is implicit in the story. Examples of (1) would be: "The boy wins the essay contest and feels *proud*." "The boy loses the contest and becomes *bitter*." "The boy *anticipates* the *glory* that will be his if he should win." An example of (2) would be: "The boy is working *very carefully* on his essay."

c. Often the standard of excellence involves no competition with others but meeting self-imposed requirements of good performance. In this case, in order to score for *AI* what is needed are words to the effect that a good, thorough, workmanlike job, and so forth is desired, or statements showing the affective concern or Instrumental Activity that will allow such an inference. Typical examples are: "The boy is *studiously* and *carefully* preparing his homework." "The boy is *worried* because he cannot quite grasp the meaning in the textbook assignment."

In the above criteria, distinction is made between statements of the *intensity* and *quality* of instrumental acts. Working hard, or working fast would be evidence of concern over achievement only when excellence at the task demanded speed or intense effort. But one may work hard to complete a task for reasons other than personal achievement. For instance, "The boy is working hard to finish his homework," may indicate only that he wants to go out and play or perhaps that he is late with his term paper and is rushing to get it in. In neither of these examples is there evidence of concern over a standard of excellence, and so there is no basis for scoring Achievement Imagery. However, a statement such as "He is working slowly with great thoroughness" implies concern with accuracy, a standard of excellence. In this instance and in ones like it, Achievement Imagery would be scored.

4.3.2 *Unique accomplishment.* One of the characters is involved in accomplishing other than a run-of-the-mill daily task which will mark him as a personal success. Inventions, artistic creations, and other extraordinary accomplishments fulfill this criterion. There need be no explicit statement of concern over the outcome or direct statement that a good job is wanted when someone is working on a new invention or is in the process of doing something unique which will be generally accepted as a personal accomplishment. Here we make the inference that the individual is competing with a standard of excellence, and that unless his goal is reached he will also experience feelings of failure.

4.3.3 *Long-term involvement.* One of the characters is involved in attainment of a long-term achievement goal. Being a success in life, becoming a machinist, doctor, lawyer, successful businessman, and so forth, are all examples of career involvement which permit the inference of competition with a standard of excellence *unless it is made explicit that another goal is primary,* e.g., food for the kids, personal security.

Often, one of the characters may be involved in attainment of some limited achievement goal, i.e., a specific task. When rather routine and limited tasks or performances are shown definitely to be related to long-term achievement interests, Achievement Imagery *is* scored. Studying for an exam would *not* be scored unless there was evidence of concern over doing well or over the possibility of failure as outlined under criterion (1) listed above, *or* unless the exam were explicitly related to "going on to medical school" or "graduating from college" —both being long-term achievement goals. *The relationship of a specific task to a long-term achievement goal must be clearly stated and not inferred by the scorer when it does not fulfill criterion (1) above.*

It is worth noting that we are able to include long-term involvement as evidence of achievement motivation only because we have knowledge that in contemporary American society, success in the career usually demands successful competition with a standard of excellence. Not everyone can be a doctor, lawyer, successful businessman, or expert machinist. Attainment of these goals is accompanied by feelings of personal success which we believe to be historically related to the pleasure associated with independent accomplishment in early childhood, in which reward (hence pleasure) is contingent upon mastery, viz., doing a good job. In scoring the stories of other cultures without knowledge of the culture, it would be necessary to adhere to the criterion of an explicit statement of concern over successful competition with a standard in order to define the achievement goals of that culture. Only with growing knowledge of the culture could other criteria be added which involve the *inference* that competition with a standard of excellence is inherent in certain cultural activities.

Only stories which fulfill at least one of these above three criteria are scored for the achievement-related sub-categories.

4.4 Doubtful Achievement Imagery (*TI*). Stories containing some references to achievement but which fail to meet one of the three criteria for Achievement Imagery are scored Doubtful Achievement Imagery (*TI*) and are not scored further for achievement-related sub-categories. The *T* chosen as a symbol for this category indicates that most frequently the stories to be classified as doubtful are ones in which one of the characters is engaged in a commonplace *task* or solving a routine problem. Whenever there is doubt about whether or not one of the three criteria for Achievement Imagery has been met, and the story is not totally unrelated to achievement, it is classified *TI*.

4.5 Unrelated Imagery (UI). Stories in which there is no reference to an achievement goal are scored unrelated and not scored further. The difference between a story scored TI and one scored UI is simply that the TI story usually contains reference to some commonplace task goal and often contains other task-related sub-categories, but fails to meet one of our three criteria for scoring Achievement Imagery; whereas the story scored UI fails to have any reference whatsoever to achievement.

The three imagery categories (UI, TI, and AI) comprise a continuum of increasing certainty that the story contains imagery related to achievement motivation. Often the scorer may feel that a story that must be scored TI because it fails to meet any one of the criteria for AI, should have been scored for AI and the other achievement-related sub-categories as well. Our experience indicates that while undoubtedly some achievement stories are lost according to the present criteria, in the long run, rigid adherence to the stated criteria is the only means of assuring high scorer reliability. The rationale for distinguishing between stories with doubtful achievement imagery and those unrelated to achievement will become clear when the method of computing the n Achievement score is discussed.

4.6 Stories illustrating various types of Achievement Imagery.

4.6.1 *Competition with a standard* (AI)

1. One fellow is the supervisor and the other the machine operator. There has been trouble with the machine, and the supervisor is attempting to repair it. The machine operator has been turning out faulty equipment and after having been called down by the supervisor, he explained what he thought has been wrong. Upon inspection by the supervisor, this theory has been proven correct. The operator has his doubts about the ability of the supervisor to repair the machine. The boss realizes this and is deter-

mined to repair it. *He wants to prove that he is capable of making minor repairs.* The boss will do part of the repairs, but due to the technicalities of the machine will be unable to complete the job, and he will have to either call in the maintenance men or a specialized repair man from the outside.

2. An operation is taking place. The persons are the doctor, patient, nurse, and a student. The patient must have been sick at one time to be on the table. The student is observing the doctor doing his job along with the nurse. The doctor is concentrating on his work. The student is attending the doctor's movements, the nurse probably thinking of her boy friend. *A good job is wanted by the doctor* and student. The doctor will complete the operation, give a lecture on it, the student will ask questions on the work, the nurse will take off on her other duties.

(The clearly stated desire to meet a standard of excellence enables one to score these two stories *AI* instead of *TI*.)

3. The boy is taking an examination. He is a college student. He is trying to recall a pertinent fact. He did not study this particular point enough, although he thought it might be on the examination. He is trying to recall that point. He can almost get it but not quite. It's almost on the tip of his tongue. Either he will recall it or he won't. If he recalls it, he will write it down. *If he doesn't, he will be mad.*

(Evidence of affective arousal as a result of non-attainment of the achievement goal in this specific task situation is all that keeps the imagery from being considered *TI*.)

4. A group of medical students are watching their instructor perform a simple operation on a cadaver. A few of the students are very sure they will be called on to assist Dr. Hugo. In the last few months they have worked and studied. The skillful hands of the surgeon perform their work. The instructor tells his class *they must be able to work with speed and cannot make many mistakes.* When the operation is over, a smile comes over the group. Soon they will be leading men and women in the field.

(The instructor's interest in accuracy and perfection is evidence of a desire for mastery in this specific task.)

5. The student is *worrying about his two exams* coming up Friday, the first night of the May frolic. The student has spent most of his time previous to this, studying information for his research paper in English 108. He is *wondering how he can ever manage to study sufficiently enough to be able to pass the exams*

while he is so preoccupied with thoughts of the Frolic. He will study "like mad" for a few hours, and then "knock off," hoping for the best.

(Note that it is the student's affective arousal [worrying] concerning the threat of not reaching his achievement goal [passing the exam] which leads to the decision to score this story *AI* and not the vigorous Instrumental Activity of the last sentence [studying "like mad"]. A distinction must be made between evidence of intense Instrumental Activity [working hard] and evidence of concern over mastery. Stories with only intense Instrumental Activity will not be scored *AI* unless one of the three criteria for Achievement Imagery is met.)

4.6.2 *Unique accomplishment* (AI)

6. Something is being heated in a type of furnace which appears to be of metal. The men are blacksmiths. The men have been doing *research* on an alloy of some type and *this is the crucial test* that spells success or failure of the experiment. They want a specific type of metal. They are working for government interests. They may be successful this time. They have *invented* a metal that is very light, strong, durable, heat resistant, etc. A *real step in scientific progress.*

7. The boy is a student and during a boring lecture his mind is going off on a tangent, and he is daydreaming. The instructor has been talking about medieval history, and his reference to the knights of old has made the lad project himself into such a battle arrayed with armor and riding a white stallion. The boy is thinking of riding out of the castle, waving goodbye to his lady fair, and *going into the battle and accomplishing many heroic deeds.* The boy will snap out of it when the instructor starts questioning the students on various aspects of the lecture, and the boy will become frantic realizing he has not been paying attention.

8. Gutenberg and his assistant, Flogman, are working on an edition of the Bible. They are working hard to get as many printed as possible. Together *they have worked on Gutenberg's idea of a printing press and now, together, they are attempting to prove its worth.* Gutenberg thinks, "Will that fifth lever in the back of the joint hold up?" Flogman thinks, "If the Cardinal approves, we are in, but it is not likely that he will." The Cardinal disapproves, but the City Council approves, and Gutenberg and Flogman receive their contracts.

9. The boss is talking to an employee. The boss has some special job that he wants done, and this man is an expert in that particular phase. The boss wants the employee, an engineer, to start *working on a specially designed carburetor for a revolutionary engine.* The employee is thinking out the problem. The job will come off "O.K.," and the engine will *revolutionize* the automobile industry.

10. *Two inventors are working on a new type of machine.* They need this machine in order to complete the work on their new invention, the automobile. This takes place some time ago. They are thinking that soon they will have succeeded. They want to improve transportation. Their *invention* will be successful and they will found a great industrial concern.

4.6.3 *Long-term involvement* (AI)

11. *The boy is thinking about a career as a doctor. He sees himself as a great surgeon performing an operation.* He has been doing minor first aid work on his injured dog, and discovers he enjoys working with medicine. He thinks he is suited for this profession and sets it as an ultimate goal in life at this moment. He has not weighed the pros and cons of his own ability and has let his goal blind him of his own inability. An adjustment which will injure him will have to be made.

12. A boy, Jim Neilson, 18 years old, is *taking an examination for entrance in the Army Air Corps.* He has studied very hard in high school *hoping all along that he will some day be a fighter pilot.* Now that he sees how difficult the examination is, he is very worried that he may fail it. He is thinking so much about his failing it he cannot concentrate on the test itself. He will just barely pass the test and will later become a cadet, then finally a pilot.

(The first sentence of this story is an example of a specific task being related to a long-term achievement goal. The second sentence reiterates the long-term concern. There is also affective concern over the possibility of failing the test that would warrant scoring this story AI.)

13. The boy is a thinker, bored with his schoolwork he is attempting to do. His mind wanders. He thinks of his future. The boy has completed all but the last of his high school career. The boy is eager to graduate. He has faith in his capabilities and *wants to get started on the job he has lined up, dreaming of advance-*

ments. The boy will graduate ranking near the middle of his class. He will do all right on the outside.

14. The boss is inquiring about a story that the young man wrote in the paper. He had claimed evidence in a murder trial that didn't actually exist. Reporter reported false evidence, and the police have raised quite a stink about it. Public opinion is clamoring for conviction. The boss wants the reporter to find new evidence which will take pressure off the paper. *Reporter is thinking he'll lose his job if he doesn't*. Reporter will find new evidence but police get conviction anyway so pressure is off paper. Man doesn't lose job.

(Here there is concern about a long-term goal, the job. The specific task of finding new evidence is related to this long-term goal of the reporter.)

15. This is a father and a son. The father is an immigrant, and his son has stopped to see his father. *The son has been successful in his business* largely because of the training he received in his home as a child and youth. The old man is looking with a feeling of pride at his son and feels that he is very fortunate to have many things he himself never had. The son realizes this pride in his father's thoughts. The son will try to give his father some of the things he gave up in order to educate him.

4.6.4 *Doubtful Achievement Imagery* (TI)

16. There are two men working in some sort of machine shop. They are making some sort of a bolt or something. One of the men's car broke down, and he has discovered that a bolt is broken. So, being a fairly good forger, he is making a new bolt. He is discussing with the other man just how he is making the bolt and telling him about all of the details in making this bolt. When he is finished, he will take the bolt and replace the broken bolt in the car with it. He will then be able to get his car going.

(This is an example of a specific task story in which there is no stated need for mastery and no evidence of affective arousal concerning the possibility of personal success or failure. There is, however, a specific achievement goal, namely, making the bolt. Therefore, the story is scored *TI* rather than *UI*.)

17. Two workmen are trying to remove one lead pig from a small blast furnace. This action was to be completed months before, but only now did the necessary material arrive. One young

man is showing the other just how to handle the pig, and perhaps a little theory is presented while they are waiting for the finished product. During the conversation, a distant bell is heard, the men quickly stop their work and prepare to adjust a number of tools before taking the pig from the furnace.

18. Jim is in the midst of deep thought trying to pick the answer to a problem on his exam out of the thin air. He is evidently having a difficult time with it. Jim probably didn't prepare himself too well for his exam and therefore doesn't have necessary things at his fingertips. Jim is trying to remember some formula. If he could just remember it, he could solve his problem immediately. Jim will skip to the next problem in a short while and then return to this one.

(Note that being in an exam situation is not scored *AI* in this instance, since there is no evidence of concern over the outcome either in the form of a stated need to do well, working carefully, affective arousal over the possibility of success or failure, and so forth.)

19. The persons are students in a school. They were studying until a distraction occurred which was the teacher who attracted their attention. The students were studying. The teacher had disciplined them for their actions in class telling them to study a story for repetition later. The students are looking at the teacher with dislike in their eyes. They don't think much of her this day and dislike her for her ways of teaching. The students will not do too well in the repetition exercise, and as a result further punishment will be applied.

(The achievement goal of the story is studying. There is no evidence of concern over mastery, perfection, or the possibility of failure, so the story is scored *TI*.)

20. An elderly man and young man with their heads together in conference. The older one is giving advice to the younger man perhaps on a matter of law. The young man, who has just entered the field of law, has come up with a difficulty in a recent case and has turned to the senior and wiser partner of his firm. They go over the situation and facts from which the elderly man will then advise. The advice will be taken by the young lawyer, and he will then proceed to form his case around the advice.

(Two lawyers are engaged in a specific, routine task, that of solving a particular problem. The mere mention of the profession of law is not sufficient to classify this story as long-term involvement. Becoming a lawyer is not the goal of the story. Rather, the solution to a specific legal problem is the goal. Unless there is evidence that perfection, the best possible solution, and so on, is wanted, the story is scored *TI*.)

21. Doctor Ingersoll is making a very difficult operation on Frank Briston's left kidney. Another doctor and nurse are present. Frank has been a drunkard most of his life which has poisoned his kidneys. The doctor is concentrating on the operation. The nurse is thinking that it is futile to try to save him. He will just go to drink again. He will recover, but as the nurse thought he will die of drinking.

(A doctor performing a routine operation is scored *TI*, unless there is direct evidence of concern over mastery, perfection, and so forth.)

22. It looks like a painting that has not been completed. The boy in the bottom of the picture is the artist. The painting has been started but has not been completed. The canvas was prepared and the rough drawing made. The boy (in the lower right-hand corner) is thinking about what to do next. He has already begun to shade in the left-hand side of the painting. The painting will be completed by the boy.

(This story is clearly not an example of a unique accomplishment. The boy is not creating a work of art. Rather he is engaged in the specific task of painting a picture, therefore, this story is scored *TI*.)

4.6.5 *Unrelated Imagery* (UI)

23. A young fellow is sitting in a plaid shirt and resting his head on one hand. He appears to be thinking of something. His eyes appear a little sad. He may have been involved in something that he is very sorry for. The boy is thinking over what he has done. By the look in his eyes we can tell that he is very sad about it. I believe that the boy will break down any minute if he continues in the manner in which he is now going.

24. The boy is daydreaming of some picture he may have seen or is projecting himself into the future, putting himself into the situation as it would be if he were a man. The boy has seen a movie. The boy is thinking of how he would like to be in the situation as seen. The daydream, if not too vivid or realistic, will be terminated so that he can engage in activity more related to his present needs.

25. An elderly man is talking to a much younger man in the study of the older man. A problem has presented itself in which the older man needs the younger man's help or advice. The younger man is listening to what is being said and seriously thinking over the situation at hand. A conclusion will be reached in which there will appear some of the advice of the younger man. But the older man will not accept everything presented by the younger.

(Here the solution of the problem is in no clearly stated way related to achievement, and hence it is scored *UI*. In Example 20 the solution of a problem related to achievement was the goal.)

4.7 **Stated need for achievement** (*N*). Someone in the story states the desire to reach an achievement goal. Expressions such as "He *wants* to be a doctor," "He *wants* to finish the painting," "He *hopes* to succeed" are the clearest examples. Very strong indications of the presence of the motive in phrases like "He is *determined* to get a good mark" are also scored. The accomplishment desired may be specific, "He wants to finish the invention"; may refer to personal status, "He wants to become a successful businessman"; or may be more general and altruistic, "He wants to be of service to mankind." Need is scored only once per story, even when it appears more than once in varying forms. *Need is not inferred from Instrumental Activity.* It may seem quite obvious to the scorer that the characters who are working furiously toward an achievement goal must want to succeed. Need is scored, however, only when there is a definite statement of motivation by one of the characters.

Not all statements of desire that appear in an achievement-related story are evidences of the presence of Need (*N*). If for example, an inventor "wants his assistant to hand him the hammer," *N* is not scored. The scorer may imagine the stated need satisfied and then determine whether or not an achievement goal has been attained. Obviously, having the hammer in hand is no personal accomplishment. If the inventor had stated that, "He hopes to get the lever in place so that the machine will be complete," *N* would be scored. Having the machine completed is an achievement goal of the inventor. Another kind of statement of need which is *not* scored is a statement by one character which defines an achievement goal for another character. Examples of this are: "The teacher wants the students to study their lesson," "A man wants the machinist to fix his car," "The machine has probably gone on the 'bum' and now needs to be fixed."

4.7.1 *Illustrative stories*

(Note that all the examples which follow also fulfill one of the criteria for scoring Achievement Imagery.)

26. A man is experimenting with a new alloy of iron, while his assistant looks on. Many years of research have lead up to this situation. The two men have experimented and failed many times over but have stuck to their job. *Both men are hoping that at last they have succeeded* in making the strongest steel possible. They will test their alloy and find that it meets with their expectations. It will then be refined in great quantities for use the world over.

27. A young person *wishes to become a doctor*. He can visualize himself performing an operation. He received a toy doctor's kit for a present several years ago, and several of his friends are planning to be doctors. He is thinking of the pleasant or glamorous side of the picture and not the long years of study. He will be unable to pass pre-medical school. He decides to become a lab. technician as he wants to stay in that field.

28. Watt and an assistant are working on the development of the steam engine. There has been a *need* for mechanical power, time, and labor saving machinery to increase production. A *need* for better and faster transportation. It looks as though they are fitting a valve or piston.

(*N* is *not* scored in this story, because the need stated does not refer to a need for achievement on the part of the characters but rather to a lack in the world.)

29. A skilled craftsman is working at his machine. A townsman *wanted* a basket woven in a certain way and asked the craftsman to make it. The craftsman is absorbed in his work and thinks that this will be another fine product worthy of his reputation. He will

work far into the night until it is finished and display it with pride the next day when the townsman calls for it.

(N is *not* scored in this story, since the statement of need for a basket by the townsman defined the achievement goal of the craftsman. When the townsman's need was satisfied, i.e., the basket handed to him finished, he did not experience feelings of personal accomplishment. Had the *craftsman* "wanted a basket woven in a certain way" and then gone on to weave it, N would be scored.)

4.8 **Instrumental Activity with various outcomes** ($I+$, $I?$, $I-$). Overt or mental activity by one or more characters in the story indicating that something is being done about attaining an achievement goal is considered Instrumental Activity and is scored $I+$, $I?$, or $I-$ to indicate whether the outcome of the Instrumental Activity is successful, doubtful, or unsuccessful. Instrumental Activity is scored only once per story even though there may be several instrumental acts stated. The outcome symbol scored reflects the net effect of all the instrumental acts which have occurred. *There must be an actual statement of activity within the story independent of both the original statement of the situation and the final outcome of the story.* If the first sentence of a story describes such a situation as "Two men are working on a new invention" and there is no further statement of Instrumental Activity in the story, I would *not* be scored. Neither would I be scored if a story went on with no statement of Instrumental Activity and ended "They will finish the invention."

The instrumental act sometimes may be successful even though the over-all outcome of the *story* is not a success. Also, a statement of Instrumental Activity within the story in the past tense may be scored so long as it is more than a statement of the outcome of previous instrumental acts. For example, after the statement of the situation "Two men are working on an invention," a statement such as "They have *worked diligently* night and day in the past with repeated trials yielding only failures" may appear. It would be scored *I* and then +, ?, or —, depending upon the rest of the story. However, if after the statement of the situation, a statement such as "They completed two important phases of their work yesterday" appeared, *I* would *not* be scored. This is considered as a description of the outcome of previous acts with no word indicating actual striving.

4.8.1 *Stories illustrating Successful Instrumental Activity* (I+)

30. James Watt and his assistant are working on the assembly of the first steam engine. They are working out the hole for a slide valve of the first successful steam engine. (Statement of situation.) All previous experiments have failed. Successful use of steam has not been accomplished. If the slide valve works, the first compound steam engine will be harnessed. *James Watt is pulling the pinion in place for the slide valve.* His assistant is watching. The purpose is to make a pinion to hold the yoke in place which will operate the slide valve. If the slide valve works satisfactorily, they will perfect it for use in factories and for use on the railway. *It will work.*

(Not until the end of the story do we learn that the Instrumental Activity which occurred earlier in the story is successful.)

31. A boy is dreaming of being a doctor. He can see himself in the future. He is hoping that he can make the grade. It is more or less a fantasy. The boy has seen many pictures of doctors in books, and it has inspired him. *He will try his best* and hopes to become the best doctor in the country. He can see himself as a very important doctor. He is performing a very dangerous operation. He can see himself victorious and is proud of it. He gets world renown for it. He will become the *best doctor in the U.S.* He will be an honest man too. His name will go down in medical history as one of the *greatest men.*

32. The two men are mechanics and are making parts for a racer. (Statement of situation.) They have found a future in driving midget cars at various tracks and are intent on trying their skill. They are thinking about the money they will get when they enter the races. A superior racing car is wanted by both men. They will eventually go to the races and will make their money. The car

will be just another homemade job, but the fans will enjoy seeing the hometown boys come through.

(This story has not been scored *I*, because there is no statement of Instrumental Activity independent of the statement of the situation and the final outcome. This story illustrates a conservative use of the manual which has been effective in producing high scorer reliability.)

4.8.2 Stories illustrating Doubtful Instrumental Activity (I?)

33. The older man is a well-known pianist giving the younger man lessons in advanced piano. He is not satisfied with his student at the moment. In the past, *the young man has worked hard* on the piano, *studying long hours,* and all his family noticed how well he was doing. He is *thinking hard and trying hard* to put into his music just what his teacher wants him to. Just because he has a famous teacher, it doesn't necessarily mean that he will be famous. *He may not do very well or also he may.*

34. The boy is in an art studio. He is probably learning to be a sculptor. Behind him is a picture of a sculptor at work. *By looking at work done before his time and by great artists, he can learn much* from their styles and mistakes. He is probably thinking someday he'll be doing great artistic work like that. The boy wants all the information he can get to better himself. *He will observe and then go to work* on some artistic work himself. He may accomplish something great and maybe not. Anyway, he is learning.

(In these two examples the outcome of the Instrumental Activity is scored doubtful, because the writer presents alternatives of both success and failure without choosing between them.)

35. The men are metal workers and they are working on a new tool for the shop. They need a sharp-edged tool and are doing work which requires tempering. A tool for the shop has worn out or broken and needs to be replaced. In the period that this picture depicts, tools couldn't be purchased but must be made in the shop. The men are probably wondering if their work will be flawless or if the tool will replace the one that has broken. *After the metal has been removed from the flame, it will be dipped into some cold water.* Doing this repeatedly serves to temper and harden the new tool.

(In the above example the outcome of the Instrumental Activity is scored doubtful, because the writer does not present an ending to his story.)

4.8.3 Stories illustrating Unsuccessful Instrumental Activity (I—).

36. The scene is a workshop. Two men are doing a very important job. They are grinding an important cog for a new jet engine which will attempt a flight to the moon. The inventor who doesn't want to let his secret out has hired these two men to work secretly for him. They are not very well known, but if the job is a success, they will be famous. They are both very tense, each knowing that one little mistake will mean *months of hard work* lost and wasted. When they are finished, they find that the piece is too small for the engine, and they have *failed* and must start again.

37. The boy is thinking that he does not know whether he can cover the material the night before the test. His roommate, seen at the right, is working. The boy is trying to decide whether to go to bed or to study all night. He has been swamped with work and has been delayed from study until a late hour because of another activity which he could not miss. He finds that the work is difficult and hasn't enough time for it. If I stay up, I'll miss much in reading later. If I go to bed, I'll get up early but maybe won't have time to finish the work. He wants to get the work covered thoroughly to pass with a good grade. He goes to bed and *gets up early and studies.* Then he covers the work, but not well enough and consequently he *doesn't do well* on the test and *shoots his average out the window.*

4.9 Anticipatory Goal States (Ga+, Ga—). Someone in the story anticipates goal attainment or frustration and failure. The Anticipatory Goal State is scored positive (Ga+) when someone is thinking about the success he will achieve, expects that the invention will work, dreams of himself as a great surgeon. The Anticipatory Goal State is scored negative (Ga—) when someone is worried about failure, is concerned over the possibility that the invention won't work, expects the worst, or is wondering whether or not he will succeed. Both Ga+

and *Ga—* may be scored in the same story, but each may be scored only once. The *Ga—* category includes all achievement-related anticipations that are not clearly positive. Thus, doubtful statements such as, "He is wondering what the outcome will be" are scored *Ga—*.

Achievement-related anticipations must be related to the achievement goal of the story.

4.9.1 *Stories illustrating Positive Anticipatory Goal State* (Ga+)

38. A research man is forming a bar. Both men are extremely interested in the operation. These two men are working together on a research problem. They have been working tirelessly up to now to get the correct ingredients for the material being used now. They are feeling satisfied with their work. A stronger metal is desired by both men. The experiment has been a successful one. They will attempt to sell their new discovery *with a feeling of surety that they will become rich*. This work has meant much in their lives.

39. The older man is advising the younger one on the choice of occupation. The older man is a doctor and *he sees prospects in the young man to become a great surgeon*. The younger man has just returned from the Army, and he is disappointed with the attitude of the civilians and has given up hope of being a surgeon. The young man is thinking that it is useless to become a great healer if people are going to fight wars which amount to nothing more than mass murder. The older man will convince him that the world is not as bad as he believes, and he will return to medical school.

(Note that the Anticipatory Goal State need not refer to the person who is ultimately going to achieve the goal in question. In this story the old doctor is anticipating a successful future for the young man.)

4.9.2 *Stories illustrating Negative (or Doubtful) Anticipatory Goal State* (Ga—)

40. A father is telling his son not to worry while in college because his health is more important, but to become a professional

man and carry on in his father's footsteps. The son has flunked a few exams and feels very bad about it. His father has noticed his unusual behavior and thinks he should talk with his son. *The boy thinks he just can't make it through college,* but he really wants to. His father wants him to continue and become a professional man. The boy will go back to college full of resolution for better studying, and he won't let the work get the best of him, for "it is not life that matters, but the courage you bring to it."

41. Two men trying out their invention for the first time. One man is tightening the last bolt on the machine before the test, while the other is giving the machine a careful eye check. These two men worked in a factory where the machines were constantly breaking down, so they decided to invent a new process for doing the work. A new machine is wanted by the factory owner, and the people who are successful will receive a boost in pay. *The two men are thinking now whether or not their efforts and time have been spent in vain.* The invention will work, and the men will receive their reward—a story-book ending.

42. The boy is doing homework. He is a student at some college. He is encountering a very difficult problem. Perhaps he has not been faced with anything as difficult as this problem. The boy is searching for a solution. *He wonders if he will succeed in solving this and future problems of college curriculum.* He will probably solve this situation but become permanently baffled by other situations.

(The above anticipation is doubtful in nature, and according to the present system would be scored *Ga—*.)

43. The older man has just told the younger one that he has a very important job he wants him to do. The younger man has had a very good record in his previous work, and the older man believes that he is the only one capable of doing the job. *The younger man is wondering if he is capable of performing this task,* and he *realizes what the results will be if he fails.* The older man knows that he is asking a great deal, but feels the younger man will come through "O.K." The young man will have a great deal of trouble with this, but he is very determined and will succeed.

(In the above story a doubtful anticipation is followed by a clearly negative anticipation. In the next sentence, a positive Anticipatory Goal State appears, "feels the younger man will come through 'O.K.'" This story would be scored both *Ga—* and *Ga+*.)

4.10 **Obstacles or blocks** (*Bp, Bw*). Stories are scored for obstacles when the progress of goal-directed activity is blocked or hindered in some way. Things do not run smoothly. There are obstacles to be overcome before the goal may be attained. The obstacles may be a previous deprivation, i.e., failure, which must be overcome before further progress towards the goal is possible, or the obstacle may be a present environmental or personal factor. If the obstacle is located within the individual (lack of confidence, a conflict to be overcome, inability to make decisions, responsibility for some breakdown in equipment, or some past failure), it is scored Personal Obstacle (*Bp*). When the block to be overcome is part of the environment, i.e., when it may be located in the world at large such as: "The invention was almost finished when the gasket broke," "His family couldn't afford to send him to medical school," "Competition was too keen for him"; or *when there is some doubt about whether it is located in the individual or in the world,* Environmental Obstacle (*Bw*) is scored. Both *Bp* and *Bw* may occur and be scored in the same story, but each is scored only once per story.

It is necessary to make a distinction between "apparent obstacles" which really define the achievement goal of the story and real obstacles to on-going goal-directed behavior. If a story began with the statement "The skilled craftsman is fixing with great care the old antique which broke," *Bw* is not scored, since the breakdown which has already occurred defines the achievement goal of the story. However, if the craftsman has the chair nearly finished when the wood snaps, then *Bw* is scored. In this latter case, the breakdown interrupts goal-directed activity in progress. This distinction is made only in the case of *Bw*. Indications of past failures are scored *Bp* whether or not they interfere with the immediate goal-directed activity.

4.10.1 *Stories illustrating Personal Obstacle* (Bp)

44. A new man is being taught how to run a machine in a factory. He is interested in the work, but he is nervous. He has been hired quite recently and has *made a mistake.* The foreman is helping him to realize what he has done. The new man is hoping that with practice he will become a skilled worker. The foreman is bored teaching him. He is required to do this every day as work hands come and go, and he feels he is wasting his time. The foreman will show the man how to do the work and then will walk off. The hired man will look around to see if anyone is watching. Then he will start to do the required work as best he can.

45. A boy is daydreaming. He is a student who knows he has to study. *In the past he has had poor marks.* Now he realizes he must study harder or else his schoolwork will just be a waste of time. He thinks of the last mark and what will happen if he doesn't improve. This man will really study and prove to himself he is not a failure but will make good.

46. Father is giving advice to his son. The son has been faced with some *trying situation or problem.* Perhaps he *is trying to decide whether to stay in college or accept a business position.* The son wants guidance. His father is trying to utilize his greater experience in life in order to help his son. The father will probably persuade the son to stay in college and reap the advantages of a higher education that he was deprived of.

(The block to be overcome in this last story is the problem of coming to a decision.)

4.10.2 *Stories illustrating Environmental Obstacle* (Bw)

47. Two workmen in a small garage. They have just completed an experiment which they hope will revolutionize the rubber industry. They have been conscious of the need for better rubber. They have worked for years at this and now have their results before them. They are wondering if success is theirs. They want success because of the remuneration to get them back on their feet. They will not be successful. *They have not the equipment needed for rubber improvements.* The improvement of rubber by merely adding a compound and heating is over. They will not give up.

48. Lawyer and client in conversation. The younger man came in for advice. He had a going business and was prospering, but a

new industry is driving his product off the market. "Shall I be forced to give up?" "Shall I sue?" "What are my chances of success?" The lawyer explains that competition is legitimate and can't be sued. The man will go out and instead of selling, will convert his industry to a specialty along the same line only one which is not jeopardized. He will try to sell out.

49. Student is sitting at his desk worrying over his grades. *He has had poor high school preparation for college,* and as a result poor semester grades. He wishes he could settle down and make a go of his college without constant failing. He eventually makes a go of his college after finding courses in which he is interested.

(In this last example the obstacle is scored *Bw* and not *Bp*, because it seems clear that the high school was to blame for the inadequate preparation and not the student.)

4.11 Nurturant Press (Nup). Forces in the story, personal in source, which aid the character in the story who is engaged in on-going achievement-related activity are scored Nurturant Press (*Nup*). Someone aids, sympathizes with, or encourages the person striving for achievement. The assistance must be in the direction of the achievement goal and not merely incidental to it. For example, "The experienced machinist is trying to straighten things out for the apprentice and is encouraging him." Press must always be considered from the point of view of the character or characters in the story who are striving for achievement.

4.11.1 *Stories illustrating Nurturant Press* (Nup)

50. *An old experienced man is giving a young green kid a little helpful advice on how to improve his work.* The kid has been slow and has had a little trouble getting into the swing of things, and the old gentleman has noticed it. The kid is thinking maybe the old boy has some good ideas, and it may help him improve and maybe even impress someone enough for a raise. The kid will take all the advice to heart and go back to work with better methods or ideas suggested by the older man.

51. The young boy is dreaming of what he hopes to do for the future. He is thinking of a great surgeon who saved his father's life and wishes to become such a man. His father needed an emer-

gency operation. He watched the surgeon save his father's life. He is thinking he must work hard to reach his goal. But he is sure that is what he wants to do in life. He will see the surgeon again and *will be encouraged in his ambitions by the great man.*

4.12 Affective States $(G+, G-)$. Affective (emotional) states associated with goal attainment, active mastery, or frustration of the achievement-directed activity are scored G. When someone in the story experiences: (1) a positive affective state associated with active mastery or definite accomplishment ("He *enjoys* painting," "He is *proud* of his accomplishment," "They are very *satisfied* with their invention"), or (2) *definite objective benefits* as a result of successful achievement which allow the inference of positive affect ("His genius is acknowledged by millions," "The people are proud of the inventor," "Fame and fortune were his," "He received a raise in pay"), $G+$ is scored. $G+$ *indicates more than mere successful Instrumental Activity.* "He works his way through college and becomes a doctor" is scored $I+$. Positive Affect $(G+)$ would be scored only when a statement of positive affect was included, i.e., "He becomes a successful doctor and experiences a deep sense of satisfaction," or if there were *adequate* indications of objective benefits associated with his success from which positive affect might be inferred with little doubt, i.e., "He becomes a *famous* surgeon." This is another example of an arbitrary distinction which was necessary to make in order to insure an objective scoring system. Positive Affect may occur within the story, or it may be associated with the outcome of the story. *It is scored only once per story and should only be scored when there is a definite statement of positive affect associated with the achievement-directed activity or a statement of objective benefits above and beyond the statement of successful instrumental activity.*

When someone in the story experiences: (1) a negative affective state associated with failure to attain an achievement goal ("He is disturbed over his inability," "He is discouraged about past failures," "He is disgusted with himself," "He is despondent, mad, and sorry"), or (2) *the objective concomitants of complete failure and deprivation* which allow the inference of negative affect ("He became a drunken bum," "He became the laughing stock of the community"), G— is scored. As in the case of positive affect, negative affect must not be inferred merely from the unsuccessful outcome of instrumental activity. Negative Affect may occur within the story or at the end, but it is scored only once per story. Both Positive and Negative Affect may appear in the same story, in which case both are scored.

Mere mention of famous persons is not sufficient evidence for scoring G+. The Affective State categories are only scored when associated with the achievement-related activities of the story, as is the case with all sub-categories.

4.12.1 *Stories illustrating Positive Affective State* (G+)

52. This is the story of the invention of a machine. One man is showing another one of his new inventions. The man approves but is recommending that some changes be made. The inventor has spent the greater part of his life working on this invention. At last he finds that his work and dream is realized. *The men are both happy* due to the new discovery. The inventor is not interested in money that can be made out of it but only the benefit it will be to mankind. The inventor, on the advice of his friend, will sell the invention to a manufacturer. He will receive little reward and will die a sick man.

(Note that G— would also be scored in this story because of the negative concomitance associated with the outcome.)

53. A father is talking to his son. *He is telling him that he is proud of him because he is doing so well in school.* He wants his son to stay on the ball and keep getting good marks. He just knows his son will be a very successful businessman. The son has just come home from college after pulling honors all through the year. He never goes out and is always in his room studying. He never partakes in sports. They are both dreaming of what the son will be in the future, a successful businessman. The son can just see

himself as the president of the biggest baby rattle company in the U.S. The boy will become meagerly and puny because of his studying. He will never have any fun out of life. He will always be a mope. Is it worth it?

54. Goodyear and his young son are getting near the end of the experiment on uses of rubber. They have been pressing different objects from rubber. They spilled a tub of rubber on the stove. Goodyear is thinking that now he is close to his goal. *They will be hailed in later years as great inventors and saviors of our country.*

(The above story is an example of our practice of scoring so-called *objective benefits* as indicating the presence of **G+.**)

4.12.2 *Stories illustrating Negative Affective State* (G—)

55. This is the night before the big economics exam, and Johnny Jones is worried. He's got to get an A. He has been taking it easy all year and now wants to bring his average up with a good grade. He is *thinking what a damn fool he has been,* and why didn't he study the months before. He must get an A or he will have to take the course over. If he has to take the course over, he knows his father will give him the devil for not working hard the first part of the year.

(Note that the phrase "Johnny Jones is worried" has a future reference and so would be scored *Ga—* rather than *G—*.)

56. The older man is about 60, and the younger man, his son, who is a writer, about 30. He is trying to encourage his son to continue. He is successful in writing. The father is a well-known writer who struggled to get where he is. The son so far has had very little work accepted, and it doesn't seem as if he ever will. The father knows that if the boy tries, he can do it. The young man has his doubts but is beginning to feel that perhaps his father is right. The boy will struggle some more. He will get work accepted, but some will come back. Because he *feels inferior to his father,* he has an emotional block and is never as successful as he might otherwise have been.

57. The man is a professor of astronomy, and the younger person is a student. They have just discovered a new planet that is headed for the earth and will end the world. These two men have been fearing this for many months and have just proved their findings. They are thinking that the earth will soon be no more and that all life must end. They want to find a way to escape from this

so that they may save a few people on earth and become heroes. The planet will change course. Their blunder will be discovered, and *they will become outcasts for putting people on earth in a dither.*

(This illustrates the scoring of G— for negative objective concomitances of failure.)

4.13 **Achievement Thema** (*Ach Th*). Achievement Thema (*Ach Th*) is scored when the Achievement Imagery is elaborated in such a manner that it becomes the central plot or thema of the story. Striving for an achievement goal and eventual attainment of the goal may be the central plot of the story. On the other hand, the plot may be primarily concerned with someone who is in need-related difficulty and never does succeed. In any case, the decision to be made by the scorer is whether or not the whole story is an elaboration of the achievement behavior sequence. If there is a major counter plot, or if there is any doubt about the achievement imagery being central to the plot, *Ach Th* is not scored. It does happen that *AI* and some of the sub-categories will be scored in stories having another *leit motif*. These stories are *not* scored *Ach Th*.

4.13.1 *Stories illustrating Achievement Thema*

58. The boy is contemplating running away from home. He has just been badly whipped, and being quite an introvert, he declines to show his emotions. This boy has been reprimanded because he has failed to conform to social approval in regard to taking a small stone belonging to another lad who has evidently attached a good deal of sentimental value to it. The boy in the picture had recognized this stone as a diamond, and he likes it so much that he wants to obtain more. He is determined to leave and go to South Africa and *get a fortune* and is now laying mental plans for his lone expedition.

(This story is *not* scored *Ach Th*. Not until the last few lines is there any evidence to justify scoring it Achievement Imagery (*AI*). This Achievement Imagery is peripheral to the central concern of the story which appeared earlier.)

59. Father and son are discussing the future of the world. The

boy has just returned from overseas combat duty, looking older and wiser than when he left four years ago. Before entering the Army, the boy never gave much time to his father and had spent most of it with the gang. Now he is changed and considers a talk with his father of extreme importance. They are discussing the peace treaties that are being drawn up, each wanting peace fervently. No matter how much they desire peace, the answer is not given them. They can only surmise as to the best way of concluding a lasting peace. Time will tell whether the son's generation will *do better than* the father's.

(Once more, the Achievement Imagery ("do better than") appears very late in the story and is hardly central to the plot of this story. Therefore, *Ach Th* would *not* be scored.)

60. The boy and his father have had a serious accident and the boy's father is being operated on. The boy and his father were having a quarrel about the boy's marks in school, and the boy accidentally caused an automobile accident by stepping on the gas pedal. The boy is thinking that if his father dies, he will be to blame. He fervently wants his father to recover and be well again so he can prove to his father that he can do schoolwork. The father dies on the operating table, and the boy makes a vow to himself that he will become a great surgeon and save lives. He does and saves many lives, but his conscience never lets him alone. At the height of his career he commits suicide.

(In this example the Achievement Imagery appears as a counter plot. Because there is a strong alternate theme, *Ach Th* is *not* scored.)

61. A young boy is daydreaming about the past wars in which doctors have participated. He is not sure of the course to follow. He cannot decide whether or not to become a doctor. He is thinking about John Drake, the great surgeon of World War I, and his great feats in it. He was certainly a remarkable man. The boy will finally become a famous surgeon himself and in turn will be an incentive to the future doctors of the world to work hard and be interested only in the welfare of mankind.

(By way of contrast, this story illustrates the Achievement Thema. No other interest is introduced.)

62. Father and son are having a serious talk. They are going into bankruptcy because of a railroad strike. They are trying to remedy the situation by borrowing money from bankers. They do get some money but not as much as they need to get the business

CHAPTER V

Effects on Fantasy of Arousing Achievement Motivation

THE PROCEDURES for eliciting different intensities of the achievement motive (*n* Achievement) have been fully described in Chapter III. You will recall that three factors were involved in these attempts to manipulate the arousal of achievement motivation: (1) the instructions that subjects were given, (2) the tasks that they were asked to perform, and (3) the experiences of success or failure on these tasks induced by manipulating announced norms. Theoretically, our efforts were aimed at gaining control of situational cues which would elicit *n* Achievement.

The Relaxed, Neutral, and Achievement-oriented conditions, presumably, provide three points on an *n* Achievement intensity continuum. In the Relaxed condition efforts were made to minimize the arousal of achievement motivation. Just the opposite was true for the Achievement-oriented condition in which the importance of the tests to be taken was magnified. The Neutral condition was what its name implies, neither very relaxing nor highly achievement-involving. For this reason the Neutral group should fall between the other two with respect to the intensity of *n* Achievement aroused.

The other conditions in which feelings of success or failure were induced by manipulating norms will, for the most part, be considered separately. We feel that these conditions, while also representing high levels of motivation, are chiefly useful for discovering the effect of success and failure on the relative frequencies of certain achievement sub-categories in the subjects' stories. That is, there is a difference between success and failure experiences and general orientation toward achievement. The cues of the achievement-related instructions and tasks can be considered relatively "unstructured" in terms of, for example, the type of affect or anticipatory affect that is elicited. They, by themselves, should evoke experiences of satisfaction $(G+)$ or dissatisfaction $(G-)$ which are characteristic of the person's past experience with success or failure in achievement-related situations. The experimentally introduced cues for success and failure should, on the other hand, evoke a *general* tendency for the appearance of either $G+$ or $G-$ in all subjects. Thus, as we can demonstrate later, the Success and Failure groups should exhibit about the same high level of motivation as the Achievement-oriented group but with a somewhat different pattern of sub-categories.

The purpose, then, of presenting the frequencies of the various achievement-related imaginative categories in the Relaxed, Neutral, and Achievement-oriented conditions is to establish which categories shift in response to an increase in achievement motivation produced by manipulation of relevant cues. We thus learn what kinds of imaginative responses are associated with achievement motivation and, hence, are in a position to develop a system of arriving at an n Achievement score for any single individual based on the frequency of certain achievement-related responses in his stories. In this way, we can move from the empirical determination of which imaginative responses are related to experimentally aroused n Achievement to a set of rules for obtaining a measure of individual differences in strength of n Achievement.

5.1 **Frequencies of all types of achievement imagery under Relaxed, Neutral, and Achievement-oriented conditions.** The definitions of various achievement-related categories have already been presented. Figure 5.1 contains a series of

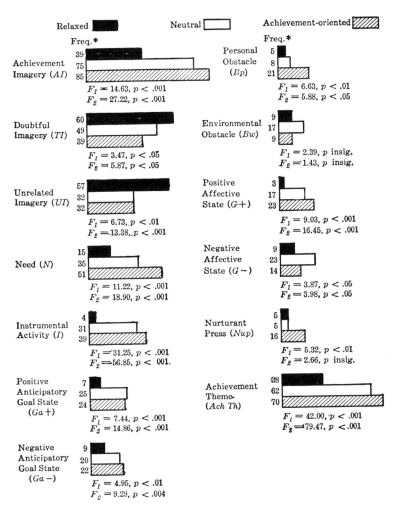

FIG. 5.1. Diagram showing frequencies of various achievement categories appearing in stories written after different conditions of experimental arousal of n Achievement with F tests showing the significance of differences among conditions. The total number of stories in each condition is 156 (39 Ss, 4 stories each).

bar diagrams representing the frequency of these various categories in stories written under different experimental conditions. There were thirty-nine subjects in each condition, and each subject wrote four stories in response to pictures B, A, H, and G (see Appendix III). To simplify the presentation of results, the total number of times a category appeared in the stories of each experimental condition is shown. The maximum total possible in each case was 156 (thirty-nine subjects with four stories each).

In addition to bar diagrams, Figure 5.1 also presents the results of an analysis of variance testing the significance of the obtained differences. In each case two F comparisons are presented. One (F_1) reflects the significance of the mean differences among the three conditions. The other (F_2) involves a comparison between the Relaxed condition, on the one hand, and the combined Neutral and Achievement-oriented conditions on the other. This latter comparison is the more pertinent one for demonstrating a shift in frequency of a particular category as a function of increased motivation, since the theory predicts that both the Neutral and Achievement-oriented conditions represent higher levels of motivation than the Relaxed condition.

The components of the analysis of variance and degrees of freedom are the same for each of the category comparisons. There were three groups of 39 subjects (116 df) involved in each comparison, divided so as to give an F test of the significance of the variance among all three (2 df) or of the first group against the second two groups combined (1 df), as follows:

Component	df	
Among Conditions	2	$F_1 = \dfrac{\text{Among Conditions}}{\text{Within Conditions}}$
Relaxed vs. (Neutral and Achievement-oriented)	1	
Within Conditions	114	$F_2 = \dfrac{\text{Relaxed vs. (Neutral and Achievement-oriented)}}{\text{Within Conditions}}$
Total	116	

For each subject the number of stories out of the four possible in which a particular category was present was noted, and the appropriate percentage assigned as his score (0, 25, 50, 75, 100). Percentages were transformed to degrees by means of the arc-sin $\sqrt{\text{percentage}}$ transformation in order that the means and standard deviations would be independent in the analysis of variance (Snedecor 1946, p. 446). Thus, the actual analysis was based on transformed data.

A word of caution is in order concerning the interpretation of the p values obtained for these category shifts. A number of categories were examined without any explicit theoretical expectancy as to which ones should shift. When a number of comparisons of this sort are made, it is desirable to adopt a more stringent level of significance before rejecting the null hypothesis (Fisher, 1951, p. 58). The usual level of confidence, p = .05, was divided by the number of comparisons made in order to arrive at an estimate of the more stringent criterion, which in this instance becomes about .004. Five of the categories (*Nup, Bw, Bp, G—,* and *TI*) do not meet this more stringent criterion. Despite this, the first four of these categories are included in the *n* Achievement scoring system and are presently accepted as indicative of *n* Achievement. Future research may well demonstrate the necessity of dropping these categories from the scoring system. However, they have been tentatively included at this time because they also shift in the previously obtained direction when the Relaxed group is compared with the combined Success, Failure, and Success-Failure groups.

5.2 **Frequencies of selected types of achievement imagery under Relaxed, Success, Failure, and Success-Failure conditions.** The data necessary to make a second test of the dependability of the increase in categories *Bp, Bw, G—, Nup* are presented in Figure 5.2 in a manner parallel to the presentation in Figure 5.1. The increase in frequency for each category

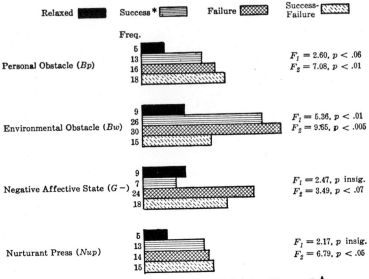

$F_1 = F$ test among conditions, $F_2 = F$ test of Relaxed vs. (Success, Failure, and Success-Failure). See text for explanation.

* The number of subjects in the Success condition was only 21, but for purposes of graphic comparison, the raw frequencies in this group have been adjusted to show what the expected frequencies would be with an N of 39. The actual frequencies were used in the analysis of variance.

FIG. 5.2. Diagram showing frequencies of selected achievement categories appearing in stories written after different types of experimentally induced success and failure with F tests showing the significance of differences among conditions. The total number of stories in each condition is 156 (39 Ss, 4 stories each).

is evident and its significance is tested in the same manner by analysis of variance, the components of which are as follows:

Component	df	
Among Conditions	3	$F_1 = \dfrac{\text{Among Conditions}}{\text{Within Conditions}}$
Relaxed vs. (Success, Failure, and Success-Failure)	1	
Within Conditions	134	$F_2 = \dfrac{\text{Relaxed vs. (Success, Failure, and Success-Failure)}}{\text{Within Conditions}}$
Total	137	

The total degrees of freedom derive, as usual, from the number of subjects involved, 39 in three of the groups and 21 in the Success group.

The F-values confirm the increase in Bp and, to a lesser extent, in Nup. In contrast with the findings in Figure 5.1, the F-values show a significant increase in Bw and a considerably less significant increase in $G-$. Since we were still in the exploratory stage, it was decided to include all four of these categories in the final scoring system, despite the somewhat ambiguous evidence for their increase. Doubtful imagery (TI) was treated differently for reasons discussed below.

5.3 **Types of imagery which do not shift with changes in conditions.** In the original analysis of the TAT stories, three other categories were investigated, none of which was ever found to be associated with increasing achievement motivation. One, *Hostile Press,* has since been partly included in the Environmental Obstacle category. The other two were called *Substitution* and *Outcome* and can be described as follows:

Substitution: A person who meets an obstacle in his achievement action sequence adopts a substitute instrumental act or substitute goal response. ("He drowns his sorrows in a tavern.")

Outcome: Outcomes of the whole story were judged according to whether they are happy ($O+$), unhappy ($O-$), or doubtful ($O?$). Finer breakdowns were made but did not prove useful. The total outcome was not necessarily the same as that for Instrumental Activity and was also separate from the final affect (G). For example, "They fixed the machine" is scored $O+$ but not $G+$ because it doesn't say they were pleased about it (cf. McClelland, Clark, Roby, and Atkinson, 1949, p. 245). Mention is made of these to save the future experimenter needless time and effort regarding them and also to indicate that no other categories have been systematically explored in these data.

We may summarize to this point by indicating which of the imaginative categories described in the previous chapter showed significant changes in frequency when n Achievement was experimentally increased. Generally speaking, we are justified in saying that as achievement motivation is experimentally increased, the imaginative stories that subjects write become increasingly more concerned with achievement, the need for achievement, anticipations of success and failure, acts instrumental to success and the avoidance of failure, affective states associated with succeeding and failing, blocks in the way of achieving, and help from other persons in the direction of achievement.

5.4 Computing the n Achievement score from the record of a single individual. The logic of combining these indexes of n Achievement in some way in order to obtain a reliable quantitative measure of the strength of any one individual's need for achievement is quite simple. Since these particular achievement-related categories have been shown to increase in frequency when motivation is experimentally increased, the individual having many of these categories in his stories is, presumably, more highly motivated for achievement than the individual who has relatively few in his stories. *The individual whose thought processes contain many of these references to achievement under normal circumstances is presumed to be generally highly motivated for achievement.* The validity of this assumption depends upon the value of the measure derived in this way when it comes to predicting differences in behavior that may be expected to be related to differences in strength of achievement motivation. A later chapter (Chapter VIII) will deal with a number of empirical relationships that have been established between the n Achievement score and various behavior measures—relationships which indicate that the n Achievement score *is* related to behavior in many meaningful ways. Thus, the argument for the validity of the n Achievement score is twofold. It is derived in part from an analysis of the experimental procedures which produced changes in imaginative responses dealing with achievement, and in part from the relationships established between the n Achievement score and behavior.

The exact method of computing the n Achievement score

presented here is actually the third method we have employed. It represents the culmination of an intensive re-analysis of the stories supplemented by consideration of thematic records written by persons in other cultures. However, we do not feel that the present method is in any sense less tentative than the other two which have been reported (McClelland, *et al.*, 1949; Atkinson, 1950). Undoubtedly, our methods of estimating strength of motivation from imaginative stories will undergo further refinements as continued research indicates the necessity of change. The particular virtue of the present method is its generality. The earlier category definitions and method of computing the *n* Achievement score leaned rather heavily upon *Long-Term Involvement* as the criterion of *Achievement Imagery.* This reflected the fact that the original criterion groups were comprised of college students, preponderantly middle-class American males, whose central achievement concerns were graduating from college and getting on in a career. Subsequent studies with younger subjects and subjects in other cultures clearly indicated that *Long-Term Involvement* could be viewed as a special case of *Competition with a Standard of Excellence,* the ultimate meaning of achievement motivation that is reiterated throughout this book.

In addition to several slight changes in the definitions of categories, there have been a number of changes in the actual method of combining the categories to get a single score for each individual. The most recent scoring system, the one outlined in Table 5.1, will be referred to as scoring system C, indicating that it is the third method to be devised.

5.5 Scoring system C. Unrelated Imagery (*UI*) is scored —1, Doubtful Imagery (*TI*) is scored 0, and Achievement Imagery is scored +1. As previously indicated, if, and *only if*, a story is scored for Achievement Imagery (*AI*) are the remaining sub-categories scored. Each sub-category is scored only once per story and is given a weight of $+1$. An Achievement score is obtained for each story by summing (algebraically) the category scores for that story. The n Achievement score for any one individual is the total of the scores obtained on all stories written.

TABLE 5.1. Scoring system C for obtaining an individual's n Achievement score

Unrelated Imagery (UI)	-1
Doubtful Imagery (TI)	0
Achievement Imagery (AI)	$+1$
Need (N)	$+1$
Instrumental Activity (I)	$+1$
Positive Anticipatory Goal State ($Ga+$)	$+1$
Negative Anticipatory Goal State ($Ga-$)	$+1$
Personal Obstacle (Bp)	$+1$
Environmental Obstacle (Bw)	$+1$
Positive Affective State ($G+$)	$+1$
Negative Affective State ($G-$)	$+1$
Nurturant Press (Nup)	$+1$
Achievement Thema ($Ach\ Th$)	$+1$

Note: Each story is scored separately with this set of categories and the total score is obtained by adding the scores obtained on single stories. Instrumental Activity may be scored $+$, $-$, or ?, depending upon its outcome. In any case, it is scored only once per story and is given a weight of $+1$ like any other category. That is, a story cannot be scored for both $I+$ and $I-$.

You will note that all of the categories shown to increase in frequency as intensity of motivation increases (Figures 5.1 and 5.2) are scored $+1$. Unrelated Imagery (UI) which decreased in frequency is scored -1. The case of Doubtful Imagery requires some further explanation. In Figure 5.1 it is shown to *decrease* fairly significantly and yet in this scoring system we have not weighted it -1 but 0. The reason for this is partly logical, partly accidental. Our original evaluations of shifts in category frequencies among conditions were made with slightly different category definitions and in terms of chi-square tests. Under these conditions, the decrease in Doubtful Imagery was of questionable significance. Therefore, we decided to score it 0. Such a decision appeared to have two further merits: (1) It reflected numerically the fact that in scoring *TI* we were often in doubt as to whether the story was really *AI* or *UI;* and (2) it seemed to justify the use of the algebraic summation system to which we were already committed; that is, if we had not had an intermediate category there would have been no point in subtracting for *UI.* Logical as all this may have seemed, we found when we made our final analysis using transformed data that *TI* really decreased fairly significantly. Rather than recompute all our scores and recalculate all our findings at this late date, we decided to leave things as they were, especially since we already knew that other slight changes in scoring systems had not made much difference. That this is true can be seen from the high inter-correlations among the various scoring systems that appear in Table 5.2.

5.6 **Refinements in the scoring system.** The original version of the scoring system as published by McClelland, Clark, Roby, and Atkinson (1949) will be referred to as scoring system A. A modification of this original system by Atkinson (1950) will be referred to as scoring system B. Some of the results to be presented later involve *n* Achievement scores that were derived from these earlier scoring systems. In each case the scoring system used will be specified. However, the inter-correlations of the different scoring systems given below in Table 5.2 demonstrate that there is very little practical difference involved. As pointed out above, the main difference is that scoring system C has wider generality.

TABLE 5.2. Inter-correlations among *n* Achievement scores obtained by three different scoring systems

39 subjects	
4 stories each	r_{AB} .95
30 subjects	
4 stories each	r_{AC} .90
32 subjects	
8 stories each	r_{BC} .87

A final note of caution should be sounded about all these systems of arriving at a total n Achievement score. None of them is constructed so as to provide an equal interval, uniform n Achievement scale along which individuals can be spaced with great precision. For one thing, sub-categories are not independent of our imagery categories. That is, if by chance there was more AI in one group, one would also expect a higher frequency for all the sub-categories in that group. What this amounts to is that the tests for the sub-categories are not independent of the F tests for Achievement Imagery and, thus, the p values yielded by these tests are not accurate indexes of the level of confidence to be placed in the obtained differences. One answer to this is that we have repeated the Relaxed or Neutral vs. Aroused conditions often enough for us to get independent confirmations of the shifts for each of the sub-categories taken one at a time. But this is not a satisfactory answer to questions about whether it is legitimate to add up sub-categories for one individual when they are not independent. We answered these questions in our original scoring system by using only those categories which shifted, *given an achievement story* in either group (e.g., with Achievement Imagery held constant). But this, too, did not seem wholly fair, since there is *some* independence between AI and the sub-categories.

Faced with these difficulties, we decided to be content for experimental purposes with a rough index which ought to give us at least a valid High-Low or High-Middle-Low breakdown even though we knew it had imperfections for finer work. Our present conviction is that if one is primarily interested in exploratory research, it is fruitful to retain and score for the presence of all the sub-categories, because they yield a wide variety of facts about qualitatively different aspects of n Achievement and they can be summed to provide a rough index of intensity level as we have done here. If, on the other hand, the main interest is in assessing strength of n Achievement and correlating it with some outside criterion like grades, it is probably better to avoid the problem of category interdependence by using more pictures (12–16), shortening the length of time per story, and scoring only for Achievement Imagery and perhaps Achievement Thema or Instrumental Activity.

5.7 The effects of Success and Failure experiences on imaginative stories. Let us examine now the effects of experimentally induced feelings of success and failure on the frequencies of various sub-categories that have been shown to be associated with achievement motivation. The Success, Failure, and Success-Failure conditions (see Chap. III) differ from the Achievement-oriented condition in that the members of these former groups calculated their scores on the paper and pencil tests and were given the opportunity to compare their scores with norms allegedly obtained from a rival college. The norms were adjusted to produce feelings of success in one group, feelings of failure in another, and feelings of success followed by feelings of failure in a third group.

The stories written following these experimental conditions should reflect both a heightening of the intensity of n Achievement and also other specific effects related to the success and failure experiences. The category frequencies and mean n Achievement scores for the Achievement-oriented, Success, Failure, and Success-Failure conditions are presented in Table 5.3. The Achievement-oriented condition represents a highly motivated group of subjects who have not experienced feelings of success or failure before writing their stories. Since there were only 21 subjects in the Success condition, expected frequencies based on an N of 39 are given in order to simplify visual comparisons.

The mean n Achievement scores following manipulation of success and failure are somewhat different. The differences may reflect real differences in intensity of motivation as well

TABLE 5.3. Frequencies of all types of Achievement Imagery and mean n Achievement scores for Achievement-oriented, Success, Failure, and Success-Failure conditions. The total number of stories in each condition is 156 (39 Ss, 4 stories each)

	Achievement-oriented	Success [*]	Failure	Success-Failure
Achievement Imagery (AI)	85	82	85	95
Doubtful Imagery (TI)	39	41	46	37
Unrelated Imagery (UI)	32	33	25	24
Need (N)	51	35	50	53
Instrumental Activity	39	43	40	30
Personal Obstacle (Bp)	21	13	16	18
Environmental Obstacle (Bw)	9	26	30	15
Anticipatory Goal States				
Positive (Ga+)	24	7	29	42
Negative (Ga—)	22	17	24	28
Affective States				
Positive (G+)	23	32	27	28
Negative (G—)	14	7	24	18
Nurturant Press (Nup)	16	13	14	15
Achievement Thema (Ach Th) ..	70	67	80	86
Mean n Achievement Score	8.77	7.92	10.10	10.36

[*] Since the N in the Success condition was 21, the raw frequencies have been corrected to show what the expected frequencies would be with an N of 39.

as specific effects of success and failure. In order to discover differences that are specifically related to success and failure, it is necessary to control in some way for the possible effects of differences in intensity of motivation. This has been roughly accomplished by considering the *relative* frequencies of the different aspects of a given sub-category. For example, one difference we might expect between the Success and Failure groups would be in the relative frequency of Positive as compared to Negative Affective States. To make such a comparison, one can count the number of times Positive Affective States $(G+)$ and Negative Affective States $(G-)$ appear in the stories of each subject. Subtracting the number of Negative Affective States from the number of Positive Affective States $(fG+ - fG-)$ for each subject provides a distribution of differences. If the mean of this distribution of differences is positive, it indicates a preponderance of $G+$. If the mean of the distribution of differences is negative, it indicates that $G-$ is relatively more frequent. In order to determine whether the balance of Positive or Negative Affective States following success is different from that following failure, we test the significance of the difference between the means of the two distributions of differences obtained by the formula $(fG+ - fG-)$.

This method of analyzing the effects of success and failure provides some control over differences in absolute number of categories which might be due to actual differences in intensity of motivation in the two conditions.

5.8 The relative preponderance of positive or negative affect following Achievement-orientation, Success, and Failure. In Table 5.4 the Achievement-oriented, Success, and Failure conditions are compared with respect to the balance of $G+$ and $G-$. The Achievement-oriented condition is included in this comparison because it represents a high level of achievement motivation without the specific effects of either experimentally induced success or failure. Examination of Table 5.4 reveals that there is a relatively greater frequency of Positive Affective States $(G+)$ in the stories written following Success than in those following conditions of Achievement-orientation alone or Failure, the latter difference being significant beyond the 5 per cent level of confidence. The comparison of Achievement-oriented and Failure conditions reveals a difference in the expected direction, i.e., relatively more Negative Affective States $(G-)$ following failure, but it is insignificant. These results can be interpreted as showing that the affective state of subjects following success is more positive than it is following failure. In addition, these results (1) provide further evidence of the sensitivity of the thematic apperception method to changes in the state of the individual produced by experimental procedures, (2) confirm the claim

TABLE 5.4. Relative preponderance of Positive $(G+)$ as compared to Negative Affect $(G-)$ in the Achievement-oriented, Success, and Failure conditions

	AROUSAL CONDITIONS		
	Achievement-oriented $N = 39$	Success [*] $N = 39$	Failure $N = 39$
Total $(fG+ - fG-)$ [*]	+9	+25	+3

DIFFERENCES IN TOTAL FREQUENCIES

	(Success)-(Failure)	(Success)-(Achievement-oriented)	(Failure)-(Achievement-oriented)
	+22	+16	−6
t	2.34	1.21	1.07
p	<.05	—	—

[*] The differences in frequencies contained in this table are based upon the raw data, but the t and p values are based upon arc-sin transformations of the data. The frequencies for the Success condition which has an actual N of 21 have been adjusted to show expected frequencies with an N of 39. The statistical analyses involving this condition were, of course, based on the actual frequencies and an N of 21.

made earlier that success and failure relative to some standard of excellence are accompanied by significant changes in affect, and (3) indicate the validity of the affect categories as presently defined.

This direct reflection of affective changes in thematic stories should provide interesting results when other motives are investigated. Gratification of the achievement motive is highly approved in our culture. There is little reason to expect anxiety, guilt, repression, displacement, or any other defense following successful consummation of this motive. However, were the present method extended to a study of sex or aggression, we might well expect different results following gratification of the motive. Following satisfaction of these latter motives, one might expect feelings of guilt or anxiety to occur which would lead to an increase in the $G-$ category. This result would be expected whenever satisfaction of some motive has been consistently punished.

5.9 The relative preponderance of environmental or personal obstacles following Achievement-orientation, Success, and Failure. A similar analysis was made of the two obstacle categories, Environmental Obstacle (Bw) and Personal Obstacle (Bp). In so far as they may be thought of as indicating where the subject places the blame for inability to achieve, Bw and Bp are similar to the extra-punitive and intro-punitive reactions to frustration elaborated by Rosenzweig (1943). Table 5.5 shows that both the Success and Failure conditions show relatively more Bw than the Achievement-oriented condition. That is, following success or failure, the blocks or obstacles to achievement met by characters in the stories are perceived to a greater degree as being due to environmental interference than due to personal shortcomings. For the Suc-

TABLE 5.5. Relative preponderance of Environmental (Bw) as compared to Personal Obstacles (Bp) in the Achievement-oriented, Success, and Failure conditions.

	AROUSAL CONDITIONS		
	Achievement-oriented $N = 39$	Success ° $N = 39$	Failure $N = 39$
Total ($fBw - fBp$) °	−12	+13	+14

	DIFFERENCES IN TOTAL FREQUENCIES		
	(Success)-(Failure)	(Success)-(Achievement-oriented)	(Failure)-(Achievement-oriented)
	−1	+25	+26
t	.22	2.66	3.34
p	—	<.01	<.01

* The differences in frequencies contained in this table are based upon the raw data but the t and p values are based upon arc-sin transformations of the data. The frequencies for the Success condition which has an actual N of 21 have been adjusted to show expected frequencies with an N of 39. The statistical analyses involving this condition were, of course, based on the actual frequencies and an N of 21.

cess condition, this seems to be a fairly accurate representation of the true state of affairs. These subjects were successful and would not, therefore, be expected to exhibit much evidence of personal shortcomings (Bp) hindering achievement.

However, this kind of argument based on the realities of the situation breaks down when extended to account for the Failure condition. The preponderance of environmental obstacles following failure may indicate the operation of a defense mechanism. The subjects who have failed may actually be blaming their failure on the tests they have taken or some other environmental condition, and this is reflected by an increase in the number of obstacles met by characters in their imaginative stories.

5.10 **The association of an affective state with the anticipation of its opposite following Success and Failure.** The same kind of analysis was made regarding the balance of Successful and Unsuccessful Instrumental Activity and the Positive and Negative Anticipatory Goal States in the three groups, and none of the differences approached significance. However, *the relatively greater frequency* of anticipations of failure in the Success condition (Table 5.6) suggests con-

TABLE 5.6. Relative preponderance of anticipations of success ($Ga+$) as compared to anticipations of failure ($Ga-$) in the Achievement-oriented, Success, and Failure conditions

	AROUSAL CONDITIONS		
	Achievement-oriented $N = 39$	Success [*] $N = 39$	Failure $N = 39$
Total ($fGa+ - fGa-$) [*]	+2	−10	+5

	DIFFERENCES IN TOTAL FREQUENCIES		
	(Success)-(Failure)	(Success)-(Achievement- oriented)	(Failure)-(Achievement- oriented)
	−15	−12	+3
t	1.44	1.43	.06
p	—	—	—

[*] Transformations of scores in this table have been made as in Tables 5.4 and 5.5 to test the significance of differences.

firmation of an hypothesis that follows from the theory of motivation elaborated earlier. It was argued (Section 2.11) that affective states probably become cues and elicit motives because they are so frequently followed by a change in level of affect. Pain, a negative affective state, is not itself a motive, but the anticipation of relief cued off by pain is a motive. Following this line of reasoning, an effort was made to determine whether affective states tended to be more associated with anticipations of a change in affect than with anticipations of the same level of affect. Specifically this means, do $G-$ and $Ga+$ tend to occur together?

One may better understand the question by imagining an affective continuum ranging from pain $(-)$ through a relatively neutral zone (0) to pleasure $(+)$. One might argue that pains are most frequently followed by relief from pains, and that pleasures are most frequently followed by decreases in pleasure. One might argue also that most of the time the individual's affective state is relatively neutral, during which time both anticipations of pleasure and anticipations of pain have a near equal probability of occurring. When, however, the individual is experiencing a negative affective state, he anticipates what has most frequently followed this, namely, relief. Similarly, when he is experiencing a high degree of pleasure, he is likely to anticipate what has most often followed this state, a return to neutral (which is relatively painful). Our theory gives rise to the seemingly paradoxical prediction that painful states can readily cue off pleasurable relief anticipations and vice versa.

Individual differences with respect to experiences of success and failure complicate our problem somewhat. For the successful individual, i.e., one who is able to accomplish a great deal, success may be followed so often by further success that an experience of success may lead to anticipations of further success. Similarly, the poor fellow who has failed consistently may anticipate further failures as he experiences the negative affective state accompanying failure. For present purposes it seems fairly safe to assume that our experimental groups sample the college population fairly randomly, and that we have relatively few of these extreme individuals to worry about. Our theory, then, should lead us to expect a greater tendency for $G-$ and $Ga+$ to occur in stories following failure, and a greater tendency for $G+$ and $Ga-$ to occur in stories following success.

Tables 5.5 and 5.6 tend to confirm this hypothesis in a general way. The Success group shows relatively more $G+$ and $Ga-$ than the Achievement-oriented group, and the Failure group shows just the reverse trends. The pertinent test involves combining in some manner $G+$ and $Ga-$, which we expect to occur together in a given individual, and comparing their frequency with $G-$ and $Ga+$ together. We may set up a formula which will give us an idea of which combination dominates in each condition. The formula $(fG+ - fG-) - (fGa+ - fGa-)$ gives us the desired measure. If the frequencies of $G+$ and $Ga-$ tend to be high together, the first quantity $(fG+ - fG-)$ will be large and the quantity subtracted from it $(fGa+ - fGa-)$ will be small or possibly a minus quantity. If the resultant quantity $(fG+ - fG-) - (fGa+ - fGa-)$ is positive, then the $G+$ plus $Ga-$ combination must predominate. If the quantity is negative, then $G-$ plus $Ga-$ must predominate. Table 5.7 shows that the anticipated result occurs. The preponderance of $G+$ plus $Ga-$ as compared to $G-$ plus $Ga+$ is greatest following success and least following failure.

This finding is consistent with many facts yielded by observation of everyday life. Ball players, for instance, are likely to expect a letdown after a big day at the plate. It is common to feel uneasy when one's luck is *too* good. In addition, it is rather obvious that the pangs of hunger $(G-)$ lead to an anticipation of eating $(Ga+)$. Many readers may recognize

TABLE 5.7. Relative preponderance of G+ and Ga— together as compared to G— and Ga+ together in the Achievement-oriented, Success, and Failure conditions

	AROUSAL CONDITIONS		
	Success $N = 39$	*Achievement-oriented* $N = 39$	*Failure* $N = 39$
$(fG+ - fG-) - (fGa+ - fGa-)$ ..	+35	+7	−2

DIFFERENCES IN TOTAL FREQUENCIES

	(Success)-(Failure)	(Success)-(Achievement-oriented)	(Failure)-(Achievement-oriented)
	+37	+28	−9
t	2.79	2.54	.94
p	<.01	<.05	—

Note: The quantities $[(fG+ - fG-) - (fGa+ - fGa-)]$ were obtained for each subject and summed to get the total scores shown. If this total for a group of subjects is positive, then $G+$ and $Ga-$ together predominate. Transformations of scores have been made here as in Tables 5.4 and 5.5 to test the significance of differences.

this phenomenon as similar to what Flugel (1945) has termed the "Polycrates Complex."

One might inquire why the positive affective state accompanying eating does not seem to produce anticipations of hunger as our theory would seem to indicate. The answer would seem to lie in consideration of the importance of the rate of affective change on the strength of an association between a cue and an affective reaction. Actually, the pleasant affective state accompanying eating is never quickly followed by the negative state associated with hunger. The change is a very gradual one. However, the first bites of even the simplest meal will suddenly stop the hunger pangs and change the affective state of the individual. Our theory would lead us to predict that for the hunger motive, at least, the $G+ \rightarrow Ga-$ association would be a great deal weaker than the $G- \rightarrow Ga+$ association.

This analysis of some of the differences attributable to the experiences of success and failure has been undertaken for two purposes. First, it maps out a method of attacking the problem of determining the specific effects of success and failure on thematic apperception. Secondly, it has provided a little evidence in support of some of our theoretical proposals. This particular analysis was not undertaken until after the theory had been developed to the point outlined in an earlier chapter. The results, tentative as they are, due to the manner in which we controlled for absolute frequency of responses, are in line with theoretical expectations and suggest a whole line of research explicitly related to the theoretical proposals.

CHAPTER VI

General Applicability of the n Achievement Scoring System

THE QUESTION of the generality of motives, or the extent to which they are common to all men, has been touched on in our proposals for a theory of motivation (Chapter II) and will be enlarged in the final chapter on the origins of the achievement motive. The broad definition of achievement imagery in the scoring manual in terms of competition with a standard of excellence emphasizes our view that affective changes early in life accompanying doing well or failing to do well in various learning situations provide the basis for motivation to succeed and to avoid failure. We have argued that our scoring categories are independent of any specific, culturally determined means of attaining these goals. Thus, we expect that the measure, as presently obtained, will reflect with a fair degree of accuracy differences in achievement motivation in subjects whose age, sex, or cultural background differs from that of our original college male criterion populations. A number of studies have been undertaken that can be used to test this hypothesis. In each of them the crucial question is, do the stories written continue to show the same characteristic changes when achievement motivation is aroused in different populations?

6.1 The effect of achievement arousal on male subjects already tested. Lowell (1950) administered equivalent forms of the measure to a group of male college students following *both* Neutral and Achievement-oriented experimental conditions. His subjects were drawn from the same general population as the original criterion groups, but his study differs from the earlier ones in that he used the *same* subjects under different experimental conditions in order to demonstrate more clearly that the category differences previously noted were actually due to the experimental manipulation of *n* Achievement and not possible differences in the populations sampled.

The question his data will answer is this: Will subjects who have been tested by this method once respond to arousal in the same way as those who have not been tested before? Or is naïveté one of the requirements for getting a valid *n* Achievement score? As part of a larger experiment, twenty-one male college students were given equivalent forms of the *n* Achievement measure (see Chap. VII) with a week's interval between the two measurements. The first occasion is referred to as the Neutral condition. The experimenter was introduced as a graduate student collecting some data for his dissertation. Subjects were given standard instructions for a Scrambled Words task following which they wrote stories in response to pictures *A, B,* and *G* (see Appendix III) under our standard TAT instructions (Chap. III).

A week later, for the Achievement-oriented condition, a different form of the Scrambled Words Test was given, preceded by the following instructions designed to heighten the achievement motivation of the subjects:

When I was here last week, I gave you a verbal test without telling you much about it. As students of psychology, you undoubtedly know the relationship between verbal ability and general intelligence. We think we have a particularly valuable test because it measures an individual's ability to perceive relationships —to make order out of an ambiguous situation. The same ability has been found necessary for executive and administrative positions. This testing program is being supported by the Office of Naval Research in the hope that we will be able to perfect techniques of selecting persons who are likely to be successful in positions demanding superior accomplishment. Today I have a slightly different form of the verbal test, and we are interested in how your performance today, when you know what we are testing, will correlate with your performance last week when you did not know. I want to urge you to do your very best on this test, and we will consider your performance on this form of the test as the best measure of your ability. Perhaps when we are finished today, we will have an opportunity to discuss these scores with you.

Then the subjects performed the Scrambled Words task after which the experimenter administered an equivalent three-picture form (pictures C, D, and E; see Chap. VII) of the TAT with the introductory remark that he wanted to finish the creative imagination test that he had started the week before. Pictures C, D, and E can be described briefly as follows:

C. Two men in colonial dress are working in a shop with an old-fashioned printing press.
D. A young man is seated at a desk in an outer office, and an older man is handing him some papers.
E. Two men, apparently conversing, are standing in a well-furnished room.

Lowell's results are summarized in Table 6.1. The mean n Achievement scores obtained under the two conditions are significantly different, and the category shifts are all in the previously obtained direction. It is clear that the measure is sensitive to experimentally induced differences in achievement motivation *on the same subjects.* In Table 6.1 and others which follow in this chapter it can be seen that the differences in frequency of certain sub-categories are not so large as previously obtained (Chap. V). However, the reader must keep in mind that almost all comparisons in this chapter are made between so-called Neutral and Achievement-oriented conditions, whereas in Chapter V a definitely Relaxed condition was used as the lower motivational limit.

TABLE 6.1. Frequencies of types of Achievement Imagery appearing in stories written by the same 21 male college students under Neutral and Achievement-oriented conditions. The total number of stories in each condition is 63 (21 Ss, 3 stories each)

	Neutral	Achievement-oriented
Achievement Imagery	30	46
Doubtful Imagery	21	14
Unrelated Imagery	12	3
Need	14	25
Instrumental Activity	14	18
Personal Obstacle	4	6
Environmental Obstacle	2	10
Anticipatory Goal States		
Positive	7	14
Negative	5	7
Affective States		
Positive	9	17
Negative	1	4
Nurturant Press	4	6
Achievement Thema	28	40
Mean n Achievement Score (C)	5.05	9.05
Mean Difference	4.00	
SE diff.	1.09	
t (paired differences)	3.67	
p	<.01	

6.2 The effect of achievement arousal on male high school students in response to pictures containing male and female figures.

Veroff (1950) administered a six-picture measure of n Achievement to two groups of high school students (aged 16–18). His groups contained both males and females. The results for the female subjects will be reported in a later section in this chapter (6.4). His measure of n Achievement contained three pictures previously described (B, E, D) and three more showing female characters which were especially chosen for this study. If we consider his results on the three male pictures only (B, E, D) we may determine whether or not the measure developed on a male college student population is applicable to younger males representing a broader socio-economic base. If we compare the stories of male subjects to pictures containing male characters, on the one hand, with their stories to pictures containing female characters on the other, we may begin to explore the effects of major differences in picture cues.

The subjects in Veroff's Neutral condition consisted of 18 boys and 22 girls. He was introduced to a high school class during a home-room hour as a former student of the school who was trying out some tests. The experimenter made the following comments to the group:

It feels great to be back at H——, and I think I'm going to have an interesting time giving you this test this morning. You see, a group of us at W—— are engaged in a project of testing imagination or story-telling. We're interested in seeing what different kinds of stories people write. I thought I would try it out at H——. I think you'll enjoy it if you give it your close attention.

The subjects in the Achievement-oriented condition consisted of 28 boys and 24 girls in the same high school. In this group, the teacher introduced the experimenter as follows:

Today during the free period, we are to be given some tests that have been given to various high school students. Mr. V—— from W—— University is going to give you these tests. Your principal, Mr. ——, is anxious that H—— do well on the tests. Pay close attention to the instructions so that you may do well.

The teacher remained in the front of the room while the experimenter gave instructions for the Anagrams Test that was given first to the students. The instructions were:

A simple process of testing has been worked out that may be a method of determining the selection of men and women for future leadership roles and other important duties. So far, the test has been given mostly to college students. We are now interested in how high school students will make out on this test. Students from M—— (a rival high school) have done very well. We would like to see what scores students from H—— will obtain in comparison.

Specific instructions for the task were then given ending with, "Try to get as many as you can. Go!" The Anagrams Test lasted for three minutes.

In both the Neutral and Achievement-oriented conditions, somewhat modified instructions were given for the TAT measure of n Achievement:

This is a test of your creative imagination or story-telling. A number of pictures will be projected on the screen before you. You will have twenty seconds to look at the picture and then about four minutes to write a story about it. Notice that there is one page before you for each picture to be shown. The same four questions appear on each page and will guide your thinking and enable you to cover all the elements of a plot in the time allotted. You don't have to answer the questions directly. They are there to help you think up a story. Plan to spend about a minute on each question. I will keep time and let you know when it is about time to go on to the next question for each story. You may go on before I tell you if you wish. You will have a little time to finish up before the next slide is shown.

Obviously there are no right or wrong answers; so you may feel free to make up any kind of story you choose. Try to make them interesting, for this is a test of your creative imagination. Do not merely describe the picture you see. Tell a story about it. Write as fast as you can in order to finish in time. You may begin writing any time after the picture is shown. Don't worry about grammar and spelling. Make them interesting. If you need more space for any question, use the reverse side. Are there any questions? So, we will begin.

The three pictures containing male characters are designated B, E, and D and have been described earlier (see Chap. III and Chap. VI or Appendix III). The three pictures containing female characters may be described as follows:

1. A woman sitting at a desk writing.
2. A woman in an office standing, handing papers to a man seated at a desk.

3. Two women seated talking. One woman has her arm resting around the shoulder of the other.

Separate n Achievement scores were obtained for each subject on the three male pictures and the three female pictures, according to the most recent scoring method, C. The mean n Achievement scores for boys, broken down according to experimental condition and sex of characters in the stimulus pictures, appear in Table 6.2.

TABLE 6.2. Mean n Achievement scores (C) obtained from male high school subjects in response to pictures containing male and female characters under Neutral and Achievement-oriented conditions

	NEUTRAL CONDITION $N = 18$		ACHIEVEMENT-ORIENTED CONDITION $N = 28$	
	3 Male Pictures	3 Female Pictures	3 Male Pictures	3 Female Pictures
Mean n Achievement Score ...	1.94	1.72	4.93	1.57
SD	3.32	3.41	3.75	2.66

The mean n Achievement score obtained from stories written by male subjects about pictures containing male characters increases from 1.94 in the Neutral condition to 4.93 in the Achievement-oriented condition. The mean difference of 2.99 is significant at the 1 per cent level of confidence ($SE = 1.08$, $t = 2.77$). Thus, we may conclude that the method of obtaining an n Achievement score which was originally developed on a population of male college students is valid when applied to experimentally induced changes in motivation in a population of younger male subjects representing a broader socio-economic base.

The mean n Achievement scores obtained from the pictures containing female characters, however, are low for high school males under both conditions. That is, the boys show the expected increase in n Achievement score as a result of experimental heightening of the motive on the male pictures, but no change and very little response at all on the female pictures. It can be concluded that, for them, the male pictures provide a measure of achievement motivation, the female pictures do not.

6.3 **The effect of achievement arousal on adolescent male Navahos.** Evidence concerning the validity of the measure in another culture has been provided by Lowell (1950) who measured n Achievement under two conditions of administration in a group of 21 ninth-grade Navaho males in New Mexico.* On the first occasion, the experimenter was introduced as a representative of one of the public services who had something for the students to do. He gave the following instructions from memory after a few friendly remarks to establish rapport:

What I have for you here today is sort of a game. I am interested in story-telling, and I'd like to have you tell me some stories. Now it would take too long if we all told stories out loud, so I have brought along some paper on which I would like to have you write stories for me. Now you might say it is sort of hard to just make up a story, so I am going to give you a little help. You see at the top of each page I have written a suggestion for a story. What I would like you to do is read the suggestion. (Experimenter reads first suggestion aloud.) Now let's think about it—make up a story about it. We don't have much time, so I have also written some suggestions on each page that will help get a complete story for me. You see the questions I have written on each page.
1. Tell what is happening.
2. Tell what happened before.
3. Tell what is being thought or wanted.
4. Tell what will happen.
If you will answer each one of those questions, we will be able to get finished this period. I have a watch here and am going to keep time and tell you just about how much time to spend answering each one of the questions. We will only have about a

* We are greatly indebted for assistance in this research to the Comparative Study of Values Project supported by the Rockefeller Foundation at the Harvard Laboratory of Social Relations.

minute to answer each question, so we will have to work rapidly. This work will not count as part of your schoolwork and will not be graded. If you make a mistake you can just cross it out and go right on so you will be able to finish in time. All I am interested in is the stories you will write for me. So now let's think about the kind of story we are going to write about the first suggestion. I don't want you to just repeat the sentence I have written, but I want you to make up your own story. Let's think about the story you are going to write, and let's all begin to write on the first question.

At the end of a minute the experimenter announced it was about time to go on to the next question, and so on.

Eight written suggestions (verbal cues) were used instead of picture cues in this study, in order to surmount the problem of specific cultural content in picture stimuli. Two forms were made of the eight verbal cues:

Form 1
1. A mother and her son—they looked worried.
2. Two men looking at something—one is older.
3. A boy has just left his house.
4. A wife with her head on her husband's shoulder.

Form 2
1. A father and his son talking seriously.
2. Brothers and sisters playing—one is a little ahead of the others.
3. A man alone at night.
4. A boy with his head resting on his hands.

Two different ninth-grade classes of Navaho boys were used to obtain the 21 subjects. One class received Form 1 on the first occasion and Form 2 on the second occasion. This procedure was reversed for the other class.

On the second occasion two days later, the experimenter announced:

Some of the stories you wrote for me last time were very good, and I was wondering whether this is because you are very good story tellers or because you are just very smart. I brought along a little test today that will show me how smart you are. It is a good test because it is simple and short, and yet it will tell me just how smart you are.

A four-minute Gottschaldt Figures test was then administered. These results are not reported, since the only purpose in giving this test was to increase the number of achievement-related cues preceding the second measure of n Achievement. Following the Gottschaldt Figures test, the other form of the "Story-Telling" test was administered with a simple explanation that more stories were desired.

The stories were scored according to system C. Lowell's results are presented in Table 6.3.

TABLE 6.3. Frequencies of types of Achievement Imagery appearing in stories written by 21 ninth-grade Navaho males under Neutral and Achievement-oriented conditions

	Neutral (21 Ss, 3 stories each)		Achievement-oriented (21 Ss, 3 stories each)
Achievement Imagery	17		32
Doubtful Imagery	21		21
Unrelated Imagery	46		31
Need	6		16
Instrumental Activity	6		11
Personal Obstacles	3		1
Environmental Obstacles	2		0
Anticipatory Goal States			
Positive	2		4
Negative	1		1
Affective States			
Positive	2		7
Negative	1		1
Nurturant Press	2		2
Achievement Thema	2		15
Mean n Achievement Score (C)	−.10		2.81
SD	3.15		3.42
Mean Difference		2.90	
SE diff.		.88	
t (paired differences)		3.30	
p		<.01	

This study suggests three important tentative conclusions: (1) Our scoring system, which was originally based on the content of stories written by predominantly upper-middle-class white American college males, is sufficiently general to pick up differences in induced achievement motivation in a group of subjects whose way of life, dominant thought pattern, system of values, and so on are markedly different from those of our college students. The differences in story content are marked, but the categories still apply. That is, it is still Achievement Imagery whether the story says he wants to be a "good sheepherder" (Navaho) or a "good doctor" (college student). (2) Achievement motivation as induced by instructions referring to intelligence, leadership, and so forth may be reflected in the same way in fantasy the world over. That is, we may be justified in thinking that achievement motivation exists in different intensities and can be measured in the same way in different cultures. Further evidence on this point appears in Chapter IX. The chief caution to remember here is that the Navaho high school boys were performing in an American school setting in which individualistic achievement values were stressed (cf. McCombe, Vogt, and Kluckhohn, 1951). (3) Lowell's study is the first in this program of research to employ written *verbal cues* rather than picture cues to elicit achievement stories. His positive results suggest the need for thorough investigation of the particular merits and limitations of the two kinds of cues. Offhand, it would seem that the verbal cue technique should allow a greater degree of control over the content of the cue, particularly for purposes of cross-cultural comparisons. This would seem to be the case because the verbal cue can be freed of elements that might lend themselves to particular cultural interpretations. For instance, the verbal cue, "A mother and her son are talking," will initiate a story about mother and son in any culture; whereas a picture of a middle-aged American woman inside a house talking to an adolescent boy might not have the desired

Achievement Imagery, as we have defined it, is associated with male picture cues more often than with female ones. Or to put this in another way, *even girls project achievement striving primarily into the activities of men.*

More significant, perhaps, is the failure of the girls to show the expected increase in n Achievement score accompanying Achievement arousal. Therefore, there is no evidence in support of the validity of the present scoring method when applied to stories written by girls. The over-all greater response to male pictures may be explained in terms of the greater association of men in office situations with achievement, but the absence of an increase in n Achievement score following achievement arousal can mean either that the scoring method is not valid when applied to women, that the instructions do not arouse achievement striving in women, or that the Neutral condition actually aroused achievement motivation to such a high degree in the girls that there was no room for further increases under Achievement-orientation. Veroff has argued that perhaps any test situation in which girls are competing with boys contains more achievement motivating cues for the girls.

6.5 **Achievement motivation in women.** To cast some light on the last of these alternative hypotheses, a study was conducted by Wilcox (1951) at the University of Michigan (See Veroff, Wilcox, and Atkinson, 1953). She decided to test female subjects under both Neutral and Achievement-oriented conditions, but with an attempt to reduce the number of achievement cues in the Neutral condition far below those existing in Veroff's study. In addition to this, Wilcox selected pictures containing female characters in situations that she thought were somewhat more achievement-related than those employed in Veroff's study.

To make the Neutral condition as relaxed as possible Wilcox

tested college women in their own dormitory rooms at night in small groups of two to ten. Her procedure for this condition is presented below:

The experimenter appeared relaxed, friendly, and treated the experiment as a routine task of no particular importance. She talked with the girls as they gathered, and was in no hurry to start the experiment. When all were present, the following instructions were given:

"I'm doing a paper on thought processes and need some imaginative stories about the pictures I'm going to hold up. I'll hold up a picture for around 20 seconds. Then you'll have about four minutes to write your story. Use a separate page of your booklet for each story. The questions on the sheets are to guide your thinking and enable you to cover all the elements of a plot in the allotted time. I'll keep time and tell you when to go on to the next question. Plan to spend about a minute on each question. There are no right or wrong answers involved, so feel free to write whatever you want. Don't sign your name. Are there any questions? If you need more space, use the back of the page."

16 × 20 inch prints were then held up in this order:

1. Male picture *D*
2. A woman typing at a desk
3. Male picture *E*
4. Heads of a man and woman facing each other in a library with a bookcase in the background
5. Group of men and women in office. Central figure is woman at desk
6. Male picture *B*

The Achievement-oriented condition consisted of testing the subjects in a classroom with both males and females present. The Achievement-orientation consisted of administering an Anagrams task with the following instructions:

We believe that there are some sex differences in this mental ability; therefore, please write your name and sex at the top of your sheet. Do this now. Please do your best, as we're interested in seeing how well people can perform when they are working at maximum efficiency. Work rapidly and try hard. Are there any questions? Here is the master word. (Experimenter writes "GEN-

ERATION" on the blackboard.) Write down all the smaller words that are contained in "GENERATION" that you can find.

The task was continued for twelve minutes with the experimenter saying "check" after each minute, at which time the subjects put a check after the last completed word. Then instructions to put name and sex on the paper were repeated and papers collected.

Following this task, the TAT was administered according to our standard procedure, employing the six pictures that were used under the Relaxed condition. Wilcox's data for male and female pictures under both conditions are presented in Table 6.5. These results constitute a direct confirmation

TABLE 6.5. Mean *n* Achievement scores (C) obtained from female college subjects in response to pictures containing male and female characters under Relaxed and Achievement-oriented conditions

	RELAXED CONDITION (N = 27)		ACHIEVEMENT-ORIENTED CONDITION (N = 26)	
	3 male pictures	3 female pictures	3 male pictures	3 female pictures
Mean *n* Achievement Score ..	5.70	.26	5.77	.38
SD	3.9	2.6	4.2	3.3

of Veroff's basic data. An analysis of variance yielded no significant differences between conditions but a significant difference between the two types of pictures ($p < .05$).

Thus, there is still no evidence demonstrating an increase in *n* Achievement score following achievement arousal for women, even though Wilcox made a concerted effort to reduce the number of achievement cues in the Relaxed condition. However, Wilcox has performance data which tend to indicate that the *n* Achievement score is valid when applied to women. As previously mentioned, under the Achievement-oriented condition the subjects performed an Anagrams task in such a fashion that the number of words produced per minute could be calculated. Table 6.6 shows the number of words produced for six two-minute periods for women with high or low n Achievement scores.

TABLE 6.6. Mean number of words produced in successive two-minute periods on an anagrams task for female college subjects above and below the mean n Achievement score

| | MEAN NUMBER OF WORDS PRODUCED ON SUCCESSIVE TWO-MINUTE PERIODS OF ANAGRAMS | | | | | | |
	1	2	3	4	5	6	Total
High n Achievement ...... ($N = 13$)	15.08	8.92	6.46	4.85	3.77	5.92	45.00
Low n Achievement ...... ($N = 11$)	15.00	6.82	5.81	4.54	3.19	4.46	39.82
Mean Difference	.08	2.10	.65	.31	.58	1.46	5.18
SE diff.		.94					2.99
t		2.44					1.73
p (predicted direction)		<.01					<.05

Note: The n Achievement score is based on the pictures containing the female characters as well as the pictures containing the male characters.

This particular experiment is almost identical with one conducted by Clark and McClelland (1950) on college males which is reported in Chapter VIII (Table 8.5). Their results showed that under Neutral conditions the superiority of the high n Achievement subjects was most pronounced in the middle portions of Anagrams (third two-minute period). Clark and McClelland argued (cf. Chap. VIII) that this was evidence of superior learning for the high n Achievement group. The college females show a similar superiority in the *second* two-minute period. The similarity suggests that the scores for females have the same functional significance as they do for males, an hypothesis which is further supported by the moderately significant over-all difference in output between women with high and low n Achievement scores. The combined evidence of Veroff's and Wilcox's studies seems to suggest that for women n Achievement is more easily engaged than for men, and that women score so highly under Neutral conditions that there is no opportunity for a marked increase under Achievement orientation.

However, some results obtained by Field (1951) at the University of M—— are not consistent with the second half of this hypothesis. Field has data for college males and females under Relaxed and Failure conditions. His "Relaxed" and "Failure" conditions are almost identical with our "Relaxed" and "Failure" conditions described in detail in Chapter III. Two of his pictures, however, differed from the ones that we used under these conditions. Field used Murray's TAT 8BM and TAT 7BM which are the pictures that we have designated as G and A. In addition, he used TAT 2 and a picture of a man and woman reclining on a beach. Thus, the absolute magnitude of Field's mean n Achievement scores are not directly comparable with ours, but the differences in magnitudes between conditions and sexes are comparable. Field's mean n Achievement scores (scoring system A) for college males and females are given in Table 6.7.

TABLE 6.7. Mean n Achievement scores (A) for college males and females under Relaxed and Failure conditions (Field data)

	Relaxed	Failure
Males	$N = 38$	$N = 41$
Mean n Achievement Score	−1.46	3.46
Females	$N = 21$	$N = 14$
Mean n Achievement Score	1.24	.93

The figures in this table reveal that the males show a large and significant increase in n Achievement score from the Relaxed to the Failure condition ($t = 5.37, p < .01$), which confirms once more what we have reported several times before. The females for this condition show a small but insignificant decrease $(t = .24)$. This, so far, is consistent with Veroff's and Wilcox's results. In addition to this, under Relaxed conditions the females score significantly higher than the males $(t = 3.10, p < .01)$. Again this is consistent with Veroff's findings under Neutral conditions. However, in Veroff's study, the females under the *Neutral* condition received a mean score somewhat higher than the males received under the Achievement-oriented condition. In Field's study the female mean n Achievement score under *Relaxed* conditions seems appreciably lower than the mean score of the males under *Failure* conditions. This would tend to argue against the hypothesis presented earlier, that the females can't show an increase in n Achievement score because they get almost maximum scores under Neutral or Relaxed conditions.

The evidence to this point may be summarized as follows: (1) women get higher n Achievement scores than men under Neutral conditions (two studies); (2) women do not show an increase in n Achievement scores as a result of achievement-involving instructions (three studies); (3) women's n Achievement scores seem as valid as men's in that they relate to performance in the same way; (4) the failure to find an increase in n Achievement score from achievement arousal is probably not due to the fact that the scores are already at a maximum. Why then don't women's scores increase under experimental arousal? This is the puzzler. Two possible explanations—invalidity of the scoring for women, scores too high to go higher—have been eliminated. Apparently the usual arousal instructions simply do not increase achievement striving in women. Fortunately, Field (1951) has collected data which demonstrate the type of instructions which *will* increase achievement motivation in women.

In addition to manipulating achievement orientation in the standard way by references to leadership and intelligence, Field had three other conditions in which the dimension of "achievement" involved was *social acceptability*. The way in which he set up Relaxed, "Success," and "Failure" groups with respect to social acceptance is best described in his own words:

The relaxed group was told only that the experimenter was a graduate student trying out some tests. The failure and success groups were run simultaneously within the same classroom. These subjects were given a rather lengthy discussion concerning the importance of their social acceptance by the group as the most important determiner of ultimate satisfaction with life. In these remarks the experimenter stressed that it had been established that the best predictor of acceptance in all social situations was acceptance in the present ones; and that if the subjects were not liked or accepted by their class group there was every reason to believe that they would not be liked or accepted by other individuals in later life.

At this point it was announced that as part of other research a committee had been selected from the members in the class. This committee supposedly included only individuals who were obviously popular and well liked by other members of the group. It was further explained that the committee, which was of course imaginary, had secretly rated everyone in the class on the basis of their social acceptability. . . . The class was also told that the committee had been instructed to consider every name carefully and then to divide the class into a socially acceptable (success) . . . group and a . . . socially unacceptable (failure) group.

While these remarks were being made, test booklets were distributed to each individual in a face down position. The subjects were then told to turn their booklets over and to remove a sealed envelope which bore their name and to examine their own rating. . . . They were then told to tear up or otherwise destroy these ratings since they were of such a personal and confidential nature. (These success and failure ratings were equally divided and had been assigned at random to individuals in the class.)

At this point the four-picture Thematic Apperception Test was administered as a test of creative imagination in the same fashion as in the standard n Achievement procedures.

In order to permit comparison of the need scores of individuals subjected to the need-Social procedures with some external measure of group social acceptance, a nominating technique was used following each of the three need-Success procedures. Before distributing the nominating forms the experimenter explained completely the false nature of the ratings and the fictitious committee, and attempted to justify the deceit by stressing the importance of the research. Each subject then had an opportunity to list the most likable and the least likable . . . members of the group. The secrecy of these nominations was assured by means of a system of coding names and test booklet numbers for each individual. On the basis of these nominations each of the primary groups was divided for purposes of data analysis into a Liked group and a Disliked group.

Field scored his imaginative stories obtained under these conditions for n Achievement (A). The results for males and females by condition are summarized in Table 6.8. There is

TABLE 6.8. Mean n Achievement scores (A) for liked and disliked males and females under Relaxed, "Failure" (rejected), and "Success" (accepted) conditions

	MALES		FEMALES	
	Liked	Disliked	Liked	Disliked
Relaxed	—.36	—.54	3.63	.79
"Failure" .... (Rejected)	—.78	2.00	5.23	2.46
"Success" .... (Accepted)	.79	1.22	4.33	5.77

one outstanding fact about this table: Variations in reported social acceptability had *no effect* on the n Achievement scores of males, whereas for females the effect was marked. Both Liked and Disliked women showed significantly ($p < .05$) higher *n Achievement scores* after being told that they were socially acceptable (Accepted) or unacceptable (Rejected) than after being told nothing in the Relaxed condition. The only exception is the Liked group which was "accepted"; their average score was higher than for the Relaxed condition but not significantly so. As for the men, none of the differences is significant, a fact which is in marked contrast to our usual finding that men's scores are more easily influenced by attempts to arouse achievement motivation. In short, the data unequivocally support the hypothesis that women's n Achievement is tied up with social acceptability, men's with leadership capacity and intelligence. To put it in another way, if you want to arouse n Achievement in women, refer, as Field did, to their social acceptability; if you want to arouse n Achievement in men, refer, as we did, to their leadership capacity and intelligence. The reason for this sex difference is not altogether clear, although we have a little evidence (Section 9.2.2) that it may be related to the greater importance of dependence on others for women and independence of others for men.

6.6 **The relation of age to achievement motivation among eminent scientists.** In an investigation of eminent scientists, Roe (1951) administered nine cards from the 1943 edition of the TAT (1, 2, 4, 6, 7, 10, 13, 15, and 11 in that order). She made her records available to us so that we could score the stories for the presence of Achievement Imagery (one of the single most diagnostic categories) according to the definitions in scoring system C. Although this procedure does not yield the full n Achievement score, it does give a rough index which correlates very highly with such a score. Complete scores were not obtained, largely because we felt that they would give undue weight to the records of those individuals who were able to enter freely into the testing situation and tell long imaginative stories. A number of her subjects found the task difficult and either refused several pictures or made very brief comments on them, a fact which suggested to us that our method of asking for brief written stories, under time pressure, in an *impersonal* testing situation may provide more directly comparable records. Certainly, we have never had as many refusals as she did, but then our subjects were all younger and our pictures less "personal."

Probably the question of greatest interest here is whether these eminent men had higher n Achievement than the ordinary run of individuals. But it is a question we cannot as yet answer, since we have no comparable data on a control group —data which would be hard to collect since the same pictures would have to be administered on an individual basis to subjects in the same age range with lower objective achievement. In anticipation of the time when such a comparison can be made, we can report that the mean achievement imagery score of these 61 men was 2.11, $SD = 1.85$. The data do permit an analysis of how n Achievement varies with age, however, since these eminent scientists ranged in age from 31–60 years. The correlation between age and number of TAT stories showing Achievement Imagery was $-.39$ ($N = 61, p < .01$). This, of course, does not necessarily mean that n Achievement declines with age. It could mean that the younger men, in order to reach a status comparable to the older eminent scientists, would have to be more highly motivated. A random sampling of non-eminent men at all different age levels might reveal no such age differential. Whichever of these interpretations is placed on these data, there is support for the validity of the n Achievement measure. If n Achievement should turn out to be related to age as such, then our data support the common observation that older people who have achieved their niche in life are less highly motivated than young people. If n Achievement should turn out not to be related to age in an unselected sample, then the fact that the younger scientists in our sample had a higher n Achievement score suggests that the score is reflecting a true motivational difference which has resulted in their early eminence.

6.7 The effect of sophistication on n Achievement score. Another interesting question related to the generality of the measure is whether or not it is possible to fake a high n Achievement score. Can an individual who knows that the test measures achievement motivation manufacture stories that will give him a high score?

This possibility was checked by having 39 students at New Britain State Teacher's College deliberately try to fake high scores. They were given the following instructions before writing four stories in response to the four pictures used in the original criterion studies (B, A, H, G).

We are doing some research on measuring achievement motivation. We have developed a test that we think will measure it. What we don't know yet is whether or not people can fake a high score on it if they know what we are trying to measure. What we want you to do is to try to make a high score, to see if you can do it.

We don't want to give you too many hints because we can't without giving away how we score the test. But just imagine that you are trying to create the impression that you have lots of drive or need for achievement.

In school or business, as you know, people may do well partly because they have brains and partly because they have lots of drive or what we call need for achievement.

Suppose, for instance, that you knew that whether or not you were selected for a job depended on your demonstrating on this test that you have high achievement motivation. We mean by achievement motivation just what you mean—just the common sense definition of the idea—nothing special.

Now I am going to read you the standard instructions for the test, but remember that when you follow them you are secretly going to try to create the impression that you have high achievement motivation. We don't have any idea if this can be done or not, but we would like to try. We will not ask you to put your names on the paper.

The mean n Achievement score for these 39 subjects was 2.79, which is slightly but not significantly higher than the score obtained from the original Relaxed condition, but is much lower than any of the other experimental conditions in the original criterion studies (see Table 6.9). The result seems to indicate that it would be difficult to fabricate a high n Achievement score without knowledge of the pertinent

TABLE 6.9. Mean *n* Achievement scores (C) for the original criterion groups and following an instruction to deliberately fake a high score

Condition	N	Mean	SD
Relaxed	39	1.95	4.30
Faking High	39	2.79	4.09
Neutral	39	7.33	5.49
Achievement-oriented	39	8.77	5.31
Success	21	7.92	6.76
Failure	39	10.10	6.17
Success-Failure	39	10.36	5.67

categories; though, of course, one can fake a low score by simply refusing to write anything or for some reason deliberately inhibiting the story that naturally comes to mind.

A number of cross-validating studies have been reported. The results of these experiments seem to justify the conclusion that the imaginative categories, as defined in the scoring manual, do provide the basis for obtaining a valid estimate of the intensity of the need for achievement in male subjects ranging in age from the ninth-grade level through college and perhaps to age 60. The one study involving another cultural group (Navahos) gave evidence in support of the claim made earlier that the scoring categories are independent of specific cultural content. The measure can be applied to women, but it apparently has a somewhat different meaning for them. The subject's knowledge that his achievement motivation is being tested does not seem to raise his score; although an unco-operative attitude could clearly lower it. With this much confidence in the general utility of the *n* Achievement measure established, we can now proceed to a more careful scrutiny of its components in the next chapter before going on to show in Chapter VIII how it relates to the behavior of the individuals in a variety of meaningful ways.

CHAPTER VII

The Measuring Instrument

OUR PROBLEM in this chapter is twofold: In the first place, we must provide data on the usual questions concerning reliability of scoring, reliability of the measure itself, the development of equivalent forms, and so forth. In the second place, we want to consider the measuring instrument and the conditions at the time of measurement in relation to what is presumably being measured. This is an often neglected area in the development of measuring devices. The problem sounds complex, but it is simple enough. Ordinarily, in testing, an effort is made to show the relation between a test score (e.g., in Block Design) and a mental function ("synthetic-analytic ability"), but often the relationship is mentioned rather casually and is not carefully worked out. Our purpose will be to go further than this and to try and show how test performance (e.g., the n Achievement score) is related to various theoretical characteristics of motivation in general or achievement motivation in particular as outlined in Chapter II. But first we must consider some of the usual measurement questions of reliability and the like.

7.1 **Reliability of scoring.** The original check of score-rescore reliability (McClelland, *et al.*, 1949) indicated that the scoring method (A) was objective enough to allow a product-moment correlation of .95 between n Achievement scores obtained from the four-story records of 30 subjects by two judges working together on two different occasions a month apart, and an average index of agreement of 91 per cent in the score-rescoring of the various scoring categories. This index of agreement was computed by dividing twice the number of agreements by the total number of times a particular category was scored on the two occasions. Both judges had extensive experience with the scoring system, having scored several thousand stories prior to the reliability check.

More recently, Atkinson (1950) scored the eight-story records of 32 subjects on two occasions six months apart. At the time of rescoring, the 256 stories of the 32 subjects were thoroughly randomized. In order that this check might be directly comparable to the earlier one when only four stories were used, two n Achievement scores (scoring system B) were computed for each of the 32 subjects. Each was based on four stories (equivalent forms). The product-moment correlation between scores assigned to these 64 cases on the first and second scorings was .95. The n Achievement scores obtained from individual stories were found to range from minus one to plus nine. In only 18 instances out of 256 (7.1 per cent) did the n Achievement score obtained from a particular story in the second scoring deviate more than plus or minus one from the score obtained from that story the first time. The average percentage agreement in score-rescoring of the various categories by the one judge (computed in the manner already described) was 84.9 per cent, only slightly less than when two judges scored together.

Further information regarding the reliability of scoring is provided in this study. A judge with limited scoring experience (approximately 400 stories) scored the eight-story records of 24 subjects. The rank order correlation between n Achievement scores (B) obtained by this relatively inexperienced judge and one with extensive experience with the method was .96. The percentage agreement between the two judges in scoring the categories was 78 per cent. Another judge achieved a similar result after about a week's experience with scoring system C, although this is unusual.

These score-rescore reliability checks were carried out with all of the usual cautions which made it impossible for the scorer to know whose story he was scoring. Our experience has shown that an average of one and one-half to two minutes is sufficient time for scoring one story when the scoring criteria have been learned. Our general attitude toward scoring is that while the majority of the scoring decisions are adequately covered by the manual definitions, there will always be a relatively small number of stories that defy the manual criteria. We have found that high scorer reliability is possible if judges agree in advance to score only what the manual covers and *not to score a particular category if in doubt.*

The four-story records of 30 subjects are presented in Appendix I. These may be scored for practice after careful study of the manual. Following the examples is our scoring of these same stories. They provide an opportunity for a reliability check in advance of individual research with the scoring method. We have made an unsystematic check of the correlations between *n* Achievement scores assigned to these same records by graduate students after perhaps a week of intermittent study on the manual examples. The correlations run between .50 and .70 after this much practice. A careful check of disagreements and further consideration of the manual usually leads to gradual improvement in scoring the same records and others. By the third or fourth batch of 30 records, the scoring reliability is usually in the neighborhood of .90 or better.

7.2 **Stability of the *n* Achievement score.** In a study conducted for the purpose of developing an equivalent form of the four-picture instrument which had been used in the original studies of criterion groups, Atkinson (1950) selected four additional pictures which seemed on a priori grounds to be reasonably equivalent. The eight pictures were then arranged in eight sequences, each sequence being presented to a separate group of subjects. The requirements of a Latin Square Design were fulfilled. Each picture appeared once and only once in each ordinal position. The eight rows corresponded to eight groups of subjects, four in each group. The eight columns corresponded to eight ordinal positions, and the eight pictures corresponded to eight Latin letters. Thus, the design provided an opportunity to determine the effect of both ordinal position of a story in the series and picture differences on the n Achievement score obtained from any one story. The measure was administered to each of the eight groups of college students at the beginning of a laboratory section in Introductory Experimental Psychology under "Neutral" conditions. The measure was preceded only by the standard instruction, "This is a test of creative imagination, and so on."

The Latin Square and analysis of variance are presented in Table 7.1. Since there was no evidence to suggest that ordinal position of a story had any significant effect on the n Achievement score obtained from that story, there was no necessity to correct for ordinal position in obtaining a correlation between n Achievement scores obtained by subjects on comparable halves of the eight-story measure.

In this study, n Achievement scores were originally obtained by method B. In order that the report of the reliability of the instrument be in complete accord with the recent changes in the method of deriving the n Achievement score, the scores were recomputed by method C. The results are practically identical for the two methods.

The correlation between n Achievement scores (C) obtained by subjects on the four original pictures ($ABGH$) and the four new pictures ($CDEF$) is .48 (see Appendix III for picture descriptions). When the Spearman-Brown correction formula is applied to determine the estimate of the reliability of the n Achievement score obtained in response to all eight pictures, this estimate is found to be .65. This agrees exactly with the estimate of reliability derived using scoring method

TABLE 7.1.   Latin square design and analysis of variance for eight-picture measure of n Achievement

ORDINAL POSITION [2]

Groups of Subjects, or Sequences [1]	1	2	3	4	5	6	7	8	Mean
1	3.50F [3]	1.25A	3.25B	4.25E	4.00C	2.50G	2.50H	3.00D	3.03 [4]
2	2.75G	3.00D	3.50C	5.75F	1.75A	3.75E	4.75B	2.50H	3.47
3	3.50C	4.25G	3.75D	3.00H	1.00E	3.75B	3.50F	2.00A	3.09
4	2.50D	3.75C	2.50A	4.00G	4.50B	3.25H	2.75E	4.00F	3.41
5	2.75H	5.00E	3.75F	5.50B	5.75D	2.25A	4.00C	3.50G	4.06
6	2.25E	4.25B	5.00H	2.50A	3.50G	5.00F	4.75D	3.75C	3.88
7	5.75B	4.00F	2.75G	5.75D	3.25H	5.25C	1.75A	2.00E	3.81
8	2.25A	5.75H	2.75E	5.00C	3.00F	3.75D	3.25G	6.00B	3.97
Mean	3.16	3.91	3.41	4.47	3.34	3.69	3.41	3.34	3.59

PICTURES [3]

	A	B	C	D	E	F	G	H
Mean	2.03	4.72	4.09	4.03	2.97	4.06	3.31	3.50

ANALYSIS OF VARIANCE

Source	Sums of Squares	df	Variance Estimate	F	P
Ordinal position	161.11	7	23.016	1.797	
Sequences	141.36	7	20.194	1.577	
Pictures	620.36	7	88.623	6.920	.01
Residual	537.91	42	12.807		
Total	1460.74	63			

Notes: 1 Rows correspond to eight groups of subjects, four subjects in each row.
2 Columns correspond to the ordinal position of the pictures.
3 Latin letters correspond to the picture presented.
4 Stories were written under Neutral experimental conditions and scored by system C plus a constant of 2 to eliminate negative numbers.

B. In order to determine whether or not the reliability of the instrument is depressed by any pictures of questionable validity, an estimate of the relative validity or internal consistency of each picture has been made. The question asked is: Does the n Achievement score obtained from one picture agree with the total n Achievement score obtained from all the other pictures in placing the subject above or below the mean in n Achievement? Thus, for each picture the total *n* Achievement score on the seven other pictures has been used as a relative validity criterion. The total *n* Achievement score, of course, has experimental validity; that is, it increases as motivation is experimentally increased.

The percentage agreement in placing subjects above or below the mean was fairly substantial in every case except for picture *F* (Boy with violin, TAT 1). Picture *F* was, therefore, dropped from the battery and the validity of each of the other seven pictures checked against the total score on the remaining six. Figure 7.1 presents the percentage agreement between each picture and its relative validity criterion in

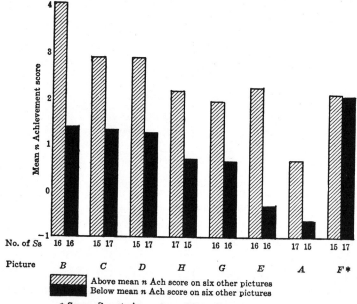

Percentage agreement between each picture and total score on six other pictures in placing subject above or below the mean.

	A	B	C	D	E	F	G	H
%	68.75	78.13	68.75	68.75	78.13	50.00	65.62	65.62

FIG. 7.1. Graphic presentation of mean *n* Achievement scores for each picture by subjects whose total score on six other pictures (*F* excluded) is above or below the mean of the distribution of total scores.

placing subjects above or below the mean, and also shows in a bar diagram the mean n Achievement score obtained in response to each picture for two groups of subjects. One group consists of those subjects whose total score falls in the upper half of the distribution of scores obtained from the remaining six pictures. The other group consists of those subjects whose total score falls in the lower half of the distribution of scores obtained from the remaining six pictures. Similar results for picture F using the other seven pictures as relative validity criterion are included. All pictures but F agree fairly well with their relative validity criterion in placing subjects high or low in the distribution of scores. Subjects having high total scores on the other pictures combined show a higher mean n Achievement score for each single picture, with the exception of picture F, than subjects having low total scores on the remaining pictures. We may conclude, therefore, that according to the present scoring method (C), all pictures but F appear to be measuring in part the same thing.

After excluding F, the seven remaining pictures were arranged in a number of ways in order to construct two equivalent forms. Data concerning the most equivalent forms, ABG (three of the original criterion pictures), and CDE (three of the new pictures) are presented in Table 7.2. The product-moment correlation between n Achievement scores (C) obtained in response to these two forms was found to be .64 ($n = 32$). The estimated reliability of the measure obtained in response to all six pictures obtained by applying the Spearman-Brown correction formula is .78.

When scoring method B was employed to obtain scores from these data, picture H also failed to discriminate adequately between subjects having high and low total scores on the other pictures. However, with the more comprehensive definition now given for Achievement Imagery, the discriminating power of picture H has improved considerably.

Lowell (1950) administered these two equivalent forms

TABLE 7.2. Comparative Achievement score (C) data on two equivalent three-picture forms

	Form with Pictures ABG	Form with Pictures CDE
Mean n Achievement score (C)	4.06	5.09
SD	4.32	4.72
Mean n Achievement score of 17 Ss above median total score	7.35	8.29
Mean n Achievement score of 15 Ss below median total score	.33	1.47
Difference between means	7.02	6.82
σ diff.	.88	1.19
t	7.98	5.73
p	<.01	<.01
Product moment r between two forms	.64	
Percentage agreement between forms in placing Ss above or below median total score	78.1%	

to the same group of 40 male college students under Neutral conditions with an interim of one week between measures. The product-moment correlation between scores obtained on the two forms was .22, which is not statistically significant. However, the two forms agreed to the extent of 72.5 per cent ($\chi^2 = 7.82$; $p < .01$) in placing subjects above or below the median score obtained from the two distributions combined. When this same procedure was applied to the data obtained in the original equivalent form study, when all six pictures were responded to on the same occasion, the percentage agreement between the forms in placing subjects high or low in the distribution is not much larger, 78.1 per cent (cf. Table 7.2).

Although every effort was made by Lowell to administer the measures under comparable Neutral conditions, there can be no certainty that the periods of stimulation immediately preceding the two measures were in fact equivalent for each subject on the two occasions. In other words, can we be sure that a few subjects exposed to considerable achievement stimulation (such as from an exam in the hour preceding) before the first measure also had a similar stimulating experience before the second measure? We have demonstrated that the instrument is quite sensitive to such conditions of stimulation preceding its application. Accordingly, a high product-moment correlation between measures on the same subjects on two occasions requires that the conditions of stimulation, whatever they may be for each subject on the first occasion, be duplicated *for him* on the second occasion. The product-moment correlation is greatly affected by a few extreme shifts in score from one occasion to the next, and this is exactly what occurred for a few of Lowell's subjects. The per cent agreement above or below the combined median is, however, affected only slightly by the few individuals showing very extreme shifts in n Achievement score. Therefore, the less sensitive measure, which considers only whether an individual tends to be high or low in the distribution on two occasions, indicates almost as much agreement between measures taken a week apart as between two measures obtained on the same occasion.

In addition to changed motivation states, this unreliability might be indicative of any one of a number of other things. Some subjects might have been unwilling to co-operate the second week if they had learned that the first measure was a "projective test." One of the major difficulties in assessing this result is that we do not know the extent to which it is a result of changes in the subject produced by having taken a prior, similar test and having thought about it. The fairly substantial relationships that are reported later between the n Achievement score and various other measures obtained at another time suggests that the test-retest unreliability of the measure may be due to the change in the subjects produced by the first administration of the test. That is, it is theoretically possible to have a test which will correlate highly with a number of other measures (high "validity") but not with itself on a second administration (low "reliability"), if the first administration has somehow "spoiled" the subjects for this type of test. We are not convinced that this is the case with our instrument as yet, but it should be considered as a possible handicap of projective tests.

In short, we conclude that the measure is, at present, unsuitable for purposes of precise prediction about the standing of individuals on n Achievement, but its stability for purposes of group comparisons is fairly well established. There seems to be no reason why further refinements in the method of administering the test and obtaining a score should not make possible a scale suitable for measuring individual differences.

7.3 An analysis of the determinants of the n Achievement score. The measure of n Achievement is derived from an analysis of the content of imaginative stories written by subjects. We assume that the thought processes of an individual are in part determined by his present state of motivation and that in complying with a request to write imaginative stories, he reveals the content of his dominant thoughts at the time of writing and hence, indirectly, his state of motivation.

Let us consider the various factors that might influence the motivation and thought processes of a subject while he is complying with the instructions to make up a story about a picture. First, there are the cues of everyday school life to which he has been responding during the period immediately before the test situation. The extent to which n Achievement is aroused by the usual, relatively uncontrollable cues in the environment is assumed to be a function of the affective changes accompanying achievement or failure to achieve which have been associated with these cues in the past experience of the subject. Closely related to the external cues of everyday environment, but not necessarily or completely dependent on them, are the thought processes of the subject which may contain intrinsic cues which elicit and maintain achievement motivation.

Next to be considered are the experimentally-controlled cues which serve either to increase motivation, as in the Achievement-oriented conditions, or to decrease it, as in the Relaxed condition. The effect of manipulating these cues depends, of course, upon the previous learning experiences of subjects. Whether or not a specific situational cue such as instructions for a "test of executive ability" will elicit achievement motivation in a subject depends largely upon the character of the culturally-defined standards of excellence in terms of which rewards and punishments for achievement and non-achievement have been meted out to him. The use of such cues in our research has been successful in changing the level of achievement motivation in groups of male college students presumably because being a good executive, demonstrating intelligence, and so forth, are achievement goals for many or most of them.

The cues of everyday life and specific, experimentally-controlled, situational cues affect the level of achievement motivation in subjects before the measure is administered. The third class of cues to be considered are those located in the pictures themselves, which apparently affect only the particular story written in response to that picture. This should follow because, as Table 7.1 shows, there were no significant sequence differences in Atkinson's (1950) study. That is, no particular order of pictures seemed more effective than any other in producing a high n Achievement score, a fact which suggests that the carry-over from one picture to the next is of minor significance here. It may not be of minor significance elsewhere, however. Clark (1952) has clearly demonstrated that certain types of pictures will arouse sexual motivation in such a way that it will influence stories to subsequent pictures. Hence, our decision not to consider sequence differences in the following discussion is based on the specific findings with this set of pictures and on a desire for simplicity, rather than on a basic theoretical conviction that sequence differences are always of minor significance.

Figure 7.2 shows how each of these three types of cues may arouse a subject's n Achievement and hence increase the number of achievement-related associations in a particular story.

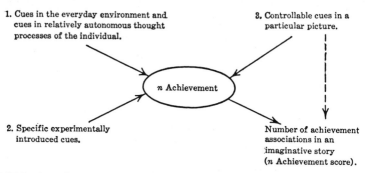

FIG. 7.2. The determinants of the n Achievement score obtained from a single story.

Evidence showing the influence of the first two classes of cues has already been presented. Thus, for example, many of Lowell's subjects who had high or low n Achievement scores under Neutral conditions on one occasion also had high or low scores under similar conditions a week later, a fact which indicates that there is some consistency in the degree to which the normal cues of everyday life arouse and maintain achievement motivation in different persons. The importance of specific experimentally-introduced cues has already been elaborated in our previous discussion of the effects of different arousal conditions. Particularly relevant is Lowell's study in which n Achievement scores were obtained from the same subjects under both Neutral and Achievement-involving conditions. The significant increase in n Achievement score following the presentation of a specific situational cue (achievement-orienting instructions and tasks) is a clear demonstration of the additional motivating effect of such cues. We will return later to a further consideration of these two sources of cues, but let us turn our attention first to the third class of cues which affect the n Achievement score, namely, those contained in the pictures. In so doing we shall have an opportunity to go over some new ground, then to see how the various factors which influence the n Achievement score relate to one another, and generally to explore in greater detail the meaning of the n Achievement score as presently derived.

7.4 **The effect of cues in pictures.** The significant picture variance in the Latin Square analysis (Table 7.1) and the evidence concerning variations in relative validity of pictures (Figure 7.1) reveal that the pictures are one of the important determinants of the n Achievement score obtained from single stories. The inadequacy of the discrimination provided by picture F (Boy with violin, TAT 1) between subjects having high and low total scores on the seven other pictures combined demands some explanation. Atkinson (1950) has argued that the achievement stories written in response to picture F may represent recollections of past events rather than the present motivational state of the subjects. The argument is based on Tomkins' (1947) summary of the results of a number of studies undertaken to determine which of the TAT pictures is most useful in eliciting accurate autobiographical material. Tomkins reports that the best pictures for this purpose are those which contain characters younger than or near the same age as the subjects being tested. In the present series of pictures, F (Boy with violin) and H (Boy with a book) were the only two pictures which contained single characters who could appear to be younger than the subjects. Picture G presents a child character but shows, in addition, the shadowy images of two adults in an operation scene in the background. A review of stories written in response to these three pictures reveals that in picture *H* the orientation was toward the *present*. The character was usually perceived as a college student (the same age as the subjects) studying or working, anticipating success or failure, graduation and a career. The stories written in response to picture *G* were more *future*-oriented and involved daydreams about becoming a doctor based on the shadowy images of adults in the background. The stories in response to picture *F* were, on the other hand, *past*-oriented and concerned nearly always a little boy practicing a violin because his parents made him. Now we have argued elsewhere (McClelland and Liberman, 1949, and Chap. VIII below) that the over-all shifts in thought patterns accompanying achievement motivation suggest *future* orientation. Thus, many of the characteristics we score (unfulfilled needs, instrumental activity, anticipated successes or failures) suggest an anticipatory state of mind. If this argument is correct, pictures allowing forward-looking identifications (like *G* and *B*) might be expected to provide a more fruitful opportunity for the expression of the motive than pictures suggesting a backward-looking or regressive identification (like *F*). Murray (1938) and others have pointed out that the content of imaginative stories may reflect specific recollections of past events as well as dynamic strivings. It is partly for this reason that we have placed a broken arrow in Figure 7.2 which leads directly from the picture cues to associated Achievement Imagery without the arousal of the achievement motive. One of our problems in this research is to eliminate Achievement Imagery which does not reflect motivation as such but only a recollection of some specific past event. The present findings suggest that one of the ways to do this is not to use pictures like *F* which provoke a regressive, backward-looking identification.

It is, perhaps, equally plausible to assume that picture *F* might have been incorrectly scored, particularly since it has been found that the discrimination provided by picture *H* is improved by the most recent extension of the definition of Achievement Imagery (method C). At present, no assumptions are made concerning the identification of a subject with a particular character in a story. It may well be that the failure of picture F to make the same discrimination as the other pictures is the result of our failure to distinguish between the wants and expectancies of the boy with the violin and those of his unseen parents. In any case, the problem is one demanding experimental investigation to determine (1) whether or not phenotypically similar achievement stories may be determined by both recollections of past events and contemporary motivation, and (2) whether it is necessary to refine the scoring procedures in order to take cognizance of the problem of identifying a "hero" or central character.

The most obvious difference among pictures is in mean n Achievement score obtained in response to them. Differences attributable to pictures in Table 7.1 are well beyond the 1 per cent level of confidence. It is possible to combine several pictures having common characteristics in the interest of organizing our observations about factors which influence the n Achievement score obtained from any one story. Five of the pictures are alike in containing only two adult, male characters ($ABCDE$). In three of the pictures the two adult characters are portrayed in situations which on a priori grounds may be considered suggestive of achievement.

B. (Two men working in a shop)
C. (Two men in colonial dress working in a shop with old-fashioned printing press)
D. (Young man seated at desk, older man handing him some papers)

Analysis of what is meant by "suggestive of achievement" reveals that these three pictures portray characters in situations containing rather obvious cues related to work situations (machinery, work aprons, tools, desks, papers). These are the kinds of cues which are likely to be associated with competing with standards of excellence in the lives of most males of our culture.

The other two pictures with two male adults do not contain as many obviously achievement-related cues.

A. (The heads of two men, "father and son," TAT 7BM)
E. (Two men, apparently conversing, standing in a well-furnished room)

For the purpose of this analysis, we will accept the notion that it is possible to objectify the measure of the "cue-value" of the picture in some fashion *independent of the achievement-related stories written to it.* For example, this might be done in terms of the number of discrete elements that could be classified by a group of judges as instrumental, achievement-related objects, or in terms of some other such scheme. On any such basis, we feel it can be safely assumed that pictures B, C, and D contain a greater number of achievement cues than pictures A and E.

When a mean n Achievement score *per picture* is computed for each subject for pictures having few or no achievement cues (A, E), and for pictures having a greater number of distinct achievement cues (B, C, D), we find the mean n Achievement score to be significantly higher in response to pictures containing a greater number of achievement cues (Mean [A, E] = .50; Mean [B, C, D] = 2.28; SE diff. = .34; t = 5.23; $p < .01$). It is clear that achievement-related cues in pictures seem to have much the same effect as cues in the situation preceding the writing of stories; they lead to an increase in the frequency of achievement-related associations in stories. It is worth while, however, to consider a probable difference in their effect on the person. The cues in the instructions and tasks serve to heighten the motivation of the person and hence lead him to think about achieving. The cues in the pictures, on the other hand, may not increase the general level of achievement motivation for the subjects. If the cues have any such motivating effect it must be temporary, since it does not carry over to subsequent pictures, as the absence of significant sequence differences shows. A more likely and by no means mutually exclusive possibility is that the picture cues provide an *opportunity* for a subject to write about achievement. In so far as cues similar to those appearing in the picture have been associated with achievement in the past experience of the person, the picture will elicit achievement-related associations in stories. The number of associations elicited will depend upon how strongly motivated the person is at the time of writing (see also Section 7.10).

7.5 The joint effect of cues in pictures and in individuals. This line of argument leads directly into a consideration of the relation between cues in the pictures and the first determinant of *n* Achievement score per story shown in Figure 7.2, namely, the interaction of "everyday cues" with the relatively autonomous thought processes that the individual brings with him to the situation. Our task here is to show how picture differences are reacted to by individuals who bring a large or small number of thought processes containing achievement cues to the situation or who, more simply, are high or low in *n* Achievement. *In all the discussion which follows, the phrase "cues in individuals" will be used as shorthand for a much more cumbersome phrase explaining each time that we believe the thought processes of individuals are conditioned by past affective experiences in connection with achievement so as to contain greater or lesser numbers of achievement cues.* In other words, some people, even if they start thinking about scrambling an egg, will end up thinking about how to scramble it well.

Figure 7.3 depicts the mean *n* Achievement scores for the two types of pictures (high and low achievement cue-value) from two groups of subjects in Atkinson's study, one of which consists of the upper half of the distribution of total n Achievement scores for the seven pictures considered together, and the other of which consists of the lower half of this distribution. Note that total score in response to a variety of picture cues is used as the best estimate of group differences in mo-

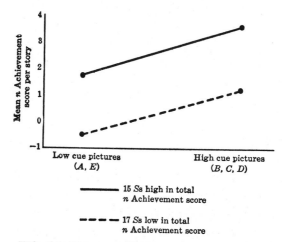

FIG. 7.3. Mean n Achievement score per story as a function of intensity level of n Achievement in subjects and number of achievement cues in the picture (Neutral condition).

tive strength produced by "cues in individuals," since this is the Neutral testing condition. The mean n Achievement scores presented in Figure 7.3 are mean scores *per picture;* they were obtained by dividing the total scores for the high and low motivation groups both by the number of subjects in a given group and by the number of pictures of a given type. Mean n Achievement scores reported earlier represented the average of a group of subjects based usually on a four-story measure. In the following sections the mean n Achievement score will represent the average per picture or per story values for a group of subjects.

Figure 7.3 shows that both the number of achievement cues

in the pictures and group differences in strength of motivation affect the score obtained from a single story. For these two groups of subjects, the effect of increasing the number of cues in the pictures seems to have the effect of adding a constant to what the n Achievement score would have been without the additional cues. In this situation, both pictures with and without achievement cues seem to discriminate about equally well between groups of subjects high and low in n Achievement. The magnitude of the difference is virtually identical. For the pictures having low cue-value (A, E), the mean difference between the high group (1.70) and low group ($-.56$) is 2.26. For pictures having high cue-value (B, C, D) the mean difference between the high group (3.53) and low group (1.18) is 2.35.

7.6 The joint effect of cues in pictures and in the experimental situation. The data just presented show the effect of picture cues and group differences in motivational level on n Achievement per story when the situational cues are held constant (all Ss from the Neutral condition). Next we can show the effect on the n Achievement score per story of cues in pictures and differences in motivational level which are produced by experimentally varying the achievement cues in the situation before the stories are written. In short, what is the effect of variations in instructional cues on achievement responses to pictures of high and low cue value? The phrase "instructional cues" is used here and hereafter to refer to cues in the instructions, experimental tasks, and so on.

Our measure of the effect of number of cues in the picture will be less reliable than in the previous comparison, since data are available on only one picture with no obvious cues (A) and one picture having such cues (B) for this comparison. In Figure 7.4 the mean n Achievement scores obtained from 39 subjects in the Relaxed condition (see Chap. III for description of conditions) and 39 subjects in the Achievement-oriented condition in response to pictures B and A are plotted. Theoretically, the subjects in these two conditions should differ in the intensity level of their achievement motivation as produced now, not by internal or everyday cues as in Figure 7.3, but by experimentally introduced cues.

The effect of increasing motivation in a group of subjects by instructions and experimental procedures is to increase the

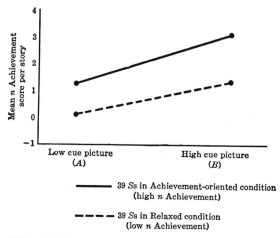

FIG. 7.4. Mean *n* Achievement score per story as a function of number of cues in the picture and differences in motivation produced by experimental manipulation of cues in the situation preceding the TAT.

mean *n* Achievement response to both pictures with and without achievement cues. The effect of differences in the number of cues in pictures remains. The mean difference between the Achievement-oriented (1.36) and Relaxed (.13) conditions on picture A is 1.23; for picture B, the mean difference between Achievement-oriented (3.05) and Relaxed (1.38) conditions is 1.67.

7.7 The effect of all three determinants together on *n* Achievement score. We have illustrated how the *n* Achieve-

ment score per story may be influenced by the number of cues
in the individual, or by the number of cues in the instructions
prior to the administration of the TAT. Have we any data
which will show the joint operation of these factors all at
once? None of our experiments was designed with the idea of
making such an analysis, but the Neutral and Achievement-
oriented conditions of our original criterion groups do provide
data which can be broken down in these various ways. That
is, there are here 78 subjects whose n Achievement scores per
story can be computed and averaged according to whether
the stories are in response to (1) a high (B) or low (A)
cue picture, (2) high or low internal cues as measured by
n Achievement score on all four pictures, and (3) high or low
achievement cues in the preceding instructions. The breakdown is not ideal, because the over-all motivational level index will be influenced by scores on pictures A and B (which
had to be included for the sake of reliability), and because we
have only a single picture in each case to demonstrate the
effect of high and low cue pictures. Nevertheless, the results
of such an analysis have seemed highly meaningful to us, if
only for their expositional value in showing how we conceive
these three factors as jointly entering into the determination
of the n Achievement score.

The results of this analysis are presented in Table 7.3 and
Figure 7.5. Each of the mean values in the Table is based on 19
or 20 cases, depending on how the 39 subjects in each group
were divided at the median, but the analysis of variance is
actually based only on the degrees of freedom in the Table.
The p values demonstrate nicely that each of the three determinants which had been isolated at first theoretically in
Figure 7.2 do contribute significantly to the total variance in
n Achievement score per story, at least so far as these data go.
It would be unwise to draw any final conclusions from such
data, but it is certainly worth noting that differences due to
"cues in the individual," in which we are usually most inter-

TABLE 7.3. Mean n Achievement score per story analyzed according to its determinants

	NUMBER OF CUES IN THE INSTRUCTIONS			
	FEW CUES (RELAXED CONDITION)		MANY CUES (ACHIEVEMENT-ORIENTED CONDITION)	
Cues in Individuals	Low Cue Picture (A)	High Cue Picture (B)	Low Cue Picture (A)	High Cue Picture (B)
High n Achievement [*] ...	.68	2.84	3.11	4.05
Low n Achievement [*] ...	−.40	.00	−.30	2.10

ANALYSIS OF VARIANCE

Source	Sums of Squares	df	Variance Estimate	F	p
Instructional Cues	4.26	1	4.26	10.39	.05
Picture cues	4.35	1	4.35	10.61	.05
Cues in individuals	10.77	1	10.77	26.27	.01
Residual	1.64	4	.41		
Total	21.02	7			

[*] As determined by n Achievement score to all four pictures.

ested, are largest with a picture of low cue value under conditions of Achievement-orientation. This suggests that the testing condition which may be optimal for getting the widest range of individual differences in n Achievement is one in which low cue value pictures are used under achievement-orienting instructions. Such a finding, if it turned out to be correct on further investigation, would bode well for the ultimate development of a practicable testing instrument for measuring achievement motivation for selection purposes, since as a matter of fact most subjects are achievement-oriented when they are being selected for some purpose or other. But not too much weight can be given such a result because, as we shall see in a moment, the ideal condition for testing individual differences in n Achievement also depends on the *kind* of n Achievement one is interested in, which in

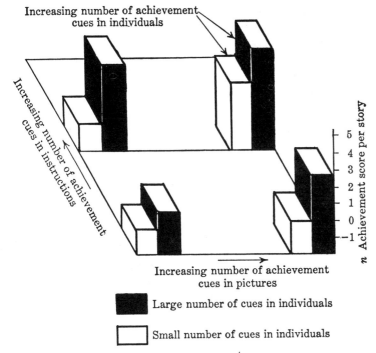

FIG. 7.5. Graphic representation of joint determination of *n* Achievement score obtained from a single story by number of achievement cues in (1) pictures, (2) instructions, (3) individuals. Based on data in Table 7.3.

turn usually depends on the kind of performance to be predicted with the help of the *n* Achievement score.

7.8 Individuals whose score is largely a function of internal cues. It is immediately apparent from our analysis of the components of the *n* Achievement score that there are several ways in which a high score can be obtained. Thus, a person's score can be high because of his internal cues, because of cues in an immediately preceding experience, or because of cues in the pictures. If this is so, questions arise as to whether scores obtained in any of these ways are equally valid measures of achievement motivation. That is, there will be some people who score high only under Achievement-oriented conditions, others who score high without external pressure, and still others who respond only to high cue pictures. Is the score obtained under any one of these conditions a more valid indicator of a man's n Achievement? Or, does the person who scores high under Neutral or Relaxed conditions have an achievement motive which is truly "stronger" than the achievement motive of a person who scores high only under Achievement-orientation?

Such questions as these serve to point up the fact that there is no single "best way" to measure achievement motivation, but rather a variety of ways to measure it for predicting behavior under different conditions. While for practical purposes we may want to treat all n Achievement scores as if they are alike, we ought to distinguish here the different meanings of scores obtained in various ways. Consider first the person who scores high even under Relaxed conditions to low cue pictures. We conclude that he is responding primarily to what we have called internal cues built up to an unusual strength out of his past experiences in achievement situations. What would we expect of such a person? He should be constantly thinking of achievement, regardless of changes in the external situation. In one sense we might think of him as having a "neurotic" achievement drive which is self-initiating and which, as far as performance is concerned, might lead him to work hard even in situations which did not obviously demand working hard. He is the kind of person that could be expected to work hard on a desert island, even when there was little chance that anyone would ever check up on his work. In short, the extensity of his motive is great since it is aroused by almost any cues.

When we first thought of this type of person, we tended to describe him as having "normally high" achievement motivation. That is, his motivation is such that it appears even under normal, everyday circumstances without any special stimulus, either from pictures or from achievement pressures. Students with such motivation should study regularly throughout the school year and not just in spurts when examinations are imminent. But, on second thought, the term *normal* seems a little misleading. One might just as well call such a person neurotic, because his achievement motivation is relatively uninfluenced by changes in reality. Instead, it seems preferable not to speak at all of a person's "normal" achievement motivation, or his "true" motivational level, but rather to measure his achievement motive under different conditions to predict what his performance will be in a variety of situations. We realize that this is a counsel of perfection as far as our present measuring instrument is concerned, but the point seems worth making in the interest of theoretical clarity.

7.9 Individuals whose score is largely a function of instructional cues. Returning to our classification of the variables influencing the *n* Achievement score, we can observe next that there will be those individuals whose score is largely determined by instructional cues. To find them we need to obtain scores under two or more conditions and pick out those whose scores are low under Relaxed conditions and high under Achievement-orientation, regardless of picture cues. As far as performance is concerned, we would predict that these are the type of people who study very hard the night before an examination. They should work hard when the situation requires it, but not when it does not. Data are reported in Section 8.3 which show that the highest correlation between our measure of motivation and grades at one college was obtained when the *difference* between *n* Achievement score under Neutral and under Achievement-oriented conditions was used as our measure of achievement motivation. In other words, at this institution those individuals whose motivation responded most readily to pressure from without for achievement got the highest grades. In other institutions, or in other types of performance situations, it is possible to get a higher correlation with the autonomous type of n Achievement measured under Neutral conditions. Thus, on a desert island the autonomous type of n Achievement score ought to be a good predictor of performance, whereas the difference score should be a poor predictor. In school or college, both types of n Achievement should lead to better grades, and for many such practical purposes it may not be necessary to distinguish between them.

7.9.1 *The effect of instructional cues on the process of writing stories.* In considering the effect of instructional variations such as Achievement-orientation on n Achievement score, there is one important point which we have so far not given the attention it deserves. It is simply this: We know the content of stories written under Achievement-orientation is different, but does the change in instructions affect the story-writing process—the way in which the stories are written? It should be recalled that the Achievement orientation is produced in connection with tests taken prior to the TAT and is *not* directed at the task of *writing good stories.* In fact, the instructions given subsequently for the TAT actually attempt to break down the "intelligence testing" set by assuring the subjects that there are no "right or wrong answers," and so on. Furthermore, we have commonly used a second experimenter to administer the TAT in order to suggest to the subjects that the TAT is not a part of the intelligence and leadership testing situation. What we were trying to do was to collect the effects of Achievement-orientation in the imaginative stories without Achievement-involving the story-telling itself.

We followed this procedure because we had once tried it the other way. We had described the TAT as "a test of creative intelligence." This apparently motivated the subjects to write *correct,* intelligent stories; that is, writing a good, intelligent-sounding story was apparently perceived as instrumental to the attainment of an achievement goal. The result was a general freezing up of the imaginative content of the stories with numerous qualifications indicating the uncertainty of subjects as to how to do well at the task in order to succeed. It was almost impossible to score these stories for *n* Achievement because of the number of alternatives offered by the subjects as to what the people in the story might "really" be doing. When the task of writing imaginative stories is itself conceived as instrumental to the attainment of an achievement goal, the free, imaginative response which would normally provide a measure of motivation is interfered with. The trick here is to create a condition of high motivation by the instructions surrounding the administration of the TAT without creating the impression that the subjects must produce intelligent or correct stories. So far we have done this by using a set of Achievement-oriented pre-tests, but there may be other ways of doing it. Even with this technique, we suspect that some individuals are guided too much in the kind of stories they write by the part of the TAT instructions which states that it is a test of "creative" imagination. Some of our subjects are probably interpreting the word *creative* to mean that they should show their ability to produce a *variety* of different types of stories. If in fact they are instructing themselves in this way, their *n* Achievement score is bound to suffer, since they will avoid telling an achievement-related story over and over again.

Have we any evidence that our attempt to separate the TAT task from the pre-tests has been successful? Of course we were successful to the extent that we obtained stories that we can score, but there is also one other small fact that encourages us to believe that the TAT is not itself directly perceived as instrumental to the attainment of an achievement goal. As far as the pre-tests are concerned, achievement-orientation usually produces an increased response output (see Table 8.3), as it should if it succeeds in raising over-all motivational level. If it affects the TAT task in the same way, there should be an increase in the length of the stories. But such is not the case. In Table 7.4 data are presented which show the mean number of words per story written by the same or very similar subjects under both Neutral and Achievement-oriented conditions. It is apparent that the Connecti-

TABLE 7.4. Mean number of words per story under Neutral and Achievement-oriented conditions

	CONNECTICUT H. S. SAMPLE SIMILAR SUBJECTS		NAVAHO H. S. SAMPLE SAME SUBJECTS	
	Neutral ($N = 18$)	*Achievement-oriented* ($N = 28$)	*Neutral* ($N = 21$)	*Achievement-oriented* ($N = 21$)
Mean No. Words	68.3	77.2	90.0	80.2
Mean Difference	8.9		9.8	
SE diff.	6.29		8.48	
t	1.41		1.15	
p	$>.05$		$>.05$	

cut subjects wrote more words and the Navaho subjects fewer words under Achievement-involving conditions, but neither shift is significant. The increase in n Achievement score, however, is significant for both groups (see Tables 6.2 and 6.3), a fact which demonstrates that the content of the stories is not systematically related to their length. This evidence, such as it is, suggests that something is happening which we hoped would happen, namely, that the stories reflect in their content the preceding Achievement-orienting experience but are not themselves Achievement-involved, at least to the extent that Achievement-involvement is indicated by increased response output.

7.10 Individuals whose score is largely a function of picture cues. Logically there is another way high n Achievement scores per story can be obtained. Suppose we find subjects whose scores do not vary much in response to instructional changes but are high only in response to pictures of high cue-value. How are we to describe these people's motivation? Or can we consider them motivated at all? Take the extreme case of a person whose score is low to low cue pictures and high to high cue pictures, regardless of instructional variations. In other words, he responds only to pictures which suggest achievement so strongly that anyone who is a member of the culture and familiar with its major themes would write Horatio Alger stories to them. One could argue that in such a case the measure indicates the *extent to which he understands the achievement values existing in the culture.* He has at least been instructed in what they are, so that they are part of his knowledge if not of his motivational system. To refer back once more to Figure 7.1 at the beginning of the chapter, this is another reason why we have placed a dotted arrow in the diagram to show that pictures may give rise directly to achievement imagery without engaging achievement motivation to the extent that instructional cues or self-cues apparently do. The distinction we are making here is ultimately between understanding certain achievement ideas and being personally involved in achievement striving. It is the same kind of distinction necessary to explain how it is that certain psychopaths understand certain values very well, but do not live by them. To sum up, we are arguing that a person whose score varies primarily with picture cues is one who *understands* achievement values but who is not himself motivated by them.

7.10.1 *Picture cues and motive extensity.* The number of picture cues to which a person responds may be considered in another light. It may indicate the *extensity* of the person's achievement motive (cf. Chap. II). In fact, it is always true that cognition and motivation interact to produce action in particular *situations*. To put it in another way, a person never has an achievement motive in a vacuum. It is always tied to one or more specific situations which are perceived as achievement-related. The number of such situations may be very small or very large. It is at least logically possible, though we have no experimental evidence to support the hypothesis, that the pictures to which a person gives achievement imagery may provide an index of the *direction* and *extent* of his achievement motivation in similar life situations. Thus, it may turn out that if he gives achievement stories primarily to pictures of athletic situations, that he will show high achievement motivation only in such situations. In the same way achievement imagery in response to academic pictures may give the best prediction of striving for grades. It is probably too much to expect that the relationship of response to pictures and to real life situations will be as simple as this, but certainly the number and kind of pictures responded to in the test situation should bear some kind of a relationship to the number and kind of situations to which a person responds in real life. Perhaps it is not too much to speculate that the number of achievement sub-categories appearing in any one story might indicate the *intensity* with which n Achievement is aroused in a particular situation. If this were so, one could imagine constructing a motivational profile for a given individual which would show the intensity of his achievement motivation in a variety of situations. Our present n Achievement score would then turn out to be a composite in which extensity and intensity of motivation are confounded. This is an area of research which clearly needs further exploration.

7.11 **Other types of achievement motives.** Even now we have by no means exhausted the varieties of achievement motivation which might some day be measured. An important typology which derives from our theoretical principles, rather than from a consideration of the components of n Achievement score, involves the distinction between an achievement motive which is characterized chiefly by a "hope of success" and one which is characterized chiefly by a "fear of failure." According to our theory, certain individuals will have been praised or rewarded primarily for successful competition with a standard of excellence. These same people may also have been predominantly successful in such striving, so that their perceived probability of success is relatively great. In such cases, the achievement motive should consist largely of the association of certain cues with positive affective changes, an association which in the language of phenomenology would be called the "hope of success." On the other hand, certain individuals will have been primarily punished for failure and perhaps have failed a good deal of the time. These people in turn should have an achievement motive characterized chiefly by a "fear of failure." In the data to be reported in the next chapter, we will resort to this distinction a number of times to explain some of the peculiar relationships we have obtained. Thus, for example, we will argue that the subjects with moderately high n Achievement scores recall relatively more completed tasks because they are defensively oriented, and recall their successes because they are primarily afraid of failure. The subjects with high n Achievement scores, however, recall more incompleted tasks because they are primarily success-oriented and want to finish the tasks.

Such analysis clearly indicates that our n Achievement score as we now obtain it is a composite which will have to be broken down into various sub-scores. Thus, in our original studies certain achievement-related responses were observed to increase in frequency in the stories of groups of subjects when motivation was experimentally increased. It is quite possible that some of these responses are representative of motivation to succeed, whereas others are representative of motivation to avoid failure. Some people would produce more of one kind than the other, but in an analysis of group results all would be taken as representing increased achievement motivation. As a result, when stories written under relatively neutral conditions are scored for the various categories, some individuals will receive moderately high scores as a result of having in their stories certain categories that are actually more representative of a tendency to avoid failure or even escape achievement-related situations than actual striving toward achievement. This may be particularly true of some of the affect responses that tend to be associated with the obstacle categories in some stories. It is quite possible that our present scoring criteria do not discriminate between (1) affective responses which allow the inference that the character in the story is really concerned about his inability to get ahead, and (2) affective responses which suggest annoyance, hostility, and other diffuse emotional reactions that appear achievement-related but may rather be the result of the author's characteristic emotional reaction in competitive situations. In the latter case, the categories would be more representative of fear of failure than the desire to succeed.

There is one final limitation of our measuring instrument which may prevent the development of a score which would accurately indicate the extent of a person's anxiety about achievement. Recently Clark has conclusively demonstrated (1952) that anxiety produced by sexual stimulation will effectively inhibit the amount of overt sexual imagery in written stories like the ones which we have been using to measure n Achievement. This strongly suggests that some of our subjects who have low n Achievement scores are really "false lows"; that is, they are people whose "fear of failure" is so great that it blocks achievement imagery out of the stories altogether. It is possible, even probable, that our rapid-fire method of collecting stories from subjects may prevent us from getting around such anxieties in the way that the more relaxed clinical method for administering the TAT does. If so, this may turn out to be one of the prices that our measuring technique has to pay in order to give a quick, economical estimate of intensity of motivation for a large number of individuals. On the other hand, the price is not so great as it might be with some motives, for the reason that the number of people whose anxiety over achievement is so great as to inhibit achievement imagery so far seems to be quite small. Furthermore, there remains the possibility that we can assess the true motivational level of such people through an analysis of the disguised or symbolic achievement imagery they produce.

Our purpose in this chapter has been to study the n Achievement measure itself a little more closely, to study it especially in relation to the psychological function or functions it is supposed to measure. It should be obvious by now that the score is only a first approximation, a composite index of a variety of types of achievement motivation which all deserve separate study and separate methods of measurement. Despite its limitations, the rough index must measure some psychological function like motivation fairly sensitively because, as the next chapter will show, there are numerous meaningful relationships between the n Achievement score and other types of behavior.

CHAPTER VIII

Relation of n Achievement Score
to Behavior

FROM THE very beginning of our research we have recognized that if the measure of motivation that we were developing did not relate to anything of importance, we would be spending our time in an interesting but scientifically unprofitable manner. Consequently, we began relating our earliest *n* Achievement scores to performance and other behavioral variables almost as soon as we were able to compute such scores. What we discovered seemed sufficiently promising to encourage us to believe that we were in fact measuring motivation.

Now our problem is to bring together these and numerous other findings in a single chapter and attempt to make some theoretical sense of them. The difficulty is that our methodological studies as reported in previous chapters have been progressing at the same time. Our scoring criteria have changed from time to time; we have decided to include or exclude a certain picture or scoring category. As a result, the *n* Achievement scores used in these various studies are not exactly comparable. It was necessary to freeze the scoring method long enough to relate our scores to other measures, but then subsequent experience forced us to revise our method of scoring which immediately put all previous work out of date. For instance, when we attempted to generalize our definition of achievement imagery to include data from other cultures, we found that the scoring criteria previously employed seemed to be merely special cases of a wider definition that we now have adopted.

What then should be done with our earlier findings? Ideally, one might suppose that we should go back and rescore all our records with the "final" criteria that have been adopted. Such a procedure would seem preferable to presenting data from several different scoring systems, but there are some arguments against it. One is the simple practical one that such an effort would involve a tremendous expenditure of time which might better be spent in *repeating* the experiments under more controlled conditions now that we better understand what we are doing. Another argument is that we have, in fact, rescored our records several times, using modifications of our scoring system for specific experiments, and have never been forced by such rescoring to modify any of our major conclusions. The fact of the matter is that the correlations between scores obtained by one method and by another are very high (see Chap. V). Most of the changes have been such as not to affect markedly the rank of a subject in the distribution of *n* Achievement scores. The third argument against rescoring is perhaps the most compelling. If we were to do so, we might be attempting to introduce a kind of precision into our results that we do not believe to be there, as yet. If our experience to date provides any forecast of the future, it would indicate that our latest way of scoring *n* Achievement will probably have to be modified again in the light of subsequent methodological studies.

The outcome of this reasoning is that we have not gone back and rescored everything but have decided to present some of the data as originally scored. In doing so, we want to make it clear that inferences based on the relationships obtained should be tempered with more than the usual number of doubts and cautions. We regard results to date as promising leads that should be checked and rechecked in a systematic way with the modified scoring definitions, with different samples of subjects, and with other refinements now so obvious in "the cold clear light of hindsight." We present our findings in the hope that they will aid and stimulate others to do research in this area. As a final safeguard, we will try to indicate in every case which method of deriving the n Achievement score was employed in a particular study and whether or not a check with the latest scoring system (C) shows that the relationship still holds. Without further ado then, let us turn to the data to see how the measure of n Achievement is related to various kinds of behavior.

8.1 **Response output.** From the beginning, we have been concerned about the possibility that we might be penalizing some relatively inarticulate people by using a verbal measure of achievement motivation. What about the fellow who is a "real hard worker" but can manage to write only a four- or five-sentence story in the time allotted to him? Is the measure as valid an index of his motivation as it is for the more verbal individual who can fill up a whole record sheet with ease? We cannot answer these questions with any degree of finality, but there are two reasons to believe that the measure should be reasonably equitable over a fairly wide range of verbal fluency. The first rests with the scoring system; we never score a category more than once per story no matter how many times it appears. This avoids favoring the persons whose imagination flows freely. The unit, "The apprentice feels bad because he didn't make the grade," is scored the same as a more elaborate treatment such as, "The apprentice, upset and angry, thoroughly disgusted with himself for not being able to perform as well as was required to do the job, goes home and complains to his wife." The second reason lies in the fact that we have not discovered any significant relationships between number of words in imaginative stories and n Achievement scores. The correlations run from .25 for a Michigan college sample to .11 for a Hartford high school sample. We view this as evidence that the subjects with higher achievement motivation do not regard the *length* of the imaginative stories they write as being achievement-related. Another possibility is that the time limit imposed on all subjects prevents any marked differences in story length due to extra persistence.

What does happen when a sample of word output is obtained under achievement-related conditions when there is greater opportunity for differences in length of written productions to appear? Zatzkis (1949) asked some subjects to write an essay in class one day in order to get a word sample for a linguistic analysis to be reported below. The title of the essay was "What I would ideally like to get out of an elementary course in psychology." The students were told that the essays were going to be read and graded in terms of the "quality of thinking" that went into them, but not for spelling, grammar, and the like. A month previously, *n* Achievement scores had been obtained for these same subjects under Neutral conditions. A simple count of the number of words in the essays written by subjects with low, moderate, and high *n* Achievement (C) produced the results in Table 8.1.

TABLE 8.1. Mean number of words written on an essay by subjects with low, moderate, and high *n* Achievement scores

| | *n* ACHIEVEMENT SCORE | | |
	Low (−4 to 3)	*Moderate* (4 to 9)	*High* (10 to 17)
N	8	12	8
Mean	491.5	424.5	543.3
SD	101.5	97.0	169.0

In three-way breakdowns of the sort presented in this table, we have decided to compare one particular third against the other two. (The rationale for choosing the breaking points will be given after data in Table 8.2 have been presented, because a comparison of Tables 8.1 and 8.2 helps to clarify this rationale.) In addition to this, at times three different comparisons are made for a three-way breakdown of a given set of data. For three groups there are, obviously, only two degrees of freedom available, and thus there are only sets of two orthogonal comparisons that can be made legitimately. However, we feel that the suggestions gained from such analyses are valuable, despite our transgression of strict statistical logic. With these considerations in mind, it appears somewhat likely from Table 8.1 that subjects with moderate n Achievement produce fewer words on the average than do subjects with high or low n Achievement ($t = 1.99$, $p < .06$). While this is the most pronounced difference among the three groups, it is also possible that the high group is significantly higher than the two lower groups ($t = 1.32$, $p < .20$).

Before attempting to interpret this result which fails to meet the accepted standard of significance, let us turn to some other measures of performance or response output. The Rorschach test was administered to 30 subjects under standard individual testing conditions. The total number of responses they gave to all 10 blots varied as a function of n Achievement score (C) as shown in Table 8.2. First, it will be

TABLE 8.2. Mean number of Rorschach responses for subjects with low, moderate, and high n Achievement scores

	n ACHIEVEMENT SCORE		
	Low (−4 to 3)	Moderate (4 to 10)	High (11 to 18)
N	8	12	10
Mean	26.8	42.1	23.7
SD	16.1	22.9	13.3

	Low vs. (Mid + High)	Mid vs. (High + Low)	High vs. (Mid + Low)
t	.90	2.18	−1.85
p	—	<.05	= .08

noted that the distribution of *n* Achievement scores has been broken at slightly different places than in Table 8.1. The fact of the matter is that whenever the results require a three-way breakdown, it is difficult to decide exactly where the cutting points should be. Obviously, the problem is much simpler when the relationship is approximately linear, and all the points can be taken into account in the statistic used. When the relationship is not linear, as in these two tables, we finally decided to use as a criterion for establishing the limits of the middle group a distance roughly equivalent in whole score units to plus or minus one-half of a standard deviation from the mean. Consequently, when the mean *n* Achievement score of different samples varies, the numerical limits of the middle *n* Achievement group will also vary somewhat. Thus, the mean *n* Achievement score for the sample of subjects in Table 8.2 is higher than for the sample in Table 8.1. The second point to notice about both tables is that the comparisons are made not between any two levels of *n* Achievement intensity but between any one level and the rest of the subjects pooled. This procedure seems to be one adequate way of determining the most probable nature of the relationship in non-linear relationships of this sort. In the present instance, it seems most likely that the middle group gives significantly *more responses* to the Rorschach test than does the remainder of the subjects. So far the results in Tables 8.1 and 8.2 appear to be contradictory.

Some data obtained by Atkinson (1950) are relevant here. As preparation for a test of recall of completed and incompleted tasks, he had groups of subjects work on a series of 20 tasks, only about half of which could normally be completed in the minute and fifteen seconds allotted for each. Subjects did vary somewhat, however, in the number they were able to complete. So it is possible to determine whether or not the subjects with high *n* Achievement completed more than those with low *n* Achievement. Furthermore, he performed the experiment with three groups of subjects under three different conditions: (1) Relaxed orientation, in which the experimenter created an informal atmosphere as a "graduate student who wanted to try out some tasks"; (2) Task orientation, in which the experimenter simply directed the students' attention to how the tasks were to be performed without any effort to create either a relaxed or highly motivated atmosphere; (3) Achievement orientation, in which the experimenter described the tasks as being measures of intellectual ability, executive capacity, and so forth, and urged the students to do their best. He obtained n Achievement scores (B) from imaginative stories written immediately after performance on the twenty tasks. The n Achievement score used was based on three pictures. The breakdown for number of tasks completed by subjects above and below the mean n Achievement score under different orientations is given in Table 8.3.

TABLE 8.3. Mean number of tasks completed by subjects with high and low n Achievement scores under three types of orientation toward the tasks

	Relaxed Orientation	Task Orientation	Achievement Orientation
High n Achievement			
N	12	17	10
Mean	8.75	9.82	10.60
SD	.93	1.49	1.20
Low n Achievement			
N	16	23	18
Mean	9.56	9.57	10.11
SD	1.02	1.79	1.78
Mean Difference ...	−.81	.25	.49
t	2.13	.47	.84
p	<.05	—	—

An analysis of variance shows that the three orientations contribute significantly to the variance in tasks completed ($F = 5.90$, $p < .01$); that is, regardless of n Achievement score, subjects completed more tasks as the atmosphere became more achievement-oriented. But Table 8.3 also shows that the subjects with high *n* Achievement show this increased output more markedly. Under the Relaxed orientation the high *n* Achievement group performs less well than the low group; but as the situation becomes more achievement-related, they complete more tasks than the low group. Under Achievement-orientation they complete 1.85 more on the average than a comparable group of subjects with high *n* Achievement did under the Relaxed orientation, a gain which is significant beyond the 1 per cent level of confidence ($t = 3.78$). At the same time, the gain shown among subjects with low *n* Achievement is much less (.55) and not significant ($t = 1.10$). The difference between these mean gains is 1.30 with a *t* of 1.85 which yields a *p* of about .07. Nevertheless, the subjects with high *n* Achievement never perform *significantly* better than those with low *n* Achievement. In fact, under the Relaxed condition they perform significantly worse. We are not sure why this is so, although it does indicate a certain reality orientation on the part of those with high motivation. After all, why work hard if the experimenter says it is not important to do so? When the atmosphere becomes a little more motivating, the high group tends to complete more tasks on the average, but the difference is not significant. Later in this chapter, fairly substantial evidence will be presented which indicates that people with high *n* Achievement do perform and learn more rapidly than people with low *n* Achievement. But this is only part of the story.

Three-way breakdowns similar to those shown in Tables 8.1 and 8.2 were also made for each of the three conditions reported here. Under Relaxed and Task orientations the number of tasks completed was essentially linearly related to *n* Achievement score (the relation for the Relaxed condition is, of course, an inverse one), but under Achievement orientation we find again the curvilinear trend. Table 8.4 underlines once more the fact that the middle n Achievement group seems to be atypical. Under Achievement-orienting conditions, whether they are writing an essay which is to be graded, or trying to complete tasks so as to appear intelligent, they appear to be somewhat inhibited in response output as compared with other subjects.

TABLE 8.4. Mean number of tasks completed for subjects with low, moderate, and high n Achievement scores under Achievement orientation

		n ACHIEVEMENT SCORE (3 STORIES)		
		Low (−2 to 2)	Moderate (3 to 7)	High (8 and above)
	N	10	9	9
	Mean	10.70	9.33	10.78
	SD	1.95	1.08	1.11
		Low vs. (Mid + High)	Mid vs. (High + Low)	High vs. (Mid +Low)
t		.89	2.61	1.30
p		—	<.05	—

Why, then, should the middle n Achievement group be so productive on the Rorschach? This finding might make sense if we made the assumptions that the subjects in the middle n Achievement group are *anxious* about achievement, and that anxiety produces a great amount of variable behavior. We might then expect a large number of spontaneous responses in a fairly free situation like the Rorschach, but interference with efficiency when an integrated series of acts is required, as in solving problems or writing a coherent essay. Specifically, we might infer that the middle n Achievement group is primarily concerned about failure, and is bothered by anticipations of failure. Although this hypothesis is no more than suggested by the data, it seems worth entertaining as we look at other relationships. As for the subjects with high n Achievement, their response output seems on the whole to be relatively high when the situation is achievement-related (words in essay, tasks completed under Achievement orientation) but relatively low when it is not (Rorschach responses, tasks completed under Relaxed orientation).

8.2 **Performance and learning.** Considering the number of tasks completed by groups of individuals with different *n* Achievement scores leads directly into the next problem, which has concerned us from the beginning of our research. What is the relationship between *n* Achievement score and learning or efficiency in various types of performance? Nearly everyone, we think, would expect that motivation should lead to some kind of faster or more efficient performance if adequate opportunity is given for such an increment in performance. (In Atkinson's experiment, because the primary interest was in the recall of completed and incompleted tasks, the situation was designed so as to restrict variation in the number of tasks completed. Therefore, the highly motivated subjects were not given a fair chance to exhibit superior performance.) If the *n* Achievement score is a measure of motivation, should it not be significantly related to work output in various types of tasks? Our first finding in this general area is reported by Clark and McClelland (1950). It concerns the relationship between *n* Achievement (A) and number of words obtained in successive minutes of an Anagrams test. The correlations obtained are reproduced in Table 8.5.

TABLE 8.5. Product-moment correlations between output on successive two-minute periods of an anagrams test and *n* Achievement score (A) under Neutral ($N = 39$) and Achievement-oriented conditions ($N = 30$)

Condition	SUCCESSIVE TWO-MINUTE ANAGRAMS TESTS					
	1	*2*	*3*	*4*	*5*	*6*
Neutral	.00	.16	.43	.23	.15	.00
Achievement-oriented ..	.11	−.05	.01	.28	.16	.17

The Anagrams test, which required the subjects to make as many words as they could out of the word *generation,* was twelve minutes in length. Subjects were required to make a check mark every minute so that the output could be computed for successive one, two, or four-minute periods. In every breakdown for the Neutral condition it was apparent that there was a significant relationship between n Achievement score and the middle section of the output curve for Anagrams. The results for two-minute periods are reported in Table 8.5, which shows that the correlations form a symmetrical pattern around the third two-minute period, at which point the correlation is significant beyond the 1 per cent level of confidence. Under Achievement-oriented conditions, none of the correlations is significant at the 5 per cent level of confidence, but again there is an indication of a fairly sizable relationship somewhere in the center of the test.

We were puzzled by this finding and wanted to discover whether there were any peculiar characteristics of the output curve for Anagrams at this point which might explain the relationship. Unfortunately, output on any particular minute in a test of this sort is a function of the number of possible words still left to be taken out of the key word. That is, it becomes increasingly more difficult to make words out of the key word as the familiar words are exhausted. In an attempt to correct for this, Clark and McClelland computed relative output curves based upon an hypothetical maximum of 80 words which could be made in the time allotted. On this basis it was apparent that the group of subjects as a whole did *relatively* poorer in the third two-minute period than at any other point in the twelve-minute period. It appeared that subjects had slackened off in their efforts somewhat in the middle of the rather long and repetitive task. Further analysis showed that the high n Achievement subjects slacked off significantly less than the low n Achievement subjects. In short, n Achievement seemed to be positively correlated with the ability to resist the "sag" in the middle of the output curve, a fact supported by the discovery that in the Achievement-oriented condition there was significantly less of a drop in absolute output ($p < .02$) from the first to the third two-minute period than in the Neutral condition. Thus, we might explain the failure of *n* Achievement to correlate significantly with the middle section of anagrams under Achievement-orientation by the fact that all subjects in this group were so highly motivated that the "sag" effect was reduced, and in consequence, the opportunity for correlation with *n* Achievement score was also reduced.

On the whole, these results were interesting but hardly conclusive. Since we had run into major difficulties with a task which imposed a limitation on output in successive time periods, we decided to repeat the experiment using a task similar in nature to anagrams but without this defect. Lowell (1952) constructed a Scrambled Words test which consisted of 240 four-, five-, and six-letter disarranged words selected from the first 500 most frequently used words in the Thorndike-Lorge Word List (1944). The subjects were handed a booklet containing 10 pages, each containing 24 scrambled words. They were allowed two minutes to work on each page. The ten different pages were arranged in ten different orders, and tests were randomly distributed among subjects in order to randomize any differences in difficulty at successive periods in the output curve. The test was administered *after* the subjects had taken one of the equivalent three-picture forms of the TAT measure under Neutral conditions.

The following instructions were printed on the outside cover:

On the following pages you will find common words that have been scrambled by changing the order of the letters. Try to make a word out of the letters and write it in the space on the right.
Example: WTSE west
If you find any of those words difficult to unscramble, skip them

and go on to the next. You may have an opportunity later to come back and work on the ones you find difficult. Please do not start until the signal is given and turn the pages when (and only when) instructed to do so.

The experimenter asked the subjects' co-operation in turning the pages promptly when asked to do so at the end of two minutes, explaining that they were not expected to be able to complete all the words in such a short time. A week later the experimenter returned, explained that he had not been able to complete his work the week before, administered the other three-picture equivalent form of the TAT measure of *n* Achievement and also an Additions test. The Additions test was set up like the Scrambled Words task, with 10 pages on each of which there were several sets of two three-digit numbers to be added and a time limit of one minute per page.

To obtain an *n* Achievement score (C) for each subject, Lowell combined the scores obtained on the two occasions. He then divided the distribution of over-all *n* Achievement scores into High and Low halves at the mean and obtained the mean word output for 10 two-minute periods for each half of the distribution shown in Table 8.6. The obvious conclusion

TABLE 8.6. Mean output of scrambled words per two-minute period for subjects with high and low *n* Achievement scores (C)

| | \multicolumn{11}{c}{Two-Minute Periods} | | | | | | | | | | |
	1	2	3	4	5	6	7	8	9	10	Total
High *n* Achievement (N = 19) ..	9.2	10.4	11.5	11.2	11.6	11.8	12.2	10.9	12.0	12.9	113.7
Low *n* Achievement (N = 21) ..	9.9	9.5	10.1	10.1	10.4	10.8	10.4	9.6	9.6	10.3	100.8
Mean Difference	.7	.8	1.4	1.1	1.2	1.0	1.8	1.3	2.4	2.6	12.9

to be drawn from this table is that the high *n* Achievement group shows evidence of increasing output or *learning*, whereas the low *n* Achievement group does not. The trend is shown clearly in Figure 8.1 in which means from adjacent periods have been combined to make it stand out more. Several tests of significance can be made to document this trend. In the first place, the high *n* Achievement group shows

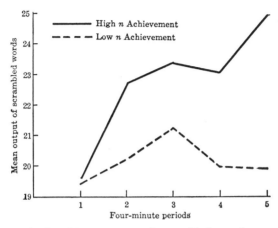

FIG. 8.1. Mean output of scrambled words per four-minute period for subjects with high and low *n* Achievement scores.

a mean gain in output from the first to the last four-minute period of 5.32 words ($SD = 3.89$); whereas, the low *n* Achievement group shows a gain of only .43 ($SD = 4.81$), a difference in gains of 4.89 which is significant well beyond the 1 per cent level of confidence ($t = 3.76$). In the second place, various tests of the significance of regression in the high and low groups and of the differences between them can be made. The difficulty is that the successive measurements are not independent, because they were made on the same individuals. There seems to be no general agreement as to the best way to circumvent this difficulty. The interested reader can consult Alexander (1946), Lindquist (1947), and Kogan (1948) for recent treatments of this problem. We have decided that a slight modification of Alexander's treatment is most appropriate for our particular data. Table 8.7 below presents this analysis.

TABLE 8.7. F tests of the significance of regression and difference between regressions for high and low n Achievement groups on the scrambled words task

Source	HIGH n ACHIEVEMENT $N = 190$ (19 individuals, 10 trials)		
	df	Sums of Squares	Variance Estimate
Total	189	3952.5	
Individual Deviations from Individual Regression	152	936.9	6.2
Between Individual Regressions	18	123.6	
Between Individual Means	18	2776.0	
Group Regression	1	116.0	116.0

$$F = \frac{\text{Group Regression}}{\text{Individual Deviations from Individual Regression}} = 18.7, \ p < .001$$

Source	LOW n ACHIEVEMENT $N = 210$ (21 individuals, 10 trials)		
	df	Sums of Squares	Variance Estimate *
Total	209	3883.6	
Individual Deviations from Individual Regression	168	1087.2	6.5
Between Individual Regressions	20	113.1	
Between Individual Means	20	2682.9	
Group Regression	1	0.4	0.4

$$F = \frac{\text{Group Regression}}{\text{Individual Deviations from Individual Regression}} = .06, \ p \ —$$

Source	HIGH VS. LOW n ACHIEVEMENT		
	df	Sums of Squares	Variance Estimate
Between Group Regressions	1	54.0	54.0
Combined between Individual Regressions	38	236.7	6.2

$$F = \frac{\text{Between Group Regressions}}{\text{Combined between Individual Regressions}} = 8.7, \ p < .01$$

* One might wonder why the variance estimate for the deviations from individual regression is so much larger than the variance due to group regression for the group with low

A detailed discussion of the rationale for this particular analysis is well beyond the scope of the present book. Let it suffice to say that several different analyses were made of these data, all of which demonstrated that the regression in the high *n* Achievement group was significantly greater than that for the low *n* Achievement group.

These results are of very great importance for two reasons. In the first place, they provide an alternative explanation for the correlation obtained between *n* Achievement score and the middle section of the Anagrams test. Output is bound to decline on successive minutes of Anagrams, because it becomes progressively harder to get words out of the key word. Consequently, the effect of learning would be to lessen the drop in output, which is exactly what we found for the high *n* Achievement group. According to this line of reasoning, *n* Achievement is correlated only with the middle section of the Anagrams test, because only there can the superior learning of highly motivated subjects show up. That is to say, in the early stages of the task the learning has not progressed far enough to cause a significant difference. In the late stages of performance there are very few words available (especially for the high *n* Achievement group), and with the supply of words just about exhausted there is no opportunity for superior learning to be exhibited. If this argument is correct, we should expect that in Lowell's Scrambled Words task the correlation between *n* Achievement and output on successive periods should increase regularly from the first to last periods as the effects of learning grow more pronounced. The correlations he obtained were as follows:

n Achievement. This is probably an artifact due to the nature of the experimental design. That is, there were ten different sequences for the lists of scrambled words and this sequence difference would enter into the component of variability due to deviations from individual regression, whereas it would not enter into the variability due to group regression. What this means is that there might be a small significant regression in the low *n* Achievement group, but the experiment was not designed to test for it. However, this defect in no way invalidates the primary objective of the analysis which is to show significantly greater regression in the high *n* Achievement group.

Product-Moment	SUCCESSIVE FOUR-MINUTE PERIODS				
	1	*2*	*3*	*4*	*5*
Correlations between n Achievement and Output on Scrambled Words ($N = 40$)	.04	.14	.16	.18	.25

Although none of these correlations reaches the 5 per cent level of significance, they show the predicted trend in a very regular fashion. Thus, the results of the two experiments seem consistent. In both cases a correlation between n Achievement and performance appears where opportunity for learning permits the higher n Achievement group to perform at a superior rate.

The second reason why these results are so important is that some theorists, notably Miller (1951), have argued that the decisive criterion for determining whether a motive is involved in performance is whether or not it can produce learning. Since there is clear evidence of learning in the high n Achievement group, it can be argued that the n Achievement score is a measure of motivation.

As one precaution, however, we should perhaps check to see whether the high and low n Achievement groups differ in intelligence. ACE Psychological Examination results were available for most of the subjects and the relevant comparisons are made in Table 8.8. Subjects having high n Achievement scores do significantly better on the linguistic section of the test. Does this mean that our differences may be entirely due to intelligence? There are a number of ways to check this possibility. One very simple way is to get the partial correlation between n Achievement and the increase in Scrambled Words output from the first to the fifth four-minute period with the linguistic score on the ACE held constant. That is to say, both the more highly motivated and more intelligent individuals should show greater speed of learning and should, therefore, have a greater gain in output from the first to the last time period. By partialing out the effects of intelligence

TABLE 8.8. Mean quantitative and linguistic test scores on the ACE psychological examination for college freshmen for subjects with high and low *n* Achievement scores

	Quantitative Score	*Linguistic Score*
High *n* Achievement		
($N = 17$)		
Mean	52.2	79.9
SD	11.69	16.15
Low *n* Achievement		
($N = 18$)		
Mean	48.8	69.5
SD	9.39	10.44
Mean Difference	3.4	10.4
SE diff.	3.69	4.71
t	.92	2.18
p	—	$<.05$

(ACE), we can determine what degree of relationship remains between *n* Achievement alone and Scrambled Words output. The results of this analysis are as follows:

1. Increase in Scrambled Words Output from First to Fifth Four-Minute Period
2. *n* Achievement Score
3. Score on Linguistic Scale of ACE

$$r_{12} = .48$$
$$r_{23} = .28$$
$$r_{13} = .25$$
$$r_{12.3} = .44$$

Thus it can be seen that even with the effects of intelligence or ability held constant, there is a significant ($p = .01$) relationship between *n* Achievement and increase in Scrambled Words output.

The above finding is doubly significant, because in partialing out the effects of the ACE we are probably washing out some contribution of motivational as well as intellectual factors. That is, the ACE is undoubtedly in part a function of past learning, and past learning (if current learning theory is correct) is a function of motivational factors.

Let us now consider Lowell's findings with respect to n Achievement and the Additions task. Although there is no significant difference in Q score for the two groups, the high n Achievement group does significantly better than the low group on an Additions task also administered by Lowell. Output on this task for successive two-minute periods is presented in Table 8.9. Notice that the superior performance of the highly motivated group is evident from the start, and there are no trends either in the high or low group means or in the

TABLE 8.9. Mean number of addition problems solved per two-minute period for subjects with high and low n Achievement scores

	Two-Minute Periods					
	1	2	3	4	5	Total
High n Achievement ... (N = 19)	31.6	32.7	29.9	31.5	31.7	157.4
Low n Achievement .... (N = 21)	26.7	26.7	25.0	26.2	26.0	130.6
Mean Difference (H-L)	4.9	6.0	4.9	5.3	5.7	27.8

differences between them. This is exactly what might be expected for a task like simple addition for which a person's skill is already at its maximum, and where the opportunity for learning new ways of doing the problems to increase speed of performance is not present. For the same reason, the over-all difference in output between the high and low groups is significant here, whereas it was not in the Scrambled Words task. The total mean difference of 27.8 has a standard error of 11.54 which yields a t value of 2.40 ($p < .05$). To put this finding in another way, additional energy in the Scrambled Words task is not enough to produce a difference in output until the subjects have learned new and better ways of unscrambling words. Thus, the two motivation groups start out about equal, but gradually the one with higher motivation pulls ahead. With the results of the early trials added in, the over-all difference is not significant. However, as we have shown, the difference between the regression lines is significant. With the Additions task, however, the effects of added motivation can be shown from the first trial since there is nothing new to be learned, and the over-all difference in performance is, as a result, significant. In summary, then, Lowell's experiments have demonstrated that high *n* Achievement score is associated with learning when learning is required (or possible) and with speed of performance when it is not.

8.3 **College grades.** The relation of *n* Achievement score to college grades is obviously a point of very great practical importance. On the other hand, it is of dubious theoretical significance, since grades in college are affected by so many unknown factors. For the sake of those who might be interested in pursuing the practical problem, we will present here some of the incidental relationships we have found in the course of our various studies. In one sample of 30 Wesleyan male students, most of whom were veterans of World War II, the correlation between *n* Achievement score (C) and the average grade for the semester during which the test was taken and the two *succeeding* semesters was .51 ($p < .01$). On these same subjects we had verbal and mathematical Scholastic Aptitude Test scores which we combined to get an over-all estimate of ability. With this measure we obtained the following relationships:

Correlation of combined SAT score and grades 48
Correlation of combined SAT score and *n* Achievement 42
Correlation of *n* Achievement and grades 51
Correlation of *n* Achievement with grades adjusted for
  SAT score 39

Again we are faced with an indeterminacy in either adjusting the grades for SAT score or partialing out its effects. When we do so, we are assuming that SAT score is not itself in part a function of n Achievement, an assumption we really are not justified in making. In any case, even when we may be taking out in this way some of the n Achievement whose effect we are interested in measuring, the relationship between n Achievement and college grades is significant.

Since this result looked promising, we checked it in the sample of subjects who had participated in the Scrambled Words and Additions tasks just reported. For these subjects from Lowell's experiment at Trinity College there was available an n Achievement score based on six stories, three of which were written on one occasion and the other three a week later, and a grade point average based on the semester in which the test was taken and the *preceding* semester. The correlation between n Achievement and grade point average was .05 ($N = 40$). What accounts for this difference? Unfortunately, there are many possibilities: (1) Picture H, which shows a boy apparently studying, was not included in the measure used by Lowell. Possibly it is necessary to introduce cues relating to the task for which achievement predictions are being made in order to get a measure of n Achievement which will predict scores for that task. This seemed especially likely, since there was a large number of subjects (eight) in Lowell's low n Achievement group who had very high grades. It looked as if the pictures had passed them by, so to speak, and not reflected their n Achievement. What may have been a relevant cue for them (Picture H) was not included in the set of pictures. This argument is not conclusively contradicted by the finding that if Picture H is subtracted from the Wesleyan group, the correlation only drops from .51 to .49, since the associations cued off by it may affect subsequent pictures in the series. (2) The subjects used in the Wesleyan group were more highly selected for co-operativeness than Lowell's subjects. This came about indirectly because a rather extensive testing program involving *n* Achievement was conducted on the very large elementary psychology class of which they were members. The selection resulted from the fact that only those individuals were used whose records were complete on all the tests administered. Records could be incomplete because the subjects were absent on the day the tests were administered, or because they failed to follow instructions accurately on some particular test. In this way we probably managed to get a group who were highly cooperative, whereas Lowell's subjects had been through no such selection procedure. Again this might explain the failure to pick up any *n* Achievement in eight subjects who had grade point averages in the eighties. They simply may not have taken the test seriously. This has suggested to us that future workers in this field introduce some kind of a screening picture which will pick out those who are not co-operating. (3) A final partial explanation might be that the Wesleyan correlation involved *predicting* grades, whereas the Trinity one involved largely *postdicting* them. It may be that the measure of motivation has a higher relation to future than to past grades. As a partial check on this hypothesis and on the simplest one of all, that our first result may have been chance after all, we were able to find 19 other subjects in the Wesleyan group who were not conspicuously co-operators and on whom we had *n* Achievement scores and college grades for the semester in which the test was given and the preceding semester. For this group the correlation was .32, which is still appreciable though considerably lower than before, and below the 5 per cent level of significance.

Lowell had another group of 21 subjects who were administered one form of the measure of *n* Achievement under Neutral conditions and another form under Achievement-oriented conditions. He found that the correlation between past grades and *n* Achievement scores obtained under Achievement-orientation was .33. But most startling of all, the correlation with the difference between Neutral and Achievement-oriented n Achievement scores was .53 ($p < .05$). Those subjects whose scores increased most as a result of Achievement-orientation had higher college grades. This finding opens up a whole new area for speculation and experimental exploration. Thus, for instance, it could be argued that if you were trying to predict excellence of performance when achievement cues are present (i.e., under pressure), then the difference in n Achievement scores between Neutral and Achievement-oriented conditions might be the best measure of sensitivity to the demands of the situation. If, on the other hand, you wanted to predict who would be most apt to work hard when the cues did not demand it, then the n Achievement score obtained under Neutral conditions might be best. It is even possible that educational institutions differ in the amount of "pressure" or emphasis that is put on academic achievement. Consequently, the n Achievement score one would use for predicting grades in a particular institution would be a function of whether it was a "low pressure" or "high pressure" institution, since it is reasonable to expect that different people would get good grades in the two places. Our preliminary experience in this field is interesting and suggestive, but no more than this. It is apparent that anyone seriously interested in this problem would have to engage in a major research program that would take into account such factors as we have mentioned.

Another relevant study has been made by H. H. Morgan (1951) as part of his Ph.D. dissertation. Morgan was interested in various personality correlates of "achievers" and "non-achievers." All the subjects in these two groups had scored at or beyond the 96th percentile on the ACE according to University of Minnesota norms. The "achievers," however, had an honor point ratio of 2.1 or better; whereas the "non-achievers" had an honor point ratio of 1.2 or less. Morgan administered a six-picture measure of *n* Achievement to 40 "achievers" and 30 "non-achievers." The mean *n* Achievement score (C) for the "achievers" was 17.80; that for the "non-achievers" was 13.47. This difference yielded a *t* of 2.3 with a *p* value of about .02. Thus, with scholastic aptitude held constant, those individuals with high academic grades obtain reliably higher *n* Achievement scores than those with low academic grades.

As a final note on the complexity of the situation, we should report that Atkinson (1950), working with University of Michigan students who volunteered to take the "test of creative imagination" a half hour before the final examination in a psychology course, obtained a correlation between *n* Achievement score (C) and general grade point average (past performance) of $-.14$ ($N = 38$). When the effects of different mid-semester standing in that particular psychology course are partialed out, the correlation becomes $-.31$.

The correlation between *n* Achievement score (C) and mid-semester standing in the course was .30, and increased to .40 when the effects of general academic standing were partialed out. Once again it is apparent that the particular conditions under which the test is taken are of very great importance. Here the subjects were motivated by situational cues, but unlike Lowell's subjects, they were not motivated by general instructions and a series of tasks purporting to measure intelligence, leadership capacity, and so on. They were motivated specifically to do well on an examination in a particular course. This specific orientation might account for the correlation with standing in the course. The negative correlation with general grade point average is a question to ponder. The plain fact of the matter is that this whole area needs much more carefully planned research than we have conducted. Our interest has always been primarily in other problems and the relationships reported here have been incidental to other findings. However, we think that they are sufficiently suggestive to warrant further study. This is espe-cially true in view of the fact that we have been working with a relatively unreliable measure of only three or four stories in most of these studies, and that correlations between n Achievement and grades or intelligence are bound to be at-tenuated by the restriction in range in both of these measures that results from employing college students as subjects.

8.4 **Level of aspiration and judgment.** Under this heading we include several studies of the effects of achievement mo-tivation on level of aspiration as measured in various ways. Practically the only thing they show in common is a tend-ency for judgment to be inaccurate in the direction of wish-fulfillment when reality factors are minimized. To begin with, let us take a look at some negative results on self-ratings of n Achievement. In Lowell's experiment (1950) in which a measure of n Achievement (C) was obtained from two sets of three pictures administered a week apart, subjects were told, after the second three-picture measure, that the primary purpose of the testing had been to obtain a measure of achievement motivation. They were then asked to fill out a brief self-rating questionnaire on their own achievement mo-tivation. He explained to them that the measure was in an experimental stage, and that he wanted to compare his esti-mate of achievement motivation with their own ratings. It was further explained that the questionnaire results would be kept confidential and would in no way affect their grades in the course. The three questions on the rating sheet were:

1. How hard do you usually strive for personal achievement?
2. How many times do you really try hard to achieve?
3. How hard did you try on these tests you took today?

The tests referred to in Question 3 included both the meas-ure of n Achievement and the Additions task. Opposite each question was a six-point rating scale with instructions to circle the number which corresponded to their answer to the question. A low number (1) indicated high *n* Achievement, and a high number (6), low *n* Achievement. The results are presented in Table 8.10. None of these differences even ap-

TABLE 8.10. Mean self-ratings on achievement motivation for subjects with high and low *n* Achievement scores

	Question 1	Question 2	Question 3	All Questions
High *n* Achievement (N = 19)				
Mean	2.42	2.52	2.84	7.78
SD	.67	.76	1.36	2.04
Low *n* Achievement (N = 21)				
Mean	2.29	2.81	2.90	8.00
SD	.88	1.04	.97	2.32

proaches significance, nor are they consistent with one another. The only trend found in what appears otherwise to be a collection of random numbers is a curvilinear relationship such that the middle third of the *n* Achievement score distribution in answer to all three questions rates itself on the average as *less* motivated for achievement than either the high or the low thirds. This trend is most marked for Question 2 (as suggested by the high SD for the low group) where the figures for the four quarters of the distribution from low to high are: 2.44, 3.00, 2.70, 2.54. In other words, if the group with the very lowest *n* Achievement scores were eliminated, there would be a fairly regular increase in self-ratings of achievement motivation as *n* Achievement score increases. Even though it might be attractive to speculate about the defensive high ratings of the poorly motivated group, we are really not justified in doing so, since the trends do not approach significance. The safest conclusion from the data we have is that there appears to be no very marked relationship between self-judgments of n Achievement and our n Achievement scores derived from projective records.

Some findings which are a little more relevant to the notion of level of aspiration concern the number of tries subjects with high and low n Achievement made in the Scrambled Words task. The subjects are the same as in the self-rating study. Lowell computed the number of incorrect words constructed by those with high and low n Achievement scores. He found that the 19 subjects in the high n Achievement group made an average of 5.4 incorrect tries ($SD = 3.8$) while the 21 subjects in the low group made only 2.6 on the average ($SD = 3.5$). The mean difference of 2.8 is significant at the 5 per cent level of confidence ($t = 2.37$), indicating that the more highly motivated subjects made more errors. This is an indirect indication that their level of achievement aspiration tended to be somewhat unrealistically high. That is, the errors could easily be attributed to "trying too hard" or to haste in their attempt to perform very well. Incidentally, the conclusions reported earlier in connection with Table 8.7 on the significant regression in the performance of the high n Achievement subjects are not changed by taking out the incorrect tries. In other words, the learning result is not simply a function of the high group throwing in an increasing number of incorrect words.

Atkinson (1950) has performed the experiment which is more directly related to techniques currently used for measuring level of aspiration. The week before the final exam in a course in elementary psychology the instructor asked his students to show up a half hour before the examination began to participate in some research in which he was engaged. It was explained that they did not have to come if they felt that it would in any way interfere with their performance on the exam, that their coming would have nothing to do with the grade in the course, but that he would appreciate as many volunteers as possible. On the morning of the final examination approximately one-half of the class showed up and was given a four-picture form of the measure of *n* Achievement (Pictures *B, H, G,* and *F*). The results on picture *F* (Boy with the violin) were not used because, as previously demonstrated (Chap. VII), this picture in terms of internal consistency is not a valid measure of *n* Achievement. As soon as the students finished writing the stories, they were given the following instructions:

The maximum score you can get on the exam that you will take in a few minutes is 100. You could expect to get 25 by chance, i.e., by sheer guessing. Under your name on the back of the story form, please indicate the score that you *expect* to make on the exam.

Also please note what quarter of the class you were in at midterm. If you were in the first quarter, write "1," second quarter, "2," etc.

Also please note your over-all scholastic average, A, B, C, D. Use plus or minus to be as accurate as possible.

Also, in a few words, write what you think the purpose of this experiment is. It is important that I know what you thought it was all about.

The *n* Achievement score (C) obtained under these circumstances was undoubtedly influenced by all the achievement cues of the week of examinations and particularly those having to do with the particular final examination that they would soon take. One of the purposes of the experiment was to see whether Achievement orientation in this real-life situation would have an effect different from the standard Achievement-orienting instructions that had been used. Presumably, the *n* Achievement scores obtained in this situation reflect motivation aroused by the specific cues in the situation. The *n* Achievement scores obtained were related to expected exam grade and various other measures. It should be remembered that whatever relationships we find may not apply when the *n* Achievement score is obtained under more normal testing conditions.

Since the level of aspiration requested ("What do you *ex-*

pect to get . . .") ought to be influenced to a considerable extent by past performance or "reality," an attempt was made to eliminate the influence of reality determinants by partial correlation as indicated in Table 8.11.

TABLE 8.11. Product-moment correlations between *n* Achievement score, expected examination grades, and grades in course ($N = 38$)

1. *n* Achievement Score
2. Expected Examination Grade (Level of Aspiration)
3. General Grade Point Average (General Past Performance)
4. Mid-Term Average in the Course (Specific Past Performance)

$$r_{12} = .24 \qquad r_{34} = .41$$
$$r_{13} = -.14 \qquad r_{34} = .43$$
$$r_{14} = .30 \qquad r_{12.3} = .30$$
$$r_{23} = .30 \qquad r_{12.34} = .19$$

$r = .33$ and $.42$ at the 5% and 1% levels of confidence respectively for both the regular and partial correlations.

The table shows that the correlation between *n* Achievement and expected exam grade is positive but low and insignificant. Comparatively, the reality factors of general grade point average and standing in the course correlate higher with expected grade. This makes sense in terms of the way the question was asked. When an attempt is made to partial out the influence of these determinants, however, the results are confusing and somewhat contradictory. If grade point average is partialed out, the correlation between *n* Achievement and expected grade increases, but if course standing is also partialed out, it decreases. In any case, most of the correlations fall below the level of significance.

Perhaps a more psychologically meaningful analysis is possible. Suppose that instead of using partial correlations, we attempt to reduce the influence of reality by choosing those subjects for whom the two reality determinants *conflict*. There will be some subjects whose standing in the course is high, but whose general academic standing is not and vice versa. In both cases the subjects should be in some doubt as to what to expect on the basis of past experience and, as a result, less influenced in their judgments by past experience. On the other hand, subjects who had done either well or poorly both in general and in this course should make their exam judgments largely in terms of these unambiguous reality determinants. To test this hypothesis, the distributions of grade point averages and mid-term class standings were each divided into thirds. Fifteen subjects appeared in the same third of both distributions. For them there should be little conflict in the reality determinants of level of aspiration. The other 23 subjects appeared in different thirds of the two distributions. For them the correlation between *n* Achievement score and level of aspiration was .45 ($p < .05$), whereas for the other 15 subjects it was —.23. The difference between the two correlations (using Z transformations) is also significant ($p < .05$). In other words, when reality determinants conflict, judgment about future performance tends to be positively related to *n* Achievement score. When, on the other hand, reality determinants are consistent, the relation between *n* Achievement and level of aspiration disappears and is perhaps even negative.

This finding is of some importance for level of aspiration theory if confirmed in other experiments. It is a customary assumption that level of aspiration is determined by motivational and reality factors. In the present instance the validity of the assumption, under certain conditions, has been demonstrated experimentally with independent measures of the two determinants.

An interesting incidental finding in the same investigation is the relationship between *n* Achievement score and discrepancy between perceived general academic standing and actual academic standing. The instructions called for an estimate in terms of letter grades (with a plus or minus) of general grade point average. This gave some opportunity for rounding errors either up or down. These letter grades were then converted into the equivalent grade point score and subtracted from the actual grade point score. The 21 subjects with n Achievement scores above the mean showed a mean positive discrepancy of .17, indicating that they overestimated their grade point standing by about .2 of a point. The 17 subjects with n Achievement scores below the mean, however, stated their averages with remarkable accuracy, their mean discrepancy score being only .018. The expected difference between the means in the given direction is not highly significant ($t = 1.31$, $p < .10$), nor is the correlation between discrepancy score and n Achievement ($r = .21$), but the relationship is in the same direction as between n Achievement and estimated future performance on an exam. In both cases high achievement motivation tends to lead subjects to overestimate their actual or expected performance, but when the reality determinants are strong, the relationship is not marked.

8.5 Perception and thought. One of the most interesting areas of investigation that we have explored with the n Achievement measure has been that which may be referred to loosely as "perceiving" or "thinking." We have tried to find out whether subjects with high n Achievement view the world differently from other people. Are they more sensitive to some kinds of stimulation, to certain types of objects or activities? Do they think habitually in different categories? Our research has employed four types of measures—linguistic usage, the Sentence Completion Test, the Rorschach test, and recognition data of the sort popularized by Bruner, Postman, and associates (see Bruner, 1951; Postman, 1951).

8.5.1 *Linguistic usage.* Language is potentially a very valuable tool for studying modes of thought, as Sanford (1942), Kluckhohn and Leighton (1947), and many others have pointed out. The frequency with which a person employs a certain grammatical category such as nouns, verbs, adjectives, and the like has been shown to be related to various personality characteristics. This makes good theoretical sense. If a person thinks vaguely, he will be likely to choose vague expressions like abstract nouns. If he is more interested in viewing life than in actively participating in it, he is perhaps apt to use relatively more adjectives than verbs, and so on. One could argue that language is the best, if not the only, operational way at present of investigating thought patterns.

Starting with this general assumption, Zatzkis (1949) attempted to predict what linguistic patterns would be shown more frequently by men with high *n* Achievement. In general, he followed the scoring categories used to obtain the measure of *n* Achievement and attempted to find linguistic equivalents for them. That is, it can be argued that since the general definition of *n* Achievement is stated in terms of *Competition with a Standard,* the frequency of *adverbs of degree* (better, very, rather, and so forth) should be higher in the records of subjects with high *n* Achievement. In a similar fashion he predicted that *abstract nouns* should reflect the general *Long-Term Involvement* scoring category; *negations* and *dependent clauses,* the *Obstacle* category; *I* references, a sort of *ego-involvement* category; and *future tenses,* the *Anticipatory Goal State* category. The way in which he obtained a language sample by asking the subjects to write an essay in class on "What I would ideally like to get out of a course in psychology" has been described earlier. It need only be added here that the essay was written about a month after the imaginative measure of *n* Achievement had been obtained, and that the nature of the topic was such as to orient students toward an achievement goal (life work, educational goals, and so on). Zatzkis did not argue that linguistic modes characteristic of high *n* Achievement would appear in all sorts of situations (in writing a love letter, for example) but only in situations which contained achievement cues. An experiment which tests the generalizations of such linguistic habits has

counts for 14 subjects, half in the high and half in the low *n* Achievement groups, and two other workers using Zatzkis' criteria scored the essays of 12 more subjects to increase the size of the sample. One subject in the high *n* Achievement group was discarded because he showed clear evidence in his essay of attempting to adopt a formal literary style (e.g., he used "the writer" whenever he meant "I") which we thought would interfere with getting a valid measure of his personally-determined, psycho-grammatical usage.

The difference between the high and low *n* Achievement groups in number of adverbs of degree used was not significant, although the difference is in the expected direction. A further check on this relationship should be made with a larger number of subjects and perhaps with other words involving comparisons (i.e., adjectives) included. The large and significant difference in the abstract noun category is particularly interesting. An abstract noun was not defined by Zatzkis in accordance with strict grammatical usage. He counted any noun as abstract whose referent could not be "pointed to," with a few specific exceptions. He really defined concrete nouns and considered anything which did not fall into this category as abstract. Thus, the words *body, machine, mesomorph, brain, book, game* are all concrete; whereas the words *personality, character, occupation, phase, belief* are all abstract. He further specifically excluded from the abstract category: (1) collective nouns if the things they referred to could be individually "pointed to" (e.g., *people*); (2) any noun derived from the sensory field (e.g., *warmth, red, sound*), since the denoting operation should not be limited to what can be seen and pointed at; (3) nouns referring to time, space, and amount (*length, month*); (4) any noun which can also be used as a verb to indicate activity (e.g., *speaking, running*), with the exception of mental activity (e.g., *thinking* which was considered abstract); (5) names of college subjects (*psychology*) or professions (*medicine*).

The interesting point about the higher number of abstract nouns in the high n Achievement group is that this is exactly what should characterize the thinking of highly motivated people, if McClelland's theoretical analysis of how motives are formed (1951) is correct. He argues that motives are acquired early in life at a time when it is difficult for the child to determine just exactly what class of cues is associated with affective change. That is, motives involve *generalized* associations in contrast to habits which involve specific associations based on easily identifiable stimuli, regular rewards and punishments, and the like. One could argue on the basis of this hypothesis that the achievement cues in the instructions for the essay elicit generalized associations or thoughts for the subjects with high motivation which express themselves in abstract nouns referring to "life and work," "one's occupation," "philosophy of life," "standard of action," "realms of knowledge," and so on. In the low n Achievement group, the same cues set off associations that deal with specific course content material rather than with general aspirations, and the nouns used to express these associations are more apt to be concrete.

The self-references are fairly evenly divided between the high and low groups. This is not too surprising, in view of the fact that the logic of how this category is derived from the n Achievement scoring system is not perfectly clear.

The significantly larger number of negations and dependent clauses in the low n Achievement group is revealing. It strongly suggests that subjects with low n Achievement tend to think more often than the subjects with high n Achievement of uncertainties, obstacles, and possible contingencies when achievement associations are aroused. They are more aware of the "ifs," "whens," "buts," and "nots" of achievement. But how can this be reconciled with the fact that we score Bw (external blocks in the way of achievement) *positively* for n Achievement? It probably cannot be. Of all the categories we have decided to score in the system presented in this book,

Bw is the only one which does not shift at or beyond the .05 probability level in our initial criterial groups (see Figure 5.1). This is true despite the fact that the *opportunity* for *Bw* to appear was considerably greater in the achievement-arousal groups since they produced more achievement-related stories. If opportunity is equalized by asking whether or not *Bw* is more likely to appear *in an achievement story* written under Relaxed or Achievement-oriented conditions, the trend is not inconsistent with what is obtained here. The achievement-related stories written under Relaxed conditions actually contain proportionally *more* instances of *Bw* (26.1 per cent) than those written under Achievement-oriented conditions (10.6 per cent). In short, we may well have to revise our scoring system once more and leave out *Bw*.

Finally, the increase in anticipatory tenses is entirely in line with our general view of the person with high achievement motivation as forward-looking and concerned about the consequences of action (*Ga+* and *Ga—*). It need only be added that Zatzkis did not restrict himself in this count to what is strictly speaking the future tense of a verb. He included very broadly any verb which suggested anticipation or expectation regardless of whether it was expressed in past, present, or future form. Thus, for example, in the sentence, "It has always been my intention to hold some sort of a social service position" the verb *has been* is scored as anticipatory. In many such cases the meaning of the sentence and particularly of the auxiliary verb had to be taken into account. By way of contrast, the verb *has been* in the sentence "This course has been most interesting" is clearly not anticipatory.

The meaning of these results seems clear. People who are highly motivated for achievement think more often in anticipatory and generalized terms. They are concerned with general and vague life goals (which perhaps can never be achieved because they are not specific enough). They want to relate the "now" to the "then," to see the connection between what they are studying and what they want to do later. On the other hand, the subjects with low n Achievement think less often in generalized terms and are more concerned about the difficulties in the way of achievement.

Methodologically it is important to note that psycho-grammatical categories have provided us with measures of "thought patterns" or "modes of thinking" which are consistent with our general theoretical notions as to how motives should influence associational processes. This confirms the expectation of a number of theorists that language is one very useful way of studying personality.

8.5.2 *Sentence Completion Test results.* Another rather commonly used instrument for getting at an individual's perception of the world is the Sentence Completion Test. For us it has the added advantage of being another so-called "projective technique," the results of which could be compared with those obtained with the picture-story or TAT projective method. A group of male college students was given a form of the Sentence Completion Test especially constructed by Dr. Jules Holzberg to get at achievement and security associations. There were 50 items in the test, some of which were phrased in the "I" form and some in the "He" form, e.g., "I feel sorry when . . ." and "When luck turned against him, Joe. . . ." Thirteen of the 50 items contained direct reference to achievement, e.g., "When he saw that others were doing better than he, Joe. . . ." It proved so difficult to score the comparative "emotional involvement" of the completions to these 13 items, as intended, that they were discarded in the final analysis. The remaining 37 items were scored simply in terms of whether or not the completion was achievement-related or not. Thus, the completions "I wish for *success*" or "He thinks of himself as *a world beater*" would be counted as achievement-related; whereas "I am afraid when *I am alone at night*" or "If Fred could only *get married*" would not be counted. Of these 37 items, 20 were cast in "I" form and 17 in the "He" form. Only 15 of the former and 16 of the latter produced at least one achievement-related response in the group of 27 subjects. As a result the opportunity for achievement-related responses to be given to self or others was approximately equal.

TABLE 8.13. Mean number of achievement-related sentence completions for subjects above and below the mean *n* Achievement score (C)

	"I" Items	*"He" Items*	*"I" Minus "He" Items*
High *n* Achievement (N = 13)			
Mean	3.23	3.69	—.46
SD	2.00	1.56	2.02
Low *n* Achievement (N = 14)			
Mean	4.79	4.29	+.50
SD	1.57	1.58	2.41
Mean Difference (H-L)	—1.56	—.60	—.96
SE diff.	.72	.40	.89
t	2.17	1.50	1.08
p	<.05	—	—

The results are reported in Table 8.13. They are somewhat surprising. To the extent that we had an expectation before we looked at the results, it was that the group of subjects with high *n* Achievement would attribute more achievement responses to others ("He" items) than would the subjects with low *n* Achievement. In short, we expected the results from the two projective techniques to be consistent; those who attributed more achievement concern to others in stories should also do so in sentence completions. But such is not the case, at least not obviously. The most striking result in Table 8.13 is the significantly higher number of "I" achievement completions made by the low *n* Achievement group. This does not, strictly speaking, contradict our hypothesis, since it had to do only with "He" completions. Nevertheless, it is somewhat unexpected. Furthermore, the same reverse trend appears in the "He" items, although not at the 5 per cent level of significance.

It is only when the "He" minus "I" achievement completions are analyzed that the trend is in the expected direction. As the table shows, those with high n Achievement give *relatively* more "He" achievement completions; whereas those with low n Achievement give relatively more "I" achievement completions. The difference between these differences is .96, which with a standard error of .89 computed from the distribution of "I" minus "He" differences for each subject yields a t of only 1.08. The trend is in the expected direction but is not significant.

The major fact in this study is that the high n Achievement group shows *fewer* achievement completions, especially in "I" sentences. Whatever interpretation is finally given this fact, it strongly suggests that the results from two projective techniques need not necessarily be the same. The interpretation which immediately suggests itself is that somebody is being defensive. But who? Suppose we start with the assumptions that the Sentence Completion Test is more easily influenced than the Thematic Apperception Test by the subject's ideas of what he ought to write, and that the "I" items are the ones which are most likely to be influenced by such considerations. Then we could argue that the subjects with low TAT n Achievement scores recognize their lack of motivation, feel ashamed of themselves, and in compensation attribute a lot of achievement concern to themselves. Exactly the same trend is apparent in the self-rating data reported in Table 8.10. When the subjects were asked to rate how hard they usually strove for personal achievement, those with low n Achievement scores tended to rate themselves as more highly motivated. Perhaps the trend is more significant here because the Sentence Completion Test is a more sensitive instrument than self-ratings. Less governed by "reality" considerations than self-ratings, it might be better at picking up the defenses of the low *n* Achievement group.

But the argument can just as well be turned around and the high *n* Achievement group made to appear defensive. For some reason (perhaps fear of failure, or ridicule, or competition with the father), they may be unaware of the real strength of their achievement motivation which can be measured in full, therefore, only in an indirect way; that is, from imaginative stories. The Sentence Completion Test, like self-ratings, is enough under conscious control to reflect only what they are aware of. Which of these interpretations is correct cannot, of course, be stated without further research. The fact of real importance that emerges from this study is that the Sentence Completion Test gives results which differ from those given by the thematic apperception method and which are more in line with conscious self-judgments.

8.5.3 *Recognition thresholds.* From projection we turn to recognition. Will the tendencies to think in characteristic ways which we have noted for subjects with high achievement motivation influence the speed with which they recognize different kinds of need-related words? McClelland and Liberman (1949) have reported a study on just this point using the technique of successive, brief exposures popularized by Postman, Bruner, and McGinnies (1948). They used 30 words— 10 neutral, 10 achievement-related, and 10 security-related— each of which was exposed for .01 second at successively increasing illuminations. Both the security and achievement words could be divided into positive words (like *nurture* and *success*) and negative words (like *threat* and *failure*). The only significant relationship they reported with the *n* Achievement score (A) alone concerned the seven positive achievement words which were recognized significantly faster by the subjects above the mean in *n* Achievement ($t = 2.15$, $p < .05$). When the same breakdown is made using the revised scoring system, the *t* is reduced well below significance to 1.18. That the trend is probably still there in the data, however, is demonstrated by dealing with frequencies and chi-square which does not involve the assumption of a cardinal scale that is inherent in the use of the t test and actual recognition scores (cf. Cronbach, 1949). That is, the distribution of the recognition time scores may be divided into those which are faster or slower than the median recognition time for the seven positive achievement words. With this breakdown, 12 of the 18 subjects with high n Achievement and only 6 of the 18 subjects with low n Achievement saw the words faster than average. The difference yields a chi-square (corrected for discontinuity) of 2.8 which is significant at about the 9 per cent level of confidence.

More interesting than this isolated and rather tenuous finding were the trends obtained by McClelland and Liberman when they combined the rank of subjects on n Achievement score (A) with the rank on the middle section of the Anagrams test. The rationale for this combined rank was that since the two measures were correlated, they might be considered to be measuring at least in part the same thing; therefore, combining them would give a more reliable estimate of the strength of the achievement motive than either one alone. Whether or not this procedure is strictly justifiable, the results they obtained using it gave the first important intimation of the difference between subjects with moderate and high n Achievement scores which we have since found in a number of other places. Figure 8.2 which is reproduced from their article tells the story. Recognition time, expressed in standard score units of the subject's distribution of recognition times for the neutral words, is here plotted separately for the positive and negative achievement words for thirds of the n Achievement rank distribution. Since the relationships are not linear, the mean recognition score for each third was compared with that of the other two-thirds of the subjects to attempt to ascertain the most probable shape of the relationship. On this basis it is the high vs. mid-low comparison which is significant for the positive achievement words ($t = 2.94$, $p < .01$), and the mid vs. high-low comparison which is significant for the negative achievement words

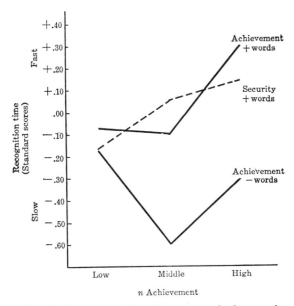

FIG. 8.2. Mean recognition times in standard scores for achievement- and security-related words plotted for the upper, middle, and lower thirds of the *n* Achievement distribution as obtained by combining ranks on the TAT and anagrams measures of *n* Achievement.

($t = 2.01$, $p < .06$). In other words, the subjects with very high *n* Achievement rank recognize words like *success, mastery,* and *perfect* more quickly; whereas subjects with moderate *n* Achievement rank are slower than others at seeing words like *unable, obstacle,* and *failure.* From this it seems logical to infer that the subjects with moderate *n* Achievement are primarily concerned with avoiding failure, an inference which is supported in part by the dotted curve in Figure 8.2 which shows the recognition times for the seven positive security words. Here it is apparent that the increase in sensitivity to security words occurs between the low and middle n Achievement groups; the low vs. mid-high comparison yields a t of 2.11, $p < .05$. The high n Achievement group continues to be as sensitive to the security positive words, but they are relatively more sensitive to the positive achievement words. Thus, McClelland and Liberman felt justified in concluding that the middle n Achievement group was more security-minded than the high or low n Achievement groups. They found further support for this hypothesis in an analysis of the pre-solution guesses made by the subjects for the different types of words. In general they argued that a structural hypothesis or guess, such as reporting *believe* for *achieve* or *master* for *mastery*, indicated a willingness to tolerate error or to take a chance when one was not quite sure what the word was. The middle n Achievement group showed a higher number of such guesses for the achievement words and a lower number for the security words than either of the other two groups. This was interpreted to mean that their tolerance for error was greater for achievement stimuli and less for security stimuli, again indicating that they were more concerned about security, provided one can assume that decreased error tolerance indicates greater concern. McClelland and Liberman found support for believing that it does by noting that the high n Achievement group showed less error tolerance (fewer structural hypotheses) for the *achievement* words than the rest of the subjects. From all this they are led to infer "that the group of subjects with moderate n Achievement are security-minded and chiefly concerned with avoiding failure, or with achieving a minimal level of aspiration, whereas the group of subjects with high n Achievement are concerned more directly with achieving success or attaining a maximum level of aspiration" (1949, p. 251).

8.5.4 *Rorschach Test results.* This difference provides an

interesting point of departure for analyzing the Rorschach Test results available on 31 subjects, especially in view of a report by Blake and Wilson (1950). These authors argue that responses which are based primarily on the form of the blot ($F, Fc,$ and FC) "might be characterized as abient in the sense that they are *descriptive* rather than interpretive." On the other hand, responses involving human or animal movement (M or FM) are "adient-like responses in the sense that the subject interprets the blots by assigning activity to them on a 'projective' basis, rather than simply describing and accounting for the objective features which he observes" (1950, pp. 461–462).

They have defined two types of responses which might roughly be described as avoidance and approach behavior in the task of interpreting blots. Furthermore, they found that subjects who were depressed, as measured by the Minnesota Multiphasic Personality Inventory, showed significantly more "avoidance" responses ($F, Fc,$ and FC) and significantly fewer "approach" responses (M and FM) than did a control group. This is exactly what would be expected if their reasoning about the nature of the two types of responses is correct. On a similar basis, we might expect that our subjects with moderate *n* Achievement would show more avoidance responses, while the subjects with high *n* Achievement would show more approach responses. In addition to this specific hypothesis we entertained two others in analyzing the Rorschach results: (1) High *n* Achievement should be indicated by a large number of whole responses, both because a whole response indicates a higher level of aspiration for the task of interpreting a blot, and because it suggests the same type of generalized thinking we found in the higher frequency of abstract nouns in the language sample and in the general "Long-Term Involvement" of imaginative stories. It is doubtful whether *popular* whole responses should be included in this tally, however, because they may indicate a very *low* level of aspiration. (2) The subjects with moderate n Achievement may show other Rorschach signs of insecurity such as FK (vista responses) or excessive concern about details to make sure they have not made a mistake.

The over-all Rorschach response output for the low, middle, and high n Achievement score (C) groups has already been presented in Table 8.2. The higher productivity of the middle group confirms the hypothesis that they may try to seek security in over-productivity or attempts to cover all aspects of the blot. Unfortunately, it also increases the opportunity for this group to show any particular kind of response, so that the over-all frequencies of appearance of various Rorschach subcategories all show the same curvilinear trend. To avoid the complexities introduced by differential productivity of responses, we adopted the device used successfully by Blake and Wilson of working only with the first response to each of the 10 blots. Each person, then, had only 10 classifiable responses except when there were rejections. The results of this analysis are arranged in Table 8.14 to test the various hypotheses advanced. They were obtained by Dr. Jules Holzberg who administered the tests individually and scored them without any knowledge of the n Achievement score standing of the individuals.

Our initial hypothesis is confirmed to some extent by these data. The subjects with high n Achievement do show a tendency to give a larger number of "approach" or movement responses than do the other two groups, but the variability is so large and the number of cases so small that the difference is significant at only the 9 per cent level of confidence. For the animal movement responses alone (FM), the difference is significant at the 5 per cent level of confidence ($t = 1.80$, $p < .05$ for the predicted direction) when the group is broken into halves instead of thirds. This trend seems sufficiently well indicated to warrant further study with a larger number of subjects.

TABLE 8.14. Mean frequency of various Rorschach categories for the first response to each blot for subjects with high, moderate, and low *n* Achievement score (C)

	F, Fc, FC	M, FM	Non-Popular W	W	D	FK KF *
High *n* Achievement (N = 10)						
Mean ..	5.00	4.40	6.40	3.70	3.60	.50
SD	2.37	2.50	1.69	1.42	1.68	.21
Middle *n* Achievement (N = 10)						
Mean ..	4.80	3.20	5.10	2.90	4.90	1.40
SD	1.72	1.25	2.17	1.45	2.17	1.20
Low *n* Achievement (N = 11)						
Mean ..	5.54	3.18	5.73	2.09	4.09	.37
SD	1.88	2.03	2.14	1.93	1.93	.18
	Mid vs. *(High-Low)*	*High vs.* *(Mid-Low)*			*Mid vs.* *(High-Low)*	*Mid vs.* *(High-Low)*
t	.64	1.32			1.25	2.31
p	—	.10			.11	.02

* In order to increase the frequencies of this relatively rare determinant, instances where it was a secondary determinant were included as well as where it was primary. Also the variance estimates from the Middle and the High plus Low groups for this category differ very significantly. Therefore a *t* test of significance is not justifiable. A bi-serial *tau* was calculated with the Mid vs. High plus Low *n* Achievement as the dichotomized variable and number of *FK* or *KF* responses as the continuous variable. The obtained *tau* was .53, which is beyond the .005 level of confidence.

At first glance it looks as if the predicted signs of anxiety in the middle achievement group do not appear. At least there are fewer rather than more "avoidance" responses (*F, Fc,* and *FC*). On the other hand, there are significantly more *FK* responses made by the middle group. Both of these findings suggest that subjects with moderate *n* Achievement are not so concerned with making responses that can be objectively justified by reference to the shape of the blot as are the anxious depressed people in Blake and Wilson's study; instead, our supposedly defensive subjects show signs which would indicate a more generalized anxiety or concern over inadequacy (*FK*), at least to the confirmed Rorschacher. To the uninitiated the problem remains of trying to determine why they should introduce the third dimension (*FK*, and so on) into their responses more often than other subjects. We might indulge in free associations about the connection between feelings of space, uncertainty, emptiness, fear of falling, and inadequacy, but it remains for future research to sharpen them into hypotheses which can be systematically tested. In the meantime, it can only be stated that our middle *n* Achievement subjects do show signs which many Rorschach experts would take to mean anxiety, including particularly the increase in vista responses, and also insignificant increases in detail and color responses (*C* and *CF*).

Finally, it should be noted that the prediction concerning the larger number of whole responses is confirmed, provided the popular wholes are eliminated, as they should be. The difference between the highest and lowest thirds is significant ($t = 2.08, p < .05$), and the correlation, as is suggested by the regular mean increase from lowest to highest *n* Achievement groups, is fairly high ($r = .36, p < .05$). Apparently the tendency for persons highly motivated for achievement to think in over-all terms is fairly general in its effects. We have found evidence of it in the content of their imaginative stories, in the kind of language they use, and in the type of response they give to an unstructured ink blot. The *n* Achievement score can be related to many other Rorschach categories and ratios. We have explored some of these relationships, but since we have no other clear-cut hypotheses or any very clear understanding of the exact significance of some of the Rorschach scores, there seems little point in presenting the data here.

8.6 **Memory.** The relationship between *n* Achievement (scoring system B) and recall of completed and interrupted tasks has been worked out by Atkinson (1950). His procedure included the following steps:

(1) Experimental Orientation—either Relaxed, Task, or Achievement-oriented instructions concerning 20 paper and pencil tasks which were to be performed; (2) Twenty paper and pencil tasks, half of which were interrupted before most of the subjects had a chance to complete them; (3) Instructions for the TAT measure of *n* Achievement; (4) A four-story measure of *n* Achievement; (5) Recall of tasks performed at the start of the period.

The three experimental instructions have already been described earlier in this chapter in connection with the analysis of the numbers of tasks completed. Also the results from one of the four pictures (*H*) were not included in the over-all *n* Achievement score because at that time results from this picture with scoring system B did not agree with the results from seven other pictures in placing subjects high or low in *n* Achievement (see Chap. VII). To minimize possible effects on recall of too great a disparity in the number of tasks completed and incompleted, only those subjects who completed between 8–12 tasks (83 subjects out of 100) were used in the analysis of recall data.

Percentages of completed and incompleted tasks recalled by each subject were computed since the number of completions had varied. Percentages were converted into degrees by means of the arc sin $\sqrt{\text{percentage}}$ transformation (Snedecor, 1946) in order to allow treatment of the data in terms of analysis of variance. There was also need for adjustment of slightly disproportionate sub-class numbers, due to the fact that subjects were classified according to experimental orientation, according to *n* Achievement (high or low), and also according to which of two forms of the 20 tasks they had performed. The forms differed only in order of tasks.

The most striking results were those obtained for the recall

of incompleted tasks as shown in Figure 8.3 in terms of un-
converted mean percentages. As instructions increase the likelihood that subjects will perceive completion to mean personal success and incompletion to mean personal failure, the
subjects with high *n* Achievement (above the mean) tend to
recall *more* incompleted tasks while the subjects with low
n Achievement (below the mean) tend to recall *fewer* incom-

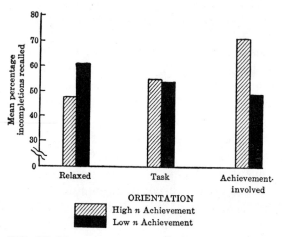

FIG. 8.3. Mean percentage recall of incompleted tasks
by subjects above and below the mean *n* Achievement
score under three types of instructional orientation

pleted tasks. The analysis of variance of transformed scores
in Table 8.15 is based on sub-class means which were derived
from the performance of 83 subjects, 27 in the Relaxed orientation, 32 in the Task orientation, and 24 in the Achievement
orientation. Since neither of the first-order interactions involving forms was significant, their sums of squares were combined with that of the triple interaction term, providing a
more stable estimate of error having five degrees of freedom.
With this estimate of error, significant *F* values are obtained
for variance in incompleted tasks recalled attributable to
Forms and to the interaction between Motivation and Orien-

TABLE 8.15. Analysis of variance for incompleted tasks recalled based on transformed scores

Source	Sums of Squares	df	Variance Estimate	F	p
1. Orientation	101.28	2	50.64		
2. Motivation	43.31	1	43.31		
3. Forms	638.86	1	638.86	9.36	.05
4. MxO	1325.96	2	662.98	9.72	.05
5. MxF	.68	1	.68		
6. FxO	206.71	2	103.35		
7. MxFxO	133.81	2	66.90		
Combined Error (5, 6, 7)	341.19	5	68.24		
Total	2450.61	11			

(From Atkinson, 1950).

tation. The latter finding is the one of particular interest to us; it is also the one illustrated in Figure 8.3 which shows how the percentage of incompleted tasks recalled *increases* for the high motivation group as a function of orientation and *decreases* for the low motivation group. Neither Motivation nor Orientation by itself has any significant effect, as can also be seen by inspection of Figure 8.3. Comparison of the most important particular differences in this Figure are given in Table 8.16, which presents the means and mean differences in percentages of incompleted tasks recalled for the two extreme

TABLE 8.16. Means and mean differences in percentages of incompleted tasks recalled, by orientation and motivational level, with tests of significance based on transformed scores

MOTIVATIONAL LEVEL	CONDITION		Difference (A-R)	t [*]	p [*]
	Relaxed	Achievement-oriented			
High *n* Achievement	47.5	71.4	+23.9	3.97	<.01
Low *n* Achievement	60.5	49.4	−11.1	2.10	∼.09
Mean Difference (H-L) ..	−13.0	22.0			
t [*]	2.35	3.81			
p [*]	∼.06	<.01			

[*] Tests of significance are based on the transformed data with standard errors of differences computed from the error term (5 *df*) in the analysis of variance (Table 8.15).

orientation groups, together with tests of significance of the differences based on the analysis of variance of the transformed data. As the p values on the right-hand side of the table show, the increase in recall of incompletions for the subjects with high n Achievement from Relaxed to Achievement orientation is more significant than the opposite trend for the subjects with low n Achievement, but the reversal in the two trends is unmistakable.

In view of our previous findings of differences between subjects in the low, middle, and high thirds of the n Achievement score distribution, it seemed worth while to present these same results according to a three-way breakdown in n Achievement score, as in Table 8.17. Since the two forms had contributed significantly to the variance, it was thought desirable to wash out this source of variation in order to simplify the analysis with smaller N's resulting from the three-way breakdown.

The steps involved in arriving at the standard scores presented in Table 8.17 may be summarized as follows:

1. The percentage of incompleted tasks recalled by each subject was converted to degrees by means of the arc sin $\sqrt{\text{percentage}}$ transformation.
2. Each subject's transformed recall score was changed to a standard score based on the mean and standard deviation for the particular form of the twenty-tasks test he had performed. This permits combining results from the different forms.
3. A constant of five was added to each standard score to eliminate negative numbers.

Exactly the same procedure was followed in the case of the percentage of completed tasks recalled. Since standard scores have been computed separately for completed and incompleted tasks recalled (i.e., since the standard scores are based on different means and sigmas), the figures in Table 8.17 do not permit analysis of the *absolute* numbers of each recalled. However, the *relative* favoring of incompleted recall over completed recall is indicated by a comparison of the difference scores at the bottom of every cell for the various orientations and levels of motivation. A minus sign has been attached to a difference in which completed tasks are favored over incompleted tasks in recall, a kind of difference which represents a reversal of the traditional Zeigarnik effect. The table shows that the differences observed in the high-low *n* Achievement

TABLE 8.17. Mean recall scores for completed and incompleted tasks for subjects in high, middle, and low thirds of *n* Achievement score distribution under three conditions of orientation toward the tasks

	ORIENTATION TOWARD TASKS		
	Relaxed	*Task*	*Achievement-oriented*
High *n* Achievement			
N	9	10	9
Completed Recall (CR)	4.75	4.87	5.30
Incompleted Recall (IR)	4.64	4.90	5.96
Difference (IR-CR)	−.11	.03	.66
Middle *n* Achievement			
N	10	11	8
Completed Recall (CR)	4.73	4.81	5.33
Incompleted Recall (IR)	5.14	4.82	4.40
Difference (IR-CR)	.41	.01	−.93
Low *n* Achievement			
N	8	11	7
Completed Recall (CR)	5.03	5.21	5.07
Incompleted Recall (IR)	5.14	5.03	4.93
Difference (IR-CR)	.11	−.18	−.14

Note: Recall scores are standard scores based on forms, plus a constant of 5, of arc sin transformations of percentages of completed and incompleted tasks recalled.

breakdown (Figure 8.3) are largely contained in the *middle* and *high n* Achievement groups, while the low *n* Achievement group shows no significant trends though it is more similar to the middle third.

The results of this analysis and the similar one based on a high-low *n* Achievement breakdown can be rather simply summarized: (1) There is a significant over-all increase in the number of completed tasks recalled irrespective of individual motivation ($t = 4.19$, $p < .01$) as the orientation goes from Relaxed to Achievement-oriented (i.e., as instructions make it increasingly more clear that completion means personal success). (2) There is a significant increase in the number of incompletions recalled by subjects in the high half ($p < .02$, Table 8.16) or high third ($p < .02$, Table 8.17) of the n Achievement score distribution as orientation goes from Relaxed to Achievement-oriented (i.e., as instructions make it increasingly more clear that incompletion means personal failure). (3) The decrease in recall of incompleted tasks by the lower half of the n Achievement score distribution from Relaxed to Achievement-oriented is significant at only the 10 per cent level of confidence (Table 8.16), and the decrease for the middle third of the distribution again misses significance ($t = 1.48$, $p = .20$, Table 8.17), but (4) the relative preponderance of completions over incompletions recalled (difference score, Table 8.17) increases significantly for this middle group ($t = 2.32$, $p < .05$) between Relaxed and Achievement orientation. In short, the middle n Achievement group becomes increasingly *defensive* as instructions make it clearer that incompletion means failure. (5) The low third of the n Achievement distribution shows no significant trends in recall, as in fact it should not, if we are correct in thinking that recall of completed and incompleted tasks is in part a function of achievement motivation. The subjects having the lowest n Achievement scores appear to be essentially *unmotivated* for achievement.

One surprising thing about these data is that although very meaningful results on the recall of tasks and number of tasks completed (see Table 8.4) were obtained, no significant increase in mean n Achievement scores occurred as the orientation became more achievement-related. The results are in the right direction, but the increases are not significant. The mean *n* Achievement scores (C) for the three orientations are as follows:

	ORIENTATION TOWARD TASK		
	Relaxed	*Task*	*Achievement-oriented*
Mean *n* Achievement Score (C)	6.18	6.62	6.88

This is the only time that we have failed to get significant increases in *n* Achievement as a result of experimental arousal. Why there should be differences in performance (Table 8.3) and memory (Table 8.17) as a function of differences in *n* Achievement score and at the same time no increase in the scores as a function of increasing involvement is something that we cannot, at present, explain. If we ignore this puzzling fact, the recall results strikingly confirm previous findings which suggest that the subjects with moderate *n* Achievement are concerned primarily with avoiding failure, whereas those with high *n* Achievement are more concerned with overcoming obstacles and eventual success. The recall results also nicely illustrate the need to consider *both* motivation and the subject's perception of a specific performance in accounting for his instrumental behavior. Thus persons having high *n* Achievement do not show real evidence of striving unless the performance is defined as one which will be considered a personal accomplishment if done well. For them Achievement orientation provides an incentive or *challenge*. They, therefore, recall more incompleted tasks as if they wanted to continue to strive to complete them. Here recall is instrumental to eventual success. For the middle *n* Achievement group, Achievement orientation is a *threat* which leads to relatively greater avoidance of failures in recall since recall of failures would serve to redintegrate the pain of failure.

Further evidence in support of this hypothesis may be found by looking at the third column in Table 8.17 which shows clearly that under Achievement orientation the middle

n Achievement group recalls fewer incompletions than either
the high or low n Achievement groups. The middle vs. high-
low comparison yields a t of 2.77 which is significant at the 1
per cent level of confidence. In short, this indicates that subjects in the middle third of the n Achievement distribution
are more defensive than the rest of the subjects. A similar type
of comparison which pits the high group against the rest of
the distribution yields a significant t value (2.98, $p < .01$),
demonstrating again that under Achievement orientation the
high n Achievement group recalls significantly more incompleted tasks than the remainder of the subjects.

It is important to remember that similar relationships were
found for number of tasks completed under Achievement
orientation (see Table 8.4). That is, subjects with moderate
n Achievement were able to complete fewer tasks than the
rest of the subjects—a result which we attributed to their increased anxiety under Achievement involvement. Now it
looks as if these same subjects are also inhibited by anxiety in
recall. This suggests the interpretation of repression offered
by Sears some years ago (1936, 1937) to the effect that anticipations of failure which may arise during performance lower
the efficiency of performance and also interfere with recall
either by reproductive interference or by disorganization of
the memory trace at the time it is formed.

Granted this is a likely hypothesis, what frankly puzzles us
at the present time is why the middle range of the n Achievement score distribution should contain people who have a
greater number of anticipations of failure. Our general theory of motivation states that there should be two kinds of
achievement motives, one characterized primarily by fear of
failure and the other by hope of success, depending on
whether achievement cues in the past history of the individual
have been primarily associated with negative or positive
changes in affective level (cf. Chap. II and Chap. VII). But
why should one type of motive be found primarily in the

middle range of *n* Achievement scores? If we had had to predict anything ahead of time, we probably would have guessed that the most highly motivated subjects would have the most anxiety over failure, just on the basis of clinical evidence that intense motives are accompanied by anxiety. We are inclined to believe at the moment that this particular association of *kind* of achievement motivation with a particular *level* of *n* Achievement score may be some kind of an artifact resulting from the way our measure of achievement motivation is derived. It has been suggested in Chapter VII that the anxieties of some subjects over achievement may be so great as to inhibit their verbalization even in fantasy. This might mean that some of the subjects in the middle or low groups are "really" high. It may be that we have been in error in simply counting the frequency of various achievement-related responses in stories without paying attention to their type or pattern (cf. Chap. V). Or it may be, as McClelland and Liberman (1949) have argued, that desire to avoid failure represents a kind of minimum level of aspiration which is first engaged on the achievement motivation continuum, that the anxiety involved is different from what the clinician means by neurotic anxiety, and that the association of the two *kinds* of motivation with different *intensities* of motivation is not an artifact after all.

Further research alone can answer these questions. At the moment we feel the need to get some better measure of the two kinds of motivation than is provided by intensity differences. We have made some exploratory studies in which two separate *n* Achievement scores are computed for each record, one based on the sum of positive characteristics, another based on the sum of negative characteristics, hoping that this breakdown would give us more direct measures of "fear of failure" and "hope of success." So far the results have proven too complex and unreliable to be worth reporting, but we believe that progress can be made along these lines.

8.7 Miscellaneous tests. In the course of attempting to explore fully the meaning of our n Achievement score, we have correlated it with a varied assortment of tests. We had no particular hypotheses to test and no reasons to expect relationships in these cases, and we got what might be expected under these circumstances, viz., nothing of any importance. For the sake of the record, however, we will present here all the things we found n Achievement *not* related to: Otis I.Q.; Masculinity-Femininity and Occupational Level scales of the Strong Vocational Interest Inventory; the six scales of the Allport-Vernon Study of Values with the possible exception of the Aesthetic scale; the Iowa Silent Reading test; the Bogardus Social Distance measure of racial and religious prejudice; the Renner scales of oral and anal tendencies; the Maslow Security-Insecurity test.

In all these analyses—made because we happened to have the test data on the same subjects—only two relationships approached significance: that between n Achievement (C) and the Aesthetic scale of the Allport-Vernon Study of Values ($r = .36, N = 31, p < .05$), and that between n Achievement (C) and the Interest Maturity scale of the Strong Vocational Interest Inventory ($r = .37, N = 36, p < .05$). H. H. Morgan (1951) also reports an indirect relationship between n Achievement and the Interest Maturity scale; so this finding may warrant further investigation.

Since these relationships do not make any particular sense at the moment, and since a certain number of significant relationships can be expected by chance, we are inclined to dismiss this whole effort as an example of the futility of "blind" empiricism.

ǂCHAPTER IXǂ

Origins of Achievement Motivation

THE STUDY OF achievement motivation would not be complete without some attempt to understand its origins. How is it that some students score high and some low? Are they simply born that way? Or are the differences in score simply temporary, reflecting momentary differences in the life situations of the individuals concerned? We can accept neither of these views if our theoretical analysis of motivation in Chapter II is correct. There we argued that all motives are learned, that they develop out of repeated affective experiences connected with certain types of situations and types of behavior. In the case of achievement motivation, the situations should involve "standards of excellence," presumably imposed on the child by the culture, or more particularly by the parents as representatives of the culture, and the behavior should involve either "competition" with those standards of excellence or attempts to meet them which, if successful, produce positive affect or, if unsuccessful, negative affect. It follows that those cultures or families which stress "competition with standards of excellence" or which insist *that the child be able to perform certain tasks well by himself*—such cultures or families should produce children with high achievement motivation. To state the same issue negatively—if a family does not set high standards of excellence, or if it does not permit the child to compete or strive to meet them on his own, then he could not be expected to have had the affective experiences connected with meeting or failing to meet achievement standards which cumulatively produce an achievement motive.

The research problem then boils down to an attempt to discover whether individuals with high and low n Achievement scores have in fact been treated differently by their families as they were growing up. Our hypothesis is that individuals with high achievement motivation will have been forced to master problems on their own more often and earlier than individuals with low achievement motivation. It has been tested in three main ways: (1) by asking students of known differences in motivation to describe their parents and their upbringing, (2) by relating objective measures of parent behavior to achievement motivation, and (3) by studying intensively a few individuals with high and low n Achievement scores.

9.1 Perception of parents and achievement motivation. The first and apparently simplest approach to the problem is to ask students to describe their parents and their upbringing. The simplicity is, of course, deceptive. It is methodological rather than interpretive, because one cannot be sure how much the student's perception or memory of his parents is determined by *his* motivation and how much by *their* actual behavior. Nevertheless, despite this difficulty, we have obtained some interesting and suggestive data from questionnaire studies dealing with perceived parent behavior and related topics—data which provided the basis for more definitive direct studies of parent behavior to be reported in the next main section.

9.1.1 *Child-rearing practices attributed to parents by sons with varying* n *Achievement.* As part of the extensive case study of 30 college students, on whom much of the test data reported in Chapter VIII was collected, a psychiatrist interviewed each student for one to two hours to obtain a life history and family background. On the basis of the interview material, the psychiatrist then rated each student on a number of variables, some of which dealt with parent behavior. Unfortunately, at the time this study was designed, our theory of achievement motivation was largely nonexistent and we were still in the exploratory stage of trying to get some ideas as to what produced it. For this reason we chose variables to be rated which had been shown by Baldwin, Kalhorn, and Breese (1945) to be key behavior patterns in terms of which parents could be differentiated. They yielded some interesting data but do not test the achievement training hypothesis directly.

The four major patterns of parent behavior found by these research workers were arranged in a rough rating scale for the psychiatrist as follows:

Democratic-Autocratic	0 1 2 3 4 5 6	
	Democratic	Autocratic
Acceptance-Rejection	0 1 2 3 4 5 6	
	Acceptance	Rejection
Indulgence	0 1 2 3 4 5 6	
	Normal	Over-protective
Casualness	0 1 2 3 4 5 6	
	Casual or Inconsistent	Consistent

The meaning of these dimensions was discussed with the psychiatrist in terms of the sub-scales characterizing them, according to the findings of Baldwin, Kalhorn, and Breese (1945). It can best be given here by reproducing the written instructions given the same subjects when they rated their parents directly on the same variables as part of another testing session.

Democratic-Autocratic: Were there restrictive regulations you had to follow more or less without questioning, or were things explained to you? Were all rules handed down in an authoritarian manner, or was family policy decided by everyone concerned? Was policy handed down without justification? To what degree was the parental direction coercive?

Acceptance-Rejection: The degree of affection, acceptance, and rapport on the part of the parent felt for you or the active dislike or hostility expressed in the manner and form of criticism, the intent and intensity of punishment, and the like.

Indulgence: The amount of protectiveness and solicitousness shown by the parent toward you. The degree to which the parent is child-centered as against self-centered. The amount of time spent by the parent with you, the amount of "anxious affection," worrying about you, and planning your welfare.

Casualness: The mildness of the parent's attitude toward you, shown by expediency (as opposed to a highly consistent policy) and inconsistency in your upbringing, but most of all by casualness in the relationship.

The students, like the psychiatrist, filled out a seven-point rating scale on each of these variables. Unfortunately, the *Casualness* dimension was treated slightly differently on the two occasions. For the students the two ends of the rating scale were labeled: *No Casualness—Extreme Casualness* as contrasted with the psychiatrist's scale which went from *Casualness* to *Consistency.* The net effect of this change was to create two different, somewhat opposed, "unfavorable" aspects of the *Casualness* dimension. Apparently the psychiatrist, faced with a *Casualness-Consistency* choice, regarded *Casualness* as "bad," as in neglect or rejection. The result, as Table 9.1 shows, is a small positive correlation of *n* Achievement score with *Consistency* for the psychiatrist and with *Casualness* for the students. As we shall see in a moment, this apparent inconsistency in the results probably reflects an over-all relationship between perceived parental severity and *n* Achievement—a severity which, because of slight changes in the description of the two scales, got attached to opposite ends of the *Casualness* dimension by the psychiatrist and by the students themselves.

The parent-behavior ratings both by the psychiatrist and by the sons were correlated with the sons' *n* Achievement scores with the results shown in Table 9.1. The sons rated each parent separately on each variable, but the most striking re-

TABLE 9.1. Correlations between n Achievement score (C) and parent behavior variables as rated by sons and by a psychiatrist ($N = 30$)

| | | RATINGS BY SONS | | RATINGS BY PSYCHIATRIST |
	Father	Mother	Both Combined	Parents Combined
Democratic— Autocratic	.10	—.03	.03	.18
Acceptance— Rejection	.49	.33	.48	.33
Indulgence	—.26	—.11	—.21	—.23
Casual— Consistent				.22
No Casualness— Extreme Casualness	.12	.30	.23	
Combined Severity ..			.40 *	.40 †

* Autocratic, Rejectant, Non-Indulgent, Extreme Casualness (Neglect).
† Autocratic, Rejectant, Non-Indulgent, Extreme Consistency (Rigidity).
Correlations of .36 and .46 are significant at the 5% and 1% levels of confidence respectively.

sult is obtained by combining the ratings into one over-all "severity" rating which, as the last line in the table shows, correlates significantly with n Achievement score. It is interesting to note that the correlation with parental "severity" is identical whether the information on it is obtained directly from ratings by the sons or indirectly from ratings by the psychiatrist based on information they gave him. Apparently the sons were equally frank on both occasions, and their standards and his standards as to what constituted severity were somewhat alike.

At any rate, perceived severity of upbringing or "felt lack of love" is associated among college students with high n Achievement. The largest single correlation involves the rejection attributed to the fathers by their sons; that is, sons who felt their fathers had rejected them had higher n Achievement scores than those who felt their fathers had loved and accepted them. Before we attempt to interpret this result, we need more data, but even now it is worth noting that what we found here is not really predictable from our theory of how achievement motivation is supposed to develop. For one thing, our theory deals only with the area of achievement training, whereas these variables cover general parental attitudes in all areas of training. For another, our theory would argue that high achievement motivation would develop as much from positive affective changes connected with independent striving as from the negative affective changes presumably associated with general severity of upbringing. In a way, this suggests that these data may have more bearing on the way sons with high achievement motivation perceive their parents than on the way in which they were actually brought up.

9.1.2 *Traits attributed to parents by sons with varying* n *Achievement.* Some further data on parental images were collected from the sons in another part of the questionnaire they filled out on family relationships. They were asked to rate each parent on a seven-point scale on the following personality traits: Self-Confident, Helpful, Domineering, Friendly, Selfish, Clever, Successful (vocationally). The ratings of traits were grouped into three clusters: one dealing with "nurturance" characteristics, one with "authoritarian" characteristics, and one with "success" characteristics. Ratings on each trait in the three clusters were combined and correlated with n Achievement scores. The results, which are summarized in Table 9.2, tend to confirm our previous findings about perceived parental severity. The *Friendly-Helpful* rating, particularly for the father, is *negatively* related to n Achievement score. In other words, sons who rank low in n Achievement tend to perceive their fathers (and their mothers to a lesser extent) as more friendly and helpful. Sons with high n Achievement tend to perceive their fathers as unfriendly and unhelpful.

TABLE 9.2. Correlations between n Achievement score (C) and personality traits attributed to parents by 30 male college students

	Father	Mother	Combined
1. Friendly, Helpful	−.56	−.39	−.57
2. Domineering, Selfish	.10	.14	.14
3. Successful, Clever, Self-confident	−.37	−.41	−.44

Correlations of .36 and .46 are significant at the 5% and 1% levels of confidence respectively.

"Authoritarian" parental characteristics, Domineering and Selfish, appear to be unrelated to n Achievement score, just as autocratic parent behavior is unrelated (Table 9.1).

The new fact added by this table is that n Achievement score is inversely related to the successfulness of parents as rated by their sons. Sons of college age who think that their parents are clever, successful, and self-confident, do not have high n Achievement scores, if the results of this sample can be generalized. An over-all picture suggested by these data is coherent. College males who give evidence of being very "close" to their parents in their admiration of them and perception of them as particularly loving and helpful do not for the most part score high on n Achievement. On the contrary, it is the students who see their parents as "distant"—unfriendly, severe, unsuccessful—who have high n Achievement scores.

Before drawing any conclusions as to the kind of parent that produces sons with high n Achievement, let us look at some similar data which were collected on high school males as part of another study. Here too the sons rated their parents on the same personality traits on the same scale as we had used for the college males. The relation between n Achievement scores and ratings on the two most significant clusters of traits is reported in Table 9.3, both in terms of mean differences and correlations. The association is now strikingly

TABLE 9.3. Mean ratings on personality traits attributed to their fathers by high school males with high and low n Achievement scores

	Friendly, Helpful	Successful, Clever, Self-confident
High n Achievement ($N = 20$)		
Mean	9.05	12.10
SD	1.24	2.61
Low n Achievement ($N = 19$)		
Mean	7.47	10.63
SD	2.13	2.70
Mean Difference	1.58	1.47
t	2.72	1.69
p	$<.01$	.10
r	$+.30$	$+.15$

reversed. Whereas the correlation between n Achievement score and perceived friendliness of the father is significantly *negative* for college age sons ($r = -.56$, $p < .01$), it is significantly *positive* for the high school age sons ($r = +.30$, $p < .05$). The reversal is also evident in the ratings on successfulness, the high school sons with high n Achievement tending to judge their fathers as more rather than less successful.

How is it that sons in high school with high n Achievement perceive their fathers as friendlier than those with low n Achievement, whereas just the reverse is true in college? Accounting for this difference remains a problem for further research, but a couple of hypotheses come readily to mind. In the first place, the range of *Acceptance-Rejection* to which high school students are exposed may be different from the range to which college students are exposed. That is, since the high school students come from lower socio-economic backgrounds, more of them may have been subjected to a degree of rejection or neglect which is relatively unknown among families from which college students come. Thus a rating of "unfriendly" for a high school student may mean behavior which is objectively much more unfriendly than what the college student means by "unfriendly." Or in similar fashion what the high school student, of lower socio-economic background, considers friendliness might be judged to be fairly unfriendly by the college student who has come to expect more attention. This hypothesis, if correct, would suggest that high n Achievement is associated with moderate levels of friendliness and success in the father and that the reversal of correlations resulted from sampling a low and a high portion of the total range of friendliness, and the like, among fathers. Thus, if the father is too rejectant, n Achievement is not apt to develop; or if he is too nurturant, it is also unlikely to develop.

Another equally plausible hypothesis explains the reversal in relationship with parental severity between high school and college not in terms of actual differences in parental behavior but in terms of the son's perception of that behavior. A high school student is in a quite different situation from a college student: he is younger, more in need of help, and normally still living at home. The college student, on the other hand, is away from home, attempting to break loose from dependency on his parents and establish himself on his own. If he has high n Achievement he may regard any attempt by the parent to help him as an unfriendly, interfering act. Because he is trying to break away from his parents, he may see them in a rather negative light, whereas when he was in high school, he might have viewed them more favorably for exactly the same behavior.

Whatever the explanation turns out to be, the fact remains that the way sons with high n Achievement perceive their parents varies from high school to college and cannot be taken as a very reliable index of how the parents actually behaved toward them.

9.1.3 *Parent-son relations suggested by the sons' views on morality.* On another part of the questionnaire used in the intensive study of 30 college students, the subjects were asked to rate themselves on six "vices"—Disrespect, General Dishonesty, Lack of Courage, Rebellion, Narrow-mindedness, and Over-indulgence. Specifically, they were asked to rate on a six-point scale the seriousness of the vice, their involvement in it, and the *guilt* that they felt if they ever "expressed" that vice. According to our knowledge, to this point, of the way college students perceive their parents, we should expect that those with low *n* Achievement should show more over-all guilt. The argument runs like this: Since the parents of such students are perceived as more nurturant and friendly, the sons should feel closer to them, should interiorize their standards more completely, and should show more guilt for being "bad"—for deviating in any way from the kind of moral demands that parents make. This in fact turns out to be the case, as the first column in Table 9.4 indicates. Subjects low

TABLE 9.4. Guilt felt over "vices" by male college students with high and low *n* Achievement scores

	Over-all Guilt	Disrespect Guilt (A)	Lack-of-Courage Guilt (B)	Difference (A-B)
High *n* Achievement (N = 14)				
Mean	17.00	2.36	3.50	−1.14
SD	6.26	1.23	1.30	1.41
Low *n* Achievement (N = 15)				
Mean	21.60	3.60	3.47	.13
SD	6.95	1.74	1.59	1.89
Mean Difference ..	4.60	1.24	.03	1.27
t	1.81	2.14	.05	1.99
p (predicted direction)	<.05	<.05	—	<.05

in n Achievement attribute more guilt to themselves for transgressing moral codes than subjects high in n Achievement; the probability of finding a difference as large or larger in the obtained direction is less than 5 in 100.

The general picture should also lead us to expect differences with regard to the way in which two of the particular "vices" are regarded. The low n Achievement subjects ought to feel much more guilty over Disrespect than the high n Achievement subjects who have gone on record as believing their parents to be unsuccessful and rejecting. This prediction is also borne out by the facts (Column 2 of Table 9.4).

On the other hand, the high n Achievement group should place much greater stock on independence, the ability to stand alone, or Courage. Here the difference expected does not occur, perhaps because the low n Achievement group is inclined to feel more guilty about everything. The last column in Table 9.4, which takes into account this general tendency by subtracting across, shows (1) that Lack of Courage is reacted to with significantly more guilt than Disrespect by the high n Achievement group ($t = 2.92$, $p < .01$), (2) that there is no significant difference in this respect ($t = .26$, $p < .50$) for the low group, and (3) that the difference between the differences is significant at the 5 per cent level of confidence. In short, college males with high n Achievement are relatively much more concerned about standing up to life's problems bravely than they are about Disrespect; whereas to those with low n Achievement both are vices which lead to equally strong guilt.

The same trend appears in less marked form for Rebellion as for Disrespect. The results are not altered if the data for individual vices are expressed as z-scores of the over-all guilt ratings, or if correlations are run between n Achievement score and an "importance index" which is obtained by adding the "seriousness" and "guilt" ratings and subtracting the "involvement" rating. In short, other analyses of the data strongly support the conclusions which can be seen most clearly in the figures presented in Table 9.4. Low n Achievement in college males seems to be associated with perceived parental nurturance, with closeness to and admiration for the parents promoted both by parental nurturance and success, and with strong guilt feelings for deviating from conventional parental moral demands, particularly for Disrespect. Subjects with low n Achievement appear to be having difficulty in cutting family ties and achieving independence.

High n Achievement in college students, on the other hand, is associated with lack of closeness to parents as reflected in the perception of the parents as rejectant, lacking in self-confidence, and unsuccessful. Disrespect is not nearly so serious a vice for the subjects high in n Achievement as is Lack of Courage. Courage is apparently symbolic for them of their independent, self-reliant achievement urges.

9.1.4 *Resistance to conformity in subjects with high n Achievement.* Confirmation of the analysis just made can be found in two widely different studies dealing with the dependence-independence of subjects with varying n Achievement. In the first, R. W. Brown (1952) demonstrated that college students in the highest third of the n Achievement score distribution were significantly lower on the F scale, a measure of authoritarianism (Adorno, *et al.,* 1950), than the remainder of the subjects. According to its authors, the F scale measures the extent to which a subject, among other things, both likes and obeys authority, strongly admires his parents, believes in conventional morality, and so on. Subjects high in n Achievement, if they are as independent-minded as they appear to be here, should therefore score low on authoritarianism, as in fact they did in Brown's study.

In quite a different field, Asch has conducted a series of experiments (1952) dealing with the ability of individuals to resist enormous social pressures for conformity. He shows a group of about seven students a card on which there is one standard line and three comparison lines of different lengths. By prearrangement with six of the seven students, he fixes it so that each of them states aloud that one of the comparison lines, which is obviously longer or shorter than the standard line, is the one which is equal in length to the standard. Under these conditions the last subject, who is not in on the deception, must, if he is to believe his eyes, choose a line which is different from the one which all his associates have chosen. Even with such strong "reality" forces at work, about one-third of the subjects yield under the group pressure and call out the same wrong line that the majority has picked. Fortunately, a number of these subjects were also given the Murray Thematic Apperception Test, and Dr. Asch kindly made available to us the TAT records of 15 "yielders" and 15 "non-yielders." The stories they told to pictures 7BM, 8BM, 9BM, 14, 18BM, 20 were scored for n Achievement without knowing which subjects belonged in which group. The results were striking. Of the 15 subjects above the median n Achievement score for the whole group, 13 or 87 per cent were "independents," whereas of the 15 below the median, 13 or 87 per cent were "yielders." The Chi square corrected for continuity is 13.33, p < .01. In short, subjects with high n Achievement not only say that lack of courage is the "vice" over which they feel the more guilt, they practice what they preach and actually more often show courageous independence when under social pressure to conform. They are independent in action as well as thought; their independence appears almost to be a consistent "way of life" which either originates or is reflected in their relationship to their parents.

The studies in this section have not been conclusive as to the origins of achievement motivation because they have relied on the reports of subjects as to their relation to their parents. These reports have all been consistent in showing that college students with high n Achievement perceive their par-

ents as distant rather than close and themselves as independent of all types of pressure toward conformity—parental or
otherwise. The students with low n Achievement are just the
opposite. They admire their parents, whom they describe as
friendly and nurturant, and tend to behave in a more dependent manner toward all types of authority. Such an analysis has added greatly to our understanding of how the achievement motive fits into or modifies a person's conception of his
relation to the world. It also strongly suggests that the origins
of achievement motivation will lie in the stress placed on independence training by the culture or family in which the
child is brought up, a notion which is directly tested in the
studies reported in the next section.

9.2 **Independent measures of parent behavior and achievement motivation.** In the studies which follow, emphasis has
shifted from the son and his perception of how he was brought
up to his parents and how they brought him up. In this way
we hope to test more definitively our hypothesis that differences in achievement motivation are learned from the different experiences that children have. Since the son's perception
of his relation to his parents should not be completely unrelated to reality, we begin with the hypothesis that achievement motivation is a function of the stress placed on independence training. Actually, the hypothesis is also supported
by our theoretical analysis of how the achievement motive is
acquired out of the way in which the child is handled as he
faces a variety of learning situations, common to all children
in all cultures at all times. That is, nearly all children have to
learn to walk and talk and all have to master some other skills
such as reading, hunting, sewing, cooking, and the like. Cultures and parents as representatives of the culture will vary
in the amount of pressure they place on their children for
early mastery of such skills. The more they insist on early
mastery, the more the child thinks in achievement terms, the

greater the affect from meeting or failing to meet achievement standards, and so on. In short, the more the child is forced to master things, the greater his n Achievement, the more independent he becomes of his parents, and the more rejectant they are likely to appear to him. The theoretical analysis joins with the data reported in Section 9.1 in supporting the hypothesis that training for early independent mastery of skills should be associated with high achievement motivation. It will be tested first cross-culturally, secondly in a U.S. sample, and finally in an individual case study, to give the concrete picture in greater detail of the relation between the two variables.

9.2.1 *Independence training and Achievement Imagery in folk tales.* The first study deals with the most general question of all: Is stress on independence training by a culture associated with higher achievement motivation for the culture as a whole? The importance of the question lies in the fact that it tests our theoretical position in its most general terms. We do not want to develop a theory of motivation or a method of scoring for achievement motivation which will apply only to middle-class White American males. The theory as stated is more general than that and should apply to children in all cultures. But is such a general question answerable? Ratings on independence training in various cultures can be obtained readily enough from the ethnographic materials available in the Human Relations Area Files, but how can an n Achievement score be obtained for a culture as a whole?

Our solution to this problem involved the use of a type of folk tale common to various North American Indian cultures. There were several reasons why we decided to use folk tales rather than actual TAT stories obtained in the field: (1) It would have been prohibitively expensive, though not impossible, to obtain actual stories in the field from a number of different tribes. (2) Even if we could have obtained stories in the field, our sample of subjects would very likely have been partly acculturated (i.e., Americanized), especially if we had taken them from our usual age groups. Folk tales, on the other hand, since they are passed on by word of mouth, are usually viewed as less altered, "purer" aspects of the culture. (3) Folk tales may be regarded as a joint product of many members of the culture, since they doubtless undergo changes which are typical of common rather than idiosyncratic cultural attitudes. Bartlett's (1932) laboratory studies of serial reproduction support this belief.

Starting with these assumptions, Friedman (1950), working with the assistance of Dr. J. W. M. Whiting and Dr. John Roberts, found in the literature brief stories from each of eight American Indian cultures: Navaho, Ciricahua-Apache, Western Apache, Comanche, Flatheads, Hopi, Paiute, and Sanpoil. Stories were selected in advance of any knowledge of the *n* Achievement scoring system. In order to reduce variability as much as possible, the stories all concerned the same central character, Coyote, who figures as a trickster hero in many of the folk tales told by these Indian tribes. Stories were fairly comparable in length and were as unitary with regard to plot as possible; that is, longer stories were broken up into episodes with a beginning, middle, and end. The stories were then scored in the usual way for *n* Achievement. The fact that no basic changes in approach were necessary to perform this feat may be regarded as evidence of the generality of the scoring system.

The major difference between these stories and those of our college students was the absence of general *Long-Term Involvement*. Career or occupational concern did not appear in the Coyote stories—perhaps because of the circumstances under which they were told. Achievement Imagery in the form of *Competition with a Standard of Excellence*, however, frequently appeared. Interestingly enough, the stories from different cultures often had the same themes, though they differed in the amount of achievement "embroidery" included. Compare these two stories, for example:

A COMANCHE TALE

Coyote was always knocking about hunting for something. He came to a creek, where there was nothing but green willows. Two little yellow-birds were playing there. He came up to them. Laughing, they pulled out their eyes and threw them on the trees, while they stood below. "Eyes, fall!" they said. Then their eyes fell back into their sockets. Coyote went to them. *He greatly admired their trick.* "O brothers! *I wish to play that way, too.*" "Oh, *we won't show you,* you are too mean. You would throw your eyes into any kind of a tree and lose them." "Oh, no! I would do just like you." At last *the birds agreed to show him.* They pulled out his eyes, threw them up, and said, "Eyes, fall!" They returned to their places. "Let us all go along this creek!" said the birds. *"Other people will see us and take a fancy to us."* They went along playing. Coyote said, "I am going over there. I know the trick well now." He left them. He got to another creek. A common willow-tree was standing there. *"There is no need to be afraid of this tree.* I'll try it first." He pulled out his eyes, and threw them at the tree. "Eyes, fall!" he shouted. His eyes did not fall. He thus became blind. He tied something around his eyes, and left.

A PAIUTE TALE

Coyote was walking along. He heard someone laughing. "Come in," they said. Wild Cat and some others were sitting there. I think Skunk was there too. Coyote asked them, "What shall I do?" "Take out your eyes. Throw them in the air. Then hold your head back, and they will fall in again."

Coyote tried to take out his eyes. He took them both out and threw them up, but not very far. He held back his head, and the eyes fell right in the sockets. Everybody laughed.

Then Wild Cat tried it again. *He threw his eyes way in the air,* and they came back. *Everybody laughed* and told Coyote to try it again. "Throw them way up in the air this time," they said. He did it. One had a stick in his hand. When Coyote's eyes were coming down, he knocked them to one side. Then everybody ran away. They took Coyote's eyes with them.

In both tales the central idea is the same, but even without going into the details of the scoring it is obvious that the first version, from a high achievement culture, contains far more achievement imagery than the second. Some of the achievement-related portions have been italicized in each story to make the contrast clearer. According to the Comanche, Coyote wants very much to perform this unusual feat with his eyes (N), is at first blocked (Bw), finally succeeds with the help of the birds (Nup), is proud of his skill ($G+$), and so on. In the Paiute version, the theme has been so changed that it appears that the other animals are now primarily interested in playing a practical joke on Coyote who is not portrayed on the other hand as having any particular achievement concern. Nevertheless, even in this story some hints of achievement imagery appear, and they were scored here and in other similar instances on the ground that some of the finer nuances of meaning may have been lost in translation.

An n Achievement score was compiled for each of the eight cultures by summing algebraically the number of different types of achievement categories appearing in each of the twelve stories, according to system C outlined in Chapter V.

As indicated already, the independence training ratings were based on ethnographic materials available in the Human Relations Area Files. Fortunately, they had already been made for Whiting and Child as part of another study (1953). Furthermore, ratings were also available on other child-rearing variables as well, so that possibly unforeseen relations of n Achievement to parent behavior could be tested. The material in the files varies in its detail from culture to culture, but it includes reports by one or more ethnographers on interviews, actual observations of how parents treat their children, and the like. There were three judges, each of whom read the same material and made his ratings separately. The individual ratings were then pooled to get the standing of the culture on a particular child-training variable. The areas of training rated were: Nursing and weaning, toilet training, sex training, independence training, and aggression control. In each training area three variables were rated. A description of the three variables as rated for independence training follows:

Initial indulgence: the degree to which the parent responds with nurturance and caretaking to dependency needs whenever the child cries or seems to need attention or want affection. This refers to the period before training starts. (Rated on a seven-point scale.)

Age of training: the age at which independence training starts.

Severity: the suddenness of training, strength and frequency of punishment for non-independence, signs of emotional conflict in the child during independence training. (Rated on a seven point scale.)

Of all the areas rated, independence training is most nearly related to what we have been calling achievement training. A child who is forced to be "on his own" and to give up being nurtured by adults is also one who will have to master his own problems and get along by himself. Furthermore, parents who stress independence are likely to stress self-reliance and individual achievement. We therefore predicted that emphasis on independence training in a culture should be positively associated with the *n* Achievement score obtained from the folk tales. It is particularly fortunate that the ratings took into account "signs of emotional conflict," since such signs of affective arousal give the evidence demanded by our theory that the opportunity for motive formation had frequently occurred.

As to the particular aspects of independence training rated, we can make several more specific predictions. *Age of beginning training* should be positively correlated with *n* Achievement score for the culture, both because parents who begin early are apt also to be the ones for whom achievement is most important—who reward their children for successful achieve-

TABLE 9.5. Rank correlations (*tau*) between *n* Achievement scores obtained from folk tales in eight cultures and ratings of child training variables in those cultures

CULTURE	n ACHIEVEMENT		INDEPENDENCE TRAINING RANK				RANKS FOR SEVERITY OF TRAINING ON OTHER VARIABLES			
	Score	Rank	Initial Indulgence	Age	Severity	Age and Severity	Nursing and Weaning	Toilet	Sex	Aggression
Navaho	19	1	3.5	1	1	1	1	4.5	4.5	7
C. Apache	15	2	8	4	2	2	5	2.5	1	2.5
Hopi	13	3	7	2	6.5	4	5	4.5	6.5	2.5
Comanche	12	4	3.5	3	5	3	5	6.5	8	8
Sanpoil	9	5	6	5.5	3.5	5.5	3	1	3	5
W. Apache	5	6	3.5	5.5	3.5	5.5	2	8	2	6
Paiute	2	7	3.5	7	6.5	7	7	6.5	4.5	1
Flatheads	1	8	1	8	8	8	8	2.5	6.5	4
Tau			−.56	.84	.64	.91	.42	.16	.16	−.18
p values *			.05	<.005	<.05	<.0005	<.15	.40	.40	.35

* In those cases involving double or triple tied ranks, exact *p* values were obtained from Sillitto's tables (1947).

ment and punish them for failure—and because the earlier such rewards and punishments are applied, the greater the affective arousal and the larger the number of undifferentiated achievement cues with which such affect is associated (cf. Section 2.11.1). Secondly, *severity of training* should also be correlated with *n* Achievement score, but probably not as highly as age of training because severity refers largely to the negative changes in affect which, according to our theory, are only part of the story. Positive changes in affect (reward for successful striving) should also contribute to motive formation and, to the extent that they are not covered by the rating for severity, the correlation should be lowered. *Age of beginning training*, on the other hand, may reflect either positive or negative approaches to achievement training and thus should produce a higher correlation with *n* Achievement than severity of training should. This last prediction, however, is less certain than the first two because our research and theorizing have not yet dealt adequately with the problem of the relative strengths of "hope of success" and "fear of failure" motives. Finally, we would expect *initial indulgence* with respect to independence training to be *negatively* correlated with *n* Achievement, because this rating indicates the degree to which a particular culture did *not* stress early mastery of problems.

The results are given in Table 9.5. All four of our expectations are confirmed by the facts. Both the *age* at which independence training is instituted and the *severity* of independence training correlate very significantly with *n* Achievement score. With age and severity combined, the relationship is significant well beyond the .001 level of significance even with only eight cases, using the rank order coefficient *tau* developed by Kendall (1948). From inspection it can be seen that there is only one inversion in rank order and one tie that prevent this relationship from being perfect. Since the raw scores in the case of the inversion are one point apart and well within scoring error, it can be concluded that the relationship is a very close one indeed. The prediction of a negative correlation with initial indulgence is borne out at about the .05 level of confidence. The expected higher correlation with *age* than with *severity* also appears, although the difference does not reach significance. The only other child-training variable in the table which approaches a significant relationship with *n* Achievement is severity of weaning. This is not too surprising. Weaning severity and independence training were found to be positively correlated in Whiting and Child's study, and in fact were not too easily distinguished by the raters since one of the criteria for insistence on independence was age of weaning.

These results are especially impressive in view of some of the methodological considerations involved. (1) The person who scored the folk tales had no accurate knowledge of the independence training ratings when he was scoring the stories. (2) Many of the folk tales were collected under adverse circumstances. It was not always possible to get 12 stories that were accurately recorded according to the best field techniques—e.g., through good interpreters, with good rapport, and the like. (3) The dates at which the stories were recorded varied roughly from 1890–1940; the child-training ratings were based on observations made roughly during this same period, but there was no certainty that the date of the folk tales and the date of the observations coincided. From all this we can only conclude that the effect we are measuring is so gross that it can be picked up readily even with our imperfect instruments.

Needless to say, we are not necessarily arguing for a direct cause and effect relationship between emphasis on independence training and *cultural n* Achievement score. That is, there are two ways of conceiving what the amount of achievement imagery in folk tales means. On the one hand, it may reflect the modal achievement motivation of the many individuals who have told and retold the stories. If so, we might argue that the stress on independence training produces higher achievement motivation which is reflected in the stories told in the culture. On the other hand, a more likely and not completely incompatible hypothesis is that the cultural *n* Achievement score reflects a general emphasis on achievement in the culture which affects *both* child training and the kind of stories which are told in the culture, particularly since the stories may often be told to educate the young.

9.2.2 *The sources of achievement motivation in mothers' attitudes toward independence training.* By far the most direct and conclusive test of our hypothesis that *n* Achievement is associated with stress on independence training has been made by Winterbottom (1953). She obtained *n* Achievement scores from stories told by 29 normal boys, 8–10 years old, in response to verbal cues (see Section 6.3) under both Relaxed and Achievement-oriented conditions. Since her findings were substantially the same for scores obtained under the two conditions, and since we have some justification for believing scores obtained under Achievement orientation are the best measure of individual differences (see Section 7.7), we will report here only the results obtained with scores obtained under Achievement orientation. The verbal cues used in this condition were as follows:

1. A father and son talking about something important
2. Brothers and sisters playing. One is a little ahead
3. A young man alone at night
4. A boy with his head resting on his hands

The average *n* Achievement score for stories (each told in 4–5 minutes) in response to these cues was 5.69, $SD = 5.05$.

The mother's attitude toward independence training was obtained from a questionnaire given the mother in an interview, the nature of which is best indicated by the "core" section dealing with training demands reproduced in part below.

Beside each statement there are two blanks. In the first one put a check mark if it is one of the things you want in your child by the time he is ten years old. In the second one put the approximate age by which you think your child should have learned this behavior. The sample below illustrates how to do this:

__V__ __10__ To obey traffic signals and street lights when he is out alone

This mother has checked this as one of the things she wants in her child and she expects him to learn this by the age of 10. . . . Lots of books have been written on how a mother should treat her child but it's surprising how little information we have on what the people on the firing-line—the mothers—actually do. We would like you to answer these questions by telling us what you find works best with your child.

___ ___ To stand up for his own rights with other children

___ ___ To know his way around his part of the city so that he can play where he wants without getting lost

___ ___ To go outside to play when he wants to be noisy or boisterous

___ ___ To be willing to try new things on his own without depending on his mother for help

___ ___ To be active and energetic in climbing, jumping and sports

___ ___ To show pride in his own ability to do things well

___ ___ To take part in his parents' interests and conversations

___ ___ To try hard things for himself without asking for help

___ ___ To be able to eat alone without help in cutting and handling food

___ ___ To be able to lead other children and assert himself in children's groups

___ ___ To make his own friends among children his own age

___ ___ To hang up his own clothes and look after his own possessions

___ ___ To do well in school on his own

___ ___ To be able to undress and go to bed by himself

___ ___ To have interests and hobbies of his own. To be able to entertain himself

___ ___ To earn his own spending money

___ ___ To do some regular tasks around the house

___ ___ To be able to stay at home during the day alone

___ ___ To make decisions like choosing his clothes or deciding how to spend his money by himself

___ ___ To do well in competition with other children. To try hard to come out on top in games and sports

These items came from some interview scales developed by Whiting and Sears at Harvard University, and each one was rephrased as a restriction in another part of the questionnaire. For example, the first item in the above list became the following restriction, to be filled out in the same way if the mother wanted it before age 10.

___ ___ Not to fight with children to get his own way

In many instances the restrictions indicated not only an absence of opportunity for independent action by the child but also positive restrictive action by the parent. The questionnaire covered a number of other matters, but these are the ones most relevant to our hypothesis.

Winterbottom's main results are summarized in Figure 9.1 and Table 9.6 which show that while the total number of demands made by mothers of sons with high and low n Achievement (above and below the median score) does not differ, the mothers of sons with high n Achievement expect their children to have met independence demands much earlier in life. Thus, as the cumulative percentage curve in Figure 9.1 shows, by age 7 the mothers of sons with high n Achievement expect that over 60 per cent of the demands checked will have been learned, whereas the mothers of sons with low n Achievement expect that only about 33 per cent of their demands will have been learned. If the distribution of ages at which demands are to be learned is broken at age 8, the results shown in Table 9.6 are obtained. The sons with high n Achievement have mothers who say they require almost twice as many skills to

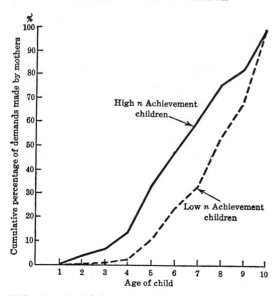

FIG. 9.1. Cumulative curves showing the proportion of total demands made up to each age level as reported by mothers of children scoring high and low on *n* Achievement (Achievement orientation).

be mastered below the age of 8 as are required by the mothers of sons with low *n* Achievement.

The "restrictions" data are also interesting although less conclusive. In general, they parallel the "demands" results but with a minor and perhaps significant difference. The mothers of children with low *n* Achievement tend to check more restrictions over all ages ($p \sim .06$, with a non-parametric test of association), while there is no difference in the total number of demands checked by the two groups of mothers. This greater restrictiveness shows up in Table 9.6 if one compares the ratio of demands to restrictions below the age of 8. Thus the mothers of "lows" make almost as many restrictions (mean $= 5.80$) as they do demands (mean $= 6.07$), and the difference between them is not significant. But the mothers of "highs" make more demands (mean $= 11.71$) than they do

TABLE 9.6. Average number of demands and restrictions required below and above age 8 by mothers of children with high and low n Achievement (Achievement orientation)

| | MOTHERS' DEMANDS | | MOTHERS' RESTRICTIONS | |
	Age 7 and Below	Age 8 and Above	Age 7 and Below	Age 8 and Above
Sons with High n Achievement ($N = 14$)				
Mean	11.71	7.43	8.79	4.50
SD	4.68	4.62	3.56	3.42
Sons with Low n Achievement ($N = 15$)				
Mean	6.07	12.13	5.80	9.60
SD	4.05	3.94	3.92	5.02
Difference between means	5.64	−4.70	2.99	−5.10
σ diff.	1.69	1.66	1.44	1.64
t	3.34	2.83	2.10	3.11
p	<.01	<.01	<.05	<.01

restrictions (mean $= 8.79$) before the age of 8 at a nearly significant level ($p < .08$). Another part of the same picture is illustrated by the way the mothers of the "highs" tend to cease making restrictions at age 8 while the mothers of the "lows" increase their restrictions. It might be argued that this is just because the mothers of the "highs" always tend to put the pressure on earlier. After all, they also drop off in the *demands* they make from age 8 on. But this is an artifact, because there are a limited number of items on the scale. Thus for the mothers of the "highs" there are only 8.29 demands left on the average for them to check to be learned at 8 or above, and they check 7.43 on the average, or nearly 90 per cent of these. The mothers of the "lows" check around 85 per cent of the demands left for them. With the restrictions it is different. Here from age 8 on the mothers of the "lows" check about 67 per cent of the restrictions left to them while the mothers of the "highs" are checking only 40 per cent of the restrictions left to them.

What this adds up to may be simply summarized. The mothers of sons with low n Achievement tend to demand less in the way of independent achievement at an early age, and they tend to be more restrictive than the other mothers. It is worth noting in this connection that the one item among the restrictions which differentiated the mothers of the "highs" and "lows" most significantly dealt with not playing "with children his parents don't know or disapprove." Significantly more of the mothers checking this item had sons with scores below the median on n Achievement. This finding is consistent with Brown's F scale results showing that low n Achievement is associated with higher F scale scores. That is, Adorno, et al. (1950) argue that high "authoritarianism" (F score) is the product of a strict home environment where conventional moral standards are stressed. The mothers of our "lows" seem to have the attitudes typical of such homes and should therefore produce children who also have high F scores, a fact which would account for the inverse correlation between F score and n Achievement, reported by R. W. Brown (1952). In short, mothers who don't want their children to play with strangers are more apt to have attitudes favoring the development of sons with low n Achievement and with high F scores or "anti-democratic" attitudes. Apparently low n Achievement comes from the same "authoritarian" or protective family syndrome which is also associated with race prejudice and the like.

The mothers of sons with high n Achievement, on the other hand, represent an "individualistic" family pattern in that they stress early independent achievement. They also make more restrictions initially, though as Winterbottom (1953) showed in another type of analysis, the restrictions tend to come *after* the demands. What is more, the restrictions fall off more markedly after age 8, presumably after the child has mastered the necessary skills. The picture here is of a parent who urges her child to master a skill early (e.g., "to know his way around the city"), restricts him until he does (e.g., "not to play away from home"), and then lets him alone. In short, she has faith in her son's ability to master something and do it on his own, whereas the mother of a son with low n Achievement tends not to have that faith and to continue restricting her child to playing around the house.

It is especially revealing in this connection to look at the "demand" items on which the mothers of the "highs" and "lows" differed and did not differ. The greatest differences appeared on the following items which were demanded significantly more often before age 8 by the mothers of the "highs" than by the mothers of the "lows":

1. To know his way around the city
2. To try new things for himself
3. To do well in competition
4. To make his own friends

The mothers did not differ on such items as these:

1. To eat well alone
2. To look after his own possessions
3. To go to bed by himself
4. To do tasks around the house

The difference between these two types of items is clear-cut. In the latter, the child is urged to do something on his own *so that the parent won't have to do it*. If the child doesn't eat alone, then the mother has to feed him. In the former, the demand seems to relate more directly to the welfare of the child, *as an end in himself*, rather than as a means to the end of freeing the parent from some "caretaking" jobs with respect to the child. If the child doesn't know his way around the city, his mother doesn't have to do it for him. The mother of the son with high n Achievement is interested in her son's developing away from her, in urging him to master things on his own, whereas the mother of the son with low n Achievement is willing to let such things slide and let him remain somewhat more dependent on her. Our initial hypothesis seems amply justified: *Achievement motivation in boys is associated with stress on independence training by their mothers.*

Before leaving this topic entirely, it is perhaps worth recording some very tentative additional findings which tend to show that the reverse is true of girls. Lowell obtained n Achievement scores in the usual way on Mormon boys and girls of high school age in a Southwest rural community. As part of another study, the mothers of a number of these children were interviewed on their socialization practices with respect to a younger child in the same family. Out of these interviews a rating on "severity of interference with a child's dependent responses" was made. In the case of the six families on whose older sons he had n Achievement scores, the correlation between n Achievement and severity of independence training was positive, as expected ($tau = +.41$, $p < .15$), but for the six families on whose older daughters he had n Achievement scores, the relationship was reversed ($tau = -.41$, $p < .15$). This is only a straw in the wind, but it is suggestive because the relationship for boys is "normal" even for so small a sample and because it is logical to assume that interference with dependency in girls, since it is more expected of women, may indicate a rejection by the mother either of the daughter or the female role. Such rejection would hardly be conducive to developing high n Achievement in the daughters, which is apparently associated with social acceptability (and possibly dependence) in women (Section 6.5) rather than with independent mastery.

9.2.3 *Affective arousal and achievement motivation.* Chapter II contains proposals for a theory of motivation which argues that a motive results from the pairing of certain cues with an affect-producing situation. Fortunately again, Winterbottom (1953) obtained data which bear directly on this problem. The questionnaire the mothers filled out contained the following item which came directly after they had answered the "demands" section:

When your child is learning how to do things like these, which of the following are you most likely to do when he does what you want? Mark your first three choices (1, 2, 3) in the space beside the ones you choose.

___ Tell him what a good boy he is. Praise him for doing well
___ Do nothing at all to make it seem special
___ Show him that you expected it of him
___ Kiss or hug him to show how pleased you are
___ Give him a special treat or privilege
___ Show him how he could have done even better

The theory makes at least one specific prediction as to how the mothers of sons with high n Achievement should check these alternatives. It is this: Primary physical affection (kissing and hugging) for fulfilling an achievement demand should produce the most certain and probably the largest affective change in young children associated with achievement situations. Therefore it should result in higher n Achievement in those children who experience it (Section 2.11.1).

Fortunately, the mothers broke about even in whether they checked this item at all or not. The results may be summarized very simply as follows:

	Mothers Reporting Physical Rewards		Mothers Not Reporting Physical Rewards
Sons' mean n Achievement score	7.60		3.64
SD	4.51		4.79
Difference		3.96	
σ diff.		1.80	
t		2.20	
p		<.05	

The hypothesis is confirmed: Mothers who use physical rewards for fulfillment of achievement demands have sons whose average n Achievement score is twice that of the sons of mothers who use more attenuated means of affective arousal. Unfortunately, not enough mothers admitted using physical punishment for non-fulfillment of demands to check any hypothesis in this area. Also it was not possible to check the possibility that giving a "special treat" might also in some cases involve primary sensory affect and hence lead to higher n Achievement.

Needless to say, this evidence does not conclusively prove that affective arousal *produced* the higher achievement motivation. It may simply reflect the fact that the mothers who used it felt more strongly about achievement and put greater pressure of all kinds on their sons. But this hypothesis seems a little less reasonable than the first, because it seems more likely that the preferred mode of handling a child—e.g., through verbal, objective, or physical rewards—is a personality or ideological characteristic of the mother rather than a direct result of the intensity of the mother's own achievement drive. Further research will have to settle this question, but as of the moment, the data appear to support the "affective arousal" hypothesis as to the origin of motives.

9.2.4 *A case study of training in independence.* Our descriptions so far have all been in terms of nomothetic relationships and, as such, have necessarily seemed rather abstract. We have had to talk of modal rather than concrete mothers and fathers. To add some "flesh and blood" to the picture of how n Achievement originates, let us look at an actual family which emphasizes independence and mastery to see how our theoretical formulation works for the individual case.

The case study to be reported was made by a field worker as part of a larger study on child-training practices for the Laboratory of Human Development at Harvard University under the direction of Dr. Robert R. Sears and Dr. J. W. M. Whiting. The family discussed is Spanish-American and lives somewhere in New Mexico. The interviewer had no knowledge of the children's n Achievement scores which had been obtained by another field worker in school two months earlier. Unfortunately, we had stories written under neutral conditions from only the second-oldest son, whom we will call José. The other children in the family wrote stories under various other experimental conditions. If our analysis of child-rearing conditions is correct, José's n Achievement score should be quite high. Here are some excerpts from the field worker's complete notes on her interviews with José's family.

I talked with Mrs. M both yesterday morning and this morning. There are five children in the family ranging in age from 5 to 16 years. The oldest is a boy who is 16, then another boy [our subject José] who is 15, then two girls, and a small boy. All the children are going to school. They have to take care of themselves. They cook themselves, take care of each other, clean the house, and keep the place going. The children have had to take care of themselves ever since they were little—since the oldest boy was about two or three. Mr. M was very ill. He had rheumatism and was bedridden for about seven years, and so the children had to take care of themselves and each other. So they are used to it. They all started working—helping to take care of the cattle and the pigs, milking the cows, and doing all sorts of work such as cleaning the house and cooking—from the age of five or earlier. When I went over there yesterday, the youngest child (who is five) wasn't feeling very well. He'd taken a bath in cold water the day before and probably had a chill. His mother was kidding perhaps, but she said he was sick because he didn't want to work.

The boy José was breast fed only for four months because it was at that time that Mr. M became ill. With all the excitement and all the work she had to do, Mrs. M lost her milk. As soon as they could sit up, which was at about three months, they would sit in a chair and eat by themselves. She said they learned early to eat by themselves. Toilet training began really quite early. They would begin about four months; she had a special high chair for them. The oldest boy taught the younger. By five months he would know where to go and she said it was the same with all the children. By five months they were all trained . . . she never picked the children up when they cried. She just turned them over in bed and if they kept crying, she just let them cry. . . . The children never woke up during the night, or if they did, she would just turn them over. If they didn't sleep, she would just let them cry it out, and they learned soon enough that they had to go to sleep. She seems not to have given very much nurturance to any of the children, and if they did get any nurturance, it was when one of the older children took care of them. She didn't think it was right to give the child attention or to pick the child up. The children learned to dress themselves shortly after they were a year old. She would just put their clothes out in a little box near their bed, and they had to dress themselves or else they didn't get dressed.

Aggression is greatly discouraged and greatly punished. Children just don't talk back to their parents. The father is the authoritative figure to the children. As soon as he says anything, they listen. That's because he has carried out his threats. Often the children have done something wrong like shirking their work or hitting each other. She has told the father and he gets after them.

As far as responsibility goes, there's quite a bit in this family. Everybody in the family can cook, including the five-year-old. The mother doesn't too often make meals for them. Whoever comes in first makes the meals—maybe the father, the boys, or the girls. Each child does his share of the work. They work from early morning to evening. Each child has a certain number of pigs and cows which are his, and which he has to take care of, and this is his property. If any of them are sold, the child gets the money to go into his bank account, and he can use this money for further education, but cannot go out and buy just anything with it. If he does, he can't have the money. She said that they enjoyed work, that it was like a game to them as they all worked together. They have to do good jobs, and the mother and father are on hand to see the jobs are done and done well.

She contrasted her child-rearing practices with others who were more indulgent with their children and played with them, while her children have lots of responsibilities such as taking care of the cattle and working on the farm, and the boys often plow. All the children can drive with the exception of the youngest one. She said that a lot of people don't like her children because they don't do jobs for other people because they're always working with their own property, taking care of their own things. This family apparently deviates a lot in the amount of ambition and importance it places on property and work by members of the family. I was also struck by the contrast between the lack of interaction in the M family, the lack of warmth, and her reports on the child training of other Spanish-American families which were definitely child-centered and in which the adults were very warm and responsive toward the children. At this point the M's seem to be quite deviant and Mrs. M did say that in her child-rearing she was different from others. The other mothers spoiled their children by paying too much attention to them.

There is much more detail in the field worker's notes, but it is all along the same lines. The M's are parents who have stressed the importance of hard work and the mastery of skills like dressing, cooking, driving, farming, and so on, at an early age. There has been minimal indulgence and nurturance, to judge by the mother's reports and the field worker's incidental observations.

Early learning experiences like these should produce high n Achievement in the children of the M family, if our hypotheses about the origin of achievement motivation are correct. Once again it appears that the stress on achievement is maintained largely by negative reinforcing agents—punishment for failure to do something for oneself, and the like. This may reflect the true state of affairs, or it may reflect, at least in part, the theoretical orientation of the research worker who might have been more interested in traumas, conflicts, and so forth. But in any case early mastery of skills was certainly stressed, and we would have to predict that the M children would have high n Achievement.

The TAT stories written by José, the second-oldest son, confirm our prediction. They yield a score of $+6$ which is definitely above average in comparison with the group of Texan boys in the same class with him (mean $= 2.30$, $SD = 4.00$) and probably even further above average in comparison with other Spanish-American boys on whom we unfortunately do not have norms as yet. José's most directly achievement-related story runs as follows:

The boys are trying to make a better house in which to play and the girls are trying to put up a little competition. They are playing in the barn on a windy day and they thought they would build themselves a small house which would do better than the barn. The girls were thinking about the house the boys had. They thought their's was better, and the boys needed some boards which they asked the girls for it. The girls were about finished and didn't have enough boards, so they brought back the boards which they had loaned so neither the boys nor the girls got their house finished although the boys beat.

Although this story deals with play activity, it involves several references to "competition with a standard of excellence"—e.g., building a better house than the barn, the boys competing with the girls to see who can do the better job. In addition to Achievement Imagery, this story contains Achievement Thema, Environmental Obstacles, Affective Goal State, Instrumental Activity, and Nurturant Press—a total score of six. The other three stories were all doubtful and were scored 0 because they do not quite meet our criteria, although they all contained references to working hard. His first story is typical of the other three and comes extremely close to being scored as an achievement story. It is especially interesting because it reflects so accurately the home situation.

They were talking about the father raising the boy's allowance because he didn't have enough to pay for something important. He had been with a couple of friends and sold a watch, which he wanted to buy back if he had the money. The father was thinking of the son working to raise the son's allowance and his son was thinking about the money he wanted for the watch. The father will lend the boy money so that the boy will have the watch and pay after he has raised the money.

In some respects the references to an "allowance," which is Long-Term Involvement for a boy, and to "raising money" would argue for scoring this story as achievement-related which would raise his over-all score even higher. His last two stories are also doubtful and might be scored. The point is that, *even with conservative scoring*, José scores very high on *n* Achievement, as indeed he should if the emphasis on independent striving which characterized his upbringing leads to high *n* Achievement as we have hypothesized.

9.3 Achievement motivation in the context of total personality development. Throughout the greater portion of this report we have been dealing with abstractions, with the kinds of general relationships useful in developing a science of personality. But we should not lose sight of the fact that the achievement motive never develops or functions in a vacuum. It is but one aspect of a complex personality structure, and only case studies of individuals can begin to give the total picture. It has already been mentioned that we made rather intensive case studies of 30 male college students in order not to lose sight of the individual personality in a maze of abstract relationships. In addition to taking a large number of tests, the results of which have been reported throughout the previous chapters, each of the students was interviewed at length by a psychiatrist and given the Rorschach, Sentence Completion, and an abbreviated form of Murray's Thematic Apperception Test by a clinical psychologist. The psychiatrist wrote brief, dynamically-oriented case summaries on each man, and in consultation with the clinical psychologist filled out a rating scale covering a number of variables including the parent behavior dimensions discussed previously.

9.3.1 *Clinical ratings and* n *Achievement score.* Clinical ratings on each of the variables were then correlated with *n* Achievement score (C) with the following results:

Need for Achievement [*] .... .08
Need for Security [*] .... .06
Insight and Self-Integration [*] .... .34
Ego-Ideal Development .... .10
Super-Ego Development .... .26
Suggestibility .... .06

[*] Joint rating by psychiatrist and clinical psychologist.

The reasons for including these variables is fairly obvious with the possible exception of *suggestibility*. Here the intention was to test the common psychoanalytic hypothesis that hypnotizability and suggestibility are symptomatic of passive dependent wishes, in which case suggestibility should be negatively correlated with n Achievement. On the whole, the correlations are insignificant and add nothing much to our understanding of the achievement motive. The only correlation which approaches significance—that with Insight and Self-Integration—is consistent with similar positive correlations found twice with the Interest Maturity Scale of the Strong Vocational Interest Inventory (H. H. Morgan, 1951, and Chap. VIII). A rationale for these relationships can be found in the hypothesis that maturity as measured in these ways represents the willingness of a person to accept responsibility and act independently like an older person—a characteristic which should, by definition, be related to high achievement motivation.

The lack of correlation between n Achievement score and clinical ratings of achievement motivation is a negative finding which requires some thought, however, especially in view of the usual assumption that clinical judgments should serve to validate testing instruments of this sort. Obviously our TAT measure of n Achievement is reflecting some aspect of the individual's motivational system that is different from what the clinical judges meant when they rated the achievement drive. This is not so surprising because the ratings were made over four years prior to this writing, at which time we had only a very imperfect understanding of what we meant by the term *n Achievement*. Thus, we were not able to give the psychiatrist and clinical psychologist a very clear definition with which to operate. As a matter of fact, a *post hoc* scrutiny of the psychiatrist's written case summaries suggests that the discrepancy in the amount of achievement drive ascribed to an individual by these two methods of measurement is not so great as the lack of correlation indicates. The psychiatrist usually was able to distinguish between a strong latent achievement motive which was blocked so that the person did not work hard and an unblocked or functioning strong motive. But when it came to reducing these two different types of cases to a rating, we had given him no instructions as to what to do, largely because at that time we did not know to what extent an inhibited motive gets expressed in the TAT. The result was that the psychiatrist's ratings represented some kind of compromise judgment which involved both the strength of the latent motive and the degree to which the person was able to express it successfully in life. A clear decision to rate in terms of one standard or the other might have produced a higher correlation with *n* Achievement score.

It is worth recording that Winterbottom (1953) found that teacher ratings of "general independence" and "pleasure in success" were significantly related to boys' *n* Achievement scores and more so than teacher ratings of "general success motivation." It looks as if judges have difficulty assessing motivation accurately, since they must make complex inferences from behavior, but when they rate "behavioral signs" (e.g., "pleasure in success" or "general independence"), their ratings may provide better indirect evidence of the strength of motivation.

9.3.2 *Case summaries of students with high and low* n *Achievement scores.* The rating data suggest that the role of achievement motivation in the functioning in the individual is probably quite complex. To show how true this is, let us take a closer look at several cases in the male college student group where there is disagreement and agreement between the n Achievement score and the psychiatrist's rating. In interpreting each case we can illustrate how n Achievement concretely develops and functions particularly in relation to the parents and the home situation.

There were three individuals who received low TAT n Achievement scores, but who had been rated as possessing intense achievement drive by Dr. Simon and Dr. Holzberg. The common factor running through these three records is the presence of a large amount of tension or anxiety related to the achievement sphere. If there is anxiety about achievement for some reason—fear of failure, fear of competition with the father, or what not—the expression of achievement imagery in the TAT may be blocked for these individuals. Thus, the achievement drive would not show up in our TAT measure, but the psychiatric interview might have been sufficiently long and "deep" to get beyond such an inhibition. This runs contrary to the rather general assumption that the TAT, as well as other projective tests, are capable of revealing the dynamics of personality that the individual consciously distorts or conceals in one fashion or another, although it must always be remembered that our form of the TAT is less searching than the usual one. As we have already pointed out several times, Clark's discovery (1952) that sexual arousal inhibits sexual imagery in these stories provides an experimental basis for arguing that some of our subjects will not be able to express their achievement concern directly because of anxiety attached to it. The possibility that they may express it indirectly, through symbols, as some of Clark's subjects did, has not been investigated as yet.

To return to our three cases again, all of them have enough anxiety over independent achievement to explain a blocking of achievement imagery on the TAT. In short, they all appear to be what we have come to call "false lows." The first one is a peptic ulcer case. His personality structure seems consistent with one of the basic patterns described by Alexander (cf. Tomkins, 1943) as being typical of individuals who develop an ulcer of psychosomatic origin. There is evidence of strong overt striving for achievement and independence with a surface rejection of dependency on the father. In the classical fashion, however, there is a strong repressed dependency need. Apparently the parents of this subject have instilled in him a strong achievement drive by making their love contingent upon his successful attainment of achievement goals. His IQ compares favorably with his classmates but his grades are below average. He has always consciously wanted to become a doctor, but with such grades he is not likely to achieve that goal. This should increase his fear of failure and fear of loss of love for non-achievement—a crippling fear which may have been partly responsible for his inefficiency in the first place, and which is certainly sufficient to account for his inability to think or write about achievement in his TAT.

The difficulty with this and other similar interpretations is that we cannot be sure what level of functioning the TAT is measuring. One might also argue in this case that the TAT is reflecting the fact that this man has no *real* need for achievement. What he wants basically is security and love and the achievement striving so obvious to the psychiatrist may be only a surface or secondary phenomenon which is not picked up by the TAT. In the present state of our ignorance we cannot decide between such alternative hypotheses, and we present them only for the value they may have in guiding further research.

Our second subject also had a low TAT *n* Achievement score, but was rated by the psychiatrist as having an intense achievement drive. This individual is described as having cold and clammy hands, as being admittedly "nervous," as talking rapidly and in bursts, and so forth. There is a lot of evidence for general anxiety, and his particular anxiety over achievement seems to be based on a fear of competition with his physician father who has pressured him into medicine against his will. The subject states openly that he feels inferior and that he doubts his chances of ever being as successful as his dad. His anxiety over achievement could be fear of failing to live up to his father's expectations, or it could be fear that he would surpass his father in the medical profession —thus symbolically displacing the father in the Oedipal triangle. Whichever interpretation is favored does not really matter for our purposes. The presence of either kind of anxiety could lead to inhibition of manifest achievement imagery in the TAT stories and give us another "false low."

The third case is similar to the second in that he has a fear of competing with others. According to the psychiatrist, he also has an intense need for love and security. One plausible explanation for the fear of competition in this case is that the subject is of German-Jewish origin and consequently may fear that successful competition will expose him to envy and lead to additional anti-Semitic attacks, rejection, and loss of love. In this case his presumed high n Achievement is in conflict with his strong need for affiliation, a conflict which could produce the anxiety over successful competition which in turn might lead to the inhibition of overt achievement imagery in the TAT. Or again, as in the first case, the conscious achievement drive may not be basic but secondary to satisfying more fundamental security needs, a state of affairs which is represented by a low n Achievement score on the TAT.

As a contrast to these cases, let us examine two other cases who have both high TAT n Achievement and high psychiatric ratings of n Achievement. The first individual, like the three preceding cases, shows an intense amount of anxiety, which is probably chronic. If our first hypothesis is correct, why doesn't this individual show inhibition of achievement imagery in his stories? One possible explanation is the absence of any evidence that the anxiety is connected with achievement. Unfortunately, we cannot be certain that there is no anxiety connected with achievement, and even if we were certain, we would be in doubt as to exactly why there is not. His parents were very strict and authoritarian, and the subject consciously *dislikes* them with *strong hatred* just at the preconscious level. Perhaps his anxiety is derived largely from a fear of rejection by loved ones. He is a solitary individual who has been badly hurt in his affiliative relations with his severe parents. In the achievement sphere, however, he has a very high IQ and also very high grades. Thus, even if there were at one time some anxiety over achievement, it could have been extinguished by a prolonged period of success, or it may have been outweighed by the substitute satisfactions of academic success in an unpleasant home situation, or it may never have developed because the parents did not use the "conditional love" formula. The data are not sufficient to decide among these alternatives.

As a startling contrast, let us look at our last case who also has high *n* Achievement as indicated by both the TAT and the rating scale. He is a sociable, well adjusted, pleasant, cooperative young man. The family situation is described as "exceptionally good," with a tolerant, acceptant, democratic atmosphere. This gives a picture of parents who administer rewards for reaching achievement goals, but who are not punishing or rejecting for failure to reach these goals. Thus, this individual's achievement motivation should be characterized by high "hope of success" rather than by "fear of failure." Therefore, in the absence of much anxiety over achievement, we would not expect inhibition of achievement imagery in the TAT.

The main function of these case studies is to underline the complexity of the origins of *n* Achievement in any particular case and to prevent the theorist from oversimplifying etiological factors. Another function is to suggest new hypotheses

⚜CHAPTER X⚜

Review

WHAT HAVE we accomplished? It is time to stop and take stock, to seek some perspective on our method of procedure, our findings, and their implications for future research. A detailed summary of the book would be tiresome and pointless, but a quick non-technical review of what we have done will serve to emphasize its major features and provide an overview of its contribution to the study of human motivation. In making such a review we shall try to suggest the directions of research necessary to complete or fill out what we have begun. For at least one major criterion of the usefulness of a work of this sort is its seminal character. Where does it lead? Does it suggest interesting research possibilities?

Our basic approach was simple: It involved attempts to alter the content of fantasy experimentally. But it soon broadened and developed in three ways—in the type of experimental variable used, in the type of fantasy sampled, and in the method of content analysis adopted for studying fantasy. With respect to the variable introduced to influence fantasy, it is obvious that any experimentally-induced condition will serve the purpose. And the simpler it is to produce in the laboratory the better—apparently. We ourselves, in fact, began with the effects of hunger on imagination. More recently the effects of such traditional laboratory variables as pain (Wendt, 1953), noise (Wendt, 1953), and sleep-inducing drugs (Mücher, 1953) have been studied. But we wanted to go beyond such simple variables in the conviction that, if we are to understand human nature, we must start operating in

319

the laboratory with the kind of motives which actually are important in the lives of human adults. The usual reason for not working with such variables is precisely because they are so difficult to manipulate in the laboratory under experimental conditions. But this should not be a crippling obstacle. Is it not sheer lack of ingenuity which forces us to fall back on electric shock or frustration as motivating forces? Shock is certainly easier to induce than the achievement motive, but it does not follow that what can be learned about motivation from working with shock is necessarily more important. On the contrary, will we not have a better chance of understanding the nature of motivation by working experimentally with the kinds of motives which constitute a large share of our everyday striving? It was this conviction which led us to experiment persistently with different methods of arousing the achievement motive in the laboratory. Whether we succeeded or not, we will have accomplished something if our efforts stimulate others to find even more ingenious ways of working in the laboratory with major human motives. Growing out of our work already have been other studies which have dealt with experimental variations in such other motives as affiliation (Shipley and Veroff, 1952) and sex (Clark, 1952). In both cases, motives were aroused in situations manipulated with considerable ingenuity by the experimenter.

With respect to the second variable—the type of fantasy measured—we have again gone somewhat beyond the traditional approach. Normally fantasy—whether it is in the form of dreams, free associations, or stories on the Murray Thematic Apperception Test—has been considered the tool par excellence of the clinical psychologist. It has been studied as the idiosyncratic product of a particular individual. It has been considered valuable almost in direct proportion to its richness, fullness, and variety. Its clinical orientation is suggested by the very term *projective technique* which has become common usage in describing all sorts of fantasy productions, despite the fact that most theorists would agree that only a small portion of fantasy involves "projection" in the strict Freudian sense. But our approach has been quite different from this. Instead of rich and full "personal documents," we collected short standardized stories. What is more we even depersonalized the testing situation so that our subjects wrote more or less anonymously in a group situation. In fact, the whole procedure is such a far cry from clinical analysis of fantasy (or perhaps from fantasy itself) that it would be the better part of wisdom to assume that the two procedures have a different purpose and deserve different names. Thus our own technique we have tended to refer to in recent years as "thought sampling." The virtues of such a term are (1) that it stresses the sampling aspect of the procedure, and (2) that it recognizes the fact that we are dealing with the association processes broadly conceived rather than just the fantasy portion of them.

The sampling problem is an interesting one. Just what is the total population of thoughts? A little simple calculation will show that it is fairly large. In analyzing one of our written protocols, we have estimated that the average person produces about 8 to 12 identifiable thought units a minute. At this rate he would produce around 600 an hour, up to 10,000 a day, between 3 and 4 million a year, or 250 million in a lifetime. Then if we are to consider the total population of the earth during any given time period it is clear that we are dealing with an order of number which is large enough to give some regularities even by the standards of the physical universe. But the concrete problem of determining what constitutes a "representative" sample of such a population is difficult. We will clearly have to deal with sub-populations and not attempt to generalize too widely. In our own case we have generally used picture cues to elicit thought samples in short bursts. But what picture cues shall we use? What variety of situations should be represented? Or are verbal cues better? Or even certain other sensory ones? What is the optimal "thought sample" length? We have answered none of these questions finally, but we raise them because it is now clear to us that there is an opportunity here to reopen an almost discarded line of psychological inquiry, namely, the analysis of ideational content which appeared to have ended in a blind alley with the demise of introspectionism a generation ago.

The third aspect of our approach—the *method* of content analysis—also came in for some rethinking. Content analysis is not new. It has been used for some time and rather widely in studies of literature and the mass media (see Berelson, 1952). Also Murray's various systems of content analysis (1938) are exceedingly rich and detailed. Our own system of scoring for *n* Achievement clearly derives from Murray. But the fact that our method of content analysis had to reflect an experimental variable added a new and significant force which influenced the shape of our final scoring definitions. That is, most content categories are derived rationally in terms of some conceptual system, but the weakness of relying entirely on a priori reasoning lies in the fact that the categories may not "fit" the data. In our own case we began with a scoring definition for achievement imagery, then mixed together the protocols written under achievement arousal with those written under neutral conditions, and tested to see whether our definition succeeded in discriminating the two types of records. Of course it did not do the job very well the first time, although on a priori grounds the definition of achievement imagery seemed good enough to us. So we revised the scoring system and went through the procedure again and so on through half a dozen successive revisions. We tried not to lose sight ever of the theoretical coherence of our final categories, but at the same time they had to be defined in such a way as to capture the effects of the variable which we had experimentally introduced. Of course, in the process of developing a definition of achievement imagery in this way, we may have come out with something that does not correspond exactly to what people think achievement imagery is. But this is not too disturbing. What people think achievement imagery is may be a significant aspect of social perception, but it need not be the way in which achievement motivation manifests itself in thought processes. Thus it appears to us that using an experimental variable to refine a method of content analysis represents a significant improvement over the usual way of obtaining category definitions, at least for many purposes.

A further aspect of our method of content analysis is its objectivity, as reflected in the high agreement that can be obtained between two trained scorers working with the same protocol independently. Probably a human measuring instrument will never achieve the reliability of a machine in recording events, but its reliability can be increased by simplifying the operations it performs. In our scoring definitions we tried to reduce *judgment* to a minimum. Thus, to take one concrete example, we tried to eliminate *rating* the strength of the achievement motive reflected in a protocol and introduced instead a *counting* operation to get a rough measure of motive intensity. It seems probable that two judges will agree more nearly on the number of different kinds of achievement imagery that appear in a record than they will agree on a judgment of the intensity of the motive in the record, because each of them might be using different unconscious cues in arriving at his judgment of intensity.

To the extent that we can develop a truly objective method of scoring "thought samples," we tend to close the gap between a psychology of "experience" and of "behavior." That is, the experimenter will be able to point to achievement imagery in a protocol with nearly the same degree of objectivity with which he can point to a "right turn" in a maze for a rat. Psychology has been impoverished by the tacit assumption that the science of human behavior must be built on muscular responses which preferably will activate a machine—all this despite the fact that man's obvious difference from other animals lies in his superior symbolic capacities. Thus if we can find and develop systematic objective ways of classifying and counting his symbolic behavior we will come much nearer getting a complete picture of man's nature. The great difficulty with earlier attempts to study man's symbolic processes is suggested by the term *subjective report* which is often used to describe this approach. It should be clear that we are not dealing here with subjective reports in the traditional sense. A subjective report often involves what the subject thinks he is thinking *in terms of his own categories of content analysis*. This obviously leads to confusion because each subject will have slightly different categories, and it would be difficult indeed to build a science on such shifting sands. Here we are collecting a thought sample under specified conditions and then applying to it a public system of content analysis which can be repeated by any observer who knows the system.

So much for our approach and some of its implications for further research. Now what did it accomplish for us? First of all, it demonstrated that the associational processes as reflected in written stories are significantly influenced by events occurring just before they are sampled. In Chapter V and elsewhere throughout the book we have reported how achievement-orienting experiences significantly increase the amount of achievement imagery in the written stories, no matter what the socio-economic or cultural background of the male subjects tested. Our ability to repeat the basic experiment with male Navaho children (Chapter VI) suggests that such an increase in an explicitly defined type of achievement imagery may be universal under certain conditions, but certainly this result is not in itself conclusive. Further research should test the generality of the phenomenon by sampling a wider variety of cultures. Also in Chapter V some data are reported on the specific effects of different kinds of achievement orientation on the content of subsequent written stories. There is evidence that experiences of success have different effects from experiences of failure, but here again our research has only scratched the surface. It ought to be possible to explore more systematically the relation between different types of antecedent achievement experiences and subsequent sub-types of fantasy associations.

Having found that references to leadership and intelligence would increase the amount of achievement imagery produced by male subjects, we then assumed that a lot of achievement imagery in the record of an individual would indicate that he was a person who was motivated for achievement. That is, we simply added the number of different types of achievement imagery appearing in his stories and obtained a total score which we considered the index of his need for Achievement. But this simple operation involves a number of assumptions, any one of which may be questioned. For example, why should the number of different references to achievement be added? Why not all references to achievement? Should some sub-types of achievement imagery be weighted more heavily than others in obtaining a total score? This problem leads to another which we never really solved. In testing for the significance of shifts in achievement sub-categories, should our base line be the number of achievement stories in each group or the total number of stories? For example, is it more significant to know that Achievement Thema as a sub-category appears more frequently in the stories of the motivated subjects or that it appears more frequently in the *achievement* stories of the motivated subjects? Obviously, since the motivated group produces more achievement stories, there will be more opportunity for such a sub-category to appear; but, on the other hand, the sub-category is not completely dependent on the basic imagery category. It does not seem proper in a case of partial dependence like this either to count all categories which increase or to count only those which increase *given an achievement story*. In short, there are many measurement problems yet unsolved in combining various types of achievement imagery to get an over-all score.

Even more important than these questions is the basic issue of whether or not a score so derived is a valid index of an individual's achievement motive. To begin with, there are some minor doubts raised by our own findings. Even if we assume that such a procedure is in general a justified way of measuring achievement motivation, we know that under certain conditions individuals with fairly high motivation will fail to express it even in fantasy because of basic anxieties about achieving. This is probably not so serious a problem as Clark has shown it is likely to be for a motive like sex (1952), but it is still a problem. There will probably always be a small percentage of every population tested for whom this measure of achievement motivation will not be adequate. This in turn raises another methodological question: What testing conditions are most likely to yield the most valid measure of motivation for the largest proportion of the population? At the present time, we believe that relatively serious, achievement-oriented instructions will provide the best measure of individual differences (Chapter VII), but we are also aware that such testing conditions will arouse sufficient anxiety in a small number to cause inhibition of achievement imagery. And last but not least, what evidence is there that our achievement index is *really* a measure of motivation?

Chapter VIII represents the bulk of our attempted answer to this last question. It is true that we were partly persuaded that the achievement imagery index ought to be a measure of motivation because of the way it was derived. That is, it increased significantly as we aroused or thought we aroused achievement motivation in groups of subjects. But the real answer to the basic question lies in the functional characteristics of the score. In short, do subjects who score high behave as if they were highly motivated for achievement? Answering such a question involved making some assumptions as to how such people ought to behave and testing them with the results reported in Chapter VIII. In general, people with a high achievement imagery index score complete more tasks under achievement orientation, solve more simple arithmetic problems in a timed test, improve faster in their ability to do anagrams, tend to get better grades, use more future tenses and abstract nouns in talking about themselves, set a higher level of aspiration if reality factors are ruled out, tend to recall more incompleted tasks, score higher on the Interest Maturity scale of the Strong Vocational Interest Test, show a slight tendency to recognize achievement-related words faster, and so on. In addition, we found evidence for differences between the subjects who are moderately high on the achievement motive index and subjects who are very high. Those who are moderately high appear to be actuated more by a fear of failure as suggested by some Rorschach indicators of anxiety, a tendency to remember completed tasks, and by a resistance to recognizing words connoting failure. Those who score very high, on the other hand, appear to be actuated more by a hope of success as indicated by greater sensitivity to success words and better recall of incompleted tasks.

Finally, it is especially interesting that the achievement index failed to correlate with two of the most commonly used validating criteria, both involving judgment. No matter how he is asked to do it, a person does not estimate his achievement motivation in a way which will correlate significantly with his achievement index score. Furthermore, a clinical judgment of his achievement motivation by outsiders—that is, in this case, by a psychiatrist and a clinical psychologist working together —also does not agree with the index score. Since we have ample evidence that the score is functionally related to various types of behavior, we are inclined to interpret these results as meaning that people's perception of achievement motivation and achievement motivation itself are two different things. In Chapter IX we have discussed some of the reasons

why we think the psychiatrist's judgment differed from the
n Achievement score we obtained for particular individuals.
This analysis suggests that the psychiatrist or perhaps even
the subject himself could be trained to make the kind of judgment of achievement motivation which would agree with our
index score, but a more interesting problem is to explore the
way in which people perceive achievement motivation. That
is, judges may all agree that an individual has high achievement motivation even though he does not by our independent
measure. This means either that we are measuring something
else or that the judgment is determined by other factors than
achievement motivation. If the latter is the case, then the
question becomes one of determining what the cues are that
the judges are responding to uniformly. Is it the fact that the
person has overcome obstacles? that he works long hours?
that he is relatively efficient in overcoming inhibitions? Such
an analysis will probably show that judges (including the
subject himself) respond to certain phenotypical evidences
of achievement motivation (see Frenkel-Brunswik, 1942)
which have become the socially agreed-upon definition of the
motive.

In Chapter IX we tested the validity of the achievement
motive measure in another way. Here, instead of asking questions about the consequences of a high n Achievement score
for behavior, we explored the antecedents of a high n Achievement score. If we are really measuring the achievement motive, we ought to be able to determine the conditions under
which it arises and develops. The data we have to date strongly
support the hypothesis that achievement motives develop in
cultures and in families where there is an emphasis on the
independent development of the individual. In contrast, low
achievement motivation is associated with families in which
the child is more dependent on his parents and subordinate
in importance to them. In both types of homes there may be
plenty of love and affection, but in the homes of the "highs"

the son is more apt to "talk back" without deep feelings of guilt and to go off on his own rather than submit to the standards imposed on him by his parents. The contrast should not be thought of too simply in terms of the autocratic-democratic dimension, currently so popular in psychological literature. The parents of the "highs" may be quite dictatorial, particularly when the son is young before he has learned to act successfully by himself; but if they are, they still act as if the child exists as an individual worth developing in his own right rather than as a subordinate part of a larger, "solidary" family unit to which he owes loyalty over and above his own individual interests. In the latter type of home from which the "lows" are most apt to come, the son must subordinate his interests for the sake of the family or even more extremely, he may not even develop a conception of himself as an individual having interests more important than his obligations to the family unit. Thus when, as an adult, the "low" is faced with the problem of going against a group all by himself as in Asch's experiment, he often cannot do it (Chapter IX). It is inconceivable.

This analysis of the origins of the achievement motive suggests several interesting lines of inquiry. For example, it has been widely assumed that German and Italian families fall predominantly in the second category, that is, are more "solidary." If so, do sons from these families show less achievement motivation than comparable children in other countries where individualistically-oriented families are more common? Or are there other factors in the family life which complicate the picture? Certainly Winterbottom's basic study on the attitudes of mothers of sons with high and low n Achievement scores should be repeated in several other cultures. Even without research in other cultures, however, our preliminary analysis strongly suggests that it is too simple to reason that a high achievement motive develops exclusively out of particular phenotypic parent behavior. To develop a strong achievement motive, a son must somewhere get the idea, for example, that he can develop friendships on his own without his parents' knowledge or necessary approval. This can happen because the mother neglects him, or perhaps because he has formed some special friendships that he wants to continue without informing his parents, or because his mother makes opportunities for such friendships to form or even urges her son to go off on his own. The rewards for forming such friendships may be intrinsic, if a boy takes pleasure in these associations, or they may be extrinsic if the mother or father praises him for being able to get along so well by himself. But the point is that the process of developing the achievement motive involves may different factors, only one of which may be the extrinsic reward and punishment given the child by the parents; and even here, the parents' own belief in the importance of the child's acting independently and developing on his own is more important probably than their overt *reaction* to such independence. Winterbottom showed that the mother is important, but primarily because of the way she structures the situation for her son and secondarily because of the way she reacts when he conforms or fails to conform to her expectations. Our own conception of motivation, outlined in Chapter II, is based on the notion that the child's achievement expectations arising from the mother's demands or elsewhere are the source of his achievement motivation, since his own actions will then interact with those expectations in ways which will yield positive or negative affect. (See Section 2.10.11.) There is no necessity, in this view, to argue that social motives are ultimately based on certain biological needs.

The importance of such achievement expectations in the development of motivation is underlined by the striking difference we found in the way men and women reacted to our achievement arousal instructions. Women were left unmoved by references to leadership and intelligence; but if they were socially rejected, their achievement motivation increased, as measured in the standard way. The men, on the other hand, were unaffected by social rejection on the achievement dimension. The reasonable way to interpret this seems to be in terms of the different expectations involved in achievement motivation for men and women in our culture. Women have achievement drives which are tied up with getting along successfully with other people, whereas men have achievement drives associated with "getting ahead" (i.e., getting a good job, being cleverer than other men, leading others, and so on). It is precisely in terms of an "expectation" theory of motivation that such differences between men and women make sense. In the same way we could interpret the falling off in achievement motivation with age, reported tentatively in Chapter VI. As men get older, more of them have "arrived," and their expectations as to further achievement will be more and more limited by reality factors. As a consequence, their activities will often provide simple confirmation of stable expectations and will therefore, according to our hypotheses, not yield much pleasure, and the achievement motive will tend to die out. Thus in the case of men, the achievement motive seems to be tied to the life cycle, but there seems less reason to assume that it should be in the case of women. At any rate, it would be worth testing the hypothesis that women show less decrease with age in their achievement motivation (as associated with social acceptability) than do men.

Concern with these differences in the types of expectation involved in an achievement motive should lead to an exploration of different types of achievement motivation. For example, our own data have indicated that some people appear to be actuated more by a hope of success, others by fear of failure. We have further speculated that for some people achievement motivation may be tied up primarily with expectations about athletics, for other people with their job, and for still others with their bridge-playing, and so on. But all of this exploration of sub-types of achievement motivation, desirable as it is, should not obscure the fact that they are simply sub-types of a more general motive for which we have succeeded in getting a definition which seems widely applicable. That is, women's achievement motivation may be aroused by references to their social acceptability, but we recognized its presence by the same methods of scoring for achievement imagery. Similarly a Navaho's achievement motive may involve expectations about being a good sheepherder or driving a faster car than anybody else, but again we score for achievement imagery in his story in exactly the same way as we do for our middle-class college students. We view it as no small accomplishment that "competition with a standard of excellence" or "affect in connection with evaluated performance" are scoring definitions for achievement imagery which are sufficiently general to be applied to records produced by all sorts of people. Does this mean that we have found a motive "common to all men" which is not simply a physiological need? There seems no logical reason to exclude this possibility, since all men are faced with learning problems from birth—with learning how to walk and talk, for instance—and the element of learning to solve these problems well or poorly enters into the experience of all men to a greater or lesser degree.

Finally, in Chapter II, more or less as a result of our experimental work with the achievement motive, we have attempted to outline some proposals for a new theory of motivation. Roughly speaking, our definition of a motive involves "redintegration of a situation involving affect." There would be no point in reviewing here the various ramifications of this definition, but if it is to be taken seriously, research must proceed along two main lines. On the one hand, it must deal more effectively with what might be called the taxonomy of affective responses, in particular with their measurement by physiological or other means. The biggest single gap in our knowledge at the present time lies in the fact that we cannot distinguish clearly a positive from a negative affective reaction, although what appear to be secondary reactions to positive and negative affect (i.e., approach and avoidance) are readily distinguished. On the other hand, research must clarify what the conditions are which produce positive and negative affect. Our hypothesis is that positive affect is normally a result of small discrepancies from an expectation, whereas negative affect is a result of larger discrepancies. The difficulties with such an hypothesis are many. In the first place, it is difficult to define what the expectation is; in the second place, it is hard to define the dimension on which a difference from it occurs; and in the third place, it is hard to know what constitutes a small and what a large difference. Despite all these difficulties, evidence is presented in Chapter II which suggests that the hypothesis is not only fruitful but testable, beginning with simple sensory adaptation levels and moving up to more complex expectations. Perhaps it is not too much to hope that we can succeed in stating a general law which will relate the size of the discrepancy which would yield maximum pleasure to the nature of the original expectation and the extent of possible deviation from it. If further research into the causes and consequences of affective arousal proceeds successfully along these lines, we believe that a significant step will have been taken toward the development of a theory of motivation which is general enough to handle simple animal drives on the one hand or complex human motives involving belief systems on the other.

❦APPENDIX I❦

Illustrative Four-Story Records from Thirty Subjects

The pictures used for the four stories in this appendix were B, H, A, G in that order. These pictures are described in Appendix III. In recording these stories a separate paragraph is used for the response to each of the four questions that were asked in order to insure complete coverage of a plot. These four sets of questions were:

1. What is happening? Who are the persons?
2. What has led up to this situation—that is, what has happened in the past?
3. What is being thought—what is wanted? By whom?
4. What will happen? What will be done?

Subject No. 1—Story 1

"Machinists are engaged in making some sort of article.

"The article has been heated and the one worker is handling it at a distance.

"The workers are hesitating momentarily to allow the object to cool.

"The heated object will be placed in the machine to be pressed or tooled toward further refinement."

1-2

"Student is contemplating the value of study.

"Something ponderous has presented itself in the reading.

"The question of values is bewildering the student. Is it likely that he can comprehend the material and successfully pass the teacher's examination?

"Reading will continue after the moment's diversion."

1-3

"Father and son are thinking about the son's actions and life in general.

"Some misdeed on the son's part had prompted a man-to-man talk.

"The son is resolving to do better and the father is assuring himself of his son's resolve.

"The same misdemeanor will repeat itself and suicide will be the only panacea."

1-4

"Young fellow is showing anxiety toward impending operation.

"Some malady has been diagnosed.

"The doctor has prescribed an operation to remove the source of illness and the boy wonders about the advisability of such a plan.

"The operation will be performed and successfully."

Subject No. 2—Story 1

"Two craftsmen are fashioning the vital part of a new invention. They have all the necessary tools and parts for it.

"These men are anxious to revolutionize the tool and die industry. They have spent months, even years working out this new tool—first on paper, later practically.

"Each waits with bated breath for the final part to be finished so they can put together the new tool—they want satisfaction, honor and financial reimbursement.

"The invention will be a failure. Discouraged, and financially bankrupt, one will commit suicide, the other will give up and go to Alaska to try his luck at farming."

2-2

"This chap is doing some heavy meditating. He is a sophomore and has reached an intellectual crisis. He cannot make up his mind. He is troubled, worried.

"He is trying to reconcile the philosophies of Descartes and Thomas Aquinas—and at his tender age of 18. He has read several books on philosophy and feels the weight of the world on his shoulders.

"He wants to present a clear-cut synthesis of these two conflicting philosophies, to satisfy his own ego and to gain academic recognition from his professor.

"He will screw himself up royally. Too inexperienced and uninformed, he has tackled too great a problem. He will give up in despair, go down to the Goodyear and drown his sorrows in a bucket of Piel's."

2-3

"The elderly gent has a scheme to pull a fast one on the market and he is putting his stooge wise to it. The old gent is a sharp Wall Street operator, and the young fellow is his flunky.

"Thru the years, by his suave manner and personality the elderly gent has built up a lot of confidence in brokers, bankers, etc., in the hope of someday fleecing the lot of them.

"The young chap is debating the possibilities of the scheme succeeding while the older gent wonders just how well the young fellow will perform. Both want money and will go the limit to get it.

"The scheme will work. The elderly gent will take the lion's share and hit Paris, Monte Carlo, St. Moritz, etc. The young chap will go on into another scheme and get tripped up, landing in jail for embezzlement and attendant charges."

2-4

"The boy is reflecting on a scene which he has read about. The doctors are barred from the profession and they take only criminals, etc., as patients. The patient has been badly wounded in a gun fight and is being operated on immediately.

"The boy has read a lot about doctors. He visualizes them as good and bad. By some quirk he would like to become a doctor of this sort depicted, so that he could experiment on people.

"The boy wants to be a surgeon so he can cut people apart and see what makes them tick. He is a sadist at heart even so young. He especially wants to cut up beautiful girls after raping them.

"He will go out at the age of eighteen or so, waylay some 12 year old girl, rape her and hack her to pieces with a butcher knife. After that he will attack an old lady, but the cops will arrive just in time and in the pursuit blow his head off."

Subject No. 3—Story 1

"The machine is being repaired by a mechanic. The person standing watching is the operator of the machine and the other is the aforementioned mechanic.

"After the machine had been broken the operator tried to fix it but was unsuccessful and finally resorted to calling the mechanic.

"The operator is watching the mechanic and feeling rather self-conscious about being unable to fix it, however, he is watching the work so he can meet the situation if it ever arises again.

"The machine will be fixed, the mechanic thanked, and the work continue."

3-2

"The students are listening to a rather boring lecture, half-heartedly.

"The inability of the student to concentrate on the lecture has caused him to pass the time by daydreaming.

"He is thinking of the house party coming up the following weekend and the fun he is going to have. All he wants immediately is the bell to ring and end that lecture.

"The bell will ring and the class will be dismissed and our friend will walk home with one of his buddies and gripe about the lecture."

3-3

"A father and son are having a very serious discussion.

"The son has gotten into serious trouble with the police. He has gambling debts and has taken some of the family jewels to pay the debt, without telling the father.

"The father suspects the son but does not accuse him directly. He wants the son to confess himself. The son is very troubled and afraid to tell the truth.

"The son will finally break down and confess in tears. The father will give him money to get the jewels back and reprimand although compassionately."

3-4

"The boy is thinking seriously about a possible accident.

"He decided to go hunting with some other young friends and his father has warned him to be careful of accidents.

"The father's lecture has had some effect because the boy thinks or imagines a shooting accident and the victim being given emergency treatment.

"The boy will snap out of the daydream and prepare for the trip, but take care to prevent accidents."

Subject No. 4—Story 1

"A machinist is working on a piece of machinery. Both men are mechanics.

"The machine has broken down and been brought to this shop to be repaired.

"The one man who is working thinks of how to accomplish the

job, while the bystander is glad it is almost finished. The first man wants to get it fixed and do a good job, while the second man wants to help but due to the nature of the work, can't.

"The first man will step back, say "that does it," and they will both gather up their tools and look to see what needs to be repaired next."

4-2

"The boy is taking an hour written. He and the others are high school students. The test is about two thirds over and he is doing his best to think it through.

"He was supposed to study for the test and did so. But because it is factual there were some items he saw but did not learn.

"He knows he has studied the answers he can't remember and is trying to summon up the images and related ideas to remind him of them.

"He may remember one or two but he will miss most of the items he can't remember. He will try hard until five minutes is left, then give up, go back over his paper, and be disgusted for reading but not learning the answers."

4-3

"The father and son are having a very important discussion of something in which the son is involved. It is a serious matter and both are highly disturbed and sobered by it.

"The son was in business and in his effort to do well he has become involved in some shady dealings. Now he discovers he is about to be found out by his partner.

"The son is angry and vicious at the partner and he seeks some way to silence or stop him from exposing the deals. The father is gravely concerned. He is worried and would like to provide a solution, but he knows there is none.

"The exposé will take place and the son will be shown as a very vicious and cruel person. The father will stick by his son but be very heartsick at the whole procedure."

4-4

"A teenager is daydreaming about an emergency operation being performed under terrible conditions behind the battle lines in the war. He is dreaming he is helping the old Army surgeon.

"The boy has read a story of medical corps heroism and now transports himself into an active role as a hero and man of experience.

"He thinks how fascinating it would be to be at such an operation, and how tough it would be and how impervious and stoic would be his action through it all.

"The operation will be successful and the dream characters will get some sleep and do it again. At this point the daydream will fade."

Subject No. 5—Story 1

"One man is working on a machine in a tool shop while another man is standing with hands on hips watching him. Tools are hanging in front of a window in the background, and both men are attired in aprons.

"The young man watching seems to be learning the trade, and the older fellow is teaching him how to handle the machine.

"The young man is disgusted and impatient, while the older man is quite absorbed in his work.

"The young man will lose interest and leave the job. The older fellow will continue his work for the rest of his life."

5-2

"A young boy dressed in a black and white checkered shirt is leaning on one arm—lost in deep thought. His face is set in a serious way, and he is ignoring the book before him.

"He just heard from the National Bird Association that his long-lost friend, the 'Bodini' bird had been shot down in a skirmish over Pango-Pango.

"He can't decide whether or not he should fly down to the Zulu Islands for the funeral or hop a pogo stick.

"He will abandon both of these ideas and go by means of a baby carriage on land and water skis for the ocean."

5-3

"Egads, another study in thought. The old boy on the right, complete with all standard equipment and a few accessories, including a sporty mustache and goatee, is gazing into space. His young chum on the left has dark hair and looks equally absorbed.

"The old man lost his soap bubble outfit and they can't find a new one.

"They are wondering if several pieces of bubble gum would not be a suitable redemption, but the old fellow isn't sure because he is afraid he might lose part of his mustache if a bubble should break on it and necessitate a quick shave.

"They, too, will give everything up and go to a burlesque show at Coney Island to see Stella, the cat-faced girl."

5-4

"I'm stumped! It appears as though a young boy is being operated on in the background, and there is an image of him in the front of the picture. Also a picture of the doctor and his assistant.

"He just swallowed a watermelon and they are performing an operation to remove it.

"The boy wonders if his mother will ever allow him to eat watermelons again, and the doctors, striking a pensive position, are wondering if they should plant the watermelon seeds in the boy's left ear after the operation is finished.

"The watermelon will give birth to six little watermelons while in the boy's stomach. This will momentarily confuse the doctors, but they will move with finality and send each little watermelon to a barber shop for shampoos."

Subject No. 6—Story 1

"It appears that the two men are machinists and one is giving instructions to the fellow standing by.

"The men are working.

"The man who was watching the other at work will feel enlightened."

6-2

"The boy is a high school student who is giving deep thought to his studies. It appears that he may be perplexed about something.

"It is probable that the boy has a philosophical mind and has been interested in a problem.

"He is thinking about a solution to the problem before him. He is striving to reach some definite conclusions.

"After continued thought he will arrive at a solution to his problem."

6-3

"The two men are politicians. The grey-haired gentleman is presenting his views in an attempt to get support from the other.

"The men have probably been colleagues in the past and have won each other's respect.

"The man on the right is attempting to get support for a bill he is introducing by explaining his position to the other.

"It appears as though the grey-haired fellow would not be successful as the other fellow looked very skeptical."

6-4

"The boy has visions of becoming a surgeon and has projected his mind to the day when he will be performing operations.

"He has had a concern for people in the past and desires to be of service to mankind.

"The boy is thinking of the day when he will be a successful surgeon. He is looking forward to that day very seriously.

"It is likely that he will strive and reach his goal."

Subject No. 7—Story 1

"The two machinists are about to place the metal into the machine to shape it into their desired shape.

"The man on the left has picked up the material from the bench with the tongs and has walked over to the machine. The man on the right has walked from the bench to the back of the machine.

"The thought of getting the piece of metal into the machine without mishap is being expressed by both men. The man on the right shows signs of apprehension as to the action of the process.

"The piece will be shoved into the machine. The machine will stamp it out. The right hand man will walk over to the bench while the left hand man removes the piece from the machine and places it on the bench again."

7-2

"The student is in the process of thinking over some incident or incidents which have occurred recently or remotely in his past.

"Some action in sight which turned the key which unlocked memories provided the impetus for the situation.

"In trying to recapture these actions through his memories, he is seeing some actions in the past—vividly.

"He will sooner or later come out of his daydream and completely forget about this thing for the moment."

7-3

"The older man is trying to give comforting advice to the younger man. The older man is acting in the capacity of a minister.

"The young man has committed a crime which has no way out but punishment by life imprisonment.

"The young man seems to resent this sympathetic advice or comfort. The old man is heartily sorry for the young man visitor.

"The young man will be sent to prison and will probably stay without getting parole."

7-4

"The boy is thinking of his fortune as a great doctor, or he may be thinking of the time when he may be operated on. He may be a hypochondriac. He is probably a doctor's son.

"He has been brought up in a medium of medicine, or he has been brought up in a home full of sickness.

"He is thinking of how he will obtain the future to a doctor, or he is thinking of the sickness which he will endure.

"He will either become a great doctor or he will become sickly and through worry become sickly."

Subject No. 8—Story 1

"Two men are inventing a new kind of round file giving it a special heat treatment. One man is Edison, the other his assistant.

"Old files were no good because they broke too easily, hence a new invention is necessary. The men have tried thousands of different treatments and compounds.

"The men are wondering if this heat treatment will really give a strong durable file. One is optimistic, the other pessimistic. Nobody wants the new file but the two men for scientific reasons.

"The treatment will be unsuccessful. There will be a long argument as to why it didn't work and the whole laborious business will begin again."

8-2

"The student is trying to get material for a very involved laborious paper. He is unable to concentrate and finds his thoughts wandering. He thinks about his girl.

"He isn't really thinking. He is just letting his mind wander. His thoughts, however, betray a want for female companionship.

"He will fritter away his time and finally at the last minute will in a burst of effort get his paper written. Thoughts about his girl will disappear."

8-3

"The elder man is a successful business man. The younger man is his son who is about to leave an important position in his father's company. They are about to go into a board meeting and the father gives advice.

"The two have not always been friendly but there has been a

great deal of mutual respect. The father has been proud of his son and now is curious. The son has been resentful.

"The son wants freedom and self-sufficiency. The father wants the son to make a big mark in order that his esteem may be enhanced.

"The son will not be successful in the board meeting. The father will be sarcastic and feel half gratification, showing he is better than his son, and half regret since he has betrayed his pride in him."

8-4

"The boy is an imaginative youngster. The men are pictured in his mind as sadistic doctors. He gets them in a reverie in a library when a shaft of sunlight comes through the window.

"In the past the boy has been extremely curious and timid. He is especially weak when it comes to cruelty of any kind, and it bothers him to be impelled to think about cruelty.

"He thinks that scientific pain in an operation is cruel but necessary. He wants to adapt himself to the conclusion this is necessary.

"He will be partly successful but cruelty will always bother him in whatever he does or whatever experience he goes through."

Subject No. 9—Story 1

"Pete Willow has come over to Jack Barnes machine and is asking him if he is working for the company or for the Union.

"Pete hasn't paid much attention to the unions and their ideas and he has needed money badly for his farm. Jack has been promoting the union and is ready to call a strike.

"Pete wants to work. Jack is trying to talk Pete into joining the union and strike for better conditions. Jack argues that in the long run Pete will be better off.

"Pete joins the strike unwillingly and is sorry that he did because Jack wants to use force against the other non-striking forces."

9-2

"Ted Markem is wondering whether he is right in coming to college. He hasn't been able to concentrate at all.

"He got through high school without much effort and he passed the college boards successfully.

"College—is it all what it's cracked up to be—Ted wonders. Nothing is clear. His purpose in life is a complete image of half ideas and dreams, none of them complete and meaningful.

"Ted made it. He passed. He has developed some self-confidence with which to carry on with. He will now pass everything."

9-3

"Professor Rosk is telling Abe Storm that his ideas for development of life in test tube are impractical.

"Abe Storm, a brilliant young biologist and doctor has come across a remarkable new use of the uranium atom.

"Professor Rosk believes that Abe has gone too far. He will be unable to carry on. Abe is trying to convince the old man.

"Abe proved himself right and he developed life in a test tube. Professor Rosk kills himself because of the future of the world."

9-4

"Allen, a young man, is seeing in his dreams what happened when he was a small boy in the old country.

"The Russians came and found his father ill. They told Allen to go outside. Allen looked through the window and saw his father being operated on.

"His father died on the table in the interest of science. Allen can't forgive nor forget.

"He will develop into a neurotic unless modern psychiatry can get ahead of him."

Subject No. 10—Story 1

"These two scientists that we see working in the workshop of their laboratory are anxiously testing the fruits of their research.

"In the approach to the problem at hand, much of their research and experimentation has taken place within their minds which . . . .

"Each man is wondering primarily will their new substance withstand the conditions which will be required by the war.

"After the successful testing of their new compound they will take steps to simplify the processes and make it suitable for manufacture on a large scale."

10-2

"As any properly adjusted liberal arts student should, we find this great mulling over the value of Aristotelian thought and ideas in the . . . .

"Following his several weeks work in classes he is now beginning to "see the light," or the worth of such studies.

"He is a searcher for the truth who feels the whole world may some time profit by his efforts if he continues with sufficient diligence and his personal problems will also receive more understanding treatment.

"After his initial enthusiasm this idea will become part of his background and make him a more learned and interested student."

10-3

"During the economic conferences these two diplomats or representatives are privately planning the lengths their nations and satellites shall . . . .

"Disorder on the continent has led to this meeting with much political unrest developing generally from the situation.

"Their only real aim is to further 'the cause' and here we find them trying to reach a decision about policy.

"On their return to their seats the same tone of general agreement will return to their faces and arguments whereas tonight the leaders shall receive a satisfactory report and recommend probable steps for tomorrow."

10-4

"This pensive fellow we here look upon is the grandson of the late _____ who is today being honored by the _____ university's dedication of the new medical school.

"Fifty-five years ago his grandfather came to this part of the country where his practice was begun and where through his efforts the first hospital was built.

"Young Edward is wondering if he could ever be able to reach the level of personal knowledge and bravery to be so. . . .

"Following this momentous occasion he shall view his future with an ever increasing intent upon medicine and the study and practice of surgery."

Subject No. 11—Story 1

"These two men are working with a machine, perhaps a printing press. It might be Tom Paine and an assistant working on the publication of his famous booklet advocating freedom for America.

"Oppression by the British has angered Paine into writing a pamphlet expressing the grievances of the Americans which is destined to make history.

"The two men are perhaps disturbed by the failure of their

primitive press and are discussing possibilities of repairing it so that their important document can be published.

"The pamphlet of T. Paine is destined to become one of the greatest of revolutionary documents and was instrumental in arousing the colonists to fight for their freedom."

11-2

"This brings to mind T. Edison who is dreaming of possible inventions rather than turning to his studies. A poor student, Edison is probably worried about his future.

"Probably he is doing poorly in school or is thinking of his girl or perhaps he is being reprimanded by the teacher for inferior work.

"I think he is dreaming of some childhood invention that he would much rather be working on than studying the boring subjects of grammar school.

"He is destined to become one of the greatest of American inventors devoting his entire life to things such as the light bulb, phonograph."

11-3

"Two senators or U.N. members discussing some problem of great world importance. They are deep in thought about the consequences of their move or the vote which is about to be taken.

"It is perhaps the Palestine problem and the rioting and bloodshed has presented a grave problem. Debate on the floor has left them worn out.

"They are both wondering about a possible solution or perhaps a compromise. They may be radically opposed to one another but both want an amicable solution to be reached.

"After much talk and thought an agreement will be reached by the two statesmen and the crisis will pass saving many lives."

11-4

"This young boy is dreaming of the day he will have completed his training and become a great and famous doctor. Perhaps this portrays someone already famous for research.

"He has been asked by his father or relative what he wants to do when he grows up and he is trying to tell them the mental picture that he has in his mind of himself in thirty years.

"The boy is thinking of the great thrill that must be experienced by a doctor when he performs a delicate operation saving someone's life.

"The boy will go out through college and eventually become a world famous doctor."

Subject No. 12—Story 1

"The man with the wrench is a plumber who is fixing a leak in the laboratory of the other man who is . . .

"The inventor has been experimenting with pressure valves for running the machine and the pipe burst due to faulty packing in the joint ruining the experiment and irking the inventor.

"The inventor is thinking what the heck went wrong and why doesn't the plumber hurry up. The plumber is thinking about how silly the whole apparatus seems.

"The plumber will fix the leak and then stand around to watch the experiment. The experiment will come off very well and the plumber will become chief engineer for the great concern that will be built up by this new discovery."

12-2

"The boys are taking an exam which is really a corker. The one in the foreground is not much interested in the exam and is worrying about his girl. Open book exam.

"The boy's girl has left him for another man who has a car. They went together for three years straight before this came up and he is all shot.

"He is wondering how he will ever get her back, and even if he does what the situation will be.

"He won't bother to get her back and will find a nicer girl. His old girl will become jealous, try to get him back. They have a fight and become enemies for life."

12-3

"The older person is Uncle Harry who is telling Jimmy who is just out of college that things really aren't as bad as they seem, and sooner or later he will be able to see his way clear.

"Jimmy has been looking for a job for three months. He hasn't had any luck, his ego has fallen, and he really feels that the world is giving him a bad break.

"The Uncle thinks Jim is a washout anyway but tries to give him courage. Jim thinks his uncle is all wrong about his ideas.

"Jim will finally go to New York to see if he can land a job. He will get mixed up in a narcotics ring and finally end up in the chair."

12-4

"The young boy is daydreaming of what he is expecting to happen to him.

"He has just been drafted into the service and actually has a deadly fear of leaving home so young in life. He has been pampered at home.

"He is thinking that he will be wounded where there are no good doctors. They will have to operate without anaesthetic and he can almost feel the pain now.

"He will go to war. Become very timid among the other more forward men. He will easily be led astray by bad men and will eventually get caught robbing the P.X. Then he will be court martialed and sent to prison where he will try to escape only to be shot in the head."

Subject No. 13—Story 1

"A broken machine is being repaired. The person whose profile is seen is the repairing technician while the man whose back is toward us is the worker who broke it.

"The worker by not obeying instructions, tried to do something which that machine was not capable of doing. He didn't know the limitations of the machine.

"The worker is unhappy—he believes it is his fault. The repairman having this particular breakdown happen to him often thinks it is fault of management not to train their workers properly.

"The technician will repair the machine and will recommend that workers be better instructed in handling that machine in being taught how to use it and what it can or cannot do."

13-2

"A 'Clyde Griffith' (An American Tragedy, by Dreiser) reads up on how to prevent the inevitable result of his irresponsible action.

"Clyde seduced one of the workers in his department. Now she is pregnant and holds him back at the point where he is about to . . .

"He is trying to solve his predicament by abortion or any other method which will leave his name out of the situation.

"He will eventually kill her and get electrocuted himself. (This I now realize was not *my* imagination but that of Dreiser. I am reading the book at the moment and 'under the grip of it.')"

13-3

"The persons are father and son, and the father is communicating some extremely disturbing news to his boy who now sees his dreams scattered and cannot yet grasp the reality of the situation.

"Father's business has gone bankrupt due to the situation beyond the old man's control. He had built it up himself, made good. Son hoped to take over.

"The son is unhappy for now instead of taking over a tailor-made job he will himself start from the beginning himself. Also he fears that he will now lose all the 'rich' friends with whom he went around with.

"The young man will do fairly well for himself but he will never reach the wealth and prestige which he would have if this hadn't happened."

13-4

"A young man, med student in college, a veteran, is nightmaring over the time he was being operated on and civilian French doctors worked over him with poor instruments and unsanitary conditions.

"He was parachuted by OSS into German occupied territory, was caught and escaped but badly wounded and now bullet removed in this poor setup.

"He is reminiscing how lucky he was that his life was saved. He is a med student in college now and realizes how the odds were against him.

"He will dedicate his life and energy to preservation of peace and international exchange of medical information."

Subject No. 14—Story 1

"Two inventors are working against time to complete their machine. Something has happened and a vital part is broken, with no spare parts they seem to be hopelessly stuck.

"They have contracted to deliver this particular invention at a certain date, but cannot now do so because of the breakdown.

"The first man is angry and disheartened, but the second is making a desperate attempt to repair the damage. Both are under great nervous strain.

"The break will be repaired in time, and the additional knowledge thereby gained will enable them to perfect an even better invention in the future."

14-2

"The boy is trying to decide whether or not to leave school and enlist in the Army.

"He has been under a great strain, but he has just about come to a conclusion.

"He is weighing the possibilities. He realizes that he is well equipped to make a good soldier but feels he should also finish his education. He does not know where his duty lies.

"He decides to finish high school then enlist, with a view toward becoming an officer."

14-3

"Both men, father and son, are trying to recover from a terrific hangover from the party the night before.

"They have lied to their wives, gone to a stag party, got themselves both girls and plenty drunk. They have since come home at ten the next morning.

"Both just want to drop dead. Also, they naturally do not want their wives to find out and are considering going out for a short beer before lunch.

"They will be found out by their wives, who will make life miserable for them, then forget about it. It will be a long time before they do it again, if ever."

14-4

"The boy is a youngster who has been impressed with his old man's war stories. He sometimes thinks about them a lot.

"His father has told him about being operated upon just back of the lines at the Battalion's aid station. The medics were working under fire, 88's were bursting over them.

"The kid is letting his mind wander on these thoughts and is getting a little nervous about the whole thing.

"The boy becomes a neurotic and the father cracks up and drinks himself to death."

Subject No. 15—Story 1

"Repairing the machine—machinists that are inventing it.

"An experiment has failed and they have to make improvements.

"Wondering how to do it—man on right is in doubt of thing left man is doing.

"Mutual compromise and the machine will be successful."

15-2

"School boy taking an exam.

"He didn't study the night before and isn't doing too well because he had a date.

"He is trying to figure out a good way to pass the test—also trying to answer one specific problem and also about the date he had last night.

"He will flunk the exam and will go on pro."

15-3

"Father and son are having a talk.

"Son had done something serious that he shouldn't have done.

"Father thinks that he should straighten him out and the son is feeling sorry for himself. Father is trying to help in a gruff way and son doesn't take to it.

"Son will repeat the misdeed and the father will disown him."

15-4

"A young boy has a vision in his mind of being a doctor. The men in the background are persons in medical world he has read about in fiction and fact.

"He is going to have an appendectomy and was wondering how they did it in the old days and wondered how they do it now.

"He was thinking that the pain he will have to go thru will be nothing to the pain that the people in the old days had to put up with.

"The boy will die from an infection in the operation."

Subject No. 16—Story 1

"The people are making or designing new woodworking products. They are machine workmen in the early 19th century.

"The need for a new product has led to an idea which is now being tried out. The men have spent hours planning and now see fruit of the work.

"Perfection is wanted by both men. They are wondering whether or not their product will fill the need. Perhaps new machines or new techniques are needed to replace antiquated methods.

"The men will find the answer. Much imagination will be put on the job, but finally something will be designed to make the average routine easier for somebody who uses the product."

16-2

"The persons are studying. The central object is daydreaming, not concentrating. He is probably in a world of fantasy, or reliving some past experience.

"The boy attended classes and got assignments to do. He has balanced his time so he has a little extra. He should be studying but he is not. Some problem is bothering him, probably lack of concentration.

"The boy wants to remember something pleasant. Perhaps he is not—perhaps reliving his past summer and the fun he had.

"The outcome will be he will snap out of it and get back to work. The daydreaming will surely become part of his subconscious to be relived again at some future time."

16-3

"The youth is being counselled by a friend or father. The younger is probably just out of college and needs orientation in business world, or in his marriage. The elder is a close friend who will answer his personal problems.

"The youth has met a situation that has thrown him, because it is different from all his past experience. His wife is probably the trouble.

"The youth wants a direct answer of what to do to make everything perfect. The sage is talking in broad terms with many modifying conditions and posing new problems.

"The youth will have to live and learn. He will either have to adjust to his wife or live an unhappy life or get a divorce."

16-4

"The fellow is trying to decide what profession to go into. The gun, symbolic of soldier—in background are symbols of doctor, teacher, and other professions.

"The fellow has grown up in a good home, gone to Sunday School and has been well sheltered. Now he has his own decisions to make about what to do.

"The fellow is weighing the relative merits of each profession, the glory, the work, the pay—what it will do for mankind.

"He will make a decision, whether good or bad. Might be just to fall into business. But he is growing up and cannot escape working for a living. College is probably in the future."

Subject No. 17—Story 1

"A worker is putting a hot piece of metal back in the oven with a pair of tongs in order to heat it up again. The gentleman beside him is a helper.

"The metal cooled off and they want to reheat it. They were making some sort of metallic object.

"They are a little expectant waiting for some sort of invention that they are working on to be realized and the hot piece of metal is necessary for the completion of the object.

"The workman putting the metal into the oven will heat it up and the two will go to the object they are working on in hopes of completing their invention successfully."

17-2

"This is a picture of a student in high school daydreaming.

"His mother died recently and he cannot seem to get his mind on his work.

"He is very depressed and wants to see his mother just once again.

"He will probably be called upon to answer a question by the teacher which will leave him very confused and he will stammer and hem and haw not even having heard the question."

17-3

"The elderly gentleman on the right is a psychologist giving a young man a test using the Freudian method of 'free association.'

"The young man found himself very depressed and couldn't understand why. The psychologist is attempting to find out why.

"The young man is earnestly trying to remember those events of his past which might have been responsible for his state. The psychologist is somewhat annoyed feeling that the patient is withholding information.

"The young man will finally come through with the true cause of his trouble—a childhood experience and will be able to take the necessary steps to correct his troubles."

17-4

"A young boy is dreaming of his future profession, that of a surgeon. The surgeon with the knife he is in his older age.

"He has been considering medical school for a long time and can't quite decide whether he wants or rather likes the idea of cutting up another person.

"He is somewhat worried wondering whether he will be capable of such a feat. He remembers the time he was wounded by fooling around with his father's rifle and remembers the blood and nauseous feeling he had.

"He will formulate his opinion one way or another, and eventually decide balancing out the relative weights of his decision to be a surgeon and his distaste for blood, etc."

Subject No. 18—Story 1

"Two men are in a machine shop—the man on the right is the boss and the man on the left is an apprentice who is taking a casting from a small furnace.

"The apprentice has not done the job in the past, he has just been hired a week before because he needed the job.

"The apprentice is impressed with the importance of doing the job right. The boss has an open mind to see if it is being done well.

"The apprentice will succeed because of his conscientiousness and will one day own the business and marry the boss' daughter."

18-2

"Boy (student) is taking an exam but has his mind on an external difficulty.

"His father has just been fired from a job because of drunkenness.

"Boy is trying to find a bright spot in the future and also trying to forget and get down to work.

"Boy's father will get a new job, reform and then slip back."

18-3

"Corrupt politician is talking to gangster and ordering his opponent smeared by a frame-up.

"Opponent is vet who is liked by people—corrupt politician is incumbent and afraid of losing out. Gangster has had terrifically bitter experiences.

"Crooked politician wants to be kept clear of entanglement with the frame job. Crook has little conscience about it.

"Crook will succeed in the frame-up but election may still be won by vet."

18-4

"Boy is high school graduate dreaming of his future as an M.D. Doctors are performing an appendectomy.

"Boy's parents have had little. He has been a high school president of his class.

"Boy wants to succeed, do good, and have comfortable income in a job he will enjoy.

"He will wander from this steadfast purpose but eventually achieve it."

Subject No. 19—Story 1

"Two men are working in a machine shop. They are the type of people who slave in sweatshops from day to day.

"The desire for men to reach material progress and control his environment has brought these men to work here.

"These men don't think. They become automatons. They are merely doing what they have been instructed to do and are producing what some one else wants them to produce.

"These men will continue to work this way from day to day until they are no longer able for want of strength. Others, perhaps their sons, will take their places and the process will continue ad infinitum."

19-2

"A young boy is deliberating on some nonsensical and insignificant thing which occurs to him as a problem.

"He has probably had a petty argument with some girl whom he is concerned with.

"He thinks that the future of the world depends upon the solution of his problem. He doesn't really want to solve the problem because it makes him feel important to think that he has grave obstacles to overcome.

"Other young men will come along with the same thoughts and problems. They will also leave the problems unsolved. We get a cyclical chain of history."

19-3

"Two men, one more experienced than the other, are considering a serious problem. They are government officials at some conference.

"The government of these men is involved in a difficulty with some other government and these men must make the decision.

"The men are thinking of a solution having the gravity of the situation in mind. They want to solve this not only to the best interest of their country but for the benefit of many.

"These men will reach a solution and perhaps there will be some agreement for a while, but new problems will nullify their achievements and new solutions will have to be found."

19-4

"Two medical men are working on a wounded or injured person. Perhaps they are giving a blood transfusion.

"There has been a war as shown by the gun on the side. This man has been wounded in battle.

"The men are thinking of saving the life of the wounded person. They are wise men and see the tragedy of the situation.

"There are two possibilities. Either the young boy on the left will also go into war and be in the same position as the wounded, or he may, in the event of war, go on to something more productive—the study of medicine for cure."

Subject No. 20—Story 1

"Two men (one subordinate to the other) are working around a hot stove with tools.

"The shop has been functioning for a long time in a small town. There is a good trade, but not a booming business.

"Production and good tools is wanted. Repairs are needed. The owner of the concern is the fellow who wants results.

"The tools will be produced or repaired. The workers will be paid their weekly salary, and things will happen over and over again in the usual manner."

20-2

"A student in a classroom is listening to a teacher explain the contents of a book which lies before the student. He is very interested in the subject.

"He has passed through all preceding school years, and is an intelligent boy. He entered the classroom with his fellows and is now listening to the teacher.

"He is trying to understand the subject which is new to him. The teacher also is trying his best to make the students understand.

"The student will understand the subject and will go out of the class, happy about his success in grasping it. He will be a success in life."

20-3

"A business executive is passing a remark to a new and bright young man during a business meeting of a corporation. There are many people in the room.

"The young fellow has recently graduated from college and the

Harvard Business School and now has a promising job in the large corporation.

"The young businessman is trying to grasp the affairs of the company in the meeting and the executive is explaining details in procedure.

"The meeting will come to a close and the usual changes in administration will be made. The young fellow will succeed and take over the executive's position in time, and will have three children."

20-4

"This is a painting, depicting a young student (13 years old) who wants to become a doctor. A test tube is seen behind him and thru it a doctor and his assistants working over a patient.

"The student has been conscientious in work and has made the best marks in his class. However, he is not an athlete and tends to be an isolationist.

"He wants to learn all about medicine and wants to be another Einstein, only in the field of medicine.

"He will be close to a genius, will make a smart doctor, but won't have the close family life that the fellow in slide #2 will have. This guy is a grind and brilliant."

Subject No. 21—Story 1

"Two workers are beside a machine, the function of which is beyond my imagination. The person on the left is fairly new on the job. He is the operator.

"The person at the right hasn't seen the machine in operation before. He is curious. The operator is somewhat nervous because he is new on the job.

"Each one awaiting outcome of the operation. The operator is hoping everything will pan out properly. The other feels sympathy and apprehension.

"Everything will turn out all right. The man on the left will do O.K. The value of the machine remains in question."

21-2

"This has all the markings of an examination, but the presence of the opened book suggests otherwise. The boy is about 16, and is having difficulty in following the instructions of the teacher.

"The boy hasn't been too punctual in his home assignments. He is tired. It is about 11:17 A.M. He is hungry. He is thinking of spring and all of its manifestations.

"He wants to get the class over with. He is bored. The subject is dry, disinteresting.

"The class will finally end. The students will close their books and get out of here as fast as possible."

21-3

"The old man is whispering some sort of restraining remark to an over-emotional young man who has nearly committed a 'faux pas.'

"The young man shares much of the ideals of the old, but his lack of experience prods him to reckless expression. The old fellow passed through the same stage.

"The old man feels sympathy, understanding. The younger is impatient, possibly mad about something.

"The younger man will go through life continually being set back by necessary compromises of his energies. Eventually he will share the cynicism or sense of reconciliation of the older."

21-4

"Two doctors are hovering over a sick patient. The boy pictured is the patient when he was younger, in good health.

"The patient's chances of living through the proposed operation are very slim. He will probably die. Maybe he is already dead. Maybe the patient is a corpse, about to have a P.M.

"The doctors feel no emotion. The body before them is just a mass of organs. The boy is innocent, looking hopefully to the future.

"If the patient is dead, I suppose the body will decay. I hope someone will bury the poor devil. The boy is but a memory."

Subject No. 22—Story 1

"An accident has just occurred in the home of the Simon brothers in their small home in Boston, 1887.

"The plunger on the first 'work-up' gasoline compression engine has come loose and smashed the cylinder.

"Both men are obviously annoyed. This is the third time this sort of thing has happened. 'Will it work?' they wonder—'Will it work?'

"Eventually, of course, the Simon Brothers will be able to make their engine run. One night, however, they will be mysteriously murdered by an enterprising scoundrel. Twenty years later this blackguard will design the first gasoline compression engine."

22-2

"A boy in a checkered sport shirt holds his head and stares dismally and miserably out through the open window of the schoolroom.

"A number of reasons can be found to have caused his present unhappiness. For a long time now he has wanted to become a garage mechanic, to get away from the dullness of Cicero and Caesar. But no! They won't let him.

"He feels miserable and trapped. He cannot get out of a mesh of emotional thought, and daydreams and worries himself to a nerve-shattering point.

"Soon he will leap from his chair, go completely berserk and be led away in a large wagon where he will sit on a piece of toast believing himself a fried egg."

22-3

"Two Frenchmen, an old one and a young one, are at a meeting of the cabinet.

"The situation has been perpetuated by a wave of strikes all over France. Now the United States Ambassador has announced that the U.S. will send no money or food to a nation unable to control itself emotionally.

"The men are unhappy. But the younger man is angry. He is listening to the silver-tongued oratory of the De Gaulist spokesman which force he fears and wants to see overcome.

"Eventually the passion of the young man will pass. The older man will not sustain his anger—he is too old to bewail, just cynical. They will go home, to starve, and to wait."

22-4

"Wilhelm Schmitzig, age 9, turns his finely chiseled features into the sunlight of another happy day and for a moment forgets the algebra lesson he has to do.

"Be a doctor—be a doctor, the passion of his idealistic youth is strong in his desire to be a surgeon like his father, now dead.

"Porato—porato—the anesthetizing machine hums on as Walter Schmitzig performs a delicate operation on a man who was doomed to die.

"Eventually Wilhelm will be tossed out of school for failing algebra. He will degenerate slowly until finally his sole income will be derived from window washing."

Subject No. 23—Story 1

"Two men are working at repairing a machine. One is doing the hammering while the other looks on, probably criticizing. Both are machinists.

"The machine has probably gone on the bum, and now needs to be fixed. The one hammering has probably been called to the task by the other.

"The man on the right wants the other man to fix his machine because something has gone wrong.

"The machine will be fixed so that the man on the right can go back to work."

23-2

"This poor boy is now worrying about something he has done recently. He is probably wondering why he did it.

"This boy has probably had his first sexual intercourse with a girl after which he was then given a lecture on V.D.

"He is probably thinking about why he has done this 'awful deed' (so they say).

"He will probably say to himself that it was wrong to do what he did and that he won't do it any more."

23-3

"Here we have father and son talking over some serious problem (probably married life).

"The son has probably been arguing with his wife, who suddenly decided to leave him, and now he resorts to his father for advice.

"The father is telling the son that he shouldn't be hasty about such things and to return to his wife and mend their argument.

"The son will probably go back to his wife and tell her that he is sorry for the way in which he had acted."

23-4

"The boy is thinking of some incident that has happened in a book which he just read. The persons other than the boy are characters of the book he has read.

"The boy has read a book in which the incidents are constantly playing on his mind.

"The boy is thinking of how these two men have just murdered another man for talking too much.

"The two men will continue in their scheme and bury their dead man, while the boy will probably have nightmares."

Subject No. 24—Story 1

"Two workmen in 1890 are in a workshop.

"One laborer has before tried to cut a certain angle on a block of steel—he has failed. He now tries again and an assistant watches.

"The man with hands on hips is hoping that the other guy can cut the precise angle that is needed. They need the block for a new machine.

"The cutting will be a success and the workshop will receive a contract from the owner, wanting the precisely cut block of steel, for other workmanship of similar nature."

24-2

"It is two days before Christmas in a New Jersey High School. A student is in a study period supposedly reading a new assignment from his economics book.

"Up to this time the student has been able to concentrate on his work and accomplish a lot in the study period, but he read about department stores in the economics book, that reminded him of presents and that reminded him of Christmas which reminded him of vacation.

"He is thinking about 1 day, 12 hours, and 45 minutes until he begins his vacation and is longing for the school bell to ring for the period to be over.

"The bell will ring in what seems to be two weeks, altho' it's only a half hour. School will be over for vacation and he will realize that the time went fast after all."

24-3

"A father and son are sitting in theatre showing a new play. The father sees someone sitting up ahead and leans over to his son to remark to him about it.

"The men are having a stag party, leaving their wives at home.

"The father tells his son about a man they see sitting further ahead (about 3 rows). The man they are talking about once accosted the father's wife and was put in prison for 30 years. He has recently been let out. The son had not learned of this before.

"The son's jaw becomes rigid and he clenches his teeth, deciding whether to take a crack at the man for insulting his mother or letting matters ride."

24-4

"A young boy thinks about a doctor in years gone by—the crude implements he had to use.

"The boy has been told that his grandfather who was in the Civil War died from an appendectomy operation because the doctor was unable to remove the appendix in time, while in the tent on the battlefield.

"The boy thinks of the scene where the doctor takes a pencil and marks off on the skin the approximate distance from the hip to navel where the appendix should be.

"The boy will then write a composition for an English class about his grandfather's heroic deeds without injury, and the irony of dying from a mere appendectomy."

Subject No. 25—Story 1

"Two men about to break the machine. They are 2 of 3 partners in a little machine shop. They were endeavoring to build up a bigger inventing company.

"Their third partner was killed by a bolt that flew from the machine. This partner was loved dearly by them and after countless endeavors to . . .

"They are thinking of their departed partner. All that is wanted is revenge at the machine that was invented. Their dream invention has turned out to be a source of great misery for them.

"They will break the machine, go on working in a small business and never again attempt to invent machines or expand their business."

25-2

"He is a student, very conscientious forced to go to school by his parents with great ambitions of becoming a lawyer. He is a 'grind' due to the fact that outside pressure is put on him. He has no girl friend.

"His fraternity brothers are having a house party with plenty of girls and fun. He has little money to ask a girl down, decides to study during the party.

"A girl or companion is wanted by this freshman. Life seems

bitter and he wishes he could be like the other fellows having a good time.

"He will get very frustrated, decide that he has just got to get a girl sooner or later if his parents expect him to do a good scholastic job."

25-3

"Father and son. The son has just finished confessing his guilt in leading some girl astray. The father is a distinguished person and the son had been thought of as one who would not stoop to such a low act of seduction.

"The boy due to his father's social importance, had to be careful of his action in society. Finally he could keep up the pretense no longer and gave vent to his natural passion.

"The father is thinking of disgrace and finds disappointment in his son. The son feels lost—almost in a daze due to his recent confession which he thought he'd never tell.

"A psychiatrist will be called in to help the fellow find himself and the father will get a polite 'bawling out' that it was mainly through his fault that the incident happened."

25-4

"The boy has just seen a movie involving a medical drama. He is now thinking of the incident and has been inspired to become a great surgeon.

"Aside from the movie, he also has been under a serious operation which saved his life and is thankful to the doctors. He hopes he can do the same some day.

"How wonderful it will be when I'm a doctor. All that is wanted is the fulfillment of becoming an M.D.

"He will be in medical school but the strain is too much for him and he will attempt suicide but will be stopped and gradually adjust himself to a happy life."

Subject No. 26—Story 1

"The two men are testing a new type of metal alloy in an electric arc furnace.

"They have had a long period of experimentation in trying to find a special alloy which will resist very high temperatures. They have met with little success in the past.

"Each is of course wondering if the specimen being tested will meet requirements they wish it to achieve. They want it to meet very high standards so as to be accepted by the government.

"The metal will not meet the test and will be rejected. The men will then continue to search for another alloy which they can test."

26-2

"This is a freshman in college. He is trying to decide which fraternity to join.

"He has been through a period of intense rushing with many varied experiences and different impressions formed.

"He is trying to evaluate the different houses he has visited and hoping he can pick the house with the best reputation on campus as an all-around good house.

"He will reluctantly make his final choice because his choices seem about equal, and pledge a house and find as time goes on he could have fitted in almost any house as well as the one he chose."

26-3

"The two men are father and son. The father is trying to console his son because of a setback the boy has received in a love affair.

"The boy had been deeply in love (or so he felt) with a very nice girl. Suddenly for no apparent reason she has jilted him and he can get no explanation from her for doing so.

"The boy is bewildered by the situation and can't think of why it has happened. He wants to talk to the girl and affect a reconciliation. The father wants to help his son over his disillusionment and spare him any hurt feelings.

"The father will by his persuasion and wisdom show the boy he shouldn't let the thing get him down and to try to forget the whole thing and start out where he left off when he began going with the girl."

26-4

"This is a young boy who has lost a brother in the war. He is thinking if there had been enough doctors his brother's life would have been saved.

"His brother was the boy's ideal and he always looked up to him. His brother went to war and was wounded and died.

"Now the boy is without his brother and he wants to make up for the loss in serving others in a way which might prevent the thing which happened to him from happening to someone else.

"The boy will take up medicine with the hope of becoming an

Army doctor but as he becomes older he will lose his burning desire to be an Army doctor and will be content to follow civilian practice."

Subject No. 27—Story 1

"A crude machine has broken down and two factory hands are trying to repair it. The man on the left knows what to do, while the man on the right stands idly by being of little help.

"The man on the right has carelessly used the machine and is responsible for the damage. He is irked by the anger and disgust of the man on the left concerning his accident.

"The man on the left desires to repair the machine, and thinks to himself that the man on the right is a blundering idiot. Man on right watches in disgust at the other's attitude—both are angry.

"The machine will be fixed unless a fight develops between the two men who are quite angry at one another. At any rate, there will be ill feeling over the incident the rest of the day."

27-2

"This man is a dejected student, vainly trying to concentrate on an overdue term paper which he must have in by the following day. It's late at night—he finds himself unable to fix his mind on any subject.

"He has let the paper slide and before this moment has been down for several fast beers. His tired mind is further fagged as a result.

"He desires to finish the paper, but his mind is wandering too much to do same. With the dreamy look on his face, he is thinking about his girl back home, and other varied, irrelevant topics.

"He will fall asleep over the book, but with typical last minute drive and a bit of luck he will make up and finish a paper (or reasonable facsimile) in time for the period concerned."

27-3

"These men are attending a stockholders meeting and are conspiring among one another with the idea of ousting the company's existing president. The older man, a hardened veteran to such corporate dealings influences the younger man greatly.

"The older man and some of his associates have been scheming for the 'turnover' for quite some time, quietly organizing and include the young man so as to influence a wider range of men toward their desires.

"The schemers desire to elect their own, corrupt leader as president of the firm, with an eye to greater personal profit.

"The young man will see his error before the 'blow off' occurs, will crusade and will defeat the schemers in a close vote at the meeting. The old man will kill the younger, and then commit suicide."

27-4

"This young boy is a decided schizophreniac, and below his innocent appearance has been a life-long mania for blood and death. He figures on becoming a medical student, performing a series of maniacal operations when a doctor.

"At a young age he was bitten by a dog in his neighborhood—he then went home in a fit of crazed rage, grabbed an axe, found the dog, and took a vengeful delight in hacking him to pieces.

"He thinks of blood, gore and the slow destruction of living things. He will have 'slips of the hand' when a future surgeon, thus filling out his crazed desires.

"In a fit of rage he will hack his parents to death, burn their home, and then die of exposure in an abandoned barn while trying to evade the police."

Subject No. 28—Story 1

"Tom Edison is giving one of the workers in his small shop hell for doing something wrong.

"The worker has destroyed his latest design thru carelessness.

"The workers thought it was a stupid invention anyway. The worker wanted fame and the publicity that Edison is getting.

"The worker will be fired and Edison will go on to new and greater heights."

28-2

"An adolescent boy on Monday morning after a big week-end party. He is worried about the strong competition that his best buddy was giving him for the girl.

"For two weeks he had been dreaming about this party. Now that it's over, he keeps thinking how much fun it was but he still can't dismiss the competition.

"The thoughts are running thru his mind and nothing very concrete is being thought. He wants to be everything that will give him a week end like that all the time.

"The teacher will call on him as they inevitably do when one's mind is wandering, and he will miss the question asked of him with the usual consequences."

28-3

"The two ministers from one of the small European countries are talking matters over at the U.N. conference.

"There is a grave question being voted on and their vote will decide the path of action to be taken. They are discussing what should be done.

"They are discussing what would be best for their particular situation. They want what is best for their particular country and the conflict in their minds is whether the best for them would be best for all.

"The vote which they will cast will decide the fate of one of the fallen states very near them and the question will be settled for the best of all concerned."

28-4

"A choice has been presented to the lad. A career as a doctor and entering the Army.

"A war in progress necessitates some time to be spent in the Army. The war shows promise of lasting some time.

"His problem is whether to enter the service at once or go to school and take a chance that the war would be over when he finished. Also the problem of facing his friends who did go into the Army at once.

"He will ponder over the question. Choose the one that will fit his emotional state."

Subject No. 29—Story 1

"One man is working a machine in some sort of workshop. They are both workers.

"Some sort of material has been given to the worker operating the machine and he is developing it further.

"The object the worker has in mind is to get his job done.

"The object being worked upon will be developed into some useful article. This article will be used for some definite purpose."

29-2

"The guy is supposed to be studying but is daydreaming instead. He is a boy probably of high school age.

"The work to be done has been uninteresting so that it is hard to concentrate.

"He is thinking of some past experience, perhaps a vacation, his girl, etc.

"He will not be prepared for the class for which the studying is to be done. He will have to stop daydreaming and concentrate."

29-3

"A father is having a heart-to-heart talk with his son about the way he has been behaving lately—probably spending too much money, etc.

"The boy hasn't been studying faithfully or has been going out too much with his girl.

"The boy is thinking about these things—the father wants him to try and make better his faults.

"The boy will think this all over. He will try hard to do better and will go back to his old faults again."

29-4

"Some poor guy is being operated on by two doctors and the boy in the foreground is thinking about a medical career.

"The boy has experienced something associated with medicine and surgery and has taken a liking to it.

"The boy is thinking of how he would like to be a great surgeon.

"He will probably end up being a great doctor and everybody will be happy."

Subject No. 30—Story 1

"Two rather insipid individuals appear to be carving or working some wooden object. It looks like one of those home factories one reads about.

"They are probably turning out these products for years, especially the one looks like an incarnation of Father Time.

"The one (the less droopy of the two) is standing by to hand any instruments to the other who is actually engaged in production. The former is probably making a mental appraisal of the work.

"He'll finish the damn thing, go on to another. Some day he may even die."

30-2

"Cogito ergo sum.

"The thinker is pondering some problem—perhaps life, or a difficult algebraic equation. He looks like a very serious individual—possibly introverted. He also has dandruff.

"A perplexing enigma is being mulled over—a solution obviously would be welcome. The next slide should certainly show him, all smiles saying, 'Aha—I have it!' (à la Gestalt.)

"Eventually an answer will permeate."

30-3

"The bearded one is trying to sell the younger an insurance policy. Putting him in a serious frame of mind by conjuring up pictures of violent death and sudden demise.

"Junior has probably just been told his blood pressure is 300 and is trying to make a good thing out of it by calling in Liberty Mutual.

"The prospective purchaser is thinking about the ephemeral quality of life. He doesn't exactly deplore it—just speculates on it.

"He will buy the insurance."

30-4

"The young boy is imagining himself a great physician. In the background are the Drs. Mayo carrying the torch of modern sterilized medicine.

"The young lad has been inspired by something he has seen or read, and wants very much to be a doctor.

"He will leave his brown study, return to it eventually and apply to college for admission."

Scoring for the Illustrative Stories

Subj. No.	Story No.	UI −1	TI 0	AI +1	N +1	+	I ? +1	−	Ga+ +1	Ga− +1	G+ +1	G− +1	Nup +1	Bp +1	Bw +1	Ach Th +1	n Ach Score
1	1		•														0
	2		•														0
	3	•															−1
	4	•															−1
Total		−2	0														−2
2	1			•	•				•	•			•			•	+6
	2			•	•				•	•			•		•	•	+7
	3			•	•		•				•	•				•	+6
	4			•	•												+2
Total				+4	+4		+1		+2	+2	+1	+1	+2		+1	+3	+21
3	1			•			•						•			•	+4
	2		•														0
	3	•															−1
	4	•															−1
Total		−2	0	+1			+1						+1			+1	+2
4	1			•	•		•									•	+4
	2			•					•				•	•		•	+5
	3			•													+1
	4			•						•						•	+3
Total				+4	+1		+1		+1	+1			+1	+1		+3	+13
5	1		•														0
	2	•															−1
	3	•															−1
	4		•														0
Total		−2	0														−2
6	1		•														0
	2		•														0
	3		•														0
	4			•	•		•									•	+4
Total			0	+1	+1		+1									+1	+4
7	1		•														0
	2	•															−1
	3	•															−1
	4			•													+1
Total		−2	0	+1													−1

Subj. No.	Story No.	UI −1	TI 0	AI +1	N +1	+	I ? +1	−	Ga+ +1	Ga− +1	G+ +1	G− +1	Nup +1	Bp +1	Bw +1	Ach Th +1	n Ach Score
8	1			•	•		•		•	•						•	+6
	2		•														0
	3			•	•						•	•	•			•	+6
	4	•															−1
Total		−1	0	+2	+2		+1		+1	+1	+1	+1	+1			+2	+11
9	1		•														0
	2			•											•	•	+3
	3			•						•						•	+3
	4	•															−1
Total		−1	0	+2						+1					+1	+2	+5
10	1			•		•				•						•	+4
	2			•		•			•		•					•	+5
	3		•														0
	4			•					•	•						•	+4
Total			0	+3		+2			+2	+2	+1					+3	+13
11	1			•		•					•				•	•	+5
	2			•					•	•					•	•	+5
	3		•														0
	4			•							•	•				•	+4
Total			0	+3		+1			+1	+1	+2	+1			+2	+3	+14
12	1			•		•					•				•	•	+5
	2		•														0
	3			•			•				•	•			•	•	+6
	4	•															−1
Total		−1	0	+2		+1	+1				+2	+1			+2	+2	+10
13	1		•														0
	2	•															−1
	3			•						•		•			•	•	+5
	4			•													+1
Total		−1	0	+2						+1		+1			+1	+1	+5
14	1			•		•					•				•	•	+5
	2			•		•					•		•			•	+5
	3	•															−1
	4	•															−1
Total		−2		+2		+2					+2		+1		+1	+2	+8
15	1			•											•	•	+3
	2		•														0
	3	•															−1
	4			•													+1
Total		−1	0	+2											+1	+1	+3

Subj. No.	Story No.	UI −1	TI 0	AI +1	N +1	I + +1	I ?	I −	Ga+ +1	Ga− +1	G+ +1	G− +1	Nup +1	Bp +1	Bw +1	Ach Th +1	n Ach Score
16	1			•	•	•			•	•						•	+6
	2		•														0
	3	•															−1
	4			•			•							•		•	+4
Total		−1	0	+2	+1	+1	+1		+1	+1				+1		+2	+9
17	1			•	•	•			•							•	+5
	2		•														0
	3		•														0
	4			•		•			•						•	•	+5
Total			0	+2	+1	+2			+2						+1	+2	+10
18	1			•							•					•	+3
	2		•														0
	3		•														0
	4			•	•				•		•				•	•	+6
Total			0	+2	+1				+1		+2				+1	+2	+9
19	1			•													+1
	2			•													+1
	3			•	•	•									•	•	+5
	4		•														0
Total			0	+3	+1	+1									+1	+1	+7
20	1			•	•											•	+3
	2			•		•					•		•			•	+5
	3			•		•							•			•	+4
	4			•	•	•			•		•					•	+6
Total				+4	+2	+3			+1		+2		+2			+4	+18
21	1			•	•				•		•	•				•	+6
	2		•														0
	3	•															−1
	4	•															−1
Total		−2	0	+1	+1				+1		+1	+1				+1	+4
22	1			•					•		•			•		•	+5
	2			•	•						•			•			+4
	3	•															−1
	4			•	•					•	•					•	+5
Total		−1		+3	+2				+1	+1	+3			+2		+2	+13
23	1		•														0
	2	•															−1
	3	•															−1
	4	•															−1
Total		−3	0														−3

Subj. No.	Story No.	UI −1	TI 0	AI +1	N +1	I +	I ? +1	I −	Ga+ +1	Ga− +1	G+ +1	G− +1	Nup +1	Bp +1	Bw +1	Ach Th +1	n Ach Score
24	1			•	•	•								•		•	+ 5
	2		•														0
	3	•															− 1
	4		•														0
Total		−1	0	+1	+1	+1								+1		+1	+ 4
25	1			•								•			•	•	+ 4
	2			•											•		+ 2
	3	•															− 1
	4			•	•				•			•				•	+ 5
Total		−1		+3	+1				+1			+2			+2	+2	+ 10
26	1			•	•			•	•						•	•	+ 6
	2		•														0
	3		•														0
	4			•	•												+ 2
Total			0	+2	+2			+1	+1						+1	+1	+ 8
27	1		•														0
	2		•														0
	3			•	•		•		•			•				•	+ 6
	4			•													+ 1
Total			0	+2	+1		+1		+1			+1				+1	+ 7
28	1			•	•						•	•				•	+ 5
	2			•	•					•						•	+ 4
	3			•	•	•								•		•	+ 5
	4			•													+ 1
Total				+4	+3	+1				+1	+1	+1		+1		+3	+ 15
29	1		•														0
	2		•														0
	3		•														0
	4			•	•				•		•					•	+ 5
Total			0	+1	+1				+1		+1					+1	+ 5
30	1		•														0
	2			•	•	•					•					•	+ 5
	3		•														0
	4			•	•	•			•							•	+ 5
Total			0	+2	+2	+2			+1		+1					+2	+ 10

Pictures and Verbal Cues Used to Elicit Stories

I. Description of pictures classified by identifying letter
   A. "Father-son." Card 7BM from the Murray Thematic Apperception Test
   B. Two men ("inventors") in a shop working at a machine
   C. Two men, in colonial dress, printing in a shop
   D. "Cub reporter" scene: older man handing papers to a younger man
   E. "Lawyer's" office: two men talking in a well-furnished office
   F. Young boy with violin. Card 1 from the Murray Thematic Apperception Test
   G. Boy with vague operation scene in background. Card 8BM from the Murray Thematic Apperception Test
   H. Boy in checked shirt at a desk, an open book in front of him
   Note: The original series in order of presentation was B, H, A, G. Pictures C, F, E, D, in that order, were chosen to be roughly comparable to B, H, A, G, but see Chapter VII.

II. Verbal cues
   Form M
      1. A mother and her son—they look worried
      2. Two men looking at something—one is older
      3. A boy has just left his house
      4. A wife with her head on her husband's shoulder
   Form F
      1. A father and his son talking seriously
      2. Brothers and sisters playing—one is a little ahead of the other
      3. A man alone at night
      4. A boy with his head resting on his hands
      Note: Cues M_2, F_4, F_1, F_2 are probably most comparable to the original picture series.

375

Bibliography of n Achievement Titles

Bold-face page references are to this book.

ATKINSON, J. W. 1950. Studies in projective measurement of achievement motivation. Univ. of Michigan. Abstract in Univ. Microfilms, vol. X, no. 4; Publication No. 1945, **147, 149, 186, 187, 195, 197, 223, 241, 244, 265, 267**

————. 1951. Recall of successes and failures related to differences in n Achievement. (Paper delivered at APA meeting, September 2, 1951.) Mss. available from the author in dittoed form.

————, HEYNS, R. W., and VEROFF, J. June, 1952. An application of approach-avoidance conflict theory to the problem of differences in generality of n Achievement score. Mss. available from the authors in dittoed form.

BROWN, R. W. 1952. Some determinants of the relationship between rigidity and authoritarianism. Univ. of Michigan. Abstract in Univ. Microfilms, vol. XII, no. 2; Publication No. 3475, **286, 302**

————. 1953. A determinant of the relationship between rigidity and authoritarianism. J. abnorm. soc. Psychol., 48, 469–476.

CLARK, R. A., and MCCLELLAND, D. C. 1950. A factor analytic integration of imaginative, performance, and case study measures of the need for achievement. Unpublished Mss. available from the authors in dittoed form, **176, 227**

DOUVAN, E. 1951. Influence of social class membership on reactions to failure. Univ. of Michigan. Abstract in Univ. Microfilms, vol. XI, no. 3; Publication No. 2583.

FIELD, W. F. 1951. The effects on thematic apperception of certain experimentally aroused needs. Unpublished Ph.D. thesis. Univ. of Maryland, **80, 177, 178**

FRIEDMAN, G. A. 1950. A cross-cultural study of the relationship between independence training and n Achievement as revealed by mythology. Unpublished Honors thesis. Harvard Univ., **290**

FROELICH, Dean K. 1953. The effect of successfully competitive experiences upon achievement motivation. Unpublished Honors thesis. Univ. of Michigan.

JACOBS, Berne. 1953. A method for investigating the cue characteristics of pictures used in projective measures of motives. Unpublished Honors thesis. Univ. of Michigan.

LOWELL, E. L. 1952. The effect of need for achievement on learning and speed of performance. J. Psychol., 33, 31–40, **229**

378   BIBLIOGRAPHY OF *n* ACHIEVEMENT TITLES

Lowell, E. L. 1950. A methodological study of projectively measured achievement motivation. Unpublished Master's thesis. Wesleyan Univ., 161, 168, 191, 242

Martire, J. G. 1953. Relationships between the self concept and differences in strength and generality of achievement motivation. Univ. of Michigan. Abstract in Univ. Microfilms, Publication No. 5702.

McClelland, D. C., Clark, R. A., Roby, T. B., and Atkinson, J. W. 1949. The projective expression of needs. IV. The effect of the need for achievement on thematic apperception. *J. exp. Psychol.*, 39, 242–255, 102, 145, 147, 149, 185

McClelland, D. C., and Liberman, A. M. 1949. The effect of need for achievement on recognition of need-related words. *J. Personality*, 18, 236–251, 198, 257, 260, 273

Morgan, H. H. 1951. An analysis of certain structured and unstructured test results of achieving and non-achieving high ability college students. Unpublished Ph.D. thesis. Univ. of Minnesota, 240, 274, 312

———. 1952. A psychometric comparison of achieving and non-achieving college students of high ability. *Jour. consult. Psychol.*, 16, 292–297.

Moulton, R. 1952. Relationship of need for achievement to perceptual sensitivity under two degrees of motive arousal. Unpublished Honors thesis. Univ. of Michigan.

Rosenstein, A. J. 1952. The specificity of the achievement motive and the motivating effects of picture cues. Unpublished Honors thesis. Univ. of Michigan.

Veroff, J. 1950. A projective measure of the achievement motivation of adolescent males and females. Unpublished Honors thesis. Wesleyan Univ., 164, 172

———, Wilcox, S., and Atkinson, J. W. 1953. The achievement motive in high school and college age women. *J. abnorm. soc. Psychol.*, 48, 108–119, 173

Weinberger, B. 1951. Achievement motivation and self concept. Unpublished Honors thesis. Univ. of Michigan.

Wilcox, S. 1951. A projective measure of the achievement motivation of college women. Unpublished Honors thesis. Univ. of Michigan.

Winterbottom, M. R. 1953. The relation of childhood training in independence to achievement motivation. Univ. of Michigan. Abstract in Univ. Microfilms, Publication No. 5113, 297, 302, 305, 313

Zatzkis, J. 1949. The effect of the need for achievement on linguistic behavior. Unpublished Master's thesis. Wesleyan Univ., 221, 249

References and Author Index

Bold-face page references are to this book.

Adorno, T. W., Frenkel-Brunswik, E., Levinson, D. J., and Sanford, R. N. 1950. *The authoritarian personality.* New York: Harper, **286, 302**

Alexander, H. W. 1946. A general test for trend. *Psychol. Bull.*, 43, 533-557, **231**

Allport, G. W. 1937. *Personality, a psychological interpretation.* New York: Holt, **8, 85**

Alper, T. G. 1946. Memory for completed and incompleted tasks as a function of personality: an analysis of group data. *J. abnorm. soc. Psychol.*, 41, 403-420, **4**

Alpert, R. 1953. Perceptual determinants of affect. Unpublished Master's thesis. Wesleyan Univ., **51**

Angier, R. P. 1903. The aesthetics of unequal division. *Psychol. Rev.* (Monogr. Suppl.), 4, 541-561, **48, 49**

Arnold, Magda B. 1945. Physiological differentiation of emotional states. *Psychol. Rev.*, 52, 35-48, **36**

Asch, S. E. 1952. Effects of group pressure upon the modification and distortion of judgements. In Swanson, G. E., Newcomb, T. M., Hartley, E. L. (eds.), *Readings in social psychology.* New York: Holt, **286**

Atkinson, J. W. 1950. Studies in projective measurement of achievement motivation. Univ. of Michigan. Abstract in Univ. Microfilms, vol. X, no. 4; Publication No. 1945, **147, 149, 186, 187, 195, 197, 223, 241, 244, 265, 267**

Atkinson, J. W., and McClelland, D. C. 1948. The projective expression of needs. II. The effect of different intensities of the hunger drive on thematic apperception. *J. exp. Psychol.*, 38, 643-658, **3, 107**

Baldwin, A. L., Kalhorn, J., and Breese, F. H. 1945. Patterns of parent behavior. *Psychol. Monogr.*, 58, No. 3, **277**

Bartlett, F. C. 1932. *Remembering: a study in experimental and social psychology.* Cambridge: Cambridge Univ. Press, **290**

Beach, F. A., and Gilmore, R. W. 1949. Response of male dogs to urine from females in heat. *J. Mammal.*, 30, 391-392, **91**

Beebe-Center, J. G. 1932. *The psychology of pleasantness and unpleasantness.* New York: Van Nostrand, **42, 44, 56, 57, 59, 64**

Berelson, B. 1952. *Content analysis.* Glencoe, Ill.: Free Press, **322**

Blake, R. R., and Wilson, G. P., Jr. 1950. Perceptual selectivity in Rorschach determinants as a function of depressive tendencies. *J. abnorm. soc. Psychol.*, 45, 459-472, **261**

Brown, J. S., and Farber, I. E. 1951. Emotions conceptualized as intervening variables—with suggestions toward a theory of frustration. *Psychol. Bull.*, 48, 465-495, **7, 12, 25, 63**

Brown, J. S., and Jacobs, A. 1949. The role of fear in the motivation and acquisition of responses. *J. exp. Psychol.*, 39, 747-759, **9, 21, 36**

Brown, R. W. 1952. Some determinants of the relationship between rigidity and authoritarianism. Univ. of Michigan. Abstract in Univ. Microfilms, vol. XII, no. 2; Publication No. 3475, **286, 302**

Bruner, J. S. 1951. Personality dynamics and the process of perceiving. In *Blake, R. R., and Ramsey, G. V.* (eds.) *Perception: an approach to personality.* New York: Ronald, pp. 121-147, **1, 248**

Clark, R. A. 1948. A factor analytic integration of projective and clinical measures of need achievement. Unpublished Master's thesis. Wesleyan Univ., **100, 102, 103**

Clark, R. A. 1952. The projective measurement of experimentally induced levels of sexual motivation. *J. exp. Psychol.,* 44, 391-399, **74, 195, 216, 314, 320, 326**

Clark, R. A., and McClelland, D. C. 1950. A factor analytic integration of imaginative, performance, and case study measures of the need for achievement. Unpublished paper, **176, 227**

Corwin, G. H. 1921. The involuntary response to pleasantness. *Amer. J. Psychol.,* 32, 563-570, **35**

Cowles, J. T. 1937. Food-tokens as incentives for learning by chimpanzees. *Comp. psychol. Monogr.,* 14, No. 71, **87**

Cronbach, L. J. 1949. Statistical methods applied to Rorschach scores: a review. *Psychol. Rev.,* 56, 393-429, **258**

Dallenbach, K. M. 1939. Pain: history and present status. *Amer. J. Psychol.,* 52, 331-347, **42**

Dashiell, J. F. 1949. *Fundamentals of general psychology.* Boston: Houghton Mifflin, **107**

Dearborn, G. V. N. 1899. The emotion of joy. *Psychol. Rev.* (Monogr. Suppl.), 2, No. 5, **35**

Dollard, J., and Miller, N. E. 1950. *Personality and psychotherapy.* New York: McGraw-Hill, **22**

Festinger, L. 1943. Development of differential appetite in the rat. *J. exp. Psychol.,* 32, 226-234, **62**

Field, W. F. 1951. The effects on thematic apperception of certain experimentally aroused needs. Unpublished Ph.D. thesis. Univ. of Maryland, **80, 177, 178**

Fisher, R. A. 1951. *The design of experiments* (6th ed.). New York: Hafner, **143**

Flugel, J. C. 1945. *Man, Morals and Society.* New York: International Univ. Press, **159**

Ford, C. S., and Beach, F. A. 1951. *Patterns of sexual behavior.* New York: Harper, **31, 56**

Frenkel-Brunswik, E. 1942. Motivation and behavior. *Genet. psychol. Monogr.,* 26, 121-265, **76, 80, 328**

Friedman, G. A. 1950. A cross-cultural study of the relationship between independence training and *n* Achievement as revealed by mythology. Unpublished Honors thesis. Harvard Univ., **290**

Garth, T. R., Moses, M. R., and Anthony, C. N. 1938. The color preferences of East Indians. *Amer. J. Psychol.,* 51, 709-713, **46**

Gwinn, G. T. 1949. The effects of punishment on acts motivated by fear. *J. exp. Psychol.,* 39, 260-269, **37, 70**

Harriman, A. E. 1952. An experimental investigation into the development of the dietary preference for salt in adrenalectomized rats and into the validity of the processes postulated to account for the manifestation of this preference. Unpublished Ph.D. thesis. Cornell Univ., **54, 55**

Heathers, G. L. 1940. The avoidance of repetition of a maze reaction in the rat as a function of the time interval between trials. *J. Psychol.,* 10, 359-380, **62**

Hebb, D. O. 1949. *The organization of behavior.* New York: Wiley, **8, 16, 18, 20, 21, 22, 23, 26, 42, 48, 59, 60, 85**

Hebb, D. O., and Riesen, A. H. 1943. The genesis of irrational fears. *Bull. Canad. Psychol. Ass.,* 3, 49-50, **59**

Helson, H. 1947. Adaptation-level as frame of reference for prediction of psychophysical data. *Amer. J. Psychol.,* 60, 1-29, **53**

Helson, H. 1948. Adaptation-level as a basis for a quantitative theory of frames of reference. *Psychol. Rev.,* 55, 297-313, **44, 58**

Hilgard, E. R., and Marquis, D. G. 1940. *Conditioning and learning.* New York: Appleton-Century-Crofts, **36**

Hull, C. L. 1931. Goal attraction and directing ideas conceived as habit phenomena. *Psychol. Rev.,* 38, 487-506, **36**

Hull, C. L. 1943. *Principles of Behavior.* New York: Appleton-Century-Crofts, **8, 13, 21, 87**

Hull, C. L., Livingston, J. R., Rouse, R. O., and Barker, A. N. 1951. True, sham, and esophogeal feeding as reinforcements. *J. comp. physiol. Psychol.,* 44, 236-245, **77**

Kendall, M. G. 1948. *Rank correlation methods.* London: Griffin, **250, 295**

Kluckhohn, C., and Leighton, D. 1947. *The Navaho.* Cambridge: Harvard Univ. Press, **248**

Kluckhohn, C., and Murray, H. A.

1948. *Personality in nature, society, and culture.* New York: Knopf, **8**

Kogan, L. S. 1948. Analysis of variance—repeated measurements. *Psychol. Bull.,* 45, 131-143, **231**

Kohn, M. 1951. Satiation of hunger from food injected directly into the stomach versus food ingested by mouth. *J. comp. physiol. Psychol.,* 44, 412-422, **16, 77**

Landis, C. 1924. Studies of emotional reactions: general behavior and facial expression. *J. comp. Psychol.,* 4, 447-501, **27**

Landis, C., and Hunt, W. A. 1939. *The startle pattern.* New York: Farrar & Rinehart, **38**

Lee, W. A. 1951. Approach and avoidance to a cue paired with the beginning and end of pain. Unpublished MSS. Wesleyan Univ., **74**

Liberman, A. M. 1944. The effect of interpolated activity on spontaneous recovery from experimental extinction. *J. exp. Psychol.,* 34, 282-301, **87**

Lindquist, E. F. 1947. Goodness of fit of trend curves and significance of trend differences. *Psychometrika,* 12, 65-78, **231**

Lowell, E. L. 1950. A methodological study of projectively measured achievement motivation. Unpublished Master's thesis. Wesleyan Univ., **161, 168, 191, 242**

Lowell, E. L. 1952. The effect of need for achievement on learning and speed of performance. *J. Psychol.,* 33, 31-40, **229**

McClelland, D. C. 1951. *Personality.* New York: William Sloane Assoc., **17, 42, 252**

McClelland, D. C., Clark, R. A., Roby, T. B., and Atkinson, J. W. 1949. The projective expression of

McClelland, D. C. (*continued*) needs. IV. The effect of the need for achievement on thematic apperception. *J. exp. Psychol.*, 39, 242-255, v, 102, 145, 147, 149, 185

McClelland, D. C. and Liberman, A. M. 1949. The effect of need for achievement on recognition of need-related words. *J. Personality*, 18, 236-251, 198, 257, 260, 273

McClelland, D. C., and McGown, D. R. 1953. The effect of variable food reinforcement on the strength of a secondary reward. *J. comp. physiol. Psychol.*, 46, 80-86, 71

McCombe, L., Vogt, E. Z., and Kluckhohn, C. 1951. *Navaho means people.* Cambridge: Harvard Univ. Press, 171

McDougall, W. 1927. Pleasure, pain and conation. *Brit. J. Psychol.*, 17, 171-180, 42, 87

McGeoch, J. W. 1942. *The psychology of human learning.* New York: Longmans, Green, 90

McMurray, G. A. 1950. Experimental study of a case of insensitivity to pain. Reprinted with additions from *Arch. neurol. Psychiat.*, 64, 650-667, 10

Maier, N. R. F. 1949. *Frustration. The study of behavior without a goal.* New York: McGraw-Hill, 15

Maltzmann, I. 1952. The process need. *Psychol. Rev.*, 59, 40-48, 62, 83

Maslow, A. H. 1953. The instinctoid nature of basic needs. *J. Personality* (in press), 8

Meehl, P. E. 1950. On the circularity of the law of effect. *Psychol. Bull.*, 47, 52-75, 34

Melton, A. W. 1941. Learning. In W. S. Monroe (ed.), *Encyclopedia of educational research.* New York: Macmillan, pp. 667-686, 13

Miller, N. E. 1944. Experimental studies of conflict. In J. McV. Hunt (ed.), *Personality and the behavior disorders.* New York: Ronald Press, 74

Miller, N. E. 1951. Learnable drives and rewards. In Stevens, S. S. (ed.) *Handbook of experimental psychology.* New York: Wiley, 21, 32, 44, 234

Miller, N. E. and Dollard, J. 1941. *Social learning and imitation.* New Haven: Yale Univ. Press, 8, 19, 53, 85

Morgan, C. D. and Murray, H. H. 1935. A method for investigating fantasies: the thematic apperception test. *Arch. neurol. Psychiat.*, 34, 289-306, 107

Morgan, C. T. 1943. *Physiological psychology.* New York: McGraw-Hill, 20

Morgan, C. T., and Stellar, E. 1950. *Physiological psychology.* New York: McGraw-Hill, 26

Morgan, H. H. 1951. An analysis of certain structured and unstructured test results of achieving and non-achieving high ability college students. Unpublished Ph.D. thesis. Univ. of Minnesota, 240, 274, 312

Mowrer, O. H. 1950. *Learning theory and personality dynamics.* New York: Ronald Press, 6, 8, 9, 10, 11, 36, 87, 95

Mowrer, O. H. 1952. Motivation. In Stone, C. P., and Taylor, D. W. (eds.), *Annual review of psychology.* Stanford: Annual Reviews, Inc., 10

Mücher, H. 1953. Psychologische Beiträge zur Untersuchung von Schlafmittelnachwirkungen, I. Analyse systematisch angeregter Vorstellungstätigkeit. *Psychol. Beiträge* (in press), 319

Murray, H. A. 1938. *Explorations in personality.* New York: Oxford Univ. Press, 4, 97, 98, 198, 322

Nissen, H. W., and Semmes, J. 1952. Comparative and physiological psychology. In Stone, C. P., and Taylor, D. W. (eds.), *Annual review of psychology.* Stanford: Annual Reviews, Inc., **11**

Nowlis, H. H. 1941. The influence of success and failure on the resumption of an interrupted task. *J. exp. Psychol.*, 28, 304-325, **4**

Pfaffman, C., and Bare, J. K. 1950. Gustatory nerve discharges in normal and adrenalectomized rats. *J. comp. physiol. Psychol.*, 43, 320-324, **54, 55**

Postman, L. 1951. Toward a general theory of cognition. In Rohrer, J. H., and Sherif, M., *Social psychology at the crossroads.* New York: Harper, **1, 248**

Postman, L., Bruner, J. S., and McGinnies, E. 1948. Personal values as selective factors in perception. *J. abnorm. soc. Psychol.*, 43, 142-154, **257**

Roe, Anne. 1951. A psychological study of physical scientists. *Genet. psychol. Monogr.*, 43, 121-235, **181**

Rosenzweig, S. 1943. An experimental study of "repression" with special reference to need-persistive and ego-defensive reactions to frustration. *J. exp. Psychol.*, 32, 64-74, **4, 155**

Sanford, F. H. 1942. Speech and personality. *Psychol. Bull.*, 39, 811-345, **248**

Schlosberg, H. 1952. The description of facial expressions in terms of two dimensions. *J. exp. Psychol.*, 44, 229-237, **33, 37**

Scott, J. P. 1945. Social behavior, organization and leadership in a small flock of domestic sheep.

Comp. psychol. Monogr., 18, No. 4, **77**

Sears, R. R. 1936. Functional abnormalities of memory with special reference to amnesia. *Psychol. Bull.*, 33, 229-274, **272**

Sears, R. R. 1937. Initiation of the repression sequence by experienced failure. *J. exp. Psychol.*, 20, 570-580, **272**

Sears, R. R. 1942. Success and failure: a study of motility. In McNemar, Q., and Merrill, M. (eds.), *Studies in personality.* New York: McGraw-Hill, **4**

Sheffield, F. D., and Roby, T. B. 1950. Reward value of a non-nutritive sweet taste. *J. comp. physiol. Psychol.*, 43, 471-481, **11, 16**

Sheffield, F. D., Wulff, J. J., and Backer, R. 1951. Reward value of copulation without sex drive reduction. *J. comp. physiol. Psychol.*, 44, 3-8, **11, 16**

Sheffield, V. F. 1949. Extinction as a function of partial reinforcement and distribution of practice. *J. exp. Psychol.*, 39, 511-526, **71**

Sheldon, W. H., Stevens, S. S., and Tucker, W. B. 1940. *The varieties of human physique.* New York: Harper, **57**

Shipley, T. E., Jr., and Veroff, J. 1952. A projective measure of need for affiliation. *J. exp. Psychol.*, 43, 349-356, **81, 320**

Sillitto, G. P. 1947. The distribution of Kendall's τ coefficient of rank correlation in rankings containing ties. *Biometrika*, 29, 332, **294**

Simon, C. W., Wickens, D. D., Brown, U., and Pennock, L. 1951. The effect of the secondary reinforcing agents on the primary thirst drive. *J. comp. physiol. Psychol.*, 44, 67-70, **84**

Snedecor, G. W. 1946. *Statistical methods* (4th ed.). Ames, Iowa: Collegiate Press, **143, 265**

Thorndike, E. L., and Lorge, I. 1944. *The Teacher's wordbook of 30,000 words.* New York: Teach. Coll., Columbia Univ., **229**

Tinbergen, N. 1951. *The study of instinct.* London: Oxford, Clarendon Press, **17, 31, 32**

Tomkins, S. S. 1943. *Contemporary psychopathology.* Cambridge: Harvard Univ. Press, **315**

Tomkins, S. S. 1947. *The Thematic Apperception Test.* New York: Grune & Stratton, **197**

Veroff, J. 1950. A projective measure of the achievement motivation of adolescent males and females. Unpublished Honors thesis. Wesleyan Univ., **164, 172**

Veroff, J., Wilcox, S., and Atkinson, J. W. 1953. The achievement motive in high school and college age women. *J. abnorm. soc. Psychol.*, 48, 108-119, **173**

Weiner, I. H., and Stellar, E. 1951. Salt preference of the rat determined by a single stimulus method. *J. comp. physiol. Psychol.*, 44, 394-401, **11, 31**

Wendt, H. W. 1953. Psychologische Untersuchungen über experimentelle Schmerzzustände, II. Schmerz als Frustrierungserlebnis und seine emotionale Verarbeitung. *Marburger Sitzungsberichte*, 75, 26-41, **319**

Wendt, H. W. 1953. Vorversuche mit Belastungsvariablen: Rechentätig-

keit unter Lärm und projektives Verhalten. Unpublished MSS University of Marburg, **319**

Whiting, J. W. M. 1950. Effects of conflict on drive. Unpublished paper, available from the author, **25, 63**

Whiting, J. W. M. and Child, I. L. 1953. *Child training and personality: a cross-cultural study.* New Haven: Yale Univ. Press, **292**

Wiener, N. 1950. *The human use of human beings.* Boston: Houghton Mifflin, **91**

Winterbottom, M. R. 1953. The relation of childhood training in independence to achievement motivation. Univ. of Michigan. (To be microfilmed), **297, 302, 305, 313**

Wolfe, J. B. 1936. Effectiveness of token rewards for chimpanzees. *Comp. psychol. Monogr.*, 12, No. 60, **87**

Woodworth, R. S. 1938. *Experimental psychology.* New York: Holt, **43, 45, 50, 86**

Yoshioka, J. G. 1930. Size preference of albino rats. *J. genet. Psychol.*, 37, 427-430, **62**

Young, P. T. 1949. Food-seeking drive, affective process, and learning. *Psychol. Rev.*, 56, 98-121, **8, 11, 31**

Zatzkis, J. 1949. The effect of the need for achievement on linguistic behavior. Unpublished Master's thesis. Wesleyan Univ., **221, 249**

Subject Index